Post-colonial Africa:
A General Survey

Godfrey Mwakikagile

Post-colonial Africa: A General Survey

First Edition

 ISBN 978-9987-16-041-9

New Africa Press
Dar es Salaam, Tanzania

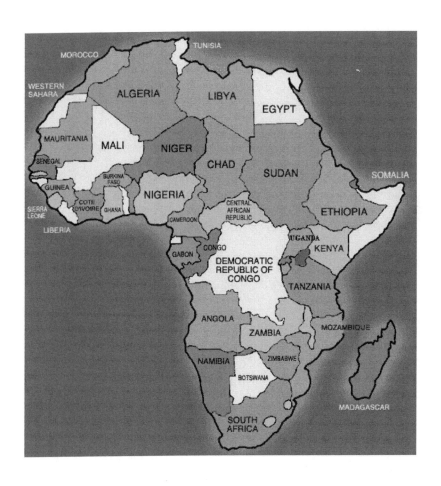

3

Contents

Introduction

THIS IS a study of statecraft and nation building in Africa in the post-colonial era.

Subjects covered include the early years of independence, the legitimacy of the state, institutional transformation, autocracy, quest for democracy, national integration, and consolidation of the state among others.

It focuses on case studies whose relevance is continental in scope.

The work has focused extensively on Uganda as one of the major case studies in the examination of Africa's transformation during the post-colonial period.

The country has gone through transitional phases characteristic of many countries on the continent: attainment of sovereign status under a democratic constitution, emergence of autocracy shortly after independence, ethno-regional rivalries, military coups, civil wars, and attempts to establish democratic institutions under very difficult conditions because of the refusal by the leaders to relinquish power.

As the highly centralised state continued to exercise hegemonic control over the people across the continent through the decades, a number of countries faced the prospect of disintegration. Civil strife ensued as a result of such mass regimentation.

Some countries descended into chaos. Many became highly unstable as the people continued to demand meaningful participation in the political process without which nation building is virtually impossible since its foundation is laid at the grassroots level requiring mass participation.

It was not until the 1990s that many African countries started to enjoy some form of democracy. But even that has been very limited in many cases.

Uganda provides a classic example of an African country that has gone through fundamental change since independence, including attempts to institutionalise democracy. And it continues to grapple with problems of democratic transformation and nation building just like other African countries do, providing an excellent case study that can help to provide some insights into the problems other countries on the continent face in their quest for peace, unity and development.

Part I

Chapter One:

One-Party System and National Unity: Consolidation of the Nation-State

SOON AFTER INDEPENDENCE, African countries faced the formidable task of nation-building, an undertaking which in most cases proved to be more difficult than the struggle for independence itself; except in a few countries where Africans had to resort to armed struggle to win their freedom.

But the Mau Mau phenomenon, if all the liberation wars in Africa may be collectively identified that way, was not continental in scope, although it had the potential to develop into one if the colonial authorities continued to ignore the demands of Africans. In the majority of cases, the colonial rulers transferred power to the nationalist leaders on peaceful terms; not because they wanted to, but because that was better than the alternative.

The prospect for mass insurrection in the colonies was real, and the colonial powers knew they would not have been able to contain it forever, as was clearly demonstrated in Angola, Mozambique, Guinea-Bissau, Zimbabwe, Namibia, and finally South Africa itself, the bastion of white minority rule on the continent.

But nation-building – which meant forging a common national identity by uniting the people in a given territory by appealing to nationalist sentiments and fostering and propagating shared values as well as invoking a common historical experience including suffering and humiliation at the hands of the colonial rulers; overcoming ethnic and regional rivalries and hostilities in pursuit of unity and stability on the basis of a common African identity and values; pursuing economic development and modernization – all that could not be done in countries which were not quite nations yet, although they identified themselves as such. It is true that Africans in the colonies fought for independence as one people.

However, that does not mean that they really considered themselves as one. As the premier of Northern Nigeria, Sir Ahmadu Bello, said during the Nigerian civil war (1967 - 1970) which threatened to split the country along ethnic lines:

"Politicians always delight in talking loosely about the unity of Nigeria. Sixty years ago there was no country called Nigeria. What is now Nigeria consisted of a number of large and small communities all of which were different in their outlooks and beliefs. The advent of British and Western education has not materially altered the situation and these many and varied communities have not knit themselves into a complete unit."[1]

It is a sentiment that was echoed by the Northern Nigerian delegation to the Ad Hoc Conference on the

Nigerian Constitution in Lagos in September 1966:

"We have pretended for too long that there are no differences between the people of Nigeria. The hard fact which we must honestly accept as of permanent importance in the Nigerian experiment especially for the future is that we are different peoples brought together by recent accidents of history. To pretend otherwise will be folly."[2]

But it was not just the Northern Nigerians who felt that way. The leaders of all the three massive regions which then constituted the Federation of Nigeria – formed in 1946 – expressed the same sentiment, only in varying degrees. In the midst of the civil war itself, the Biafran leader Colonel Odumegwu Ojukwu made an impassioned plea before the Organization of African Unity (OAU) in Addis Ababa, Ethiopia, on August 5, 1968, for recognition of his secessionist region as an independent state on grounds of incompatibility:

"The former Federation encompassed peoples of such vast political, economic, religious and cultural differences as could hardly ever have co-existed peacefully as one independent political entity."[3]

As far back as 1947, the leader of Western Nigeria, Chief Obafemi Awolowo, stated in his book *Path to Nigerian Freedom*: "Nigeria is not a nation. It is a mere geographical expression. There are no Nigerians."[4] And in the 1950s, the decade preceding independence, Northern Nigerians talked seriously about pulling out of the federation and establishing their own independent state, as did Awolowo in 1953 when the British Colonial Secretary Oliver Lyttelton ruled that Lagos shall remain federal territory as capital of the federation.

Awolowo wanted Lagos to be incorporated into the Western Region under his jurisdiction, since it was located in Western Nigeria, his tribal homeland of the Yoruba. When the British colonial secretary ruled against that at the constitutional talks on the future of Nigeria attended by all Nigerian leaders in London in August 1953, Awolowo stormed out of the conference and threatened to pull the Western Region out of the federation. Only Eastern Nigeria did not threaten to secede. Ironically, it was also the first to secede, but only after it was compelled to do so by the massacres of tens of thousands of its people – 30,000 to 50,000 – in Northern Nigeria in 1966, and by the unwillingness of the northern and the federal authorities to intervene and stop the pogroms.

But such secessionist sentiments were not peculiar to Nigeria. The history of the former Belgian Congo during the turbulent sixties is well-known when Katanga Province, led by Moise Tshombe, seceded only 11 days after Congo won independence on 30 June 1960. South Kasai Province, home of the Baluba tribe, also seceded in December 1961 under the leadership of Albert Kalonji who declared himself king of Kasai. And the remaining four provinces also tried to establish themselves as independent states in the early sixties.

In Ghana, the Ashanti were resolutely opposed to a unitary state established by Dr. Kwame Nkrumah, and made unsuccessful attempts to have a federal constitution which would have enabled them to retain their independence through extensive devolution of power short of sovereign status. For centuries before the advent of colonial rule, Ashanti, also known as Asante, had existed as an independent nation ruled by the Asantehene (king).

It was also one of the most powerful kingdoms in pre-colonial Africa before it was finally conquered by the British in one of the bloodiest wars in colonial history.

Uganda was also seriously threatened by the attempted

secession of the Buganda kingdom. Like Ashanti, Buganda was also an independent nation before the imposition of colonial rule, and was ruled by a king known as *kabaka* in the local Kiganda language. Even after independence, the kingdom considered itself to be a separate nation. On 20 May 1966 almost four years after independence, the kingdom's parliament known as Lukiiko demanded Uganda's expulsion from Buganda by May 30th because it did not fully recognize the national government's jurisdiction over the kingdom. And it did not relent until Ugandan Prime Minister Milton Obote, in a swift military move, took over Kabaka Edward Frederick Mutesa's palace.

The *kabaka* went into self-imposed exile in Britain where he continued to rail against Ugandan authority over his kingdom until his death in November 1969.

Other kingdoms in Uganda – Toro, Bunyoro, Ankole, and the princedom of Busoga – were also opposed to the national government. They considered themselves to be autonomous entities with their own political systems and institutions independent of central authority, as had been the case before the conquest of Africa and imposition of colonial rule by Europeans.

Zambia also had to contend with secessionist threats, especially by Barotse Province also known as Barotseland, home of the Lozi people, ruled by its own king known as *litunga* in the Lozi language. Other provinces and different tribes were also embroiled in ethnoregional rivalries. But the greatest threat to national integrity came from Barotseland. However, they all posed great danger to national unity and, for a short period in February 1968, President Kenneth Kaunda resigned as head of state. As he put it, he was "upset by a terrible provincial and tribal approach to our national problems."[5]

It was true elsewhere across the continent, and such ethnoregional loyalties caused a lot of problems for the

13

young nations which had just won independence as "one people," yet had to contend with tribalism – hence secession in a number of cases – as the biggest threat to national unity. Compounding the problem was the fact that, contrary to what many people had expected, independence did not bring immediate relief to millions of Africans trapped in poverty and suffering from disease and ignorance; even decades after the end of colonial rule, millions across the continent have yet to enjoy the fruits of independence.

Such rising expectations only fuelled resentment against central authority, as Africans grappled with the problems of nation-building with only scant resources in countries which are the poorest of the poor in the world. And they could not expect to survive as nations if they were structured along tribal lines. Therefore, even before nation-building in terms of economic development could be seriously considered, every African country had to contend with another formidable task: forging a sense of common identity and loyalty to the nation composed of different tribes, many of which were suspicious and jealous of each other or one another, and sometimes outright hostile towards each other.

So, tribes "had to go." They could no longer exist as autonomous entities for one simple reason. Tribalism is incompatible with nationalism, and nation-building is impossible without nationhood. And you can't have nationhood without a genuine feeling of common citizenship and identity which goes beyond saluting the same flag and travelling on the same passport.

Therefore, right from the beginning, consolidation of the nation-state – institutions of authority over national territory – went hand-in-hand with nation-building. One could not be given priority over the other, and the state could not be consolidated without containing or neutralizing tribalism. Tribalism was, and still is, a constant threat to the existence of African countries, almost all of which were artificially created during the partition of Africa by the European powers about 130 years ago at the Berlin Conference which lasted from November 1884 - February 1885.

With the exception of the Arab countries in North Africa, and Somalia which is almost entirely composed of ethnic Somalis except for a small number of people from Bantu tribes in Kenya, Tanzania and Mozambique who were taken there as slaves by the Arabs during the slave trade more than 300 years ago, none of the countries on the continent are ethnically homogeneous entities, as is the case in most countries around the world.

Even Botswana is not entirely Tswana, although it is about 80 percent; nor is Swaziland entirely Swazi, although it is in overwhelming numbers in black Africa's last kingdom.

After the partition of Africa, the countries created were no more than a collection – not even an amalgamation – of different, often antagonistic, tribes just lumped together by the colonial powers to satisfy their imperial ambitions. The colonial boundaries were arbitrarily drawn without the slightest concern for the interests and well-being of Africans. All the tribes, not just some, saw themselves as independent entities or nations – even if held captive by other tribes – and would secede anytime if they got the chance to do so.

Besides their skin colour and hair texture, they saw themselves as different from each other, and the nation-state a mere imposition by alien intruders from Europe, thus making the task of nation-building a very complicated one. As Obafemi Awolowo said, the people who are called Nigerians – a collection of more than 250 different ethnic groups – are as different from each other as much as the people of different European countries are.[6]

But African countries have survived as political entities despite the odds against them through the decades

15

since independence. Therefore, just holding them together, preventing them from falling apart, is a great achievement even though they have survived as weak nations. But Africa would have been even weaker, much weaker, had the countries broken up along tribal lines, with each tribe ruling itself as was the case in precolonial times, except for conquered tribes which were ruled by others.

Yet African countries are not given credit for that. Keeping the tribes together is an enormous task even today. And maintaining the countries as functional units where members of different tribes and races work together and even identify themselves as one people, is an even greater achievement, considering the fact that the disruptive forces inherent in such complex multi-ethnic societies are beyond the capacity of the state to contain them without using a skillful combination of persuasive and coercive power. There is no army that can stop all the tribes in a country from tearing it apart if they decide to go their own way. Only a few can be destructive enough, wreaking havoc nationwide.

Therefore in fairness, if African leaders are considered to be a failure in many areas, which they are, frankly speaking, they should at least be given credit for keeping their countries united and, in some cases, for creating a sense of common identity among different tribes within their national boundaries. As Julius Nyerere said many years after he stepped down as president of Tanzania, his greatest failure was that although he managed to unite Tanganyika and Zanzibar to create Tanzania in 1964, he was never able to persuade the leaders of neighbouring countries to form a larger federation, a move he believed would have made the region a powerhouse:

"I felt that these little countries in Africa were really too small, they would not be viable – the Tanganyikas, the Rwandas, the Burundis, the Kenyas. My ambition in East Africa was really never to build a Tanganyika. I wanted an

East African federation. So what did I do in succeeding? My success is building a nation out of this collection of tribes."[7]

He also went on to say: "A new leadership is developing in Africa....The military phase is out. I think the single-party phase is out."[8]

A few years after independence, the one-party state was introduced in most African countries and was justified by the leaders on the grounds that it was the most effective apparatus for mobilizing different tribes under one leadership to achieve national unity. And it proved to be a potent weapon, although in more than one way, including suffocation of legitimate dissent in most cases. But, in spite of its shortcomings, the one-party system did eliminate one danger which threatened practically all African countries during the early years of independence when peoples of different tribes did not identify with each other as one people: formation of political parties along ethnic and regional lines in the name of democracy under a multi-party system, despite constitutional bans against formation of such parties. There would always have been ways to circumvent that, including formation of ethnoregional alliances to the exclusion of others.

That would have been the end of African countries. Besides Nkrumah, Nyerere was probably the most articulate exponent of the one-party state on the continent, and its most successful practitioner for two decades; Tanzania became a *de jure* one-party state in 1965, and Nyerere stepped down from the presidency in 1985, although he continued to be chairman of the ruling party (Chama Cha Mapinduzi - CCM - Party of the Revolution) until 1990, two years before multi-party politics was introduced with his full support. As he said in an interview not long before he died:

"I really think that I ran the most successful single-party system on the continent. You might not even call it a party. It was a single, huge nationalist movement....I don't believe that our country would be where it is now if we had a multiplicity of parties, which would have become tribal and caused us a lot of problems. But when you govern for such a long time, unless you are gods, you become corrupt and bureaucratic.... So I started calling for a multiparty system."[9]

Few would say it would have better for African countries to have split up along tribal lines, plunging them into chaos and civil wars, than to have peace and unity under one-party rule that guaranteed their survival as nations even if that meant curtailed freedom, suffocating dissent. There was not one African country that was safe then, or is safe today, from the danger of tribalism. And that includes those composed of small tribes, such as Tanzania whose 126 tribes – except one or two – are too small, weak and poor to survive as viable entities even if they wanted to secede. But if tribalism is widespread, even small tribes can be just as disruptive. Aware of the danger of tribalism, President Nyerere addressed the subject in his annual radio broadcast to the nation on the seventh independence anniversary on 9 December 1968. He spoke in Kiswahili, the national language:

"I have begun to hear whispers about tribalism. Just after independence, we got complaints that people were being appointed to government positions on the basis of tribalism, and we immediately appointed a commission to look into the allegations. The commission proved without any doubt that there was no tribalism in the allocation of jobs in government.

But just recently, I began to hear this complaint again. I did not treat it lightly. We called some of these people who were saying there is tribalism, and told them to give their evidence either to me or to Chief Mang'enya (the ombudsman). We promised to investigate immediately. But they have not given us one shred of evidence....

Tanzanians who had the opportunity for higher education during colonial rule were mostly Wahaya, Wachaga, and Wanyakyusa. And because most of the education was provided by missionaries, most of these people are also Christians. And when we replace Europeans who hold responsible jobs, and give those jobs to Tanzanians, the people who get them come mostly from these three tribes. Therefore, if you ask me why Wahaya, Wachaga, and Wanyakyusa have most of the jobs which require higher education, the answer is very obvious. They are the ones who got higher education during colonial times.

I would say, look at the positions in politics, where a person is not asked about his educational qualifications. Look at Parliament, the National Executive, the Central Committee of TANU (ruling party), and at the Cabinet. How many Wanyakyusa, Wahaya, or Wachaga are members? You will find that perhaps there aren't any, or there is one or two....

It is the job of the government to help, even favour, the more backward parts of the country, especially regarding education. We are doing this and will continue to do so. But if a Mchaga, a Mhaya or a Mnyakyusa young man were denied a job because of his tribe – when he is capable and there is no other Tanzanian with the necessary qualifications – then we would be practising a very stupid and very evil kind of tribalism which led to the establishment of Biafra."[10]

It would have been very easy for such people, who were complaining about tribalism yet could not prove it was a factor in the allocation of jobs as President Nyerere said, to form their own political parties on tribal and ethnoregional basis – and even forge alliances with other "victimised" tribes – under the multiparty system and ignite tribal conflict; a potential catastrophe the one-party system, which embraced and accommodated all the tribes under the same political tent, was able to contain and neutralize in many African countries, especially in the early years of independence when the countries were in their formative stage trying to forge a true sense of national identity among the different ethnic groups.

This should not, in any way, be misconstrued as a defence of dictatorship but an objective appraisal of the functional utility of the one-party system and the positive role it played in saving African countries from splitting along tribal lines. And that entailed curtailment of freedom in many cases; a sad necessity, not in all but in some cases, when it was critical to avert the catastrophe of national disintegration. In most cases, it was sheer abuse of power, with many leaders invoking the specter of national disintegration to perpetuate themselves in office.

But that does not mean that the positive role played by the one-party system as a unifying force during those critical years should be ignored; a positive contribution even some African leaders don't want to acknowledge simply because they are so much opposed to one-party rule, although for good reasons, mostly abuse of power. As Nicephore Soglo, former president of Benin, stated after losing the election in 1996:

"The West African country of Benin held elections in March (1996). I lost the presidency....

While former President Mathieu Kerekou has returned to power, there is a difference now. Twenty-four years ago, he came to power by the barrel of the gun. This year it was by way of the ballot box....

Many claim that Africa is different, that it is not ready for democracy. Ethnic tensions are pointed to as poisoning

20

democracy. We have ethnic tensions in Benin. We have managed them. Sadly, many African leaders of the early independence years used these same arguments to justify their repressive rule."[11]

Yet Benin itself, then known as Dahomey, was almost torn apart by ethnic strife during the early years of independence, something Soglo conveniently overlooks. It is a subject I have also addressed in one of my books, *Military Coups in West Africa since the Sixties.*[12]

Would a multiparty system, with several parties formed on ethnic and regional basis as was the case in Dahomey in the sixties, have served the country better? Or would it have made things worse, exacerbating ethnoregional rivalries and hostilities? It is true that Nicephore Soglo conceded ethnic tensions still exist in Dahomey today, as they do in other African countries. And Benin has survived under those tensions in a democratic environment of multiparty politics. But that is today.

African countries are stronger today as political entities than they were during their early years of independence, although all are still vulnerable to ethnic conflicts; but not as vulnerable as they were when they emerged from colonial rule. They were very young then, newly born. They did not have strong governments. They did not command full allegiance from different tribes which regarded central authority as an alien institution imposed on them to destroy their tribal and traditional values and leadership. And all their political institutions, inherited from the departing colonial masters, were not restructured to reflect African realities and accommodate or harmonise conflicting ethnoregional interests.

They were not firmly established and could have collapsed any time from the slightest push by tribalists if these tribal chauvinists had the opportunity to form opposition parties to promote their agenda. And being tribalists and regionalists, they naturally would have appealed to tribal sentiments to achieve their goals which would have been at variance with national aspirations.

The situation is different today across Africa. African countries are more mature. They have survived an entire generation since independence; most of them half a century. And they don't need one-party rule as they did before, except – and that's may be – in some cases such as Rwanda and Burundi where the one-party system embracing both the Hutu and the Tutsi may be the only way to guarantee justice and equality for all. The Tutsi will never win an election against the Hutu majority under a multiparty system.

Political parties in both countries have always been structured along ethnic lines, excluding the Hutu majority from power, except in Rwanda from 1962 to 1994 when the Hutu were in control. Both Rwanda and Burundi have historically been dominated by the Tutsi for about 400 years since they came from the northeastern part of Africa and conquered the Hutu.

The one-party system may also be a temporary safeguard against national disintegration when a country faces total collapse, requiring the need for a united or coalition government under strong leadership.

Although it is true that African countries today are ready for multiparty democracy, Soglo's contention that such a system would have been appropriate for Africa even in the sixties after independence, does not correspond to reality even in his own country. How could it have contained tribalism and ethnoregional rivalries in Dahomey, as Benin was then called, during those early years of independence?

Dahomey won independence on 1 August 1960, under the leadership of Hubert Maga, a northerner. His main support came from the north because the country was plagued by ethnic rivalries, especially between northerners and southerners. Because of such ethnoregional rivalries,

President Maga did not have clear mandate to rule the country, since he hardly had any support in the south. And as expected, southerners also had their own leaders who enjoyed little support in the north, President Maga's ethnoregional stronghold. Justin Ahomadegbe had solid support in the south, while another leader, Migan Apithy, commanded allegiance in the central part of the country and in some parts of the south. Such divisions made it virtually impossible for the national leaders to govern effectively. In October 1963, President Hubert Maga was overthrown in a military coup led by Colonel Christophe Soglo, a southerner.

But the coup did not end ethnic and regional rivalries. Democracy was tried but thwarted by ethnic rivals. When Dahomey tried to hold elections in 1970 after the results of the 1968 electoral contest were annulled, northern and southern politicians were so bitterly divided that the elections were cancelled. It would, of course, be an oversimplification to blame all of Dahomey's problems on ethnic rivalries. Economic problems and social unrest across the country caused by a number of factors also played a significant role and made it it difficult for the government to exercise effective control. They were one of the main reasons why President Hubert Maga's government was overthrown.

But all those problems were exacerbated by ethnic rivalries which have always plagued African countries since independence, even in times of economic prosperity and political stability rarely enjoyed on this troubled continent.

Contending that the multiparty system would have served African countries better than the one-party system in the early years of independence when they were most vulnerable to ethnic and regional rivalries, is to ignore the destructive nature of ethno-nationalism; the most potent force in the world even today, as much as it has been throughout history. It is also to ignore the potential for

23

disruption unscrupulous politicians always exploit in multiparty politics, a term synonymous with multi-tribal politics in the African context. Because of its tolerance of dissent, the multiparty system enables – even if it does not legally allow – almost anybody, including tribalists and regionalists and other disruptive elements, in the name of democracy to form political parties with a hidden partisan agenda while professing national unity. And Africa has already suffered and continues to suffer from some of the worst excesses of this ethno-nationalist impulse.

In the sixties, ethnic hatred of the Igbos in Nigeria exploded with such unconstrained fury that it almost destroyed Africa's largest nation at a cost of more than one million lives, mostly Igbo. It also exploded in Rwanda where almost one million Tutsis were slaughtered in only three months, and in neighbouring Burundi where hundreds of thousands of Hutus – at least 300,000 – were massacred by the Tutsi in the 1990s alone. And the massacres continued as the Tutsi refused to share power with the Hutu on meaningful basis. Where was the multiparty system to avert such catastrophe? Instead, it fanned flames in all three countries.

When Nigeria exploded during the sixties, it was a multiparty state. But all the parties were regionally entrenched with a strong ethnic bias. Even the National Convention of Nigerian Citizens (NCNC) – until 1960 known as the National Council of Nigeria and the Cameroons – which was led by Dr. Nnamdi Azikiwe and had supporters in all three regions of Nigeria, was strongest in the Eastern Region dominated by the Igbos. The Action Group led by Chief Obafemi Awolowo enjoyed overwhelming support among the Yorubas who dominate the Western Region. And the Northern People's Congress (NPC) led by Sir Ahmadu Bello, the Sardauna of Sokoto, was firmly entrenched in the Northern Region dominated by the Hausa-Fulani; Bello was Fulani.

Would a one-party state, under a single party of

national unity, have helped Nigeria in its turbulent times through the years? No one knows, given its size and complexity as a multi-polity of more than 250 ethnic groups and religious differences especially between the predominantly Muslim north and Christian as well as animist south. But one thing is certain, however controversial it may be. Militocracy – or military rule also known as stratocracy – as a kind of "one-party state," at least kept the country united, through coercion, and prevented the genocidal rampage that took place during the sixties and which was triggered by tribalism.

This is not to justify military rule – soldiers do not have the mandate to rule, they should stay in the barracks, and obey the rule of law under democratically elected leaders; it is simply to point out that an ethnically diverse population with a history of tribal conflicts needs strong leadership under one central government that is capable of accommodating all groups on equal basis but which also should be willing to decentralise power to diffuse tensions.

The alternative is national disintegration, or a weak federal system – or confederation – under which different ethnic groups become autonomous entities with the right to secede; a subject I have addressed in the last part of the book. A weak federal system is better than total disintegration of African countries into hundreds of independent ethnostates. But most lleaders across the continent chose one-party and authoritarian rule to contain tribalism and maintain national unity. And it worked.

Even today, when most African countries are trying to experiment with multiparty politics, a case can still be made for one-party rule. If the multiparty system is going to enable people to form political parties on ethnic or regional basis and even form alliances to prevent members of some ethnic groups from winning public office, then one-party rule is justified to maintain national unity and guarantee equality for all. Or let some people go, if they are excluded from power by their fellow countrymen. They have the right to establish their own independent state and rule themselves, as the Igbos did in the late sixties.

It is true that one-party rule has been a tragedy in most African countries for decades. But when you have ethnoregional rivalries accentuated by multiparty politics, one-party rule may be a better alternative. It may be the only way members of all tribes and all regions can compete for office on equal basis because the single party is open to everybody, as was the case in Tanzania under President Julius Nyerere. In fact, Tanzania's ruling party was more than just a political party. It was a national movement.

In defence of multiparty politics, an argument can be made that the constitution prohibits formation of tribal or regionally entrenched parties. And it can. But in practice, how effective is it? Tribal and regional parties – or parties with a hidden agenda to promote tribal and regional interests – have ways of legally qualifying for the ballot under the constitution by merging with other ethnoregional parties to win national mandate. They may seem to be nationally representative. But they will continue to be tribalist if their purpose of forming a coalition is to exclude members of some regions or tribes from winning elections. And such alliances have been formed in the past, although in the case of Azikiwe's NCNC, its decision to form an alliance with the Northern People's Congress (NPC) at independence in 1960 was not in pursuit of a tribal agenda.

Dr. Azikiwe's NCNC and the Northern People's Congress (NPC) led by Sir Abubakar Tafawa Balewa but dominated by Sir Ahmadu Bello, formed an alliance which excluded Awolowo's Action Group from the first African federal government formed at independence in October 1960. It would, of course, be wrong to characterize the alliance as tribalist deliberately intended to exclude

Yorubas from power. It was a marriage of convenience for political expediency. Azikiwe's party, the NCNC, was not ethnic but national in character. It was the only party which had members in all three regions and even won seats in the Northern and Western Regional Assemblies, the regional strongholds of the Hausa-Fulani and the Yoruba, respectively.

Therefore Azikiwe's move was a tactical alliance with a party – the Northern People's Congress – which had the largest number of representatives in the federal legislature, although it represented only one region: Northern Nigeria. It was also the most tribalistic, and most conservative, of all the Nigerian political parties dominated by northern Muslim traditional rulers who brooked no dissent. Even the Action Group, led by Awolowo, an uncompromising Yoruba bigot who died in 1986 at the age of 76, had some members in the Eastern Region, although not many.

But in spite of its virulently ethnoregional bias, the Northern People's Congress emerged as Nigeria's ruling party, since it dominated the federal legislature because of the structural imbalance of the federation favouring the north.

The British colonial rulers formed a structurally flawed federation of three massive regions – instead of several – dominated by the country's three largest ethnic groups. The smaller ones were left out of the equation and never became a factor in determining the future of the country. They were frozen out of power.

The Northern Region had the largest population, officially, although the other two regions disputed the 1956 census figures taken just four years before independence. The census was deeply flawed.

And because of the numerical preponderance enjoyed by the north, based on those census figures, the region also produced the largest number of representatives in the national legislature.

An entire half of the members of the Nigerian

parliament were northerners who, by simple majority rule, were legally entitled under the constitution to form the federal government. And that meant a national government dominated by the Northern People's Congress whose dominant figure was the Sardauna of Sokoto, Sir Ahmadu Bello. The federal prime minister, Tafawa Balewa, also a northerner and titular head of the Northern People's Congress and the Nigerian Federal Government, was no more than a puppet manipulated at will by the Northern Premier Ahmadu Bello.

Nigeria emerged from colonial rule with a federal constitution which theoretically guaranteed justice and equality for all. But its future looked bleak because of the lopsided nature of the federation favouring the north at the expense of the other regions, and excluding minority groups from the centre. And it had catastrophic consequences, plunging the country into civil war only a few years later, a conflict that almost destroyed the nation.

The flawed structure of the federation continued to be a source of many problems and instability even after the federation was restructured several times; it now has 39 states, the last added by democratically elected President Olusegun Obasanjo, a southerner.

And because of historical inequalities in the allocation of power, northerners dominated the federation for almost 40 years since independence. Most of the rulers were soldiers from Northern Nigeria. Tribalism and regional biases continue to be some of the major problems Nigeria faces, and northern military rulers only made the situation much worse. As Professor Crawford Young stated in his article, "The Impossible Necessity of Nigeria: A Struggle for Nationhood," in *Foreign Affairs:*

"During most of Nigeria's 27 years (almost 30 years until May 1999 when Olusegun Obasanjo took over as elected president) of military rule, the senior autocrat has been from the north. The two civilian prime ministers (one was actually a president, Shehu Shagari, 1979 – 83) – from 1960 to 1966, and 1979 to 1983 – (the only civilian rulers the country had since independence in 1960 before Obasanjo, a former military head of state, was elected as a civilian president in 1999) were both Hausa-Fulani, the politically and demographically dominant ethnic category in the north. Even though Generals Yakubu Gowon (1966 – 1975), Ibrahim Babangida (1983 – 1993), and Sani Abacha (1993 –1998) are not themselves Hausa-Fulani, (they are all northerners and) Nigerians view them as integral parts of what Wole Soyinka terms 'a self-perpetuating clique from the yet feudally oriented part of the country.'"[13]

Soyinka goes on to denounce this ruling clique in his book, *The Open Sore of A Continent: A Personal Narrative of the Nigerian Crisis:*

"(It is an) infinitesimal but well-positioned minority....In denouncing the activities of this minority, described variously as the Sokoto Caliphate, the Northern Elite, the Kaduna Mafia, the Hausa-Fulani oligarchy, the Sardauna Legacy, the Dan Fodio Jihadists, et cetera, what is largely lost in the passion and outrage is that they do constitute a minority – a dangerous, conspiratorial, and reactionary clique, but a minority just the same. Their tentacles reach deep, however, and their fanaticism is the secular face of religious fundamentalism."[14]

And when Sani Abacha, a demented Kanuri – not Hausa-Fulani – from Kano, annulled the results of the June 1993 presidential election won by Moshood Abiola, a Yoruba from the southwest but who was able to garner impressive support in the eastern and northern parts of Nigeria as well, in addition to overwhelming backing in his native Yorubaland in the west, he only confirmed fears

29

among many Nigerians that he was determined to perpetuate northern domination of the federation and pushed the country to the brink of disaster. The country almost split along ethnic lines, and would probably have, had he not suddenly died of a heart attack in July 1998, reportedly after being poisoned by a prostitute.

The results of the June 1993 elections had actually been annulled by his predecessor, Ibrahim Babangida, but Abacha sealed the annulment instead of reversing it after he seized power and imprisoned Abiola when he claimed office the following June as the legitimate president of Nigeria. Abacha had the chance to rectify the situation. But he chose not to, and made the annulment final. And as Soyinka said about this betrayal and denial of the people's mandate: "(It was) the most treasonable act of larceny of all time: It violently robbed the Nigerian people of their nationhood."[15]

Soyinka is not alone in doubting that Nigeria will continue to exist as a single political entity. Many other Nigerians share the same sentiment. They include a significant number of Yorubas, Igbos, Ogonis, Ijaws and others in the Niger Delta who have been marginalised, especially under northern military rulers who dominated the federation for decades. Even the three titans of the Nigerian independence movement – Nnamdi Azikiwe, Obafemi Awolowo, and Ahmadu Bello – did, at different times, question the viability of the structurally flawed federation, and even the wisdom of preserving Nigeria as one country.

Ethnic rivalry and mistrust was, and still is – together with religious fanaticism among some Muslims such as Boko Haram and others in the north – the fundamental problem threatening the existence of Nigeria.

Soyinka, like many Nigerians and other Africans including this writer, still would like to see Nigeria remain united, but admits: "I...frankly could not advance an invulnerable reason for my preference for a solution that did not involve disintegration."[16]

Even more tragic for Africa is the fact that Nigeria is not the only country facing this bleak prospect. The Democratic Republic of Congo, the giant nation that has become the bleeding heart of Africa right in the middle of the continent, was virtually partitioned into fiefdoms dominated by rebel groups in the east and by an inept and powerless central government that exercised virtually no control over the remaining parts of the country since 1998 when the insurgents launched a rebellion – ignited by Rwanda and Uganda, with Burundi's involvement – to overthrow President Laurent Kabila.

The rebellion continued after his son Joseph Kabila took over, following his assassination in January 2001. This former Belgian colony, which lost at least 10 million people under the brutal imperial rule of King Leopold II, has been the scene of carnage for more than a century. Between August 1998, when the rebellion started, and June 2001, about 3 million people died in eastern Congo as a result of the war. And the carnage continued. The Congo should never have been one country. And as Professor Crawford Young wrote about another giant African nation: "Nigeria has little cultural logic; its peoples would never have chosen to live together."[17]

Most of the tribes in other African countries would never have chosen to live together either. Before the advent of colonial rule, each had its own leaders. And had it not been for the European colonial rulers who partitioned Africa and lumped different tribes together, they would have continued to live the same way as independent micro-nations or ethnostates. The secessionist attempts by all three regions in Nigeria dominated by three main ethnic groups is instructive in this context.

Yet, in Nigeria like everywhere else across the

continent, attempts were made by African leaders to transcend tribalism and regionalism for the sake of national unity. When Dr. Nnamdi Azikiwe formed an alliance with Federal Prime Minister Tafawa Balewa, a northerner, it was with the hope that although Nigerians "would never have chosen to live together," they could at least try to contain or even submerge their tribal and regional differences in order to live together. Therefore this alliance was different from many others in one fundamental respect: It was not formed to promote tribal interests or deliberately exclude Yorubas from power but to save Nigeria as a collective entity, with the predominantly Yoruba party, the Action Group, forming the official opposition.

However, there have been other alliances in Nigeria and other African countries that have been formed deliberately to promote tribal interests and exclude members of some ethnic groups from holding public office; for example the Igbo in Nigeria. Tribal and regional parties forming such alliances in order to technically qualify as "national parties" under the constitution which expressly forbids formation of such parties are not complying with the constitution – they are circumventing and subverting the constitution.

And if there is no other way members of excluded groups can be protected and qualify for office, then – short of secession – the one-party system is totally justified under those circumstances, since it is capable of accommodating members of all tribes and regions on equal footing. It is in this context that the one-party system should be viewed as a very effective weapon against tribalism in African countries. And that was especially the case when they were just new nations trying to establish themselves shortly after independence.

Even as late as the 1990s and beyond, many people in Tanzania questioned the functional utility of the multiparty system because of the divisions and the violence it caused in what had been one of the most peaceful and stable countries in Africa for decades when it was under one-party rule. Tanzania was a one-party state for almost 30 years under the leadership of President Julius Nyerere. And not once in those years was the country rocked by violence caused by political factions pursuing partisan interests as happened after the introduction of multiparty democracy which has even provided an opportunity for many tribalists to form tribal associations; a phenomenon unheard of under Nyerere.

Even students at the University of Dar es Salaam, who are supposed to be liberal-minded, have formed tribal organizations. As one student from Tanga complained in an interview with one of Tanzania's leading newspapers, *The Guardian,* on 20 July, 2002, the situation on campus was so bad that even a sick student could not count on getting help from a roommate who was not a member of the same tribe. Help had to come from his or her fellow tribesmen and their organization.

And that is tragic, posing great danger to national unity that was carefully nurtured by the nation's founding father Mwalimu Julius Nyerere for almost half a century.

If Tanzania is to remain a strong, stable, and united nation, then tribal associations should be banned, and should not enjoy legal protection from the government in the name of pluralism. People of different tribes should belong to the same civic organizations, which may be called the Tanzania Brotherhood Associations, or whatever other names they choose, in place of tribal associations. Otherwise Tanzania may be headed towards catastrophe, with prospects for tribal conflict and national disintegration being a distinct possibility.

That is the main reason why, in a national survey conducted before the introduction of multiparty politics in the early 1990s, the majority of Tanzanians who participated in it were resolutely opposed to the adoption of the multiparty system. They feared it would divide the country and threaten national stability and were vindicated a few years later when violence erupted following the general election in 2000 which resulted in a number of deaths, prompting President Benjamin Mkapa to publicly wonder if the people were not wiser than the leaders when they rejected the multipatry system in the early nineties.

But the multiparty system was introduced, anyway, against prevailing national sentiment and in defiance of the people's will. Yet the people, popularly known as *wananchi* in Kiswahili meaning citizens or owners of the country or the land, were vindicated by subsequent events, including the irresponsible conduct of some opposition parties such as the Democratic Party under the leadership of a fiery fundamentalist minister, Christopher Mtikila, inciting violence and preaching racial and religious intolerance.

The people of Tanzania should have voted in a referendum to determine their wish, although the national survey conducted in the early 1990s was comprehensive enough as a statistical tool to gauge collective national sentiment towards divisive politics legitimized by multiparty democracy. And they should have been allowed to continue living under a one-party state if that is what the majority wanted. The electoral mandate won by the ruling Chama Cha Mapinduzi (CCM) – Party of the Revolution or Revolutionary Party – which virtually constitutes a *de facto* one-party state, seems to indicate that. It is the same party that has ruled Tanzania since independence: Tanganyika African National Union (TANU) on the mainland, and Afro-Shirazi Party (ASP) on the isles, until the two parties merged in 1977 to form CCM, as urged by Nyerere.

But there is really no need for one-party rule in any African country, except in extreme cases when nations are in danger of collapsing because of ethnic conflicts or violence between political parties pursuing partisan interests at the expense of national unity and stability. That is an emergency involving national survival and can not be dismissed lightly. Even Western multiparty democracies submerge their differences in times of national crisis.

Therefore African countries should be not be expected to act differently when their survival is at stake. And when opposition parties are so weak, unable to win national mandate because of rivalry and lack of direction within the opposition camp, they lose the rationale for their existence and even resort to subversive tactics to win power. They also do everything they can to weaken or frustrate the government in order to make it look bad before the electorate from whom it won the mandate to rule. And incumbents also invoke this to stifle legitimate dissent and justify repressive rule and a return to the status quo ante in order to re-institute one-party rule, mostly *de facto*, in this era of multiparty democracy.

There are, of course, exceptions to this common trend towards multiparty democracy sweeping across the continent. Rwanda and Burundi are prime examples. The Hutu and the Tutsi in both countries may be beyond the point where they could have genuinely tried to resolve and submerge their differences amicably, if they ever took that route. Even one-party rule intended to forge national unity and guarantee peace and security for all, is not going to work in these two countries.

The hostility between the Hutu and the Tutsi runs so deep, and has been going on for so long, that partition of Rwanda and Burundi along ethnic lines seems to be the only solution to this problem; although it is going to be a Herculean task, given the integrated nature and interwoven structure of both societies, if it is ever attempted; which is highly unlikely.

And it is impossible for slaves and masters to live together as equals. The Tutsi have been holding the Hutu in feudal subjugation for 400 years in spite of the fact that they are a small minority who comprise about 14 percent of Burundi's population, and only about 9 percent of

Rwanda's; while the Hutu constitute a formidable 90 percent of Rwanda's population, and 85 percent of Burundi's, with the Twa (pygmies) making up 1 percent of the population in each of the two countries. Ultimately, numbers will determine the fate of these twin states, with dire consequences for the Tutsi minority if they continue to subjugate the Hutu majority.

However, the solution of partition suggested here in the case of Rwanda and Burundi is not appropriate in all contexts where African countries are torn by ethnic conflicts, as many of them have been since independence in the sixties; nor does it mean that the solution is viable today, as ethnic strife continues to threaten the integrity of African nations.

Like secession, partition should only be the ultimate solution, as a last resort, if nothing else works; for example in the case of Sudan where the Arabs in the north want to perpetually dominate and enslave blacks in the south and forcibly convert them to Islam in order to transform the country into a fundamentalist theocratic state based on a radical interpretation of the Koran.

Had such a solution been implemented in the past, it would have split up African countries along tribal and regional lines, creating non-viable mini-ethnostates. It was avoided because of the one-party system and the coercive power of the state which helped to forge national unity on the anvil of uniformity. And such uniformity was possible only under the one-party system because of its monolithic nature, contrasted with the multiparty system which many politicians and their supporters unscrupulously exploit to pursue ethnoregional interests at the expense of national unity.

Therefore, in spite of its shortcomings, and there are many, there is no question that the one-party system saved African countries from falling apart and, indeed, saved Africa. And history is highly instructive in this context when we look at some cases involving multiparty politics across Africa soon after independence in the sixties. The relevance of these cases is continental in scope.

Immediately after independence, Ghana's leader Dr. Kwame Nkrumah faced strong opposition from political parties which were regionally entrenched. He was the founder of the Convention People's Party (CPP) which led the country to independence. The strongest opposition during the 1950s and after independence came from the Ashanti region spearheaded by Dr. Kofi A. Busia and Dr. J.B. Danquah of the United Gold Coast Convention (UGCC), the first party to campaign for independence before the CPP was formed by Nkrumah in 1949.

Compounding the problem was the fact that there were strong secessionist tendencies among the Ashanti. The secessionist threats were particularly strong in the late fifties, and when Ghana won independence, celebration among the Ashanti was muted. The Ewe in eastern Ghana also threatened to secede and unite with their fellow tribesmen across the border in Togo. This irredentist movement started even before Ghana won independence and continued thereafter. Also in northern Ghana, separatist tendencies threatened to break up the nation. And different political parties capitalized on all those secessionist sentiments in the name of multiparty democracy.

But Nkrumah suppressed the secessionist movements by instituting a unitary state under one-party rule. Otherwise, there probably would be no Ghana today. In 1964, the people of Ghana voted in a referendum – although the results were controversial – and gave President Nkrumah the mandate to establish a one-party socialist state, effectively ending multiparty politics which encouraged secessionist and irredentist movements.

In Dahomey (renamed Benin in 1975) in the sixties, three major leaders represented various ethnic groups and regions as we learned earlier: President Hubert Maga in the north, Migan Apithy in the central and parts of the south, and Justin Ahomadegbe in other southern areas. Without solid support in the north, Maga would not have become Dahomey's president when the country won independence from France in 1960. And the other two leaders, Apithy and Ahomadegbe both of whom briefly served as president at one time or another, would not have served in that post had it not been for the overwhelming support of their tribal members and allies in their respective regions.

In fact, tribal and regional divisions were so strong that the three leaders were forced to form a coalition government – triumvirate – to prevent civil war from breaking out, due to resentment among the tribes and regions which would have felt, and rightly so, that they had been left out of power if one of the regionally-entrenched parties or two in alliance ruled the country. The political parties led by the three leaders were strongly ethnic and regional in character under a multiparty system which was supposed to promote democracy for the sake of national unity. Instead, it ended up dividing the nation purely on tribal and regional basis.

In The Gambia, Prime Minister – later President – Sir Dawda Jawara's ruling People's Progressive Party (PPP), which ruled for 32 years until 1994 when Jawara was overthrown, was predominantly Malinke, the largest ethnic group in the country, and could not even be voted out of office because of the numerical superiority of its supporters who belonged to the dominant ethnic group and allied tribes.

By contrast, opposition parties drew most of their support from smaller ethnic groups. Gambia was said to be democratic, yet elections became useless when the smaller parties, hence tribes, could not dislodge the main party – read, Malinke – from power by electoral means. It was said to have a multiparty system, yet, in practice, it was a de facto one-party state because of the dominant position of the Malinke-backed People's Progressive Party.

In Sierra Leone, the Sierra Leone People's Party (SLPP) led by Dr. Milton Margai, the country's first prime minister, and next by his brother Sir Albert Margai who succeeded him as the nation's leader, was primarily composed of members of their ethnic group, the Mende, one of the two largest constituting at least 30 percent of the country's population. In the same way, Dr. Siaka Stevens' All People's Congress (APC) was mostly supported by members of the Temne tribe (although his father was a Limba and his mother a Mende), which also makes up about 30 percent of the population.

Hostility and rivalry between the two ethnic groups and their allies continued through the decades and was a major factor in the ouster of President Ahmad Tejan Kabbah, although a Mandingo but staunch member of the Mende-dominated SLPP, in 1997, and subsequent persecution of the Mende by the military junta of Major Johnny Paul Koromah, a member of the Limba tribe. The mutliparty system has not been able to contain or defuse such tension between members of different tribes in Sierra Leone but has, instead, thrived on it.

In Nigeria, before and after independence, all of the country's major political parties owed their existence to solid regional and ethnic allegiance as we learned earlier. Even after years of military rule, and after political parties were again allowed to operate and explicitly prohibited by the constitution from appealing to regional and tribal sentiments, Nigerians still overwhelmingly voted for candidates from their own tribes and regions in national elections, clearly demonstrated by the 1979, 1983 and 1993 general elections.

The Hausa-Fulani voted for their own kind for president, as did the Yoruba and the Igbo, the country's dominant groups which constitute a triad that virtually props up the Nigerian federation. The same pattern was repeated in the 1998 - 1999 general elections because of the toxic politics of ethnic loyalties.

In the Belgian Congo before independence, Joseph Kasavubu – who became the country's first president when the country won independence in 1960 – drew his strongest support from members of his own ethnic group, the Bakongo. And the political party he led, ABAKO - *Alliance des Bakongo* - was solidly Bakongo, yet claimed to be nationally representative in a country of more than 200 ethnic groups which were not Bakongo. In fact, Kasavubu, who was partly Chinese, dreamt of reuniting the Bakongo people who had been split up by the colonial borders of the French Congo (now Congo-Brazzaville), the Belgian Congo, and Portuguese Angola, and rebuilding the old Kongo kingdom. And under his leadership, ABAKO became a militant organization which advocated secession for the Bakongo more than it fought for Congolese independence as one country.

Moise Tshombe also mobilized his supporters into a powerful tribalistic and secessionist party known as CONAKAT – *Confederation des Associations Tribales du Katanga* – which had its strongest support in southern Katanga, the copper mining area which produced the country's most valuable export. The secessionist leader, who was related to the royal family of the Lunda ethnic group in his home province of Katanga, was solidly supported by members of his tribe, the Lunda. And his party, CONAKAT, dominated Katanga Province which he led into secession on 11 July 1960, only 11 days after Congo won independence on June 30th under the leadership of Patrice Lumumba. Tshombe's secessionist move plunged the country into chaos and anarchy and claimed more than 100,000 lives.

Neither Tshombe nor Kasavubu was interested in transforming his party into a truly national party transcending ethnic and regional loyalties. The multiparty system encouraged the two leaders and their parties to exploit and fortify regional allegiances to the detriment of national unity. In fact, every political party in Congo had been formed to protect and promote tribal interests, with the exception of Patrice Lumumba's Congo National Movement – *Movement National Congolais* – which campaigned from a Congolese nationalist and Pan-Africanist platform.

But even the highly popular Lumumba himself, the only Congolese leader of national stature with significant support in different parts of the country, could not overcome or suppress regional sentiments among his supporters in his home province. He had no control over that. Among all the country's six provinces, he drew his strongest support from Orientale Province in the east whose capital was Stanleyville (renamed Kisangani), his political base, and from members of his own tribe, the Batetela, although he did not encourage such ethno-regional loyalties like the other Congolese leaders did. But he could not make his regional and ethnic supporters overcome their biases, or stop them from throwing their weight behind him purely on the basis of regional and ethnic loyalties, because of the tremendous influence of ethnoregional allegiances in Africa's highly volatile cauldron of ethnic politics.

However, Lumumba's politics was examplary and transcendent. He led the Congo National Movement, the most nationalist and Pan-African-oriented political party in the history of the country, and became Congo's first prime minister and minister of defence when the country won independence.

But the multiparty system which fuelled ethnic and regional rivalries thwarted his efforts to unite the country, weaknesses outside powers exploited during the turbulent sixties to try and break up the country.

In Uganda, Dr. Milton Obote, a northerner from Lango district, drew his strongest and biggest support from fellow northerners: the Langi, the Acholi and other ethnic groups including Idi Amin's small Kakwa tribe. However, his ruling party, the Uganda People's Congress (UPC) he formed in 1960, was the only party which had the largest number of supporters in other parts of the country embracing all ethnic groups and championed nationalist causes.

By contrast the official opposition, the Democratic Party led by Benedicto Kiwanuka, was mostly supported by members of his tribe the Baganda and was regionally entrenched in the Buganda kingdom. In addition to being tribal and regional, the opposition party was divisive in another respect. It deliberately appealed to Catholic voters across Uganda and exploited religious sentiments to the detriment of national unity.

The other party in Uganda was the Kabaka Yekka, meaning Kabaka Only. It was led by the Kabaka (King) Edward Frederick Mutesa II and was unabashedly tribalistic, composed almost exclusively of members of the Baganda ethnic group who constituted the Buganda kingdom. And it was secessionst, demanding full independence for the kingdom. Although the two opposition parties – the Democratic Party and the Kabaka Yekka – both entrenched in the Buganda kingdom were intentionally divisive and therefore a threat to national unity, they were able to continue their activities in the name of multiparty democracy. The multiparty system clearly fostered and thrived on tribalism despite professions to the contrary.

In Rwanda, after centuries of subjugation and oppression by the Tutsi, the Hutu majority rose against their minority oppressors and deposed the Tutsi aristocrats in the mass uprising of July 1959. More than 100,000 Tutsis were massacred, and at least just as many fled to Burundi, Uganda, and Tanganyika (now Tanzania).

Just two years earlier in 1957, the Hutu had formed two political parties demanding a voice in the country's affairs commensurate with their numerical strength: the Association for the Social Improvement of the Masses led by Joseph Gitera, and the Party of the Hutu Emancipation

Movement (Parmehutu) led by Gregoire Kayibanda who became Rwanda's first president when the country won independence from Belgium on January 1, 1962.

Automatically, the dethroned Tutsi constituted the opposition in the national legislature, a case of unmistakable ethnic rivalry and hostility sanctioned by by the multiparty system in the name of democracy at whatever cost to peace and security and national integrity. It is an almost identical situation in neighbouring Burundi where the same ethnic groups, the Hutu and the Tutsi, have locked horns. And multiparty politics has fuelled ethnic hostilities in Rwanda and Burundi because the Hutu and the Tutsi vote strictly along tribal lines, threatening national unity, already fragile.

In Zambia also, like in many other African countries, the multiparty system proved to be divisive soon after the country won independence from Britain on 24 October 1964. President Kenneth Kaunda's United National Independence Party (UNIP) was national in scope, while the opposition African National Congress (ANC) led by Harry Nkumbula, and the United Party (UP) led by Maluniko Mundia, were based on regional loyalties with strong separatist tendencies, and appealed to tribal and regional alliances.

The two opposition parties were strongest in the south and in the west, respectively, where separatist tendencies were also strongest. Secessionist sentiments were strongest in Barotse Province, also known as Barotseland, in the west dominated by members of the Lozi tribe. Nkumbula was the favourite son of the Tonga and the Ila tribes in the south, and Mundia of the Lozi in the west.

And they organized their parties on that basis under the multiparty system, hardly a basis for national unity, yet one that acquires legitimacy in the name of multiparty democracy.

In Zimbabwe, the Shona and the Ndebele, traditional rivals and the country's largest ethnic groups, were neatly split along ethnic lines even during the struggle for independence. Their support for the two nationalist movements which waged guerrilla warfare for 15 years against white minority rule in the former British colony of Rhodesia was solidly ethnic, yet in pursuit of a nationalist cause. The Zimbabwe African National Union (ZANU) led by Robert Mugabe was and still is mostly Shona. And the Zimbabwe African People's Union (ZAPU) was overwhelmingly Ndebele and entrenched in the southwestern part of the country, Matebeleland.

ZAPU became the official opposition after the country won independence in 1980, and the two parties even fought in the early 1980s, with Matebeleland being the bloodiest battleground where more than 20,000 people, mostly Ndebele, were killed by government soldiers and security forces in a brutal campaign launched by the Shona-dominated government to crush the opposition.

The conflict erupted mainly because of ZAPU's refusal to accept ZANU as the legitimate government of Zimbabwe in spite of the fact that its leader Robert Mugabe won the general election just before independence. But it is also true that ZANU won because of overwhelming support from the Shona, the country's largest ethnic group constituting a formidable 70 percent of the total population, and the Ndebele about 20 percent; a case of clear ethnic rivalry exacerbated by the multiparty system.

The two parties merged in 1987 to form one ruling party, ZANU-PF (Patriotic Front). But the unity remained fragile at best because of the hostility between the two ethnic groups, much of it rooted in history when the Ndebele, who came from what is now Kwazulu-Natal Province in South Africa, emigrated north and conquered the Shona in the 1830s, forcing them to pay tribute. The Shona were not only subjugated but also humiliated. Many of them have not forgotten that.

In Kenya, ethnic loyalties were so strong in the 1992

and 1997 general elections that the opposition parties failed to defeat President Daniel arap Moi who won only about 40 percent of the vote in both elections. They failed to unite behind a single candidate because they were split along tribal lines; a lesson they remembered well during the 2002 elections when they formed a coalition and united behind a single candidate, Mwai Kibaki, to defeat Uhuru Kenyatta, Jomo Kenyatta's son, who was the KANU (Kenya African National Union) candidate, a party that had ruled the country for almost 40 years since independence in December 1963.

Yet, the parties which formed the coalition, NARC, were *still* tribal and regional in orientation and in pursuit of ethnoregional agendas in their quest for the national pie. It was essentially a coalition of the main tribal parties, representing the largest ethnic groups in the country, although smaller ones were also represented.

The coalition collapsed within three years, and tribalism again reared its ugly head when Kenya exploded during the December 2007 general elections which were rigged by President Mwai Kibaki and his fellow Kikuyus to deny Raila Odinga, a Luo, victory and perpetuate Kikuyu hegemonic control of the country. About 2,000 people were killed in the violence which tore the country apart along ethnic and regional lines and more than 600,000 people ended up homeless, refugees in their own homeland: Kenyans refugees in Kenya.

National unity has been an elusive goal in Kenya's history since independence and even before then.

In fact, the quest for national unity was clearly evident during the struggle for independence when KANU was formed. It was formed in May 1960 as a merger of three major parties: the Kenya African Union (KAU) formed in 1944 and led by Jomo Kenyatta; the National People's Convention Party (NPCP) formed in 1957 and led by Tom Mboya; and the Kenya Independence Movement (KIM) formed in 1959 and led by Oginga Odinga and Dr.

45

Gikonyo Kiano.

KAU was founded by James Gichuru. He stepped down from the party's leadership in favour of Jomo Kenyatta who returned to Kenya in 1946 from 15 years of self-imposed exile in Britain campaigning for independence. Kenyatta became the leader of KAU the following year in 1947.

But because KANU was dominated by the Kikuyu, and to a smaller degree by the other major tribes such as the Luo and the Kamba, smaller tribes feared that they would be left out of the equation as one of the determining factors in the country's future. This led to the formation of the Kenya African Democratic Union (KADU) in 1960, under the leadership of Ronald Ngala, which favoured a federal system of government with a weak central government as opposed to a strong unitary state advocated by KANU under Kenyatta.

KADU was preceded by the formation of another party for smaller tribes, the multiracial Kenya National Party (KNP), in 1959, with the support of European settlers apprehensive of the rise of African nationalism spearheaded by the major tribes which also had the largest population in a country of 42 tribes. The Kalenjins – an alliance of different small tribes in the Rift Valley Province – in the KNP were led by Daniel arap Moi and Taita Towett; the Baluhya-Bukusu by Masinde Muliro, and the smaller tribes in the Coast Province by Ronald Ngala. The KNP evolved into KADU the following year, led by Ngala.

However, in the 1963 general elections a few months before independence, KADU lost and, in the following year, its leader Ronald Ngala announced the voluntary dissolution of his party. This paved the way for the establishment of one-party rule by KANU which lasted until 1990 when the Kenyan constitution was amended to allow the re-introduction of multiparty politics.

The tragedy is that such liberalisation of the political

system only led to a return to the status quo ante of tribal politics reminiscent of the pre-independence era, tragically demonstrated by the prominence of ethnoregional loyalties and rivalries as well as violence in the general elections of the 1990s.

In the 1992 and 1997 presidential elections in Kenya, each major tribe – except the Kisii who did not field a presidential candidate – voted for its own candidate. The Kikuyu, Kenya's largest, overwhelmingly voted for Mwai Kibaki; the Luo for Raila Odinga, son of former Vice President Oginga Odinga under Jomo Kenyatta; the Luhya for Kijana Wamalwa; and the Kamba for Mrs. Charity Ngilu. They all lost, of course, because of tribalism among themselves and kept in power an unabashedly tribalistic president, Daniel arap Moi of KANU, whose government was dominated by his fellow Kalenjin tribesmen.

Those are just some of the countries whose political parties were split along ethnic and regional lines under the multiparty system despite professions of national unity, and despite a constitutional ban explicitly forbidding tribal politics and appeal to regional sentiments.

Yet ethnoregional alliances prevailed, and the multiparty system failed to transcend such sectarianism. In fact, it accomplished exactly the opposite. And little has changed.

Still, uncompromising proponents of the multiparty system contend that it is the only system which can maintain national unity and sustain robust democracy, despite evidence to the contrary, especially with regard to national unity. For example in Ghana, Dr. Kofi Busia, the opposition leader in parliament during Nkrumah's tenure, railed against Nkrumah's "one-party dictatorship" and presented himself as the embodiment of democratic ideals and the best alternative to despotic rule.

Yet, he not only ended up being a dictator himself – like Frederick Chiluba in Zambia in the 1990s, and other African leaders – under the multiparty system, of all systems, when he became prime minister in 1969, but led a party, the Progress Party, whose strongest support came from his ethnic group (and home region), the Ashanti, which is also the nation's largest.

That is something Dr. Nkrumah fought against, ethnoregional allegiances, when he led Ghana. Still, the multiparty system under which Dr. Busia won the election in 1969 did little to neutralise such ethnic and regional loyalties in national politics like Nkrumah did.

That is a significant number of countries where the multiparty system has played such a divisive role by thriving on tribal and regional sentiments in the name of national unity and democracy. And that is still the case today in a number of countries across the continent which have adopted multiparty democracy, thus putting the whole matter in its proper perspective necessary for one to understand *why* African leaders instituted one-party rule soon after independence in the sixties.

And the tragedy is that we Africans don't seem to have learned much from all this, as our countries continue to fan flames of ethnic hatred fuelled by multiparty politics.

Contemporary cases where ethnically-based political parties have caused conflict, sometimes leading to catastrophe, include Somalia, whose clan-based political interests and quest for power plunged the country into civil war after the fall of dictator Siad Barre in 1991, leaving it without a national government; Ethiopia, whose government was dominated by the Tigrean People's Liberation Front, an ethnically-based group representing only 10 percent of Ethiopia's population (Tigreans in Tigre Province in the north), since the ouster of dictator Mengistu Haile Mariam in 1991.

There is also Kenya, where – even after the coalition government was formed following the 2002 general elections – the Kikuyu mostly supported the Democratic Party. The Luhya, now the second-largest ethnic group after surpassing the Luo, were solidly behind FORD (the

Forum for the Restoration of Democracy); the Luo fiercely loyal to the National Development Party, and the Kamba to the Social Democratic Party; and Tanzania, where the Civic United Front (CUF) is mostly supported by opponents of the union of Tanganyika and Zanzibar and by a large number of Muslims who see it, rightly or wrongly, as a party fighting for the interests of Muslims.

There are other political parties in Tanzania which get their strongest support from specific regions where their leaders come from, thus tainting them with regional bias regardless of the positions they articulate as truly national parties. They include the United Democratic Party, the Tanzania Labour Party, and CHADEMA (Chama cha Demokrasia na Maendeleo - the Party of Democracy and Progess or Development).

Compounding the problem, and the felony, of ethnoregional biases of different political parties in different African countries is the fact that the governments themselves – with very few exceptions – have been dominated by a few ethnic groups through the years at the expense of others who end up playing a peripheral role in national affairs because of their marginal status.

In Zaire under Mobutu, the government was dominated by members of his tribe, the Gbande, from Equateur Province, as was the ruling party which for all practical purposes was the government across the spectrum.

In Congo-Brazzaville, also known as the Congo Republic, you have the Bembe and the Bakongo ethnic groups and their political parties in the southern part of the country competing with the Mbochi, the Sanga and other ethnic groups from the north. Gabon is dominated by the Mbochi, President Bongo's tribe. They have dominated the ruling party and the government since November 1967 when the then 32-year-old Bernard (renamed Omar) Bongo became president.

Across the border in Congo-Brazzaville President

Denis Sassou-Nguesso – who overthrew democratically elected President Pascal Lissouba (a member of the Bakongo tribe in the south) in October 1997 after a four-month civil war in which more than 10,000 people were killed and the capital Brazzaville destroyed – is a member of the Sanga tribe and has a daughter who was married to the late President Omar Bongo. Thus, you had two oil-rich countries ruled by a father-in-law and a son-in-law, also with strong ethnic ties. The Sanga and the Mbochi are strong allies, an alliance that has proved critical to the assumption of power by the northerners in Congo-Brazzaville through the years.

In Angola, the opposition party UNITA was compromised in its claim as a national party because it was supported almost entirely by the Ovimbundu tribe against the democratically elected government of the MPLA, the party which also fought for independence more than any other in the country. In Mozambique, RENAMO, the opposition party, draws its largest support from ethnic groups and regions opposed to the democratically elected government of FRELIMO.

In South Africa, the Inkatha Freedom Party (IFP) is supported almost entirely by the Zulu and rules Kwazulu-Natal Province, one of only two provinces where the governing African National Congress (ANC) had not been able to win elections before winning in the Western Cape. By contrast, the ANC, once led by President Nelson Mandela and next by President Thabo, enjoys enormous support across the country. Yet it is also worth remembering that ethnic loyalty is clearly evident even in the ruling ANC itself despite its stature as a truly multi-ethnic and multi-racial party. The vast majority of the Xhosa, the second largest ethnic group in South Africa after the Zulu, support the African National Congress. Also both Mandela and Mbeki were Xhosa.

But the first president of the African National Congress when the party was founded in 1912 was a Zulu,

Dr. John Dube. And the man who presided over the conference at the founding of the party, Dr. P. ka Seme, also belonged to a group closely related to the Zulu; in fact even the Xhosa themselves are closely related to the Zulu.

Therefore the ANC has never been an exclusively or even remotely a Xhosa party, unlike the Inkatha Freedom Party which is Zulu and openly advoctes Zulu interests, especially in Kwazulu-Natal Province.

In Malawi during Dr. Kamuzu Banda's life presidency, the ruling Malawi Congress Party (MCP), hence the government, was dominated by the Chewa, his tribe. In Kenya, when Mzee Jomo Kenyatta was in power, his tribe the Kikuyu dominated the ruling party, KANU, and the government. After he died and was succeeded by Daniel arap Moi, it was Moi's tribesmen the Kalenjin who became dominant in the government and in the ruling party KANU. In Cameroon, it is the Beti, President Paul Biya's tribe, which is dominant both in the ruling party and in the government; in the Ivory Coast, it was the Baoule, of which President Felix Houphouet-Boigny was a member. He ruled from 1960 until his death in December 1963, only to be succeeded by another Baoule, Henri Konan Bedie.

After a brief tenure of General Robert Guei who overthrew Bedie on Christmas eve in 1999, another Baoule, Lawrence Gbagbo became president. The Baoule is a predominantly Christian and southern tribe which treated the government of the Ivory Coast as its exclusive domain since independence, incurring the wrath of northern tribes who are also mostly Muslim; an injustice which led to civil war in 2000 and beyond and which virtually split the country into two: Muslim north versus Christian south.

In Liberia, after a military coup in 1980 by some of the country's indigenous tribesmen overthrew the Americo-Liberian oligarchy which dominated the country for 150 years since its founding, the Krahn, the tribe of military

51

ruler Samuel Doe, came to dominate the government during his tenure which eventually plunged the country into civil war from which it has not fully recovered, just as Somalia has not, and may not for decades to come.

In Togo, the Kabye, a northern tribe to which the late President Gnassingbe Eyadema belonged, as does his son who succeeded him, dominates the country and the army, versus the Ewe most of whom live in the southern part of the country, as well as other groups.

That is the depraved nature of ethnic politics in Africa on which the multiparty system thrives.

It is true that under the multiparty system, groups that have been excluded from power also get the chance to form their own political parties; which is good, since they get the opportunity to ventilate their grievances from political platforms and speak up for their rights. But tribalism also becomes legitimized and institutionalized as an integral part of multiparty democracy.

Even when political candidates rise above tribal politics, they are still constrained by the partisanship of their parties and supporters. For example, in the 1996 general election in Ghana, which was also the last for him, Jerry Rawlings again won the presidency in a free and fair election, although his victory in 1992 was controversial. And most Ghanaians voted across ethnic lines. But still, Rawlings' National Democratic Convention (NDC) ruling party also drew massive support from the Ewe, his mother's ethnic group in the Volta Region, his home in the eastern part of the country; while his leading opponent John Kufuor of the New Patriotic Front (NPF) also got support from different parts of the country but mostly from the Ashanti Region, his stronghold fortified by ethnic loyalty.

So, regardless of how nationalist or Pan-African-oriented some candidates may be, ethnic and regional divisions don't only remain a prominent feature of electoral contests under the multiparty system but are, in fact, exacerbated and legitimized by the very nature of multipartyism as a contest between competing interests, be they class, tribal or regional. Tribes take advantage of that by promoting their ethnic and regional interests through political parties they form or support in the name of multiparty democracy, which really means multiparty tribalism.

It is against this background that the establishment of one-party rule in Africa must be looked at, especially in the early days of independence, in order to understand why truly nationalist and Pan-Africanist leaders such as Kwame Nkrumah and Julius Nyerere chose the one-party system and became its most articulate exponents; and why they felt it was the best system under the circumstances. It helped Tanzania to become one of the most stable, and most peaceful, countries in Africa for almost 30 years under the leadership of Nyerere.

And it is a legacy that continues today, although the country has now and then been threatened by the fractious nature of multiparty politics since it was re-introduced in 1992 and led to incidents of violence especially during the 2000 general election and thereafter, including threats by some opposition leaders that they would resort to violence to achieve their political objectives under the multiparty system.

Therefore, both systems have major pitfalls. And both must be looked at objectively. Yet, given a choice between the two, there is no question that after decades of one-party misrule in most countries, the multiparty system must be given a chance to work in Africa, now that it has been adopted across the continent. But it must be adapted to the realities of African politics characterized by ethnic and regional rivalries.

There is no better argument for forming coalition governments in all the countries riven by ethnic tensions to replace the winner-take-all system common in all African countries which only fuels ethnic hostilities when some groups are excluded from power. The result is perpetual conflict, paralyzing the nation. It can even lead to civil war, as it already has in many countries across the continent. Coalition government composed of winners and losers in general elections should be institutionalized as a permanent feature of democracy in Africa in order to contain hostilities and defuse tensions among ethnic groups competing for power.

There is no question that the multiparty system is good and, in most cases, is even better than one-party rule. But it is contextual in relevance and application, depending on local circumstances and the nature of society. Having a multiparty system just for the sake of it, even when it is going to tear the country apart along tribal and regional lines with members of different parties appealing to ethnoregional loyalties, is not very good statesmanship. In countries threatened by ethnic rivalries, as almost all African countries are including Tanzania where – despite its excellent reputation for peace and harmony – some opposition parties thrive on ethnoregional loyalties, it is utterly naive, or rank dishonesty, to discount that.

And it has been vindicated by history: the former Belgian Congo, although at the instigation of Western powers and financial interests, exploiting local rivalries; Nigeria, because of the massacre of the Igbos which forced them to secede; Uganda, Ghana, and even Zambia, are some of the countries which were seriously threatened by ethnic conflicts and rivalries in the sixties, although – especially in the case of Nigeria and may be even the Congo – the one-party system would probably not have prevented the horrendous tragedies that befell these two giant nations and almost destroyed them in the turbulent sixties.

It was with those problems in mind that most African countries adopted the one-party system soon after independence; knowing full well that if they did not submerge the tribe, the tribe would destroy the nation. The rationale was extended even to the individual level. The primacy of the community, hence the nation, was invoked over the interests of the individual; admittedly, with dire consequences in many cases.

But this approach had a perfectly rational basis. Forging a national ethos that would fuse the people of different tribes into an organic whole, and not just as a collection of antagonistic groups, entailed placing the interests of the community above those of the individual including his freedom. It was not done for political expediency but for national survival; an imperative underscored by President Sekou Toure when he said:

"We have chosen the freedom, the right, the power, the sovereignty of the people, and not of the individual. Before this people you should have no individual personality. Our personality becomes part of the personality of the nation."[18]

And anyone who was not ready to submerge his personality and freedom in the supra-entity called the nation in the interests of the people was considered to be more than just a dissenter – he was a "traitor"; although he himself, like everybody else, was one of the people constituting "We the people," without whom there would be no people. And that was one of the most tragic aspects of the one-party state, its benefits notwithstanding. Thus, the ethic of individual freedom became anathema to the nationalist ideologies of the young African countries whose existence and survival was predicated on the inculcation of the primacy of a collective ethos throughout the populace.

In a very tragic way, individual freedom was considered to be as dangerous to national integrity and survival as tribalism was. As Sekou Toure put it:

"Tribal, ethnic, and religious (as well as political) differences...have caused so much difficulty to the country and people....We are for a united people, a unitary state at the service of an indivisible nation."[19]

Therefore, it is critical to understand the context in which such nationalist sentiments were articulated across the continent before one passes judgment, condemning African leaders as dictators just lusting for power. Most of them were despotic or authoritarian rulers. But inculcation of the ideal of collective will and spirit, as opposed to individual liberty, was critical to the very survival of African countries during the early years of independence. These were countries which did not really even "exist" as countries, except on the map and as a mere collection of tribes, many of them hostile towards each other and haphazardly put together by the colonial rulers, with little in common in terms of loyalty to higher authority; each having its own princes, chiefs, and other traditional rulers. It was a herculean task to build a nation out of such an amorphous whole.

Even some ardent critics of Africa in Western countries concede that much. As Robert Greenberger wrote about Tanzania – a country the size of Texas, Oklahoma and West Virginia combined, or bigger than Nigeria in terms of area, and made up of more than 120 tribes – in *The Wall Street Journal*:

"Nyerere was a skilled nation builder. He fused Tanzania's 120 tribes into a cohesive state, preventing tribal conflicts like those plaguing so much of Africa."[20]

Jomo Kenyatta, the Grand Old Man (called Mzee in Kiswahili) of the African independence movement, accomplished the same feat in Kenya, although to a smaller degree, compared to Nyerere; so did Nkrumah in

Ghana, Sekou Toure in Guinea, Obote in Uganda, Kaunda in Zambia, and other African leaders elsewhere on the continent, but in varying degrees of success.

Yet, there was also abuse of power in most countries across the continent under the one-party state and military rule during those years of national consolidation, and all the way through the decades since independence. That is what makes the multiparty system so appealing in all African countries today, including Tanzania which was very peaceful and stable, and relatively free, under President Nyerere's one-party state for almost 30 years.

Curtailment, and in most cases total denial, of individual freedom was not always necessary to maintain national unity and stability in the fledgling states. Most African leaders invoked the specter of national disintegration just to perpetuate themselves in office and suffocate dissent, as they still do today.

Yet, without putting a premium on national interest, and inculcating the ideals of a collective national spirit, a common identity, and commitment to national unity even at the expense of individual freedom in some cases, there probably would be no African countries as we know them today.

We would have hundreds of "nations": micro-states, none of them viable, structured along tribal lines, making it impossible for Africa to survive let alone develop. Therefore, the emphasis on national survival was justified. But it did not justify dictatorship, although it justified curtailment of freedom in some cases.

The invocation of slogans such as "national survival," "national unity," "One Zambia, One Nation," "Harambee! - Let's Pull Together," "Uhuru na Umoja – Freedom and Unity," "the people, not the individual, come first," and many others, has always been an integral part of the indoctrination process for which African countries are despised in the West as a diversionary tactic to justify dictatorship.

And in many cases such criticism by Westerners and others is justified. But let us also be brutally frank: We all practice indoctrination. Western countries do, communist countries do. So do all the rest, including African countries.

Inculcation of individual and national values is indoctrination. Even glorification of a nation's practices and beliefs, values and traditions, ideals and ideology, is a form of indoctrination. When Americans are taught that capitalism is better than socialism or communism, that is indoctrination, even if it is true; which it is, in terms of producing wealth but *not* in terms of protecting the weak from exploitation since capitalism is predatory by nature and thrives on greed. When they are taught that America, the first republic since Rome, was founded on the twin ideals of liberty and equality, that is indoctrination, even if it is not true; which it isn't. America was founded on slavery, and thrived on slavery.

Millions of Americans were not taught - and are still not taught - in school and when growing up that African slaves and their descendants helped to build America more than anybody else, especially in its early years, and without being paid. As Malcolm X said, African slaves worked "from can't see in the morning to can't see in the evening without being paid a dime. Yet we built this country...and we aren't American yet. As long you and I have been here, we aren't American yet."

African slaves built America's foundation without which the country would not have survived and thrived as a nation. And it would not be what it is today, as the richest nation in history, had it not been for the forced labour extracted from African slaves and their descendants. They made America rich. Yet they were never paid one cent for it.

But a number of black American conservatives contend otherwise. One is Dr. Thomas Sowell, an economics professor and a prolific author, who argues in

58

his book, *Race and Culture,*[21] that there is no conclusive evidence showing that America derived net economic benefits from slavery.

He and a number of other blacks, especially conservatives, are opposed to reparations for slavery for various reasons. They are mostly middle-class and upper-class blacks who are detached from their own people in a desperate attempt to be accepted by and integrated into white America. Yet, they are not accepted by whites as equals. Alienated from their own people, and rejected by white America, they are caught in a predicament similar to the situation many educated Africans were trapped in during colonial times. Western education "de-Africanized" them, mentally. Yet it did not elevate them to the same status enjoyed by their colonial masters and other whites; a subject I have addressed in one of my books, *Africa and the West.*[22] It is also a subject – in the American context – black nationalist scholar, Professor Harold Cruse, has tackled in his magnum opus, *The Crisis of the Negro Intellectual.*[23] And as he said about slavery and the myths being propagated to distort American history, in another book, *Rebellion or Revolution?*:

"America lies to itself that it was always, from the beginning, a democratic nation when its very constitution sanctioned and upheld chattel slavery. Moreover, America conveniently forgets that the first capitalist 'free enterprise' banks and stock markets in the land were made possible by accumulated capital accrued from the unpaid labor of Negro slaves. But it would be too much to expect contemporary America to go back over its own history and reassess all these racial facts."[24]

America does not want to face that because it still has a serious racial problem – although it is no longer a racist society in the legal sense – and wants to continue propagating the myth that African slaves and their descendants did not significantly, if at all, contribute to the economic growth of the United States. This myth is an integral part of America's racist ideology, and it is indoctrination. Yet, all this indoctrination which started as soon as Africans were taken to America in chains, has not always worked.

Even slaves knew better; they had to, they were the ones doing all the work on the plantations without pay. As Bailey Wyat, a former slave and although illiterate, put it poignantly in broken English when arguing for redistribution of land to former slaves not long after the Emancipation Proclamation:

"We has a right to the land where we are located. For why? I tell you. Our wives, our children, our husbands has been sold over and over again to purchase the land....And then didn't we clear the land, and raise the crops?....And then didn't them large cities in the North grow up on the cotton, on the sugars, on the rice that we made?....I say they has grown rich and my people is poor."[25]

When America denies that, to insulate itself from reality and its ugly past, it is practising indoctrination that is no better than the kind that is practised by many African leaders and their people when they blame American imperialism for all their problems; nor is it wrong for Americans to say capitalism is better than communism, just as it is *not* wrong for Africans to say Pan-Africanism is better than nationalism, and nationalism *better* than tribalism.

Indoctrination serves a purpose, good or bad. Hitler preached a racist ideology. It was even taught to the young. It was indoctrination, at its worst, with dire consequences at a cost of more than 6 million lives of people who belonged to the "wrong race," mostly Jews. But it could have served a good purpose under a different kind of leadership, with a different ideology, unlike that of Nazi Germany.

In Africa, indoctrination has also served a purpose. And it has served Africa well in many areas when it corresponds to reality. And that included justifying centralisation of power "in the name of the people" during the early years of independence under one-party rule. That is because a strong central government was vital and critical to national unity and survival, in pursuit of economic development by mobilizing resources at the national level under one leadership.

That was also the case in the United States when Alexander Hamilton argued that a strong central government was necessary for the young nation. It is doubtful that America would have survived without it. This was clearly demonstrated when the states constituting the union adopted a federal constitution at the Philadelphia convention in 1787 to replace the Articles of Confederation in order to establish a strong central government.

In addition to instituting a unitary state, most African countries also adopted a common or similar ideology to develop their economies and consolidate national unity. The approach most took towards development was socialism, and its concomitant, centralisation of power, as the most effective mechanism for rapid mobilisation of resources at the national level; and as a weapon against tribalism and regionalism. As Professor Ali Mazrui states in his book *Towards A Pax-Africana*:

"A former Labour Party Colonial Secretary, Arthur Creech Jones, once remarked that he did not consider it the duty of that office to impose socialism on the colonies. In the case of Africa it has now turned out such an imposition was not necessary.

61

No ideology commands respect so widely in Africa as the ideology of 'socialism' – though, as in Europe, it is socialism of different shades. In Guinea and Mali a Marxist framework of reasoning is evident. In Ghana Leninism was wedded to notions of traditional collectivism. In Tanzania the concept of *Ujamaa*, derived from the sense of community of tribal life, is being radicalized into an assertion of modern socialism.

In Kenya there is a dilemma between establishing socialism and Africanizing the capitalism which already exists. In Nigeria, Senegal and Uganda some kind of allegiance is being paid to the ideal of social justice in situations with a multi-party background.

There are places, of course, where no school of socialism is propagated at all. But outside the Ivory Coast there is little defiant rejection of the idea of 'socialism' in former colonial Africa.

Yet the kind of socialism which Arthur Creech Jones would have propagated was a socialism operating in the context of a multi-party system of politics. What is more common in Africa, however, is a socialism wedded to a one-party structure of government."[26]

Dr. Mazrui's book was first published in 1967, the same year Tanzania adopted its famous Arusha Declaration in February, outlining the country's socialist policies. It was a period – throughout the sixties – when interest in socialism among African leaders was at its peak, with most countries across the continent having adopted the socialist ideology in one form or another within that decade of euphoria which also marked the end of colonial rule. By 1968, most African countries had won independence.

But their war against tribalism, ignorance, disease, and poverty had just begun. African countries saw socialism as the best solution to these problems, with central planning being one of its most attractive features. And it is easy to understand why. When all tribes and regions are brought together under one leadership, there is no room for division along ethnoregional lines. If power is too decentralized, it can help strengthen tribal and regional institutions to the detriment of national unity. That is the argument African countries used to justify concentration of power at the centre. And they made a rational choice under the circumstances when they instituted the unitary state during those years when African countries were so fragile, and national unity virtually non-existent.

And their belief in socialism as the best means to achieve rapid economic development was not without foundation. There was the example of the Soviet Union, with all its faults, yet persuasive enough that development could indeed be achieved in a relatively short time – as opposed to the centuries it took the West to develop – if decision-making on the allocation of the nation's resources, which include people, was centralised.

Even some of those who criticized African leaders for taking the socialist path felt that the leaders were vindicated in their belief because of the rapid industrialization the Soviet Union was able to achieve within 40 years under socialism; although the foundations of the future great nation had largely been built by Peter the Great in the preceding years.

There was another equally compelling argument why African leaders chose socialism over capitalism: equitable distribution of wealth to achieve social justice. They saw capitalism as a predatory system for survival of "the fittest" under which people sought to accumulate wealth without the slightest concern for the poor and for the well-being of others. "I got mine, you get yours. Each to his own," is the underlying logic of capitalism.

Although it is true that capitalism capitalizes on greed, there is no question that it provides incentives to production more than socialism does, much as some of us may hate its predatory instincts. But that is part of its nature. If you like its virtues, be prepared to accept its vices.

By contrast, socialism emphasizes sharing. Therefore, with its redistributive ethic, it was seen as morally superior to capitalism which nurtures and nourishes predatory instincts in man; pursuit of profit being incompatible with social justice, since people exploit others to accumulate wealth. In short, capitalism is based on inequality, and is therefore the very antithesis not only of social justice but of human equality.

But probably the biggest attraction to socialism among African African leaders was that – as the only ones who "knew what was best" for the people and the nation – it enabled them to control all the nation's resources in order to plan and direct economic development; something that is impossible under capitalism where economic development of the whole country is mostly left to the invisible hand of the free market. Under socialism, they were not only able to choose development targets and allocate resources to achieve national goals; they even used coercive means to achieve these goals. All this was seen as necessary to achieve economic development. As Dr. Kwame Nkrumah put it:

"The economic independence that should follow and maintain political independence demands every effort from the people, a total mobilization of brain and manpower resources. What other countries have taken three hundred years to achieve, a once dependent territory must try to accomplish in a generation if it is to survive....

Capitalism is too complicated a system for a newly independent nation. Hence the need for a socialistic society. But even a system based on social justice and a democratic constitution may need backing up, during the period following independence, by emergency measures of a totalitarian kind. Without discipline, true freedom cannot survive."[27]

Most African leaders did not explicitly say they were going to employ "measures of a totalitarian kind," as Nkrumah bluntly stated. But they ruled that way, and still do. And besides saying "capitalism is too complicated a system for a newly independent nation," Nkrumah, like most African leaders, also believed that the capitalist system would only perpetuate exploitation of their countries by the metropolitan powers.

Capitalism was not only identified with colonialism; it was organically linked to their former colonial masters who were determined to continue exploiting Africa; capitalism, by nature, being an exploitative system and an integral part of colonialism and imperialism as the history of Africa clearly demonstrated since slavery and colonisation. If it was adopted by the newly independent nations as the best path towards economic development, local capitalists would continue to work with foreign capitalist interests to exploit the people. Even African leaders such as Tom Mboya found much that was desirable in socialism. As he stated:

"It might be argued that African socialism stands in a class by itself. This is not true. The basic tenets of socialism are universal and we are either socialists by these basic principles or not at all....I strongly believe that in the field of economic relations we can be guided by the traditional presence of socialist ideas and attitudes in the African mental make-up."[28]

Yet, Mboya was not a socialist, at least not in the same way Nyerere, Nkrumah, and Sekou Toure were, in terms of policy formulation and implementation. If Mboya was a socialist, then Nyerere was a capitalist. They were poles apart. And his socialism must have been shelved when he was a cabinet member in Kenya's capitalist government under Kenyatta where he held key ministerial posts including economic planning.

But articulation of his feelings on the relevance of socialism to Africa shows the kind of strong appeal the socialist ideology had across a broad spectrum of African leaders during the sixties and through the decades. Today, of course, with the collapse of the Soviet Union and its satellites, it is a discredited ideology. But that does not diminish the significant role it played in the establishment and consolidation of the African nation-state through the years under the one-party system which also has been replaced by the multiparty system in most African countries, although only in theory. Most are *de facto* one-party states.

But there is also no question that both socialism and the one-party system had a negative impact on African countries in terms of diminished freedom and retarded economic growth. There were some notable achievements in the economic arena, but not as significant as they would have been had African governments adopted a free-market approach even with limited state intervention in the economy.

However, when looked at in the context of the sixties when most African countries won independence, and even in the seventies when they were still struggling to consolidate their nation-states as much as they are still struggling to do so today, the negative impact of both socialism and the one-party system should be weighed against the fact that the African nation-state was established against overwhelming odds and would probably not exist today had African leaders taken a different path.

In Africa, unlike in Europe, nationalism preceded the establishment of the nation-state. The leaders who campaigned for independence had to appeal to nationalist sentiments of non-existent nations in order to create a sense of collective identity among different and antagonistic ethnic groups which constituted the colonies. And it was a formidable task.

Convincing members of different tribes that they were the same people – as Tanganyikans and not just Sukumas, Nyakyusas, Zanakis, Digos, Chagas, Ngonis, Gogos, Makondes, Nyamwezis, Yaos, Hayas, Pares, Hehes, Benas, Makuas or Kingas; Ghanaians and not just Ewes, Fantis, Ashantis, Gonjas, Dagombas, Nanumbas, or Konkombas; Kenyans and not just Kikuyus, Kambas, Luos, Luhyas, Samburus, Masais, Pokots, Merus, or Somalis – required strong central authority at the national level under a unitary state with no room for divisive politics and partisanship so typical of the multi-party system.

The one-party system as well as socialism, both with an instinct for mass mobilisation under one strong leadership at the national level, provided just the kind of institutional tools and mechanisms which enabled Africans to establish, build, and consolidate the nations which exist today across the continent, however fragile they may be.

This is not to gloss over the negative impact of socialism and one-party rule on African countries. Both had tragic consequences. They stifled individual initiative, lowered productivity, and curtailed freedom. But they also taught and enforced discipline, similar to army discipline, to maintain national unity which would have been impossible without mass regimentation in societies fragmented along ethnic lines.

Therefore, the positive contribution of socialism and one-party rule must also be acknowledged, at least in the African context where, instead of the 53 countries we have today, we probably would have hundreds, equal to the number of tribes or ethnic groups and racial groups on the continent.

If that is what multi-party "democracy" is going to do, weaken or split up countries, then it is recipe for disaster.

67

African countries should therefore not rule out a return to the status quo ante if circumstances dictate, and temporarily re-institute one-party rule before returning to multi-party democracy. But the decision to form such government of national unity must be by popular consent approved in a referendum. Otherwise, when faced with the prospect of national disintegration and bloodshed as a result of ethnic conflicts, let the people learn the hard way; if they want their countries to dissolve in anarchy under the multiparty system which thrives on divisive politics in the name of democracy even when national survival is at stake.

African nationalists of all ideological stripes have always been very much aware of the danger our countries face because of their pluralistic nature as multi-ethnic societies or multi-national states. As Dr. Nnamdi Azikiwe, who was no admirer of the one-party system, said when he warned against the Pakistanization – Balkanization – of Nigeria:

"It is essential that ill-will be not created in order to encourage a Pakistan in this country. The North and South are one, whether we wish it or not. The forces of history have made it so."[29]

Preservation of national integrity is better than the ghastly alternative of total disintegration which can also be averted by extensive devolution of power to the regions and districts, but while retaining strong central authority. One-party rule, with all its faults, has been able to maintain national unity across much of Africa.

Only time will tell whether or not its antithesis, the multiparty system, will be able to do the same. And it can, if it effectively contains tribalism and regional loyalties, as the one-party system has done, by establishing parties that are truly national in character cutting across regional and ethnic lines.

Unfortunately, few tribes in Africa have demonstrated the capacity to transcend ethnoregional loyalties for the sake of national unity. The perennial ethnic rivalries which continue to threaten the very existence of African countries is a rueful reminder of that.

Probably the best solution to this seemingly intractable problem is for African countries to limit the number of political parties, preferably to three, to broaden the base of support cutting across ethnic lines.

Members of different tribes will then have to learn to live together, and work together, as members and supporters of those few parties in order to build strong African nations without promoting tribal and regional interests at the expense of their fellow citizens. As Mrs. Charity Ngilu, the first woman to be a serious contender for Kenya's presidency, lamented after the 1997 general elections which the incumbent Daniel arap Moi won because the opposition was hopelessly divided along tribal lines and failed to rally behind a single candidate:

"Honourable Mwai Kibaki got most votes in 1997 from the Kikuyu, Honourable Raila Odinga from the Luo, Honourable Kijana Wamalwa from the Luhya and I myself from the Kamba. President Moi got most of his votes from the Rift Valley. Is this the Kenya we want?"[30]

Is this the Africa we want for the sake of multi-party politics?

The adoption of the multiparty system should not blind us to reality. And the reality in this context is that ethnic politics, and manipulation and exploitation of tribal loyalties in the quest for national office, is a dominant feature of the African political landscape. And it is going to remain that way for a long, long time in most countries across the continent.

How to address this problem is going to be one of the main challenges Africa will have to face in the twentieth-first century, which South African President Thabo Mbeki declared to be the century of the African Renaissance.

Chapter Two:

Milestones:
Africa Since the Sixties

AFRICA has come a long way since the sixties, and still has a long way to go. The tortuous journey has been marked by important milestones which can help us look at Africa in its proper historical context, as we recall some of the major events which have taken place on the continent since independence.

The year 1960 occupies a special place in the annals of the continent probably more than any other in one fundamental respect: It was the year when an unprecedented number of African countries won independence, a feat that was never duplicated in any of the following years.

A total of 17 countries won independence in 1960. The United Nations called it Africa's Year. The attainment of sovereign status by so many African countries in a single year ushered in a new era for the continent whose most celebrated decade was the euphoric sixties.

But 1960 was also a tragic year for Africa. It was a year marred by the Congo crisis, an unprecedented catastrophe at the dawn of Africa's post-colonial era. The Congo tragedy was engineered and fuelled by Western powers. Communist countries stepped in at the invitation of the nationalist forces in their desperate attempt to oust a puppet regime backed by the United States and spearheaded by the CIA. It was also supported by Belgium, the former colonial power, apartheid South Africa, France and other Western powers and financial interests. It was a coalition of forces, and a concerted effort, determined to perpetuate domination and exploitation of Africa and dismember the Congo in pursuit of Western interests.

The crisis erupted right in the middle of Africa, earning the Congo the unenviable distinction as the bleeding heart of Africa. More than 100,000 people, mostly Congolese, perished in the early sixties alone in this conflict which also had ideological dimensions involving super-power rivalry between the United States and the Soviet as well as the People's Republic of China. Among the casualties was Congo's first and popular prime minister, Patrice Lumumba. Compounding the tragedy was Africa's inability to do anything to end the conflict right on its own soil. As Julius Nyerere said about the Congo crisis in a speech in August 1961 about three months before he led Tanganyika to independence:

"I am an advocate of African unity. I believe firmly that, just as unity was necessary for the achievement of independence in Tanganyika or any other nation, unity is equally necessary to consolidate and maintain the independence which we are now achieving in different parts of Africa.

I believe that, left to ourselves, we can achieve unity on the African continent. But I don't believe we are going to be left to ourselves! I believe that the phase through which we are emerging successfully is the phase of the first scramble for Africa - and Africa's reaction to it. We are now entering a new phase. It is the phase of the second scramble for Africa....

I used the phrase 'the second scramble for Africa.' It may sound farfetched, in the context of the Africa of the 1960's....But anybody who thinks this is farfetched has been completely blind to what is happening on the African continent....

There were obvious weaknesses in the Congo situation, but those weaknesses were deliberately used in a scramble for the control of the Congo....So I believe that the second scramble for Africa has begun in real earnest. And it is going to be a much more dangerous scramble than the first one."[1]

The assassination of Lumumba, like the Congo tragedy itself as a whole, was an important milestone in the history of Africa. Much is known about the CIA's and Belgium's involvement in Lumumba's assassination which American President Dwight Eisenhower wanted carried out as soon as possible. A team of CIA agents worked on a covert operation which involved more than one assassination scheme including poisoning and shooting the Congolese leader with a high-powered telescopic rifle.

Even the CIA station chief in the Congo, Laurence Devlin conceded that much after Lumumba was killed. He also confirmed this in an interview as late as 1996 from Princeton, New Jersey, where he lived; so did Dr. Sidney Gottlieb, a CIA doctor, who went to Congo in September 1960 with a poison kit to kill Lumumba. Many people have written about the subject, which I have also addressed in one of my books, *Africa after Independence: Realities of Nationhood*,[2] in a chapter devoted to the Congo crisis. And as John Reader states in his book,

"An agent (of the CIA) was dispatched to Leopoldville. An initial assassination plan required someone to apply a dose of poison to Lumumba's toothbrush; alternatively, a high-powered rifle with telescopic scope and silencer was proposed....

In a radio broadcast on 5 September (1960), President Kasavubu, urged by American diplomats, Belgian political advisers, and Congolese supporters, announced that he had dismissed Lumumba as prime minister. When the news reached Lumumba, he in turn rushed to the radio station and announced that he had dismissed Kasavubu as president. Confusion ensued. Some parts of the Congo declared their support for Lumumba, others for Kasavubu and Ileo (the new prime minister), and parliament voted to annul both decisions.

With arrests and counter-arrests by the contending parties threatening yet another round of violent disturbance, the impasse was resolved on the evening of September 14 when the twenty-nine-year-old army chief of staff, Colonel Joseph Mobutu, announced that he was taking power in the name of the army....Then, in a move that warmed the hearts of the CIA agents who had been indoctrinating him for weeks, Mobutu ordered the Soviet and Czechoslovak embassies to get out of the Congo within forty-eight hours....

Though deposed by Mobutu on 14 September 1960, after just seventy-six days in office, Lumumba continued to live at the prime minister's residence in Leopoldville, guarded by an inner ring of UN troops in the garden to prevent his arrest and surrounded by an outer ring of Mobutu's troops on the perimeter to prevent his escape. Hence the difficulty of obtaining access to his toothbrush that the CIA agents had experienced."[3]

But his days were numbered, and he fell right into the hands of his enemies, the most powerful of whom were the Belgians and the Americans helped by their Congolese henchmen, including Mobutu:

"Meanwhile, Lumumba's supporters regrouped in Stanleyville. At the end of November Lumumba decided to join them – a fatal move. He was arrested en route and handed over to Mobutu's army.

Lumumba was consigned to a military prison, but his supporters continued to have an unsettling effect on the country at large....Kasavubu and his (American and Belgian) advisers decided that he should be sent to Elisabethville, the Katangan capital, where the errant Tshombe was in charge.

On 17 January 1961, Lumumba and two colleagues (Maurice Mpolo and Joseph Okito) were flown to Katanga, where a Swedish warrant officer with the United Nations forces witnessed their arrival:

'The first to leave the aeroplane was a smartly dressed African. He was followed by three other Africans, blind-folded and with their hands tied behind their backs. The first of the prisoners to alight had a small beard [Lumumba]. As they came down the stairs, some of the *gendarmes* ran to them, pushed them, kicked them and brutally struck them with rifle butts; one of the prisoners fell to the ground. After about one minute the three prisoners were placed in a jeep which drove off....'

Neither Lumumba nor his colleagues were ever seen again. It is believed they were taken to a farmhouse on the outskirts of Elisabethville, where they died at the hands of Katangese officials and Belgian mercenaries."[4]

It was also said that Lumumba was killed in the presence of Tshombe himself. And there was ample evidence showing that the United States and Belgium had conspired to eliminate Lumumba; further confirmed by intelligence and diplomatic messages coming from each other's capital. One was a cable from the American ambassador in Brussels, on 19 July 1960, advising Washington that Lumumba had "maneuvered himself into a position of opposition to West, resistance to United Nations and increasing dependence on Soviet Union and on Congolese supporters who are pursuing Soviet ends....Only prudent, therefore, to plan on basis that Lumumba government threatens our vital interests in Congo and Africa generally. A principle (sic) objective of political and diplomatic action must therefore be to destroy Lumumba government as now constituted, but at the same time we must find or develop another horse to back which would be acceptable in rest of Africa and defensible against Soviet political attack."[5]

That horse turned out to be Mobutu, one of the most loyal servants of the West who started working for the CIA even before he became head of the Congolese army. At the time of his appointment as head of the army, he was Lumumba's private secretary and already on the CIA payroll. And both the Americans and the Belgians – as well as others including the French, and the apartheid regime of South Africa – supported Mobutu. Therefore, they were all responsible for what happened in Congo; the Americans and the Belgians being the most culpable.

The West did not want any truly independent nationalist to lead any African country. They wanted puppets they could manipulate at will. Lumumba was not one of those stooges. On independence day, June 30, 1960, Lumumba gave a fiery response to Belgian King Baudouin's racist and patronizing speech which even Joseph Kasavubu, a conservative leader and friend of the West, found to be offensive and demeaning.

Lumumba's speech was not well-received in the West. Western governments saw Lumumba as a threat to their economic, political and strategic interests in Congo and on the entire continent. A true nationalist and Pan-Africanist, he believed that political independence was meaningless without economic independence. Therefore Africa had to cease being an economic colony of Europe or a plantation for the metropolitan powers.

Yet, Western powers, especially Belgium, the United States and France, had invested heavily in Congo to exploit its vast amount of minerals and other resources. And Lumumba, because of his independent and pro-African policies, was a direct threat to this hegemonic control of the Congolese economy by the West. As Professor Adam Hochschild of the University of California-Berkeley stated about the CIA's involvement in Lumumba's assassination in his book, *King Leopold's Ghost: A Story of Greed, Terror, and Heroism in Colonial Africa*:

"An inspired orator whose voice was rapidly carrying beyond his country's borders, Lumumba was a mercurial and charismatic figure. His message, Western governments feared, was contagious. Moreover, he could not be bought. Anathema to American and European capital, he became a leader whose days were numbered.

Less than two months after being named the Congo's first democratically chosen prime minister, a U.S. National Security Council subcommittee on covert operations, which included CIA chief Allen Dulles, authorized his assassination. Richard Bissell, CIA operations chief at the time, later said, 'The President [Dwight D. Eisenhower]...regarded Lumumba as I did and a lot of other people did: a mad dog...and he wanted the problem dealt with.'

Alternatives for dealing with 'the problem' were considered, among them poison – a supply of which was sent to the CIA station chief (Laurence Devlin) in Leopoldville – a high-powered rifle, free-lance hit men.

77

But it proved hard to get close enough to Lumumba to use these, so, instead, the CIA supported anti-Lumumba elements within the factionalized Congo government, confident that before long they would do the job. They did. After being arrested and suffering a series of beatings, the prime minister was secretly shot in Elizabethville in January 1961. A CIA agent ended up driving around the city with Lumumba's body in his car's trunk, trying to find a place to dispose of it...

The key figure in the Congolese forces that arranged Lumumba's murder was a young man named Joseph Desire Mobutu, then chief of staff of the army and a former NCO in the old colonial *Force Publique.* Early on, the Western powers had spotted Mobutu as someone who would look out for their interests. He had received cash payments from the local CIA man and Western military attaches while Lumumba's murder was being planned."[6]

Hochschild was in the Congo during that time, and had first-hand knowledge of some of the events that went on and which had to do with Lumumba's assassination:

"I had been writing about human rights for years, and once, in the course of half a dozen trips to Africa, I had been to the Congo.

That visit was in 1961. In a Leopoldville apartment, I heard the CIA man, who had too much to drink, describe with satisfaction exactly how and where the newly independent country's first prime minister, Patrice Lumumba, had been killed a few months earlier. He assumed that any American, even a visiting student like me, would share his relief at the assassination of a man the United States government considered a dangerous leftist troublemaker."[7]

The CIA and the Belgian government not only worked

together to assassinate Lumumba; they plotted to get rid of him in the most gruesome manner. New revelations about the assassination by some of the people who were directly involved in it only add to our understanding of the sinister plot as one of the most diabolical deeds in the history of post-colonial Africa, conceived by some of Africa's worst enemies.

Some of these revelations come from a Belgian sociologist, Ludo de Witte, who quotes some of the killers in his book, *The Assassination of Lumumba,*[8] published in 1999. And they were right on target, although it took them some time to get to Lumumba. But the objective was clear. As CIA Director Allen Dulles wrote: "In high quarters here, it is the clear-cut conclusion that if [Lumumba] continues to hold high office, the inevitable result will [have] disastrous consequences...for the interests of the free world generally. Consequently, we conclude that his removal must be an urgent and prime objective."[9]

De Witte explains in detail the prominent role the Belgian government played in Lumumba's assassination. According to *U.S. News & World Report*:

"De Witte reveals a telegram from Belgium's African-affairs minister, Harold d'Aspremont Lynden, essentially ordering that Lumumba be sent to Katanga. Anyone who knew the place knew that was a death sentence.

When Lumumba arrived in Katanga, on 17 January (1961), accompanied by several Belgians, he was bleeding from a severe beating. Later that evening, Lumumba was killed by a firing squad commanded by a Belgian officer. A week earlier, he had written to his wife, 'I prefer to die with my head unbowed, my faith unshakable, and with a profound trust in the destiny of my country.' Lumumba was 35.

The next step was to destroy the evidence. Four days later, Belgian Police Commissioner Gerard Soete and his brother cut up the body with a hacksaw and dissolved it in sulfuric acid. In an interview on Belgian television last year (1999), Soete displayed a bullet and two teeth he claimed to have saved from Lumumba's body....

A Belgian official who helped engineer Lumumba's transfer to Katanga told de Witte that he kept CIA station chief Laurence Devlin (in Leopoldville) fully informed of the plan. 'The Americans were informed of the transfer because they actively discussed this thing for weeks,' says de Witte. But Devlin, now retired, denies any previous knowledge of the transfer."[10]

Other sources give similar and sometimes almost identical accounts of the assassination, thus corroborating each other. According to one such source: "A U.N. investigating commission found that Lumumba had been killed by a Belgian mercenary in the presence of Tshombe."[11]

The Belgian mercenary was said to be a CIA agent. Other CIA agents (American) were also probably at the scene, including one American agent who tried to get rid of Lumumba's body before they decided to dissolve it in acid. In addition to that were Congolese henchmen and their Belgian masters.

Also present was Godefroid Munongo, Tshombe's confidant and a member of his cabinet. Although a Congolese, Munongo was a Nyamwezi, a large ethnic indigenous to what is now western Tanzania some of whose members migrated to Congo in the latter part of the 1800s and founded the Yeke kingdom whose ruler, Msiri, was Munongo's ancestor.

Lumumba went down in history as one of the most admired political martyrs in modern times. To many people, especially in Congo and other parts of the continent, he was and still is one of the most revered political figures in the history of post-colonial Africa, together – even if not necessarily in the same league – with leaders such as Julius Nyerere, Kwame Nkrumah, and Nelson Mandela.

The Congo crisis was one of the biggest tragedies that befell Africa during the sixties. And its domino effect and devastating impact is still being felt today, as the Congo lies in ruins. It is, indeed, the bleeding heart of Africa.

The assassination of Lumumba ushered in a new era of political assassinations and military coups in sub-Saharan Africa. On 13 January 1963, almost exactly two years after Lumumba was brutally murdered, another prominent African leader, President Sylvanus Olympio of Togo, was assassinated in a military coup led by a 25-year-old sergeant, Etienne Eyadema, who became one of Africa's longest-ruling and most brutal dictators re-named Gnassingbe Eyadema.

I remember President Olympio's daughter came to live in Tanzania and taught French at our school, Tambaza High School in Dar es Salaam, when I was there from 1969 – 1970 in Form V (Standard 13) and Form VI (Standard 14). She was married to a Tanzanian, Professor Anthony Rweyemamu, now deceased, who was then head of the political science at the University of Dar es Salaam. Her father was shot at the gates of the American embassy in Togo's capital, Lome. It was the first military coup in black Africa.

Although Lumumba was ousted earlier in 1960 when another soldier, Mobutu, seized power, his ouster was not a typical military takeover – like the one in Togo in 1963 – but part of a larger conspiracy by Western powers to dominate and break up Congo and at a time when Lumumba and Kasavubu were competing for power, both claiming to be in charge. Mobutu seized power only later in November 1965 in a typical military coup.

It was Western powers who engineered and supported the secession of mineral-rich Katanga Province in July 1960, only 11 days after Congo won independence on June

81

30th under the leadership of Prime Minister Lumumba, plunging the country into chaos and full-scale civil war. And they continued to support Katanga's secessionist leader Moise Tshombe until 1963 when his forces were defeated by UN peacekeeping troops sent to Congo at the request of Lumumba and other African leaders to keep the country united.

Tshombe died in Algiers, Algeri,a on 29 June 1969 where he was held in captivity since July 1967 after his plane was forced to land, en route to Congo, to cause more mischief. He was 49. He was travelling from Spain. And he did everything he could to break up Congo. He was buried in Belgium.

Ironically, his Western masters accused him of being a racist who didn't like whites; the same people who supported him in his diabolical schemes to destroy Congo.

Had Congo disintegrated, it would have set a dangerous precedent for the rest of Africa, encouraging secession in other parts of the continent.

Tragically, another dangerous precedent was gaining prominence on the continent in the form of military coups when Eyadema assassinated President Olympio and seized power in Togo. Olympio's assassination drew swift condemnation from other African leaders. The government of Tanganyika under Julius Nyerere sent an urgent message to the UN Secretary-General, questioning the dubious credentials of Togo's new leadership:

"After the brutal murder of President Olympio, the problem of recognition of a successor government has arisen. We urge no recognition of a successor government until satisfied first that the government did not take part in Olympio's murder or second that there is a popularly elected government."[12]

At the founding of the Organization of African Unity (OAU) in May 1963 in Addis Ababa, Ethiopia, attended by African heads of state and government, the seat that would have been occupied by the late Togolese President Sylvanus Olympio was conspicuously empty in the conference hall, known as Africa Hall; sending a chilling message to the assembled leaders and future ones on how vulnerable their governments were to subversion by a mere handful of soldiers. But it was also a warning to aspiring coup makers that coups and assassinations would not be tolerated on the continent.

The new Togolese president was Nicholas Grunitzky, Olympio's brother-in-law and opposition leader who had been living in exile in neighbouring Dahomey, re-named Benin in 1975. He was invited by Eyadema to return to Togo and assume leadership; only to be ousted by Eyadema himself four years later on 13 January 1967, on the fourth anniversary of Olympio's assassination.

Unfortunately, the stern warning by African leaders at the OAU summit in May 1963 to soldiers intent on overthrowing governments fell on deaf ears. And military coups became a continental phenomenon and a ritual of African politics for almost 40 years from the sixties to the nineties.

A total of 32 independent African countries were represented at the summit and signed the OAU Charter establishing the Organization of African Unity. They were: Algeria, Burundi, Cameroon, Central African Republic, Chad, Congo-Brazzaville, Congo-Leopoldville, Dahomey, Ethiopia, Gabon, Ghana, Guinea, Ivory Coast, Liberia, Libya, Madagascar, Mali, Mauritania, Morocco, Niger, Nigeria, Rwanda, Senegal, Sierra Leone, Somalia, Sudan, Tanganyika, Togo, Tunisia, Uganda, United Arab Republic (Egypt), and Upper Volta (now Burkina Faso).

Of the 32 countries, 26 had experienced military coups by the end of the 1990s, most of them more than once and sometimes within the same year. For example, three governments were overthrown in Sierra Leone within a month, in April 1968, and two in Nigeria in January and July 1966.

Only Cameroon, Gabon, Morocco, Senegal, Tanganyika (renamed Tanzania after uniting with Zanzibar in 1964), and Egypt, among the OAU founders, escaped this scourge between the sixties and the nineties. But they all had, at one time or another, been targeted by soldiers trying to seize power. Egypt had already experienced two military coups before then: one in 1952, and another in 1954. And it was the only country represented at the 1963 OAU summit that had been under military rule.

Almost exactly a year after the assassination of President Olympio on 13 January 1963, the armies of the three East African countries of Tanganyika, Kenya, and Uganda, mutinied in January 1964. The mutiny started in Tanganyika on January 20th and spread to Kenya and then Uganda in only a matter of days. President Nyerere asked Britain for help to suppress the mutiny in Tanganyika; so did President Jomo Kenyatta of Kenya, and Prime Minister Milton Obote of Uganda. All three countries were former British colonies.

But British troops did not stay long in Tanganyika. Uncomfortable with the presence of foreign troops on African soil, and in an independent country on top of that, Nyerere called for an emergency session of the Organization of African Unity (OAU) in Addis Ababa, Ethiopia, to ask for help from fellow Africans to replace British soldiers as soon as possible. Soon thereafter, Nigeria under President Nnamdi Azikiwe sent troops to Tanganyika to replace the British. Kenya and Uganda continued to rely on British assistance until the situation return to normal.

The army mutinies in the three East African countries helped inspire military coups on the continent when soldiers in other countries saw how they could use guns to extract concessions from civilian governments and even overthrow them at will. And they were some of the earliest manifestations of the intrusive power of the military in African politics as a continental phenomenon, and of what was yet to come in an even more violent way: coups and assassinations spanning four decades.

The 1964 military crisis in the three East African countries occurred around the same time when two major political developments took place in what came to be known as Tanzania. On 12 January 1964, the Zanzibar revolution ended the political dominance of the Arabs when the Arab government was overthrown in one of the bloodiest conflicts in post-colonial Africa. Thousands of people, probably no fewer than 4,000, were killed.

The revolution was supported by Tanganyika. And according to Thabit Kombo who became secretary-general of the Afro-Shirazi Party (ASP) which assumed power in Zanzibar after the revolution, President Kwame Nkrumah of Ghana also helped finance the Zanzibar revolution, as Andrew Nyerere, President Julius Nyerere's eldest son, told me when I was working on the expanded edition of one of my books, *Nyerere and Africa: End of Era*, which I discussed with him throughout the project.

Only about a month before on 10 December 1963, Zanzibar won independence from Britain. But the Arab leaders to whom power was transferred by the departing colonial masters excluded blacks from the government. Not long after the revolution, Tanganyika united with Zanzibar on 26 April 1964. The Union of Tanganyika and Zanzibar was renamed the United Republic of Tanzania on October 29 the same year.

However, some people in the region and elsewhere expressed strong reservations about the union, fearing that it was communist-inspired and would become a launching pad for communist penetration of Africa. Apprehensive of the situation, Ronald Ngala, leader of the Opposition – and of the federalist Kenya African Democratic Union (KADU) – in the Kenyan parliament, had the following to say:

"I hope...that the overseas influence infiltrated into Zanzibar will not spread to Tanganyika in any malicious way."[13]

He made the comment on the same day Tanganyika united with Zanzibar, and mentioned "communist" influence on the former island nation because the Zanzibar revolution had been supported by some communists, including Fidel Castro, and some of the Zanzibari revolutionaries were communist or communist-oriented. But Ronald Ngala's fear of communist penetration of Tanzania, shared by others including the eccentric president of Malawi, Dr. Hastings Kamuzu Banda, proved to be unfounded.

Through the years, Tanzania remained non-aligned – maintaining strong ties with both the East and the West – under President Nyerere and his successors, Ali Hassan Mwinyi (1985 – 1995), and Benjamin Mkapa who became president in 1995 not long after the collapse of communism except in a few countries such as China, Cuba, and North Korea where it remained a state ideology, even if not a functional one in all aspects.

The union of Tanganyika and Zanzibar was the first between independent states on the entire continent, and the only one that has survived for decades.

Consummation of the union between Tanganyika and Zanzibar was a step towards African unity and consolidation of African independence.

But only about a year-and-a-half later, Africa suffered a reversal in its quest for freedom. In November 1965, the same year and month in which General Joseph Mobutu overthrew President Joseph Kasavubu, the white minority government of the Rhodesian Front party led by Ian Smith in the British colony of Rhodesia declared independence illegally, totally excluding the black majority from power.

The unilateral declaration of independence, which came to be known as UDI, was in outright defiance of the wishes and aspirations of not only the black majority in the colony but of the entire continent except the other white minority regimes in South Africa, South West Africa (Namibia) which was ruled by apartheid South Africa, and in the Portuguese colonies of Angola, Mozambique and Portuguese Guinea (Guinea-Bissau), and in other colonial territories. Rhodesia was on the way to becoming another state like South Africa: a bastion of white supremacy on the continent.

Since Rhodesia was a British colony, African leaders urged Britain to intervene and end Smith's rebellion. But Britain did nothing, prompting most African governments to break diplomatic relations with London, in protest. Yet the British government conceded it had jurisdiction over Rhodesia and the constitutional mandate to intervene in the rebellious colony, but still used twisted logic to justify non-intervention. It was neither impressive logic nor clever semantics, and triggered the following response from President Nyerere:

"What has Britain done since 11 November (when Rhodesia declared independence)? On that date Mr. Wilson (the British prime minister) used some strong words: he said 'it is an illegal act, ineffective in law; an act of rebellion against the crown and against the constitution as by law established.' But he then went on to instruct the civil servants of Southern Rhodesia to 'stay at their posts but not to assist in any illegal acts.' He was unable to explain how they could do that when they were serving an illegal government.

As regards the use of force Mr. Wilson repeated his stock phrase despite the changed circumstances. Britain would not use force to impose a constitutional settlement, he said, but he went on to say that the British Government 'would give full consideration to any appeal from the Governor (of Rhodesia) for help to restore law and order.' Mr. Wilson refrained from explaining how the law could be more broken than it had been by the usurpation of power, that is to say, by treason. He refrained later from explaining how the Governor was to transmit his appeal once the telephone had been taken from him as well as all the furniture of his office, his staff and his transport."[14]

African countries continued to uphold what came to be known as the NIBMAR principle: No Independence Before Majority Rule. But rebel Prime Minister Ian Smith saw the future of Rhodesia from an entirely different perspective. He vowed, at different times, there shall be no majority rule in Rhodesia "not in my lifetime; not in one hundred years; not even in a thousand years." History proved him wrong within his own lifetime.

As the world entered the 21st century, Ian Smith was still living on his farm, but as an ordinary citizen this time, in a country he once ruled defiantly with a tight grip on the black majority. He was now living under his nemesis, Robert Mugabe, a black president, a man he once kept in prison for more than 10 years. Mugabe's crime was simple, yet profound in its implications for white minority rule. He was imprisoned for demanding independence on the basis of majority rule: one man, one vote, regardless of race, gender, class, religion, or national origin. He won, and Rhodesia became Zimbabwe. It was a crowning achievement after a long, bitter struggle, and one of the bloodiest in British colonial history. But, back in 1965, no one foresaw that realization of this goal would be many years away.

It was also in the same year that Africa witnessed another military coup. The coup was the second military takeover on the continent, after the first one in Togo only about two years earlier, and from which Africa had not yet recovered. On 24 November 1965, General Joseph Mobutu overthrew the government of President Joseph Kasavubu in Congo-Leopoldville, coincidentally only 13 days after the white minority regime of Ian Smith illegally declared independence for Rhodesia.

Among the casualties was Evariste Kimba, appointed prime minister by President Kasavubu in October 1965 to replace Moise Tshombe who was invited in 1964 to return from exile to become Congo's premier as fighting intensified in Katanga Province, hoping that his appointment would help to end the fighting in his former secessionist province. Kimba was hanged on orders from Mobutu; so were other opponents, soon after the coup.

As Africa was still grappling with the Rhodesian crisis, and with the Congo which was still in turmoil, two major developments of political and historical significance for the continent took place in 1966.

On 15 January 1966, Nigeria, Africa's most populous country, was rocked by its first military coup in which Federal Prime Minister Sir Abubakar Tafawa Balewa and two regional premiers and other top government officials were assassinated.

The coup was led by a group of young army officers from Eastern Nigeria. And it triggered a violent reaction against easterners living in Northern Nigeria after the Northern Premier Ahmadu Bello, Federal Prime Minister Abubakar Tafawa Balewa, also a northerner, and a large number of northern military officers were killed.

The other premier who was killed was Chief Samuel Ladoke Akintola of Western Nigeria.

Tens of thousands of Eastern Nigerians were massacred in retaliation, pogroms which largely contributed to the secession of the Eastern Region and subsequent civil war in the following year, as did Nigeria's second military coup only a few months later in July 1966 in which the head of the federal military government, Johnson Aguiyi Ironsi, an easterner, was assassinated.

Another major political event in Africa in 1966 was the military coup in Ghana, only about a month after the first coup in Nigeria which may have helped to inspire it. On 24 February 1966, Dr. Kwame Nkrumah was overthrown when he was in Peking on his way to Hanoi at the invitation of Ho Chin Mihn to help end the Vietnam war. The coup was masterminded by the CIA. Black American ambassador to Ghana, Franklin Williams who was Nkrumah's schoolmate at Lincoln University, a historically black college in Pennsylvania, played a critical role in facilitating the coup. The coup makers were reportedly given at least $6 million by the CIA through the American embassy in Ghana to oust Nkrumah; his ouster partly inspired by his increasingly dictatorial rule, and by a deteriorating economy drained by expensive projects and failed socialist policies.

Dr. Nkrumah's downfall was significant in a number of respects. Not only was he one of Africa's most controversial presidents because of his daring and policy initiatives; he was also one of the most influential.

Nkrumah was the first leader in sub-Saharan Africa to lead his country to independence on 6 March 1957. He was the most ardent proponent of immediate continental unification. He was the first black African head of state to institute a one-party state and adopt socialism. He was one of the strongest supporters of African independence and liberation movements. He articulated an ideology and concepts which stimulated debate and had profound impact on the course of political events on the continent. And he remains, even today, the most influential African leader besides Julius Nyerere and Nelson Mandela; with Mandela's influence mainly as a moral authority, and not as a political theorist like Nkrumah and Nyerere.

In a poll conducted by the BBC in 2002, the majority of Africans who participated in the survey voted for Nkrumah as the most influential African leader in the twentieth century.

While many people in Ghana were debating the legacy of Dr. Nkrumah and adjusting to new life under military rule for the first time in their lives, Nigeria was hurtling towards disaster, inexorably propelled by the spiraling wave of violence as a result of the two military coups in 1966.

The hour of reckoning came on 30 May 1967, when the leaders of Eastern Nigeria declared independence and renamed the secessionist region, the Republic of Biafra, "land of the rising sun." Secession of Eastern Nigeria from the rest of the federation was the biggest threat the country had faced since independence in 1960. And it had serious implications for the entire continent.

Nigeria was seen as an anchor of stability on a continent of weak states, and, because of its sheer size and enormous wealth mostly from oil, had the potential to become one of the most powerful countries in the developing world. Should it collapse, its weaker neighbours would inevitably be sucked into the vortex and suffer tremendously from the spill-over effects of the implosion.

This dreadful prospect seemed to be a distinct possibility when, not long after Eastern Nigeria declared independence, hostilities broke out between the two sides in July 1967, plunging the country into civil war. From then on, until 1970, the Nigerian conflict became the dominant story dominating headlines across the continent.

The secessionist forces capitulated to federal might on 12 January 1970, and the war officially ended three days later, on January 15, when the Biafrans finally surrendered.

More than one million people, mostly Igbo, perished in the conflict. Most of them died from starvation which the federal military government used deliberately and effectively as a weapon against the Biafrans. Chief Obafemi Awolowo, vice-chairman of the Executive Council, hence vice-president of Nigeria under General

Yakubu Gowon, unequivocally stated that starvation was a legitimate instrument of war against the secessionists to force them to surrender. Other estimates, including those of the BBC and other news organizations and relief agencies, put the death toll at 2 million.

It was, until then, the deadliest conflict in modern African history and one of the biggest humanitarian disasters the world had ever seen, evoking memories of the Jewish holocaust in Nazi Germany when 6 million Jews were exterminated.

The conflict in the Middle East also had direct bearing on Africa. When the third Arab-Israeli war broke out in June 1967, just one month before the Nigerian civil war erupted, almost all the Arab countries in North Africa became directly involved in the conflict. Egypt, the leader of the Arab world and the most powerful Arab nation, played the most dominant role, sending to the front the largest number of troops among all Arab countries comprising North Africa and the Middle East; in fact, most Arabs in the world live in Africa, not in the Middle East, and Arab countries in Africa constitute the largest percentage of Arab land in the world.

In addition to Egypt, two other North African countries, Algeria and Libya, also sent troops. And most African countries supported the Arab cause, especially at the Organization of African Unity (OAU), the United Nations and in other international forums. It was also during this period that one of the most dominant political figures in the Arab world and on the African continent, President Gamal Abdel Nasser, died. He died of a heart attack on 28 September 1970. He was 52.

The year 1971 witnessed the emergence of a new political phenomenon on the African continent: Idi Amin. Ignorant and arrogant with only a standard two education – Americans call it second grade; flamboyant and comical, he earned himself a place in history for his atrocities and buffooneries – including antics unheard of – few would envy. An eccentric and bizarre character, he admired Hitler and tried to emulate him. He even wanted to build a monument to the Fuhrer, in his likeness, in Uganda's capital Kampala.

Yet he did not have a policy of systematic ethnic cleansing involving extermination, although he initially targeted members of the Langi and Acholi ethnic groups whom he thought were loyal to deposed President Milton Obote who was a Langi.

The Acholi and the Langi constituted a disproportionately large number of enlisted men and officers in the Ugandan army whom Amin swiftly replaced with men loyal to him from his home region, West Nile Province, in the northwest. And through the years, he also targeted assorted groups, including real and perceived enemies, across the spectrum, and praised Hitler as a true nationalist for persecuting and exterminating Jews. He even expelled almost all Asians from Uganda in 1972, including Ugandan citizens of Asian – mostly Indian and Pakistani – origin, and gave them only three weeks to leave the country. About 70,000 left Uganda.

I remember the expulsions well. I was on the same flight, East African Airways (EAA), with some of the expelled Asians in November 1972 on my way to Britain, and got the chance to talk with an elderly Indian sitting next to me. He was one of those kicked out of Uganda by the burly dictator and talked about this forced exodus, about which I had known when I was a reporter at the *Daily News* in Dar es Salaam, Tanzania.

The flight originated from Dar es Salaam, Tanzania's capital, where I caught the plane on my way to the United States for the first time as a student. Our first stop was Nairobi, Kenya; next, Kampala, Uganda, where the expelled Asians boarded the plane on their way to Britain and whatever other countries would take them in.

Stripped of their possessions including financial assets, they landed in Britain, and in other countries such as

Canada and the United States, destitute. Most of them ended up in Britain, Uganda's former colonial ruler. Almost all the passengers on the flight I was on from Uganda were Asians expelled by Idi Amin, as were those on subsequent flights, booked full.

President Julius Nyerere of Tanzania publicly condemned Idi Amin for expelling the Asians and called him a racist. Two other African leaders, President Kenneth Kaunda of Zambia and President Samora Machel of Mozambique, also criticized Amin for his brutalities and eccentric behaviour in general.

But it was Nyerere who was most explicit in his condemnation of Amin, and strongly criticized other African leaders for their silence and tolerance and even their admiration of the Ugandan despot and for practising tyranny in their own countries.

He reminded them that had Idi Amin been white, and had the apartheid regime of South Africa gone on a genocidal rampage, slaughtering blacks across the country, these same leaders would have been furious. There would have been an outcry across the continent, calling for severe sanctions and even military action against the white murderers. But because Amin was black, other African leaders simply looked the other way, as they did when other atrocities were being committed across the continent by fellow Africans. Black leadership had become a license to kill fellow blacks.

Idi Amin was one of the most brutal tyrants Africa has ever produced. And he was probably the most notorious, grabbing international headlines every few days – sometimes everyday – for his antics and brutality. He went on a genocidal rampage, killing an estimated 300,000 – 500,000 people during his eight-year blood-soaked reign of terror in a relentless campaign viciously prosecuted across ethnic lines by his henchmen.

Anybody, including his wives, was fair game as he sought to eliminate all his enemies, real and imagined.

And he himself participated in many of those killings, personally delivering the final blow. He also reportedly bragged about eating the flesh of some of his opponents, although this was never confirmed. As David Lamb stated in his book, *The Africans*, Amin could be as playful as a kitten and as lethal as a lion:

"Ugandans coined a word – Aminism – to describe the terrible happenings in their country, and by the time the Aminisms ended in 1979, an estimated 300,000 Ugandans - or one Ugandan in every forty - were dead. The carnage was tantamount to murdering the entire population of Louisville, Kentucky.

It was as though Amin had studied presidential protocol in Papa Doc's Haiti or Pol Pot's Cambodia. And in the process the Ugandan people learned how to survive but forgot how to feel. 'Killing was so commonplace,' a grocer in Kampala told me, 'that if you heard your brother had been picked up by the police, you knew that was the end of him. You'd say, 'Too bad,' and you'd feel bad for a few days, then you'd just go back to work and forget about him.'

A single human beast, as playful as a kitten, as lethal as a lion, had managed almost single-handedly to destroy a nation of 13 million people." – (David Lamb, *The Africans*, Vintage Books, New York, 1987, p. 78).

After he was chased out of Uganda eight years later in April 1979 by Tanzanian troops and Ugandan exiles, he left the country in tatters; a monument to the incalculable damage he had inflicted on that beautiful land and on his fellow countrymen during his brutal reign, drenched in blood on a scale unparalleled in the history of post-colonial Africa.

Other brutal dictators who earned notoriety in the seventies included President Masie Nguema of Equatorial Guinea. During his 11-year reign from 1968 – 1969, he terrorized the entire country and left it in ruins. About one-third of the population, at least 100,000 people, fled into exile, and an estimated 40,000 were tortured and killed. His nephew, 33-year-old Colonel Teodoro Obiang Nguema overthrew him in August 1979. President Nguema tried to escape but was captured, tried for genocide and witchcraft, and executed with six aides in September 1979.

Another brutal tyrant with a knack for grabbing headlines like Idi Amin was President Jean-Bedel Bokassa of the Central African Republic. In January 1966, Colonel Bokassa overthrew President David Dacko, his cousin. He dissolved the national legislature, abolished the constitution, and banned political parties. Suspected political opponents were routinely arrested and summarily executed or tortured indefinitely. He was also said to practice cannibalism like Idi Amin, his friend.

In December 1976, Bokassa crowned himself Africa's first socialist emperor at a sports stadium in the capital Bangui in a ceremony that cost $20 million and drained the coffers of his impoverished nation. His official title was Emperor Bokassa I. His brutality knew no bounds. When school boys demonstrated against a government decree ordering them to buy uniforms from a shop partly owned by one of his three wives, the notorious dictator ordered them arrested. About 100 of them were brutally murdered in April 1979. Bokassa himself personally killed 39 of the students.

The seventies also witnessed a series of other tragedies on the African continent. In 1972, a campaign of ethnic cleansing in Burundi by the Tutsi military rulers claimed more than 200,000 Hutu lives within three months; a genocide which presaged what was to happen 22 years later in neighbouring Rwanda which has roughly the same ethnic ratio and composition and whose holocaust claimed even more lives than the massacres in Burundi. At least five times as many lives were lost in Rwanda, but of Tutsis this time, and at a rate five times faster than Hitler killed the Jews.

In 1974, one of Africa's most influential and revered leaders, Emperor Haile Selassie of Ethiopia, was deposed in a military coup. He died in 1975 in captivity, reportedly smothered with a wet pillow, and was buried in an unmarked grave, symbolically intended to shunt him into oblivion. Other reports said he was buried under a toilet in his former imperial palace in Addis Ababa where he was detained and where his remains were found in 1992. President Julius Nyerere intervened and tried to save his life but did not succeed in convincing the military rulers to free the deposed emperor and spare his life.

One of the reasons for his ouster was his unwillingness or refusal to admit that tens of thousands of his people were starving – he was ashamed, as an emperor. Also known as the Lion of Judah, and King of Kings, Haile Selassie was said to be a descendant of King Solomon and the Queen of Sheba, and the 250th king in that line of succession, although some people dispute this claim to royal lineage.

But the military regime which ended the monarchy turned out to be ruthless on a scale unheard of during Emperor Haile Selassie's reign. In June 1974, Ethiopian troops overthrew the government and declared "war on feudalism." At least 200 former cabinet members and advisers to the emperor were arrested. Haile Selassie himself was deposed in September 1974, ending his 58-year reign as Africa's only emperor and one of the most respected leaders on the continent and in the entire world.

The military junta officially abolished the Ethiopian monarchy in March 1975. After a protracted power struggle, Lieutenant-Colonel Mengistu Haile Mariam emerged as Ethiopia's ruler. A dictator, he went on to institute a reign of terror that claimed more than 5,000 lives in 1977 – 1978.

Nine assassination attempts on Mengistu were reported by his government in 1978, leading to the execution of many members of the ruling military junta. In 1981, Amnesty International estimated that 10,000 to 40,000 political prisoners remained in Ethiopian jails and prisons. Many were tortured and killed.

The famine in Ethiopia went on to claim more than one million lives through the seventies and early eighties. In 1982 – 1985, Ethiopia had one of the worst droughts in its history. More than 9 million people faced starvation.

A major international relief effort mobilized more than $700 million in government and private aid for the famine victims who received thousands of tons of grain and other supplies including medicine.

Famine in other African countries such as Niger, Mali, Chad, and Upper Volta (renamed Burkina Faso in 1984), also claimed hundreds of thousands of lives during the same period.

Civil wars also dominated headlines in Africa during that period.

In 1975, the Portuguese colonies of Angola and Mozambique won independence after 500 years of colonial rule; Portuguese Guinea, also the oldest colony on the continent, won hers as Guinea-Bissau in 1974, becoming the first Portuguese colony in Africa to emerge from colonial rule.

But immediately after that, Angola was plunged into full-scale civil war – the war actually never stopped between the three contending parties, the MPLA (Popular Movement for the Liberation of Angola), UNITA (Union for the Total Independence of Angola), and FNLA (National Front for the Liberation of Angola), which had been fighting for control of Angola while at the same fighting against the Portuguese.

The FNLA withered in the late seventies, not long after Angola won independence, but UNITA continued to fight against the ruling MPLA through the decades and into the twentieth-first century. By the end of 2000, the war had cost more than one million lives and devastated the country. It ended in April 2002 after rebel leader Dr. Jonas Savimbi was killed by government soldiers in February the same year.

While the war in Angola was raging in the seventies, another major conflict erupted between Ethiopia and Somalia in 1977 after Somalia invaded its neighbour to reclaim the Ogaden Region in the southeast – which is predominantly ethnic Somali – annexed in 1896 by Ethiopian Emperor Menelik II; he also annexed several other provinces to the west during the same period.

The two countries continued to fight intermittently through the years until 1988 when Somalia surrendered. The Somali army was devastated back in 1978 after eight months of intense warfare, but was still able to sustain a protracted conflict between the two countries through its surrogates, Somali guerrillas in the Ogaden, until 1988 when Somalia conceded defeat and signed a peace agreement with Ethiopia virtually on the victor's terms.

It was also during the same period that Tanzania and Uganda went to war after Idi Amin invaded Tanzania in October 1978 and annexed 710 square miles of its territory in the northwest Kagera Region bordering Uganda. He also had other territorial ambitions to seize and annex a corridor of Tanzanian territory and what then was the country's second largest city, Tanga on the east coast, ostensibly to have an outlet to the sea.

But his imperial ambitions didn't get very far. Tanzania drove out the invaders and, together with an army of Ugandan exiles, marched all the way to Kampala, forcing Amin to flee the country in April 1979. He sought refuge in Libya, welcomed by another mercurial leader, Muammar al-Qaddafi who earlier sent troops and weapons to Uganda to help Amin fight Tanzania.

The war, which lasted for six months and finally ended Amin's brutal dictatorship, inflicted a heavy blow on Tanzania and cost the poverty-stricken country more than $500 miilion.

Africa entered a new decade, the 1980s, with some good news. In April 1980, white minority rule in Rhodesia came to an end after a 15-year intense guerrilla war of independence in which tens of thousands of people were killed. The country was renamed Zimbabwe. But the euphoria of independence was marred by the massacre of more than 20,000 people by government troops in the early 1980s in the opposition stronghold of Matebeland in southwestern Zimbabwe; a brutal campaign that exacerbated tensions between the country's two major ethnic groups, the Shona who constitute about 70 percent of the population and dominate the government, and the Ndebele who make up about 20 percent and once ruled the Shona before the advent of colonial rule.

But more than any other country in Africa, Sudan has suffered the longest from the scourge of war. Its war began in 1955, just before the country won independence from Britain and Egypt in 1956, and cost more than 500,000 lives by 1972 when the Arab-dominated government in the north reached a cease-fire agreement with the black insurgents in the south who had been fighting against Arab domination and for autonomy.

The war re-ignited in 1983 and claimed more than two million lives by 1999 in that 15-year period alone. With about three million dead since 1955, it was the bloodiest conflict in African post-colonial history up to the end of the twentieth-century and beyond, and came to be known as the world's longest, bloodiest, and most forgotten war.

In July 2002 , the two sides signed the Machakos Agreement – in the town of Machakos, Kenya, under the auspices of Kenyan President Daniel arap Moi – and agreed to share power; allow the south to enjoy extensive autonomy; and hold an internationally supervised referendum after six years, in 2008, to enable the people of the south decide if they wanted to remain an integral part of Sudan or secede and establish their own independent state.

In a referendum that was held in January 2011, southerners overwhelmingly voted for independence. On 9 July 2011, the south became independent as the new nation of South Sudan.

The mid-eighties saw the eruption of another major civil war in Africa, besides the conflict in Sudan that was already going on. In 1986, a rebel group called RENAMO (Portuguese acronym for Mozambique National Resistance) started waging a sustained military campaign against the FRELIMO government of Mozambique; FRELIMO is an acronym for Front for the Liberation of Mozambique, an organization which waged guerrilla war and ended Portuguese colonial rule in the country.

The conflict between RENAMO and FRELIMO started earlier, before 1986, but escalated in the mid-eighties. RENAMO was created with the help of the Rhodesian security forces and was supported by apartheid South Africa, the United States, and right-wing organizations in the West. Other countries including Saudi Arabia also supported RENAMO.

The war went on for 16 years. When it ended in 1992, more than one million people had been killed and at least five million ended up as refugees mostly in Tanzania and Malawi. It was one of the most brutal wars in modern African history characterized by gruesome mutilation, chopping off limbs, ears and lips as in Sierra Leone where the rebels also chopped off buttocks and branded civilians with hot iron and steel.

Chad was also embroiled in civil war in the 1980s. Civil conflict in Chad began in the sixties between Arabs in the north, who are mostly Muslim, and blacks in the south who are predominantly Christian. In the seventies and eighties, outside powers were involved in the conflict and switched sides supporting one side and then the other whenever it suited their interests. The United States and France were allies against Libya and her clients throughout the conflict. Tens of thousands of people died in the war in the seventies and eighties alone.

The government of Hissene Habre, a northerner, killed more than 40,000 people and tortured more than 100,000 in southern Chad, his opponents' stronghold. The conflict was political as much as it was racial as has been the case since the sixties when Arabs in the north, a minority in the country, tried to secede or establish an autonomous state with the help of Libya after they failed to dominate the country following the end of French colonial rule in 1960.

Famine also continued to ravage Africa in the 1980s and many countries in a belt stretching across the north-central part of the continent from Mali to Ethiopia faced massive starvation. They were helpless and could only count on international relief efforts to alleviate their plight. Hundreds of thousands of people died. Drought was responsible for most of the famine and also wiped out livestock. But mismanagement, corruption, wrong policies and inept leadership also played a major role in aggravating the situation.

The collapse of communism in the late 1980s and early 1990s ushered in a new era round the globe. Just as the sixties saw most African countries become one-party states and socialist or socialist-oriented, the early nineties witnessed a reversal of that when almost all the countries embraced multiparty democracy and capitalism, once considered their nemesis in the quest for unity and development.

After the end of communism, free-market policies were adopted in countries – including Russia and former Soviet satellites – which had pursued socialist policies for decades even before African countries won independence. And multiparty democracy found ready acceptance where it had been reviled by leaders as a tool of the capitalist West to divide and dominate weaker countries. African countries shared this view after they attained sovereign status.

And when change came, showing that communism had

failed, Africa was no exception from this reconfiguration of the political landscape. In the early 1990s, a wave of democratisation swept across the continent which had been dominated by one-party states since the sixties, and socialism was renounced as a state ideology even by countries which had been the strongest exponents of this politico-economic philosophy.

The early nineties also witnessed the beginning of the end of apartheid in South Africa, the bastion of white supremacy on the continent. In February 1990, South Africa's most prominent political prisoner, Nelson Mandela, was released from prison after being incarcerated for more than 27 years. The apartheid regime finally collapsed in May 1994 when Mandela became president after the first multiracial democratic elections in the country's history. However, the transition to the new dispensation had also been marred by political and ethnic violence in the early nineties that cost more than 10,000 lives within three years before the April 1994 elections which were a spectacular success.

But in spite of the good news about the end of apartheid whose demise was celebrated across the continent, 1994 was also a tragic year for Africa. It was the year when about one million people, mostly Tutsi, were massacred by the Hutu in Rwanda within three months at a rate five times – some say six times – faster than Hitler killed the Jews.

The massacres took place from April to July 1994, around the same time South Africa was emerging from her nightmare of apartheid. It was a strange coincidence, "the best of times,...the worst of times," in the words of Charles Dickens. As Wole Soyinka stated in one of his articles, "The Blood-soaked Quilt of Africa," in May 1994: "Rwanda is our nightmare, South Africa is our dream." Tragically, the nightmare has not yet ended, not only in Rwanda but in many parts of Africa.

The bloodshed in Rwanda was only one of the

tragedies that befell Africa during the nineties. It was a decade of wars, and AIDS, and other calamities. Besides having the largest number of AIDS victims and casualties, Africa also had the largest number of civil wars in the 1990s more than in any other period since independence in the sixties. At least 25 countries were torn by civil conflicts: Algeria, Sierra Leone, Liberia, Guinea-Bissau, Sudan, Somalia, Ethiopia, Uganda, Rwanda, Burundi, Congo-Kinshasa (Zaire), Congo-Brazzaville (Congo Republic), Angola, Mozambique, Kenya, Chad, the Central African Republic, Cote d'Ivoire (Ivory Coast), Nigeria, Mali, Senegal, Niger, the Comoros, Lesotho, and South Africa during the transition from apartheid to democracy.

Some of the bloodiest conflicts which erupted in the nineties took place in Liberia and Sierra Leone. The war in Liberia started in December 1989, and in Sierra Leone in March 1991. Both countries were totally destroyed. About 200,000 were killed in Sierra Leone, more than 100,000 maimed, and tens of thousands were uprooted from their homes and ended up as refugees in neighbouring countries. In Liberia, also more than 200,000 were killed, more than 800,000 ended up as refugees, and about 6 to 8 percent of the total population perished in the seven-year conflict.

In Sierra Leone, the rebels of the Revolutionary United Front (RUF) earned international notoriety because of their gruesome tactics, chopping off limbs, ears and lips, gouging out eyes, chopping off buttocks, and other brutalities inflicted on innocent civilians including the elderly, women, and babies only a few weeks old. They all met the same fate, sometimes with both arms and legs chopped off.

As the century came to an end, the wars were still raging in both countries. The war in Sierra Leone formally ended in January 2002. But there was no guarantee that peace would be maintained after British troops, which ended the war, left the country. UN peacekeeping troops, the largest force ever deployed anywhere in UN's history, also helped restore peace but were not as effective as British combat troops. In Liberia, the war formally ended in 1996 but low-intensity warfare – and sometimes pitched battles in sporadic fighting in different parts of the country – continued through the years in an attempt by rebel groups to overthrow President Charles Taylor; a brutal warlord and dictator who intimidated his fellow countrymen into voting for him in 1997, with the implied threat that he would plunge Liberia back into war if he did not win the presidency.

A thug even in office, he continued to use brutal tactics against real and perceived enemies, torturing and killing them. The brutalities helped fuel the war against his regime. In February 2002, he came perilously close to being overthrown when one of the rebel groups advanced towards the capital, Monrovia, and was within striking range – only about 20 miles – when government forces fought back.

The conflict escalated into full-scale war in different parts of the country, forcing tens of thousands of refugees to flee and seek shelter elsewhere within Liberia and in the Ivory Coast and other neighbouring countries.

Finally, rebels belonging to two groups – LURD (Liberians for Reconciliation and Democracy) and MODEL (Movement for Democracy in Liberia) – entered the capital Monrovia and forced Taylor to relinquish power in August 2003. He left Liberia and was granted political asylum in Nigeria as part of an agreement to end the civil war. But he was later arrested, handed over to the Liberian government which, in turn, sent him to a UN court in Sierra Leone to be tried for crimes against humanity. Hew was finally transferred to stand trial at The Hague in the Netherlands. On 26 September 2013, he was sentenced to 50 years in prison and was sent to Britain to serve his sentence.

The 1990s were tragic in another respect. These were also the years when Somalia died as a nation, pulverized from within, the only African country to "disappear" from the map; and the only country in the world that had no government and remained stateless from 1991 – when it first collapsed – well into the 21st century.

It was also during this period that another nation, Eritrea, was born out of Ethiopia in May 1993. Ethiopia became the first African country to break up peacefully, and Eritrea the first to be born out of another since the advent of colonial rule and in the post-colonial era, although it once was an Italian colony and was forcibly incorporated into Ethiopia in 1952 by the United Nations as a condition for its "independence." Ethiopia ended up absorbing it, turning it into one of its provinces and a virtual colony. It was, for all practical purposes, the last "colony" on the continent, colonised within the "mother country," Ethiopia, and ended that status as Africa, with all her problems, staggered towards the beginning of another century, with hope and despair.

Some of the deadliest conflicts hardly made headlines outside Africa. In Congo-Brazzaville, a four-month civil war from 5 June – 15 October 1997, devastated the capital, Brazzaville. Entire parts of the city were reduced to rubble, and more than 10,000 people were killed in the capital alone when government troops of President Pascal Lissouba fought a militia group, the Cobra, supporting former miltary dictator Denis Sassuou-Nguesso.

Lissouba, a former professor, won the presidency in a democratic election in 1992 but fled to Burkina Faso where he was granted asylum after he lost the war in 1997.

Sporadic fighting continued in different parts of the country in the following years, with the Ninja rebels and other forces loyal to former President Lissouba and to the former Brazzaville mayor Bernard Kolelas who once served as prime minister under Lissouba, trying to oust President Denis Sassou-Nguesso.

In 1998, another major civil war erupted in Guinea-Bissau between government troops loyal to President Joao Bernardo Vieira and rebel soldiers led by former army chief Ansumane Mane. The rebels seized most of the country and much of the capital, Bissau, and finally toppled the president in May 1999. Tens of thousands of people fled their homes, creating a major refugee crisis in one of the world's smallest and poorest countries. General Ansumane Mane was eventually killed by government troops in November 2000 for allegedly trying to launch a coup d'etat.

The last two years of the decade (1998 - 1999) also witnessed the bloodiest conflict on the continent since World War II when Ethiopia and Eritrea went to war over a barren piece of land. The war involved tanks, fully mechanized battalions, combat jets and other modern weapons, but was mostly fought as trench warfare like World War I.

The war cost more than 100,000 lives in a combined total of only a few weeks of intense fighting, sometimes claiming as many as 5,000 – 10,000 lives within a few days.

Although the war was fought intermittently, it drained the economies of both countries, some of the poorest in the world. Both countries spent hundreds of millions of dollars, buying expensive and highly sophisticated weapons, while their people, especially in Ethiopia, were starving.

The 1990s were also a period when the AIDS epidemic wreaked havoc across the African continent more than anywhere else and continued to do so well into the 21st century, with no cure in sight. The statistics were appalling, and AIDS became an acronym for Africa Is Dying Slowly.

Since the beginning of the epidemic in the early 1980s, more than 20 million people in sub-Saharan Africa had died of AIDS by the end of 2000; more than twice the number of those who died in World War I. For example, in Zimbabwe, at least 5,000 people were dying everyday. And about half of all 15-year-olds infected with the HIV virus that causes AIDS will eventually die of the disease even if infection rates drop substantially through a combination of therapies and education on AIDS prevention.

Thus, even with the combined casualties from all the African wars since the 1950s and 1960s, including liberation wars against colonial regimes, the death-toll in those conflicts comes nowhere close to the number of people who died of AIDS in Africa by the end of the 1990s; a casualty rate that was bound to grow exponentially through the years, short of divine intervention or some miracle cure including combination therapy to stop the pandemic.

There was also another dimension to some of the African conflicts during that period. There were secessionist threats which led to skirmishes between the insurgents and government troops on the independence-prone island of Bioko in Equatorial Guinea in 1998, and in Caprivi Strip in Namibia in 1999 and beyond. However, they were not major threats.

But there were other secessionist attempts on the continent that were far more deadly and escalated into full-scale war on the separatist islands of Anjouan and Moheli in the Comoros in September 1997, while the conflict in Casamance Province in Senegal had been going on as a full-scale guerrilla war since 1983 when secessionist forces in the region resorted to violence to achieve their goal.

There were other appalling statistics in the 1990s on this embattled continent. The civil war in the Democratic Republic of Congo, formerly Zaire, which drew armies from at least nine African countries, cost almost 2 million lives in Eastern Congo alone between August 1998 when the latest round of fighting started and May 2000. By June

2001, more than 2.5 million people had died, and no fewer than 3 million by mid-2002 in the same region. By 2013, the war and ts accompanying disasters, including hunger and disease, had claimed 6 million lives.

When the war started, the countries involved were Congo itself, Zimbabwe, Angola, Namibia, Rwanda, Uganda, Burundi, Chad, and Sudan. Rwanda, Uganda and Burundi supported the rebels trying to overthrow the government of Laurent Kabila, while the rest backed up the Congolese army in its war against the insurgents; also, there were about 20 rebel groups involved in the war, with conflicting interests.

The intervention by foreign armies from other African countries internationalized the conflict which some people called "Africa's First World War"; a hyperbolic statement whose outlandish nature did not help to put the conflict in its proper historical context. Although it was an inflated statement, there was no question that the war was a major conflict and catastrophe with serious implications for the stability of the continent. And it was still going on as Africa entered the 21st century, as did other wars on the continent. Africa had declared war on itself.

Even in a continent used to wars, the casualty list is staggering. Millions of Africans have died in these conflicts: Angola, more than 1 million; Mozambique, more than 1 million; Congo, formerly Zaire, about 6 million in the Second Congo War from 1998 – 2013; Rwanda, about 1 million killed within 100 days; Burundi, between 250,000 – 500,000 killed within 5 years since the mid-1990s; Somalia, more than 500,000 dead in the 1990s; Ethiopia, tens of thousands dead; Eritrea, also tens of thousands dead in a senseless war with Ethiopia over some tiny, barren piece of land, two bald-headed men fighting over a comb; Sudan, more than 3 million dead since 1983; Sierra Leone, more than 200,000 dead, and more than 100,000 left limbless, their limbs, and even buttocks, ears and lips, chopped off by rebels in an 11-year civil war from 1991 – 2002; Liberia, more than 200,000 dead, about 6 – 8 per cent of the entire population, equivalent to 16.2 million – 20.6 million Americans dead in a civil war within the same period. And this is not an exhaustive list of the number of people killed in wars in this mangled continent.

Some of the least known wars have also been some of the deadliest. Uganda has, relatively speaking, a reputation for stability in a region torn by conflict; although not like neighbouring Tanzania which is far more peaceful and more stable than all the countries in East Africa. Yet, for years, it had to contend with several rebel groups since the eighties when President Yoweri Museveni assumed power in 1986 after waging a successful guerrilla campaign against the government.

One of the bloodiest conflicts was in northern Uganda where rebels of the Lord's Resistance Army (LRA) backed by Sudan killed tens of thousands of people and abducted just as many, mostly children, forcing them to join the rebel army to work as sex slaves and as porters, in addition to fighting. The rebel group continued to wage war as late as 2007 and remained the deadliest among all the insurgents in Uganda including those waging a sporadic guerrilla campaign in the western part of the country.

In neighbouring Kenya, more than 10,000 people were killed within three weeks in a tribal war between the Pokot and Turkana tribesmen in the northern part of the country in 1998.

Earlier in 1992, ethnic cleansing in the Rift Valley Province, home of President Daniel arap Moi and his fellow Kalenjin tribesmen, claimed hundreds of Kikuyu lives, at least 1,300, and forced 300,000 others to flee for their lives, while their property was ransacked and destroyed by the Kalenjins.

Other tribal conflicts in Kenya, including those during the 1997 general elections in the Coast Province and again in the Rift Valley Province, claimed more lives in different parts of the country through the years.

In Nigeria, communal and ethnic violence threatened to tear apart Africa's biggest nation and continued to do so well into the 21st century. Within only three years since the inauguration of President Olusegun Obasanjo in May 1999, the violence claimed more than 10,000 lives in different parts of the country. The conflicts were exacerbated by the introduction of Islamic law, know as *sharia* (in Kiswahili, a language which is about 25 - 30 percent Arabic, *sheria* - not *sharia* – simply means law, any law), in the predominantly Muslim states in the north, triggering clashes between Muslims and Christians originally from the south.

Besides the religious dimension, the conflict was also ethnic. The Christians from the south living in Northern Nigeria are mostly Igbo and members of other ethnic groups, while the Muslims in the north are mostly members of the Hausa and Fulani ethnic groups which are so close to each other – ethnically, culturally, and religiously – that they are simply and collectively known as Hausa-Fulani; with the Fulani mainly constituting the ruling class.

The conflicts in Nigeria, especially in the oil-rich Niger Delta, were ignited and fuelled by government neglect, prompting some people to call for secession.

The end of the 1990s were also marked by another tragedy. Famine threatened the lives of millions of people in East Africa. About 18 million people faced starvation in Ethiopia; 13 million in Kenya faced the same dreadful prospect, prompting one elderly Kenyan photographed and quoted by *The Washington Post* to say, "It's only you white people who can save us," a searing indictment against African governments in general for their inability and unwillingness to help their people. And 13 million people in Tanzania, about 40 percent of the population, were threated by famine during the same period.

Hardest hit were the countries of southern Africa

which faced massive starvation at the dawn of the new century, especially in 2001 - 2004. Malawi, Zambia, Zimbabwe, Angola, Botswana, Mozambique, Swaziland, Lesotho, Namibia, and even South Africa, all faced famine, only in varying degrees. Malawi, Angola, and Zimbabwe whose crisis was aggravated by the seizure of white-owned farms by President Robert Mugabe's government, were the hardest hit, and an international relief effort was launched to help alleviate the plight of millions of people in the region.

But there was also a glimmer of hope, at least for future generations, when the defunct East African Community (EAC) which collapsed in 1977 was revived in 2001 and became functional in 2002 in pursuit of stronger regional integration including federation.

The original member states are Kenya, Uganda and Tanzania which, together with Rwanda and Burundi which joined the EAC in July 2009, may one day form an East African federation that has been an elusive dream since 1963 when Julius Nyerere, Jomo Kenyatta and Milton Obote tried to unite their countries.

The prospects for regional integration also gave some hope to the people of West Africa when the countries in the region decided in 2000 to institute a common currency known as the Eco by 2004; unfortunately, they did not.

It was an ambitious project whose fulfillment would have to depend on the commitment of the member states – Economic Community of West African States (ECOWAS) – to the ideal of regional integration.

The goal towards integration on a continental scale assumed another dimension in June 2001 when the Organization of African Unity (OAU) founded in May 1963 was replaced by the African Union (AU) to facilitate the establishment of a common market, a common currency - the Afro? - and other institutions including a continental parliament.

The OAU officially came to an end at an annual

summit of the African heads of state and government in Lusaka, Zambia, in June 2001 under the chairmanship of Zambian President Frederick Chiluba. It was skillfully led for an unprecedented three consecutive terms by Dr. Salim Ahmed Salim of Tanzania who served as OAU secretary-general from 1989 to 2001, the longest term ever served in that capacity.

The African Union (AU) was formally launched in Durban, South Africa, in July 2002 under the chairmanship of South African President Thabo Mbeki.

The Southern African Development Community (SADC) composed of 14 countries in East and Southern Africa, which is also the strongest economic bloc on the continent because of South Africa's membership, the continent's powerhouse, continued to grow and took further steps to achieve full economic integration in the region. Measures proposed included establishment of a common market, a common currency, and a regional parliament.

On a continent dominated by bad news, the trend towards regional integration was some of the best news to come out of Africa as the 20th century came to an end.

But there was more bad news. Africa suffered another tragic loss at the end of the 1990s that was also an important milestone in the history of Africa. Tanzania's first president, Julius Nyerere, died of leukaemia at a hospital in London, England, on 14 October 1999. He was 77.

Nyerere was one of the most prominent African leaders in the 20th century who spearheaded the independence movement across the continent. He was also one of the most articulate and ardent spokesmen for the Third World. His death marked the end of an era in the history of post-colonial Africa, and the dawn of a new one in terms of ideological orientation and leadership.

He was one of the last of the most prominent African leaders who led their countries to independence in the

113

fifties and sixties. They included Kwame Nkrumah, Jomo Kenyatta, Nnamdi Azikiwe, Patrice Lumumba, Ahmed Sekou Toure, and Modibo Keita. He outlived them all, except Kenneth Kaunda, Milton Obote, Leopold Sedar Senghor, and Ahmed Ben Bella.

His belief in socialism remained unshaken, and he died with his reputation for integrity intact.

Nyerere will be remembered for generations as one of the founding fathers of independent Africa and a staunch advocate of Pan-Africanism whose ideology and philosophy was embraced by those in the diaspora as well, comparable in stature to another uncompromising Pan-Africanist, Dr. Kwame Nkrumah. As one South African journalist wrote about Nyerere's role in the liberation of the countries of southern Africa from white minority rule:

"All these countries are now free, with their liberation sprung from Dar es Salaam."[15]

Another one stated:

"From Dr. Nyerere's commitment flowed the liberation first of Mozambique, Angola, Guinea-Bissau and Cape Verde in the early '70s, followed by Zimbabwe in 1980, Namibia in 1990 and eventually South Africa."[16]

And as Nyerere himself said about some of his achievements:

"We took over a country with 85 per cent of its adults illiterate. The British ruled us for 43 years. When they left, there were two trained engineers and 12 doctors. This is the country we inherited. When I stepped down, there was 91 per cent literacy and nearly every child was in school. We trained thousands of engineers, doctors and

114

teachers."[17]

The death of Julius Nyerere evoked strong feelings from many people in different parts of the world, most of it positive. One of the most memorable tributes came from Ghanaian member of parliament, Hackman Owusu-Agyemang, who was also minority spokesman for foreign affairs, later minister of foreign affairs under President John Kufuor:

"Dr. Nyerere even in death at the state-owned St. Thomas Hospital in London, symbolised the humility and modesty that had come to be associated with his life-style.... That he retired from politics with nothing more than a second-hand tractor and a bicycle showed that as President he neither dipped his hands into state coffers nor private pockets. Nor were his hands covered with anyone's blood....

His Ujamaa community-based farming collective which was conceived with due acknowledgement of the African communal way of life, in spite of its failure as a concept, demonstrated his sensitivity to the plight of his people and his desire to provide the needed leadership.... Dr. Nyerere indeed personified selflessness, sincerity and sensitivity.

An avowed fighter against colonialism and apartheid, Mwalimu who played a pioneering role in the O.A.U. will forever be remembered as an African leader with his name engraved in gold.

By his retirement from the Presidency of Tanzania in 1985, Dr. Nyerere lived up to his title as Mwalimu since he not only taught but demonstrated the virtue in bowing out even when the applaud is loud....

As we mourn the loss of this gem and giant of a statesman, we take consolation in the fact that death, coming at this time, has been the crown of a historic, rich and fulfilling life for Mwalimu Julius Nyerere.... The death of Dr. Julius Nyerere has robbed Africa of a leading light, whose exploits as a politician and statesman filled the hearts of Africans with joy and inspiration.

We...recall with nostalgia the passion and zeal with which a young Dr. Julius Nyerere together with our own Dr. Kwame Nkrumah and other African nationalists, prosecuted the anti-colonist and independence struggle to liberate Africa from foreign domination. That today, the last vestige of colonialism has been routed in Africa, is to a large extent, due to the untiring efforts of Dr. Nyerere and his co-fighters in the African liberation struggle."[18]

Tragically, he died when Africa, mired in conflict, needed him most. As he himself said not long before he died: "Africa is in a mess."

But in spite of all the tragedies the continent has endured through the years, there was also some good news out of Africa at the end of the 1990s, although not much. And it inspired many people across the continent. Africa's giant nation, Nigeria, finally returned to democracy in May 1999 after 15 years of uninterrupted brutal military dictatorship.

Where Nigeria is headed, and what the future has in store for the rest of Africa, was never meant for us to know. But we know one thing. We have come a long way since the sixties. And we still have a long way to go. We will keep on going, even if we don't get there. We have no other choice. And that is Africa's only choice.

Chapter Three:

Africa After Independence:
Realities of Nationhood

IT HAS BEEN almost 50 years since most African countries won independence. But their independence was and in most cases remains more apparent than real.

Attributes of sovereignty and nationhood were not and could not have been derived from a constitutional text simply because the colonial rulers transferred power to Africans at independence. They had to be given concrete expression, which was by itself a herculean task compounded by the unwillingness of the former imperial powers to totally relinquish control of their former possessions.

When most African countries won independence in the sixties, the former colonial powers wanted to maintain close ties with their former colonies for a number of reasons: economic control; political domination; strategic interests; Cold War imperatives; and national prestige. They still considered their former colonies as their property and spheres of influence. Colonialism was transmuted into neocolonialism but in essence it remained the same as a system of political domination and economic exploitation through indirect rule.

The most glaring example of such hegemonic control was France. To hang on to their colonies, the French formed the French Community in 1958. That was the same year when France granted internal autonomy to all her colonies. It was also the same year in which Guinea demanded and won full independence and pulled out of the French Community.

But the Community collapsed two years later in 1960 when all the French African colonies attained sovereign status. The French Community was formed to replace the imperialist French Union formed in 1946 and which was more brazen in its operations and pursuit of its imperial goals.

The notion that the former colonies would be satisfied only with internal self-government – granted in 1958 – and let the French formally control their defence, foreign policy, finance, communication and other vital matters, was contrary to the nationalist aspirations for full independence; although that is exactly what almost all of them allowed to happen except Guinea which voted for independence in 1958, and Mali among countries which won independence in 1960, as well as Algeria which became independent in 1962.

Tunisia and Morocco, which won independence in 1956, also did not submit to the dictates of France although her influence in both countries was still substantial even after they won independence mainly because of their economic ties with the former imperial power.

But they all publicly expressed a strong desire for independence, partly to gain credibility especially among other Africans as genuinely nationalist countries and France was aware of that. The former French colonies have through the years been known for their subservience to Paris. Nkrumah called them "client states." And as Nyerere stated in an interview:

"I went to Addis (in May 1963 when the Organisation of African Unity (OAU) was formed) and it was an incredible meeting.

Here is this continent of young nations coming from colonialism and so forth and the debate is awful, and really what provoked me was the French-speaking countries, you know.

With all their French culture, training in rationalization – you can't really argue with those fellows.

And I discovered some of these fellows have their visas – *their visas* – signed by the French ambassadors in their own countries! And I said, 'Oh, but I thought you were fighting for freedom?'"

Nyerere was interviewed by Bill Sutherland and the interview is published in a book by Bill Sutherland and Matt Mayer, *Guns and Gandhi in Africa: Pan African Insight on Nonviolence, Armed Struggle and Liberation in Africa,* Africa World Press, 2000.

So when Mali, led by the militant Pan-Africanist leader Modibo Keita, demanded full independence in 1960, France, determined not to repeat the mistake she made with regard to Guinea in 1958 when that country refused to bow to her wishes, acceded to that demand. And she proceeded to dismantle the entire Community apparatus in the same year in order to grant independence to almost all her colonies.

However, the decision by France to fulfill Mali's demand for independence infuriated Felix Houphouet-Boigny, the leader of the Ivory Coast and an unabashed Francophile, who also went on to demand independence for his country, succumbing to nationalist agitation among his own people who did not want to remain under French rule, contrary to his wishes and belief that his country was not ready for independence.

Houphouet-Boigny was so subservient to France that even years after his country won independence, he refused to attend meetings of the Organization of African Unity (OAU) claiming that he was afraid of flying. Yet he did not show any fear when he flew to Paris every year.

Another leader, Dr. Hastings Kamuzu Banda of Malawi, also refused to attend OAU meetings because he saw them as useless, as did Houphouet-Boigny although he was not as blunt as Dr. Banda was on the subject. Banda went on to forge links including diplomatic ties with the apartheid regime of South Africa in defiance of OAU resolutions against any relations with the white minority government.

The Ivory Coast under Houphouet-Boigny also established ties with South Africa, although the Ivorian leader was not openly defiant as Dr. Banda was. And his capitulation to demands for independence among his people in the Ivory Coast had domino effect, as did Mali's demand for full independence. Other French African colonies followed suit.

Houphouet-Boigny's hostility to full independence demanded by Mali in 1960 was also evident two years earlier when Sekou Toure pulled Guinea out of the French Community after 95 percent of the electorate[1] endorsed his demand for total independence.

The Ivorian leader took sides with France and even fuelled her hostility towards Sekou Toure because of Guinea's demand for full independence. But the French did not need to be urged, exhorted or prompted by Houphouet-Boigny to adopt such a hostile attitude and try to destroy Guinea. They were already furious on their own because Guinea refused to be a satellite in the French orbit by remaining under the neo-colonial umbrella of the French Community.

However, that does not exonerate Houphouet-Boigny

from what he did or justify his anti-pan-African stance against Sekou Toure. As Professor Fred Greene, although he overstates his case about Houphouet-Boigny's role, states:

"In the 1958 vote all but Guinea chose to stay in the (French) Community, and the French, at the urging of Houphouet-Boigny, influential leader of the Ivory Coast, adopted a hostile attitude to that recalcitrant state."[2]

The French burned government files, severed communication links to the outside world and within the country itself, and cleaned out the treasury before leaving Guinea, not because Houphouet-Boigny urged them to do so, although he was obviously delighted; they did that, and tried to cripple Guinea, because they were infuriated by what they saw as Sekou Toure's defiance of their wishes when he refused to be subservient to the metropolitan power.

Therefore, they would have done what they did, anyway, even without Houphouet-Boigny encouraging or urging them to do so.

When Sekou Toure pulled Guinea out of the French Community, the French took that as an insult and saw it as a challenge to their authority over their empire, a dangerous precedent they feared others would follow by also withdrawing from the "French family" of nations which were no more than puppets of Paris.

The French may have been the most brazen in exercising control over their imperial possessions. But they were not the only ones who were openly determined to stay in Africa as masters of their sphere of influence.

In order to perpetuate imperial control over their possession like the French did through the French Community, the Belgians also formed a nominal, formal union with their huge colony, the Belgian Congo, which was the size of Western Europe. They also devised a network of financial and defence agreements to bind the Congo to Belgium after the country won independence in order to perpetuate their hegemonic control over this vast expanse of territory in the heart of Africa.

But all those arrangements and the union itself were disrupted when the Congo slid into anarchy immediately after independence and the two countries severed diplomatic ties. However, because of Belgian intervention during the Congo crisis ostensibly to help stabilize the situation but in reality to dismember the Congo and take full control of the country's mineral resources in Katanga Province, the weak government of Prime Minister Cyrille Adoula resumed diplomatic relations with the former colonial power in 1962.

Adoula's government had no national following; nor did Adoula himself have his own power base of loyal supporters or a strong regional backing which would have given him some clout and leverage.

His position was in sharp contrast with that of the other Congolese leaders such as President Joseph Kasavubu who had a strong backing among his people, the Bakongo who also constitute the largest ethnic group in the country; Moise Tshombe based in the mineral-rich secessionist Katanga Province and who was related to the royal family of the Lunda, one of the largest ethnic groups in the Congo; and Albert Kalonji who in 1962 declared himself King of South Kasai dominated by his people, the Luba, also one of the largest ethnic groups in the entire country.

The appeal to ethno-regional loyalties and sentiments was strong throughout the whole country. And all the leaders mentioned – with the exception of Patrice Lumumba who was assassinated on 17 January 1961 – exploited those differences and conflicting interests to pursue their partisan agendas and helped fuel the Congo debacle in the sixties.

Although the Congolese had their own problems and

conflicting ethnic and regional interests, the Congo crisis itself was engineered by Western powers – led by the United States and Belgium – who intervened in one of Africa's biggest and richest countries to secure their economic and geopolitical interests – vis-a-vis the Soviet Union and China – at the expense of the Congolese and other Africans in general.

Just as the Congo crisis was a significant event in the history of post-colonial Africa with far-reaching consequences for many years, the end of colonial rule in Africa from 1951 when Libya won independence from Italy until 1968 when most African countries had won independence was one of the most contentious periods during the Cold War era.

Western powers, apprehensive of their declining influence on the continent because Africans had won their freedom, did everything they could to keep the Russians and the Chinese out of there. On the other hand, the Soviet Union and her satellites in the Eastern bloc, as well as the People's Republic of China, saw in that "vacuum" – created by decolonization – opportunities for penetration and even counter-mischief against the West.

In the midst of all this were the Africans themselves who, determined to maintain their newly-won independence, forged links with both the East and the West in the areas of trade, education, diplomatic representation, and technical assistance. But whenever they tried to assert or demonstrate any degree of independence from both power blocs, they were either threatened or thwarted by one side or the other.

The greatest threat came from Western countries which, having ruled Africa, felt that they had the first and final say on what Africans were supposed to do. And that intensified the Cold War between the two ideological camps. African countries, weak and caught in the middle right on their own continent, could only remonstrate or try to play one power bloc against the other.

But their desire and determination to remain independent and keep the Cold War out of Africa was evident from the beginning as soon as they emerged from colonial rule. As one Nigerian scholar, Dr. Okon Udokang, stated:

"By the 1960s, a period that witnessed the unprecedented proliferation of independent states on the continent of Africa, there arose a powerful upsurge of pro-nonalignment sentiments in Afro-Asian countries. It is significant that this development coincided with the period when the Cold War seemed to have reached its apogee, and in certain regions of the world was already taking on an explicit and pronounced military character, as in Vietnam and the Congo.

It was indeed fashionable for the leaders of the new African states to argue that in the Cold War African states belonged to neither camp, but only to Africa. President Nyerere of Tanzania, one of the more perceptive leaders of contemporary Africa, declared that the fledgling African states 'must struggle all the time to stay out of the great power competition.' This sentiment was echoed in the capitals of nearly all the new African states, as their governments attempted to consolidate their individual domestic political base, while grappling with the taxing problem of economic and social reconstruction."[3]

And as Nyerere stated about two years earlier on December 19, 1961, just ten days after he led Tanganyika to independence from Britain, Africans wanted to be friendly with countries in both ideological camps and in the Third World: "(But) we have no desire to have a friendly country choosing our enemies for us."[4]

Nyerere's commitment to non-alignment and his determination not to submit to ideological dictates from either the East or the West was tested in 1964 when West

Germany demanded that the newly-formed United Republic of Tanzania should not allow East Germany to establish a diplomatic mission on her soil; to which Nyerere responded:

"When our people united to win independence...they wanted to have a government responsible to them, so that it would consider their interests and not the interests of people thousands of miles away who had a separate government....The case in which this principle was most openly challenged was the one relating to the recognition of East Germany....

The West Germans...put heavy pressure on the Government (of Tanzania). When diplomatic pressure failed to move Tanzania,...the West German Government unilaterally and without notice, broke a five-year training and aid agreement relating to the new air wing, and returned all their technicians overnight. They went further, and threatened to cut all their aid if we continued with our declared policies."[5]

The actions taken by West Germany because of Tanzania's determination to maintain her political independence remind us of what the French did to Guinea in 1958 when Guinea refused to be a client state and pulled out of the French Community. Had Guinea succumbed to pressure from Paris, her independence would have been compromised and rendered meaningless; so would have Tanzania's, had Tanzania bowed and capitulated to West German demands.

The Cold War had entered Africa with a big chill and the world was watching with interest if Tanzania, one of the the first test cases on the continent during the early years of independence, would be able to withstand it. As Nyerere explained:

"The choice before Tanzania was then clear; we could either accept dictation from West Germany and continue to receive economic aid until the next time we proposed to do something they did not like, or we could maintain our policies and lose the aid immediately. In effect, therefore, we had to choose whether to become a puppet state of Germany in return for any charity she cared to give us....

East Germany wanted Tanzania to give diplomatic recognition to her, and West Germany wanted us to ignore the existence of the German Democratic Republic and pretend there is no such administration over the Eastern part of Germany....As a result of our decision West Germany withdrew some types of aid and announced that other aid was under threat if Tanzania did not change her policies. Tanzania refused to do this and told the West Germans to withdraw all their federal government aid."[6]

In this diplomatic confrontation, Tanzania as the weaker country was supposed to back down, given the harsh realities of realpolitik where power means everything, and morality means nothing. Tanzania's insistence on asserting her independence was perceived by some observers and others as recklessness and not in the best interest of the nation desperately in need of help; power politics is not the kind of game weak nations play. And Nyerere was aware of such criticism. But the issue was bigger than that, more than just bread and butter. As he put it in perspective:

"It has been suggested that the Government made a mistake by telling the Germans to withdraw all their aid, without waiting for them to do this on their own. Yet even in this regard the Government had little alternative if it was to uphold the dignity of our independent country. For there is no doubt that had we simply maintained our policy and waited for the Germans to react by withdrawing aid as

126

and when they liked, they would have been misled into believing that economic pressure would eventually make us change our minds, and there would have been a great deal of intrigue designed to undermine the unity of the country. It is also clear that only by taking this very strong stand could our determination to defend our independence be recognized - both by the Germans and by others."[7]

Guinea faced a similar situation, although the parallels are not exact. After the former French colony severed ties with France in 1958, it sought and obtained economic assistance from the Communist bloc, mainly from the Soviet Union. But gradually, Guineans became disillusioned by Communist attempts to interfere in their affairs and, in December 1961, Sekou Toure expelled the Soviet ambassador, a move which surprised those who considered Guinea to be a Soviet satellite or a strong ally of the Soviet Union.[8]

In 1964, Tanzania also expelled some diplomats from a major power, the United States. Tanzania was also involved in another diplomatic wrangle with the United States for her involvement in an attempt to overthrow the Tanzanian government. As Nyerere stated:

"We have twice quarrelled with the US Government, once when we believed it to be involved in a plot against us, and again when two of its officials misbehaved and were asked to leave Tanzania....The disagreements certainly induced an uncooperative coldness between us."[9]

Attempts by the American Central Intelligence Agency (CIA) to undermine, destabilize and overthrow the Tanzanian government in the mid-sixties were an integral part of a global strategy by the United States during the Cold War intended to install a puppet regime which would dance to the tune of Washington and the West in general;

Nyerere was fiercely independent and took an uncompromising stand on matters of principle even if such a stance offended world powers, as it always did. There were even suggestions by the American government to arm groups in Tanzania opposed to Nyerere. As John Prados states in his book, *Safe for Democracy: The Secret Wars of the CIA*:

"The Special Group (at the CIA) reportedly considered a State Department proposal to supply arms to certain groups in Tanzania, where secret-war wizards saw President Julius Nyerere as a problem, in the summer of 1964....Like Nyerere, Washington viewed Ghana's leader Kwame Nkrumah as a troublemaker." – (John Prados, *Safe for Democracy: The Secret Wars of the CIA*, Ivan R. Dee, Publisher, Chicago, Illinois, USA, 2006, p. 328).

In addition to American hostility towards Nyerere and his socialist-oriented government, the conflict between Tanzania and West Germany over East Germany's diplomatic representation also demonstrated the intensity of the rivalry between East and West and which both camps were more than prepared to wage on African soil by proxy if they could find surrogates on the continent. After all, it was on German soil that the Russians had built the Berlin Wall dividing that city in East Germany between East and West, a move that threatened to trigger a nuclear confrontation between the two super powers.

The Berlin crisis of 1961 which started when the Berlin Wall was built in August in the same year was later linked with the Cuban missile crisis of October 1962. In both cases, the rest of mankind looked with apprehension at how the two super powers were determined to secure their interests even at the risk of a major military conflict which could have escalated into a nuclear conflagration engulfing the whole world.

That Africa, the world's weakest and poorest continent

could be converted into a theatre of conflict between the two ideological camps showed not only how intense but also how reckless the competition was. Aware of the gravity of the situation, African countries and other Third World nations tried to diffuse tensions between the two super powers when the Belgrade Conference of Non-Aligned Nations in 1961 sent Modibo Keita, president of Mali, to Washington, and Dr. Kwame Nkrumah to Moscow.

But as leaders of weak countries, they could only count on moral appeal to influence the leaders of the two super powers. Their role was only peripheral because of their weakness as leaders of weak countries and both were ignored by President John F. Kennedy and Soviet Premier Nikita Khrushchev in their attempts to resolve the Berlin crisis. As President Kennedy told Modibo Keita:

"Are you finished? Well, let me tell you that I, on behalf of the people of the United States, subscribe 100 percent to the objectives of the conference (of Non-Aligned Nations) in spite of the tone of the language....I support your views. Now you have a much harder job - you go and sell this to Chairman Khrushchev in Moscow. Is there anything further you want to say?"[10]

President Modibo Keita was accompanied by President Surkano of Indonesia. As Richard Reeves states in his book *President Kennedy: Profile of Power*:

"Two of the neutrals came to Washington on September 12 (1961): President Surkano of Indonesia, short and volatile, and President Keita of Mali, a tower of dignity almost seven feet tall. Their mission was to inform Kennedy of the results of the Conference of Non-Aligned Nations, just completed in Belgrade, Yugoslavia."[11]

The marginal role played by Modibo Keita and Dr. Nkrumah in power politics during the Berlin crisis painfully underscored one harsh reality about power because of the weakness of Africa in the international arena: If you are weak, no one pays you any attention, and you are always wrong because might is right and morality means nothing.

Professor Oran Young also describes in similar terms the two African leaders as peripheral actors in the conduct of international diplomacy during the Berlin crisis. As he states in his book *The Politics of Force: Bargaining During International Crises*:

"Informal and often rather indirect means of communication appear to have played a somewhat greater, though frequently ambiguous, role during the 1961 crisis. Some contacts of this kind were largely perfunctory and therefore relatively inconsequential. This seems to be the most reasonable assessment...of the September missions of Nehru and Nkrumah to Moscow and Surkano and Keita to Washington....

The Belgrade Conference clearly demonstrated the new-found concern of the nonaligned states about the dangers of the Berlin crisis, but it also emphasized both the peripheral quality of their deliberations on the subject and the limitations on their abilities to influence the behavior of the great powers."[12]

Although Keita and Nkrumah, two of Africa's leading statesmen, played only a marginal role during the Berlin crisis, their role in the Congo crisis was different even if most of the time it was more symbolically than qualitatively substantive in terms of influencing events and the outcome of what transpired in the Congo.

The Congo crisis thrust them and other African leaders as well as the entire continent into the international spotlight precisely because they could not keep the major powers out of the Congo due to their weakness; painfully aware as they were of the danger power politics posed to the security of Africa. As Dr. Nkrumah stated in his speech to the UN General Assembly on 7 March 1961, just two months after Lumumba was assassinated, Africa had the right to know what the United Nations was doing in the Congo and demanded accountability for its actions:

"Unless at this juncture the United Nations acts in full consultation with the African states and in accordance with the needs of Africa, the same results will flow from the United Nations' intervention in the Congo as flowed from the intervention of the great powers in African affairs."[13]

To Nkrumah and other African leaders such as Nyerere, the Congo imbroglio was a chilling reminder of what the imperial powers did almost a century earlier at the Berlin conference (November 1884 - February 1885) which led to the partition of Africa. During the sixties, in the second half of the twentieth century, the big powers were competing for control of the Congo; while during the latter part of the nineteenth century, the colonial powers competed – during "the cold war of those days" as Nkrumah put it – for colonies in Africa.

The Congo during the early sixties was a tinder box which could have ignited and escalated into global warfare due to super-power competition. It was a major international crisis, demanding immediate attention and direct intervention by a large number of UN forces and was therefore more than just an African problem.

But it was during the Cuban missile crisis in October 1962 that the world came perilously close to nuclear war and went through one of its most dangerous periods in history, a debacle that was inextricably linked with the super-power rivalry over Berlin.

In their book, *The Kennedy Tapes*: *Inside the White House During the Cuban Missile Crisis*, Ernest R. May and Philip D. Zelikow, quote President Kennedy as he ominously warned his colleagues about the consequences of any conflict between the two super powers and on what would happen if the United States invaded Cuba. They would have to be ready for a forceful response from Khrushchev and his colleagues in the Kremlin:

"He'll grab Berlin, of course....I'm not so worried about the air. But the atomic bombs, they can get a couple of them over on us anyway....

If we attack Cuban missiles, or Cuba, in any way, it gives them a clear line to take Berlin....If we do nothing then they'll have these missiles and they'll be able to say any time we ever try to do anything about Cuba, they'll fire these missiles....If we go in and take them out on a quick air strike, we neutralize the chance of danger to the United States of these missiles being used....On the other hand, we increase the chance greatly, as I think - there's bound to be a reprisal from the Soviet Union, there always is - (of) their just going in and taking Berlin by force. Which leaves me only one alternative, which is to fire nuclear weapons - which is a hell of an alternative - and begin a nuclear exchange....

They can't let us just take out, after all their statements, take out their missiles, kill a lot of Russians (in Cuba) and not do anything....The problem is not really so much war against Cuba. But the problem is part of this worldwide struggle with the Soviet Communists....

If we invade Cuba, we have a chance that these missiles will be fired on us....When you talk about the invasion, the first (point), excluding the risk that these missiles will be fired, (is that) we do have the 7 or 8,000 Russians there....Ambassador Thompson (to the Soviet Union) has felt very strongly that the Soviet Union would regard, will regard the attack on these SAM sites and missile bases with the killing of 4 or 5,000 Russians as a greater provocation than the stopping of their ships. Now, who knows what?....We are going to blockade Cuba."[14]

But few people, including advisers to President Kennedy such as Defence Secretary Robert McNamara, knew how close the world came to the brink of nuclear catastrophe. And even today, most people still don't know.

After the end of the Cold War, Fidel Castro said in 1992 and later that had the Americans attacked Cuba, the Soviets would have fired the Cuban-based missiles which had already been targeted at the United States. McNamara himself was shocked when he learnt this after the collapse of the Soviet Union and when he attended a conference in Cuba on the Cold War.

Had it not been for Kennedy's and McNamara's restraint – as opposed to the hawkish attitude and the recommendation of most of his advisers including the joint chiefs of staff who favoured an air strike and an outright invasion of Cuba – the Cuban missile crisis would have ended in a nuclear exchange between the two super powers with dire consequences for the entire world.

The Americans had also – despite their intelligence capabilities and constant surveillance over Cuba – grossly underestimated Soviet strength on the Cuban island and the Russians' resolve to use nuclear weapons already on the island if the United States launched an invasion.

Had the United States known the actual number of Soviet combat troops and technicians, and Soviet nuclear capability on the island, they probably would never have contemplated an air strike against the missile sites. As Professor Jorge G. Castaneda states in his book *Companero: The Life and Death of Che Guevara*:

"It is now known - because Soviet participants insinuated as much at the Moscow meeting of 1989, and Fidel Castro stated so categorically at the Havana

133

conference of January 1992 - that twenty of the forty-two Soviet missiles deployed in Cuba were armed with *nuclear warheads*. And six tactical missile launchers, loaded with nine missiles with *nuclear tips*, were ready to be used in the event of a US invasion....Arthur Schlesinger and Robert McNamara, who both attended the Havana conference, almost fell off their seats when they heard this.

Furthermore, the number of Soviet troops sent to Cuba was much larger than the Americans suspected. They estimated 4,500 in early October, 10,000 at the height of the crisis, and 12,000 to 16,000 at its end. In reality, 42,000 soldiers entered Cuba, disguised with winter clothing and even snow skis. Castro confirmed this figure, also put forth by Alexeiev and Mikoyan.

In other words, the Soviets were able to deploy missiles, atomic warheads, troops, and sophisticated antiaircraft equipment in Cuba before American intelligence caught on. So much so that Walt Rostow, then a State Department adviser, reported to President Kennedy in a 'top-secret and sensitive' memorandum dated September 3, 1962 - less than a month before the crisis - that 'on the basis of existing intelligence the Soviet military deliveries to Cuba do not constitute a substantial threat to US security'....

The problem was not keeping the missiles secret, but what the Soviets were willing to do with them once they had been introduced into Cuba....Soviet military officers in the field were authorized to launch the missiles with nuclear warheads....in the event of a US invasion; and the U-2 (American) spy plane shot down over Cuba on October 27 was attacked under instructions from the Soviet base in Cuba - not Moscow."[15]

Although Soviet prestige around the world may have suffered in what some people perceived to be capitulation to American demands to withdraw Russian missiles from

Cuba, in exchange for a pledge by the United States not to invade the island, Kremlin leaders knew that in some areas – especially in a number of Third World countries including African – their reputation was not, for historical reasons, as bad as that of the West.

Western countries were identified with colonialism. By remarkable contrast, the Soviet Union never had colonies in Africa or anywhere else in the Third World. Western countries were also identified with imperialism in developing countries which they continued to dominate even after those countries won independence. Such domination included exploitation of the Third World by Western conglomerates which has now reached its peak in this era of globalisation, with globalisation itself being dictated by Western countries which dominate the global economy under capitalism. Globalization is the new imperialism in this post-Cold War era in a unipolar world dominated by the United States.

Countries dominating Africa and other parts of the Third World included the United States, the leading Western power, which also had and still has the largest number of corporations with tentacles extended to all parts of the world. As Americans say, what is good for General Motors is good for America; and for the world, they might as well add, as some of them probably do, since the United States dominates the world economy.

But as a super power itself, the Soviet Union was not entirely blameless. Together with the United States, the Soviet Union had twice pushed the world to the brink of a nuclear holocaust: over Berlin in 1961, and during the Cuban missile crisis in 1962, the most dangerous crises since World War II. And coincidentally during the same period was the Congo crisis, which became a major international crisis right in the heart of Africa, again involving the two nuclear giants and other world powers.

While the Berlin and Cuban crises were eventually contained, although not entirely resolved (the United

135

States continued with its attempts to undermine Castro surreptitiously through surrogate forces and more brazenly by economic means including imposition of an embargo on the island nation), the Congo crisis continued to pose great danger to Africa and threaten world peace. The threat continued at least until the mid-sixties when the West finally gained the upper hand over the Soviets and the Chinese in that troubled African country. Because of their weakness, the other independent African countries could not do anything about Western imposition of its will on the Congo.

It was Western powers led by the United States which ousted and assassinated the popular Congolese prime minister, Patrice Lumumba, installing Colonel Joseph Mobutu in his stead. Mobutu was already on the CIA payroll when he was working under Lumumba before he became army chief.

However, the Soviets never gave up on Africa despite the setbacks they had suffered in the Congo. Western countries also, because of their history of colonialism in Africa, and even of American enslavement of millions of Africans earlier during the slave trade, all of which tarnished the West, feared that the Soviets had great advantage over them in winning friendship among Africans during the Cold War since the Soviet Union had never owned any colonies anywhere on the African continent.

Compounding the problem for Western countries was continued colonialism and white minority rule in the countries of southern Africa and Portuguese Guinea (Guinea-Bissau) in West Africa. The colonial powers were Western, and the racist minority regimes were also Western in origin and ideological orientation. All that worked to Soviet advantage, as did the intransigence of the white minorities in relinquishing control of the countries they dominated.

Not all African countries had won independence during

the sixties or even the seventies and eighties; not even the early nineties. The last African countries to win their freedom were Zimbabwe in 1980; Namibia ten years later in 1990; and finally South Africa in 1994. They all had been under white minority rule.

Even after the collapse of the Soviet Union in 1991, the West was still tarnished in the eyes of many Africans because of the continuing racist policies of its strongest ally on the continent, apartheid South Africa, which during white minority rule had always been an integral part of the Western world and the main custodian of Western values and traditions – and civilization – on a continent many Westerners considered to be "backward and uncivlized."

The Congo crisis also tarnished the West among Africans because of its involvement in the assassination of Patrice Lumumba and its support for the secession of Katanga Province which had in fact been engineered by the West. The Soviets tried to exploit that, showing that they were on the side of Africans and the nationalist forces opposed to Katanga's secession.

But Africans did not want to exchange one master for another and wanted both sides – East and West – out of the Congo. Instead, they supported UN intervention to keep the Cold War out of Africa.

Among all the colonial powers, France maintained the strongest and most pervasive influence in her former colonies not only during the early years of independence but also all the way through the years until the 1990s when that influence began to decline in a few of those countries.

One of the countries under very strong French influence – and with a presence of no fewer than 40,000 Frenchmen – was the Ivory Coast which also considered itself to be the leader of Francophone Africa; although Senegal, especially under its Francophile President Leopold Sedar Senghor, also claimed that "eminent" status and mantle of leadership.

When the Mali Federation formed in 1959 and

comprising Mali and Senegal – it collapsed the following year after Senegal pulled out – demanded and won independence in 1960, Ivorian leader Houphouet-Boigny became furious. He wanted all French African colonies to remain under French tutelage.

However, because the French had acquiesced in the Federation's decision to become independent, Houphouet-Boigny – as a protest against France but mainly because of pressure exerted on him by his own people who wanted to end colonial rule – also demanded independence for his country in the same year. And together with Dahomey, Niger, and Upper Volta – all of which also won independence in 1960 as did most of the other French African colonies – Ivory Coast formed a weak association known as *Counseil de l'Entente*.

France's enormous influence over the Ivory Coast was clearly visible even to a casual observer. For example, in 1965 and thereafter, more than 120,000 Frenchmen were living in Abidjan alone, the nation's capital. They led the army and the police, ran the country's administration and even occupied ministerial positions in the cabinet including the most influential ones. Like most of the former French African colonies, Ivory Coast was independent in name only. As Henry Tanner stated in his report from the Ivory Coast published in *The New York Times* on 25 March 1962:

"The most striking anachronism to the radical African nationalists is that M. Houphouet-Boigny has practically abdicated sovereignty in the military field. The Ivory Coast has only a small force for internal security. And even this force has French officers. The French army assures the external defense of the country. It has been asked to do so, M. Houphouet-Boigny says, because 'we wish to devote our modest means to economic and social development.'"[16]

138

It was that kind of subservience which prompted Dr. Nkrumah to describe the former French African colonies as "client states," with the exception of Guinea under Sekou Toure, Mali under Modibo Keita, and Algeria under Ben Bella later under Boumedienne. The former vice president of Kenya, Jaramogi Oginga Odinga, also articulated the same sentiment about his country in his book *Not Yet Uhuru* which he wrote after he fell out with Kenyatta during the late sixties. Nyerere wrote the introduction to the book.

Odinga went on to form an opposition party, the Kenya People's Union (KPU), and accused the Kenyan leadership of ignoring the interests of *wananchi* (the people) and of selling the country to the imperialists.

But he did not last long as a political force. His party, formed in March 1966, was effectively neutralized within two years and banned shortly thereafter. And that ended an illustrious political career of a leader of continental stature who was also one of the most prominent figures in the struggle for African independence and one of the strongest advocates of African unity. He was an ideological compatriot of Nyerere and Nkrumah and shared their socialist and Pan-Africanist vision.

Ironically, independence for the largest number of the African colonies came first to the least nationalistic and least pan-African-oriented countries, those of Francophone Africa, which cherished their ties with the metropolitan power, "mother" France, more than they did their natural ties with their African brethren in other African countries.

Another irony was that the French-speaking African countries which also had a reputation as the least militant in pursuit of continental unity were also among the first to forge links among themselves although they were also, individually and collectively, institutionally linked to "mother" France; thus casting serious doubt on their commitment to African unity. For example, their common currency (CFA) and airline (*Air Afrique*), were not formed

139

on their own initiative but France's in order to enable the former colonial power – which never left – to perpetuate her domination over her former colonies.

Therefore soon after independence, there was an effort, however lukewarm, by different African countries to pursue the goal of African unity even if such pursuit meant forming different regional and sub-regional groups which were mutually antagonistic; hardly a path towards continental solidarity which had to be achieved even before the idea of unity could be seriously considered. In spite of all that, they proceeded along that path nonetheless.

In 1960, the same year they won independence, twelve of the former French African colonies formed what came to be known as the Brazzaville Group. They were tied to the franc zone and received financial, technical, and military assistance from France. The group was named after Brazzaville, the capital of Congo-Brazzaville where the group was formed and had its headquarters.

The Brazzaville Group, also known as the UAM or the Union of African and Malagasy states, went on to establish – on French initiative – a common currency, the CFA; a common bank, common monetary policy, telecommunication links, and an airline, *Air Afrique*. But they refused to form a federation.

The original members were Cameroon, the Central African Republic, Chad, Congo-Brazzaville, Dahomey, Gabon, Ivory Coast, Malagasy Republic, Mauritania, Niger, Senegal, and Upper Volta. They were later joined by Rwanda, a former Belgian colony but French-speaking, which won independence in 1962.

Another Pan-African group that was formed was the Casablanca Group with a reputation as a group of radical states. It was formed in Casablanca, Morocco, in 1961 and was the most diverse in ts composition – racially, historically, linguistically, and even ideologically – among all African groups; a microcosm, in terms of diversity, of what was yet to come only about two years later when the Organization of African Unity (OAU) was formed in Ethiopia's capital, Addis Ababa, in May 1963.

The Casablanca Group was composed of the most militant states with the exception of one member. The member-countries were Egypt, Ghana, Guinea, Mali, Morocco, and Algeria even before Algeria won independence from France in 1962 after one of the bloodiest liberation wars in colonial history which cost an estimated one million lives, mostly Algerian.

Morocco was the least militant member of the Casablanca Group - ironically the group was formed in Morroco's largest city – except for her support of the Algerian independence struggle, a position which made the conservative North African Arab state as "militant" as the rest of the members in the group. Ghana was, of course, also an oddity as an Anglophone member in a predominantly Francophone group and the least-Muslim country. Not only were most of them French-speaking but also overwhelmingly Muslim. Another exception was Egypt – Muslim but not Francophone.

And racially, of course, the Casablanca Group was "split" in half. Three member-countries, Ghana, Guinea and Mali were mostly black; and the other three – Egypt, then officially known as the United Arab Republic (UAR), Morocco and Algeria – were predominantly Arab with a population of Berber minorities especially in Algeria and Morocco. However, Mali also provided a bridge between the two racial groups.

Unlike the other two black members, Ghana and Guinea, Mali has a large number of its citizens, especially in the northern part of the country bordering Arab North Africa, who are Berber and Arab. About 10 percent of Malians are Tuareg and Moors; 6 percent Songhai, and a smaller percentage Arab. The first three groups are mainly Berber mixed with Arabs. Tuareg nomads alone in northern Mali constitute a substantial population of more

141

than 700,000.

Yet, in spite of its diversity, the Casablanca Group was also one of the most cohesive. It was also one of the most influential because of its leaders such as Nkrumah and Nasser who were formidable political personalities of international stature.

Later in the same year, 1961, when the Casablanca Group was formed, the Brazzaville group joined Nigeria, Liberia and other moderate states to form the Monrovia Group, later known as the Lagos Charter Group, in order to formulate plans for the establishment of an All-African organization on continental basis.

The Casablanca Group, which was militant, refused to attend meetings of the Monrovia Group – formed in Monrovia, Liberia – and talked about continental unification, a radical proposition in pan-African rhetoric and diplomacy even today. The group even proposed formation of an African High Command for continental security. Nkrumah was the first African leader to propose that.

The Monrovia Group considered such propositions by the Casablanca group not only too radical but also too dangerous for Africa.

In reality, the Monrovia Group was politically weak. It even failed to take a firm stand on the Algerian war of independence which lasted for seven years at an enormous cost. By contrast, the Casablanca Group fully supported the Algerians in their struggle against France.

Yet, in spite of its weakness and moderate stand, it was the Monrovia Group which laid the groundwork for the establishment of the Organization of African Unity (OAU). It also proposed that African heads of state and government should meet every three years; sought to establish a permanent secretariat and headquarters for the organization, and a permanent supervisory council of ministers. The group also proposed the creation of an African common market and a permanent tribunal for conflict resolution among African countries with the mandate to settle both intra- and inter-state disputes.

The quest for African unity under one government as advocated by the Casablanca Group of radical states – all of which were in West and North Africa – got a boost from another part of the continent, East Africa, when in June 1963, Kenya, Uganda and Tanganyika agreed to form an East African federation before the end of the year. President Julius Nyerere of Tanganyika, Prime Minister Milton Obote of Uganda, and Prime Minister Jomo Kenyatta of Kenya, issued the following statement in Nairobi, Kenya, on June 5, 1963:

"We, the leaders of the people and governments of East Africa assembled in Nairobi on 5 June 1963, pledge ourselves to the political Federation of East Africa.

Our meeting today is motivated by the spirit of Pan-Africanism and not by mere selfish regional interests....Within this spirit of Pan-Africanism and following the declaration of African unity at the recent Addis Ababa conference (from May 22 - 25, which led to the establishment of the Organization of African Unity - OAU), practical steps should be taken wherever possible to accelerate the achievement of our common goal. We believe that the East African Federation can be a practical step towards the goal of Pan-African unity...and wish to make it clear that any of our other neighbours may in future join this Federation."[17]

Nyerere was the strongest proponent of an East African federation and even offered to delay independence for Tanganyika so that the three East African countries – Kenya, Uganda and Tanganyika – would attain sovereign status on the same day and unite under one government.

But the federation was never formed. Nationalism won over Pan-Africanism.

An even bigger federation including Ethiopia, Somalia,

143

Zanzibar, and Nyasaland, was also discussed. But it also got nowhere.

Nkrumah vehemently opposed formation of an East African federation and dismissed it as "Balkanization on a grand scale."

Nyerere responded to Nkrumah's argument by saying "those are attempts to rationalize absurdity."

Nkrumah also he did everything he could to try to block formation of the federation.

Nkrumah's interference infuriated Nyerere so much that he wrote Nkrumah directly about it:

"His meddling became so apparent that on 6th August, 1963, President Nyerere of Tanzania wrote him a very angry letter on this subject." – Donald S. Rothchild, *Politics of Integration: An East African Documentary*, Institute of Development Studies, University College of Nairobi; East African Publishing House, Nairobi, Kenya, 1968, p. 112).

Nkrumah strongly denounced attempts to form an East African federation because he would not be in a position to control it. He wanted to be the driving force behind any kind of regional integration in Africa so that if the leaders of those regional blocs eventually decided to unite, they would choose him to be the head of a continental government.

Therefore he was not really opposed to regional federations; only if he could not control them. He himself had attempted to unite his country with Guinea in 1958 to form the Ghana-Guinea Union and with Mali as well in 1960 to form the Ghana-Guinea-Mali Union. But the unions were not successful.

Had the Ghana-Guinea-Mali Union evolved into a functional entity under one government, it is inconceivable that Nkrumah would have denounced it as an obstacle to continental unification. Ghana does not even share borders

144

with Guinea and Mali. Yet Nkrumah was willing to form a political union with them; the latter two share a common border. But when Nyerere tried to do the same thing, form a regional union in East Africa, Nkrumah denounced the move not only as an obstacle to African unity and as discriminatory; he contended it would divide Africa even further, on a grand scale. As Professor Ali Mazrui stated:

"Nkrumah pointed out that his own country could not very easily join an East African federation. This proved how discriminatory and divisive the whole of Nyerere's strategy was for the African continent.

Nyerere treated Nkrumah's counter-thesis with contempt. He asserted that to argue that Africa had better remain in small bits than form bigger entities was nothing more than 'an attempt to rationalize absurdity.'

He denounced Nkrumah's attempt to deflate the East African federation movement as petty mischief-making arising from Nkrumah's own sense of frustration in his own Pan-African ventures.

Nyerere was indignant. He went public with his attack on Nkrumah. He referred to people who pretended that they were in favour of African continental union when all they cared about was to ensure that 'some stupid historian in the future' praised them for being in favour of the big continental ambition before anyone else was willing to undertake it." – (Ali A. Mazrui in his lecture "Nkrumahism and The Triple Heritage: Out of the Shadows" at the University of Ghana-Legon in 2002; Ali A. Mazrui in Opoku Agyeman, *Nkrumah's Ghana and East Africa: Pan-Africanism and African Interstate Relations*, Fairleigh Dickinson University Press, 1992, p. 16; Ali Al'Amin Mazrui, *Nkrumah's Legacy and Africa's Triple Heritage between Globalization and Counter-Terrorism*, Ghana Universities Press, 2004, p. 35).

Nkrumah also used President Milton Obote to

undermine Nyerere in his regional venture to form an East African federation. Obote was a friend of both.

Nkrumah argued that such a federation would not be in the best interest of Uganda because Uganda would be no more than a junior member in a union dominated by Kenya and Tanzania. As Philip Ochieng, a veteran Kenyan journalist and political analyst, stated in his article, "Did Nkrumah Kill Off the First EA Community?," in *The East African*, Nairobi, 28 March 2009:

"In the late 1960s, when Yoweri Kaguta Museveni was the leader of the 'revolutionary' wing of the University of Dar es Salaam's student movement, he and his group militantly rebuked the governments of Uganda, Tanzania and Kenya for failing to federate as they had promised.

The Ugandan leader still appears passionate about that union. Last week, he told a news conference that, instead of fighting over an island smaller than a football pitch, Nairobi and Kampala should fight to make Kenya and Uganda one political entity.

Topical again after a lull of many years, one East African republic was a nationalist, pre-Independence theme. Indeed, a treaty of commitment to it was signed by Jomo Kenyatta, Julius Nyerere and Milton Obote just before Kenya's independence.

So what happened? Why hasn't that great idea panned out for us nearly 50 years after the Uhuru fanfare of the early 1960s? I ask this question because, in truth, Museveni may be in a better position than any of the present East African leaders to answer it....In the Ugandan capital's archives – now controlled by his government – there may lie documents that can enlighten us.

Let me jog the president's memory. He and I were in Dar es Salaam in the late 1960s and early 1970s. He will have heard Obote – whom he still deeply admired – being publicly accused as the chief saboteur of the proposal to federate. Official Tanzania was, of course, mum about this accusation. But it came from top-level academics known to enjoy direct links with Mwalimu's State House. The certainty is that it was Nyerere who was feeding them with the lowdown on Kampala.

What did Mwalimu Nyerere and his Cabinet know about Dr Obote that we did not know? The accusing finger I constantly saw whenever I visited the campus at Ubungo was explicit.

Somebody else – far away from East Africa – was extremely unhappy about an East African union and worked tirelessly – mostly through Kampala – to nip it in the bud, so the story went. No, it was not the British (though they would play a central role in frustrating the federation).

So who could it be? The answer: None other than the great Kwame Nkrumah.

This may sound paradoxical because that redoubtable intellectual and nationalist was the father of the pan-Africanist movement. So you would have expected him to be the chief sponsor of all the regional initiatives that might lead to a pan-African government. That again was paradoxical.

According to the story that I kept hearing, it was because Dr Nkrumah wanted to be the father figure of all the regional initiatives, that he sabotaged the East African chapter....

Nkrumah himself sponsored a West African initiative similar to the proposed East African federation...composed of his Ghana, Ahmed Sekou Toure's Guinea and Modibo Keita's Mali....As long as he was the paramount leader of such an initiative, there was no problem.

In East Africa, Nyerere was also taking serious steps to restructure his society. Tanzania (under Nyerere), indeed, is the African country that has gone farthest in dismantling the political, economic and intellectual pillars of colonialism....

Nkrumah...wanted to be the dominant figure in every

regional initiative. Like Joseph Stalin for all of the world's non-Maoist communist parties, Nkrumah wanted to be chief policy-maker and policy implementer for every one of the regional groupings. The probable idea was that, if all those regional groupings decided to unite into a single continental government, no individual would be in a position to vie with the Ghanaian leader to be its first president.

That was why Nkrumah could not trust Mwalimu Nyerere as the intellectual spirit behind the East African proposal. For, although they seemed like ideological comrades, the old Tanganyikan schoolteacher was completely independent-minded and would never have been prepared to act as Nkrumah's regional poodle.

With Nyerere thus dismissed and Mzee Kenyatta accused of having surrendered Kenya as a backyard of corporate Britain, the Ubungo intellectuals explained that, in Nkrumah's eyes, Obote now appeared as the only one not too committed one way or the other. That was why – according to the story – it was Obote that Nkrumah latched onto to frustrate all the plans to federate."

Nkrumah's interference in East Africa to neutralise Nyerere's attempt to form an East African federation was a big mistake and portrayed Nkrumah as a trouble maker who was determined to undermine other African leaders who did not agree with him. As Basil Davidson states in his book, *Black Star: A View of the Life and Times of Kwame Nkrumah*:

"Some, like Julius Nyerere of Tanzania, chastised Nkrumah for his interference. East Africa, Nyerere believed, could best contribute to continental unity by moving first towards regional unity. Although knowing little about East Africa, Nkrumah not only disagreed but actively interfered to obstruct the East African federation proposed by Nyerere.... It was one of Nkrumah's worst mistakes." – (Basil Davidson, *Black Star: A View of the Life and Times of Kwame Nkrumah*, Allen Lane, London, 1973, cited by Geoffrey Mmari, "The Legacy of Nyerere," in Colin Legum and Geoffrey Mmari, eds., *Mwalimu: The Influence of Nyerere*, Africa World Press, Trenton, New Jersey, 1995, pp. 179 – 180).

During the OAU summit conference in Accra in 1965, Nkrumah even had listening devices installed in Nyerere's room and in the rooms of the other Tanzanian delegates and those of other African leaders he did not trust or who were a threat to his quest to become the paramount leader of the whole continent. But the director of the Tanzanian intelligence service, Emilio Mzena and his colleagues who accompanied Nyerere to the conference, detected the listening devices. The spying on Nyerere and other delegates from Tanzania by Ghana's intelligence service is one of the subjects addressed by Professor W. Scott Thompson in his book, *Ghana's Foreign Policy 1957 – 1966: Diplomacy, Ideology, and the New State* (Princeton University Press, 1969).

After Nkrumah was overthrown, his espionage activities came to light and were exposed by the new military rulers of Ghana:

"Special attention was devoted to some of these delegates who were thought to be critical of Nkrumah....

Chalet C-4, one of the largest on the grounds of the Star Hotel, also housed Emilio Charles Mzena, a delegate from Tanzania....

At the conference President Nyerere was attended by his personal physician, Dr. A. Nhonoli, who was also an occupant of Chalet C-4." – (*Nkrumah's Subversion in Africa: Documentary Evidence of Nkrumah's Interference in the Affairs of Other African States*, Ghana's Ministry of Information, Accra, Ghana, 1966).

Nkrumah had continental ambitions. He wanted to exert his influence on the entire continent. But he also focused on some parts, especially East Africa where he wanted to undermine Nyerere, the most influential leader in the region and one of the most respected across the continent:

"East Africa was high on Nkrumah's list of subversion priorities. At one point, early in 1965, an attempt was made to recruit two sources close to Tanzania's President Julius Nyerere to 'exploit the political contradictions in the East African area.'" – (*Atlas*, a journal, Worley Publishing Company, New York, 1966, p. 22).

One of them was Oscar Kambona, Tanzania's minister of foreign affairs. Perhaps the other one was Kassim Hanga, Kambona's close friend, who briefly served as vice president and prime minister of Zanzibar (January – April 1964) before he became a cabinet member in the union government after Tanganyika united with Zanzibar on 26 April 1964.

They developed their close friendship when they were roommates in London during their student days.

Kambona even sent Nkrumah some money in Conakry, Guinea, where the Ghanaian leader went to live in exile after being overthrown on 24 February 1966. In his book, *Dark Days in Ghana*, Nkrumah thanked Kambona for sending him some money. Only a small amount is mentioned in the book. But sources in the Tanzanian government said the amount Kambona sent Nkrumah was large.

As Tanzania's minister of foreign affairs, and as someone who was so close to Nyerere, Oscar Kambona played a major role in attempting to form an East African federation. Yet he was at the same time secretly working to undermine Nyerere and even wrote Nkrumah telling him any attempts to form an East African federation was an

150

imperialist scheme which would not be in the best interest of Africa. He later became a bitter enemy of Nyerere and was behind an attempt to overthrow and assassinate him.

Kambona told Nkrumah about the plot against Nyerere and Nkrumah supported it, according to sources in Tanzania who saw the letters exchanged between the two leaders when Nkrumah was living in exile in Guinea.

Kambona left Tanzania in July 1967 and went into exile in Britain.

The failure to form an East African federation and other attempts elsewhere on the continent also showed that African countries were more willing to cooperate in the economic and technical fields than they were to form political unions under regional governments, let alone under one government on a continental scale.

Still, the quest for unity remained a perennial ambition. But the mere fact that African countries formed regional groupings or continued to maintain regional institutional structures formed during colonial times showed that they were all aware of the imperative need for unity even if it did not mean forming regional governments.

It is also worth noting that the groups they formed after independence were not strictly regional. The Casablanca Group was formed by North and West African states. The Brazzaville Group – admittedly, more of a neo-colonial than a pan-Africanist institution inspired by France – spanned Francophone Africa, all the way from West Africa to the island nation of Madagascar in the Indian Ocean in East Africa.

The Lagos Charter Group, better known as the Monrovia Group, was also continental in scope and in inspiration. As Dr. Nnamdi Azikiwe, the governor-general of the federation of Nigeria, stated in his speech to the Lagos conference of African heads of state and government on 25 January 1962:

"The main reason for convening this conference is to

exchange views among African leaders at the highest possible level for the unity of the political entities comprising the continent of Africa.

There have been conferences of this nature in the past, but this particular conference is very significant because it is the first time in African history that so many heads of state and government have assembled to confer among themselves for the future security and stability of African countries....

The Lagos Conference looks at the continent of Africa as a miniature United Nations....At Monrovia, in May, 1961, the participants of this conference evolved a *modus vivendi* for African states....The principles enunciated in Monrovia include...the right of African states to federate or confederate with any other state or states."[18]

Tanganyika, which won independence on 9 December 1961 – shortly after the Monrovia Group was formed in May the same year – and which was among the first African countries to win independence, attended the conference of the Lagos Charter Group held in the Nigerian capital, Lagos, in January 1962; so did the only other independent East African country, Ethiopia.

Therefore the group was not restricted to West or North African countries which constituted the largest number of the independent African countries during that period.

But Tanganyika, which became increasingly radical taking a militant stand on a number of issues especially on the Congo crisis and the liberation struggle in southern Africa, did not attend subsequent meetings of the Lagos Charter Group. Her increasing militancy led her to identify with the members of the Casablanca Group who together – with the exception of Morocco – even constituted their own group within the Organization of African Unity (OAU) to pursue common goals. As Jorge Castaneda states in his book *Companero*: *The Life and Death of Che*

Guevara:

"Moise Tshombe was despised by the leaders of the OAU, especially its most radical ones - the so-called Group of Six, consisting of Nasser, Ben Bella, Kwame Nkrumah of Ghana, Sekou Toure of Guinea, Julius Nyerere of Tanzania, and Modibo Keita of Mali - who still blamed Tshombe for Lumumba's death....According to Ben Bella, - in an interview with the author in Geneva, on November 4, 1995 - these leaders had a group of their own within the OAU; they regularly consulted and conspired among themselves."[19]

Even before independence, African nationalists from different countries forged links to pursue common goals. For example, in 1958 they attended the Accra Conference convened by Kwame Nkrumah to formulate a common strategy for coordinating the independence struggle across the continent.

The conference was attended by independent African countries – there were only a few then: Egypt, Libya, Tunisia, Morocco, Sudan, Ethiopia, Liberia, Ghana, and Guinea – and by representatives from the countries still under colonial rule. It was held in December and was chaired by Tom Mboya from Kenya, who was then 28 years old. He was one of the most prominent leaders in Africa and was assassinated ten years later in Nairobi, Kenya, in July 1969. He was 39.

One of the organizations which played a critical role in laying the foundation for the establishment of the Organization of African Unity (OAU) was PAFMECSA: the Pan-African Freedom Movement for East, Central and Southern Africa. It was preceded by PAFMECA – the Pan-African Freedom Movement for East and Central Africa – which was the original group founded at its first meeting in September 1958 in the town of Mwanza on the shores of Lake Victoria in what was then Tanganyika under the stewardship of Julius Nyerere.

PAFMECA was an umbrella organization for thirteen African nationalist parties in Kenya, Uganda, Tanganyika, Zanzibar, Ruanda-Urundi, the Belgian Congo, Northern Rhodesia, Southern Rhodesia, and Nyasaland.

It lasted until February 1962 when it was replaced by PAFMECSA after the umbrella organization was extended to the countries of southern Africa still under white minority rule. Nelson Mandela addressed a conference of PAFMECA delegates in Addis Ababa, Ethiopia, in February 1962, where he asked for assistance for the liberation struggle in South Africa after he secretly left the land of apartheid to attend the meeting. The African National Congress (ANC) was invited to the conference and Mandela led the ANC delegation to Addis Ababa. As he stated in his speech:

"The delegation of the African National Congress, and I particularly, feel specially honored by the invitation addressed to our organisation by the PAFMECA to attend this historic conference and to participate in its deliberations and decisions.

The extension of the PAFMECA area to South Africa, the heart and core of imperialist reaction, should mark the beginning of a new phase in the drive for the total liberation of Africa - a phase which derives special significance from the entry into PAFMECA of the independent states of Ethiopia, Somalia, and Sudan.

It was not without reason, we believe, that the Secretariat of PAFMECA chose as the seat of this conference the great country of Ethiopia, which, with hundreds of years of colorful history behind it, can rightly claim to have paid the full price of freedom and independence. His Imperial Majesty, himself a rich and unfailing fountain of wisdom, has been foremost in promoting the cause of unity, independence, and progress

154

in Africa, as was so amply demonstrated in the address he graciously delivered in opening this assembly.

The deliberations of our conference will thus proceed in a setting most conducive to a scrupulous examination of the issues that are before us.

At the outset, our delegation wishes to place on record our sincere appreciation of the relentless efforts made by the independent African states and national movements in Africa and other parts of the world, to help the African people in South Africa in their just struggle for freedom and independence.

The movement for the boycott of South African goods and for the imposition of economic and diplomatic sanctions against South Africa has served to highlight most effectively the despotic structure of the power that rules South Africa, and has given tremendous inspiration to the liberation movement in our country.

It is particularly gratifying to note that the four independent African states which are part of this conference, namely, Ethiopia, Somalia, Sudan and Tanganyika, are enforcing diplomatic and economic sanctions against South Africa.

We also thank all those states that have given asylum and assistance to South African refugees of all shades of political beliefs and opinion. The warm affection with which South African freedom fighters are received by democratic countries all over the world, and the hospitality so frequently showered upon us by governments and political organizations, has made it possible for some of our people to escape persecution by the South African government, to travel freely from country to country and from continent to continent, to canvass our point of view and to rally support for our cause.

We are indeed extremely grateful for this spontaneous demonstration of solidarity and support, and sincerely hope that each and every one of us will prove worthy of the trust and confidence the world has in us.

We believe that one of the main objectives of this conference is to work out concrete plans to speed up the struggle for the liberation of those territories in this region that are still under alien rule. In most of these territories the imperialist forces have been considerably weakened and are unable to resist the demand for freedom and independence - thanks to the powerful blows delivered by the freedom movements.

Although the national movements must remain alert and vigilant against all forms of imperialist intrigue and deception, there can be no doubt that imperialism is in full retreat and the attainment of independence by many of these countries has become an almost accomplished fact.

Elsewhere, notably in South Africa, the liberation movement faces formidable difficulties and the struggle is likely to be long, complicated, hard, and bitter, requiring maximum unity of the national movement inside the country, and calling for level and earnest thinking on the part of its leaders, for skilful planning and intensive organisation.

South Africa is known throughout the world as a country where the most fierce forms of colour discrimination are practiced, and where the peaceful struggles of the African people for freedom are violently suppressed.

It is a country torn from top to bottom by fierce racial strife and conflict and where the blood of African patriots frequently flows.

Almost every African household in South Africa knows about the massacre of our people at Bulhoek, in the Queenstown district, where detachments of the army and police, armed with artillery, machine-guns, and rifles, opened fire on unarmed Africans, killing 163 persons, wounding 129, and during which 95 people were arrested simply because they refused to move from a piece of land on which they lived.

Almost every African family remembers a similar

massacre of our African brothers in South-West Africa when the South African government assembled aeroplanes, heavy machine-guns, artillery, and rifles, killing a hundred people and mutilating scores of others, merely because the Bondelswart people refused to pay dog tax.

On 1 May 1950, 18 Africans were shot dead by the police in Johannesburg whilst striking peacefully for higher wages. The massacre at Sharpeville in March 1960 is a matter of common knowledge and is still fresh in our minds. According to a statement in parliament made by C R Swart, then Minister for Justice, between May 1948 and March 1954, 104 Africans were killed and 248 wounded by the police in the course of political demonstrations.

By the middle of June 1960, these figures had risen to well over three hundred killed and five hundred wounded. Naked force and violence is the weapon openly used by the South African government to beat down the struggles of the African people and to suppress their aspirations.

The repressive policies of the South African government are reflected not only in the number of those African martyrs who perished from guns and bullets, but in the merciless persecution of all political leaders and in the total repression of political opposition. Persecution of political leaders and suppression of political organizations became ever more violent under the Nationalist Party government.

From 1952 the government used its legal powers to launch a full-scale attack on leaders of the African National Congress. Many of its prominent members were ordered by the government to resign permanently from it and never again participate in its activities. Others were prohibited from attending gatherings for specified periods ranging up to five years. Many were confined to certain districts, banished from their homes and families and even deported from the country.

In December 1956, Chief A J Lutuli, President-General

157

of the ANC, was arrested together with 155 other freedom fighters and charged with treason. The trial which then followed is unprecedented in the history of the country, in both its magnitude and duration. It dragged on for over four years and drained our resources to the limit.

In March 1960, after the murderous killing of about seventy Africans in Sharpeville, a state of emergency was declared and close on twenty thousand people were detained without trial.

Even as we meet here today, martial law prevails throughout the territory of the Transkei, an area of 16,000 square miles with an African population of nearly two and a half million. The government stubbornly refuses to publish the names and number of persons detained. But it is estimated that close on two thousand Africans are presently languishing in jail in this area alone. Amongst these are to be found teachers, lawyers, doctors, clerks, workers from the towns, peasants from the country, and other freedom fighters. In this same area and during the last six months, more than thirty Africans have been sentenced to death by white judicial officers, hostile to our aspirations, for offences arising out of political demonstrations.

On 26 August 1961 the South African government even openly defied the British government when its police crossed into the neighboring British protectorate of Basutoland and kidnapped Anderson Ganyile, one of the country's rising freedom stars, who led the Pondo people's memorable struggles against apartheid tribal rule.

Apart from these specific instances, there are numerous other South African patriots, known and unknown, who have been sacrificed in various ways on the altar of African freedom.

This is but a brief and sketchy outline of the momentous struggle of the freedom fighters in our country, of the sacrifice they have made and of the price that is being paid at the present moment by those who keep the freedom flag flying.

For years our political organizations have been subjected to vicious attacks by the government. In 1957 there was considerable mass unrest and disturbances in the country districts of Zeerust, Sekhukhuniland, and Rustenburg. In all these areas there was widespread dissatisfaction with government policy and there were revolts against the pass laws, the poll tax, and government-inspired tribal authorities.

Instead of meeting the legitimate political demands of the masses of the people and redressing their grievances, the government reacted by banning the ANC in all these districts. In April 1960 the government went further and completely outlawed both the African National Congress and the Pan-Africanist Congress.

By resorting to these drastic methods the government had hoped to silence all opposition to its harsh policies and to remove all threats to the privileged position of the Whites in the country. It had hoped for days of perfect peace and comfort for White South Africa, free from revolt and revolution. It believed that through its strong-arm measures it could achieve what White South Africa has failed to accomplish during the last fifty years, namely, to compel Africans to accept the position that in our country freedom and happiness are the preserve of the White man.

But uneasy lies the head that wears the crown of White supremacy in South Africa. The banning and confinement of leaders, banishments and deportations, imprisonment and even death, have never deterred South African patriots. The very same day it was outlawed, the ANC issued a public statement announcing that it would definitely defy the government's ban and carry out operations from underground. The people of South Africa have adopted this declaration as their own and South Africa is today a land of turmoil and conflict.

In May last year a general strike was called. In the history of our country no strike has ever been organized under such formidable difficulties and dangers. The odds against us were tremendous. Our organizations were outlawed. Special legislation had been rushed through parliament empowering the government to round up its political opponents and to detain them without trial.

One week before the strike ten thousand Africans were arrested and kept in jail until after the strike. All meetings were banned throughout the country and our field workers were trailed and hounded by members of the Security Branch. General mobilization was ordered throughout the country and every available White man and woman put under arms. An English periodical described the situation on the eve of the strike in the following terms:

'In the country's biggest call-up since the war, scores of citizens' force and commando units were mobilised in the big towns. Camps were established at strategic points; heavy army vehicles carrying equipment and supplies moved in a steady stream along the Reef; helicopters hovered over African residential areas and trained searchlights on houses, yards, lands, and unlit areas. Hundreds of White civilians were sworn in as special constables, hundreds of white women spent weekends shooting at targets. Gun shops sold out of their stocks of revolvers and ammunition. All police leave was cancelled throughout the country. Armed guards were posted to protect power stations and other sources of essential services. Saracen armored cars and troop carriers patrolled townships. Police vans patrolled areas and broadcast statements that Africans who struck work would he sacked and endorsed out of the town.'

This was the picture in South Africa on the eve of the general strike, but our people stood up to the test most magnificently. The response was less than we expected but we made solid and substantial achievements. Hundreds of thousands of workers stayed away from work and the country's industries and commerce were seriously damaged. Hundreds of thousands of students and schoolchildren did not go to school for the duration of the strike.

The celebrations which had been planned by the

government to mark the inauguration of the republic were not only completely boycotted by the Africans, but were held in an atmosphere of tension and crisis in which the whole country looked like a military camp in a state of unrest and uncertainty. This panic stricken show of force was a measure of the power of the liberation movement and yet it failed to stem the rising tide of popular discontent.

How strong is the freedom struggle in South Africa today? What role should PAFMECA play to strengthen the liberation movement in South Africa and speed up the liberation of our country? These are questions frequently put by those who have our welfare at heart.

The view has been expressed in some quarters outside South Africa that, in the special situation obtaining in our country, our people will never win freedom through their own efforts. Those who hold this view point to the formidable apparatus of force and coercion in the hands of the government, to the size of its armies, the fierce suppression of civil liberties, and the persecution of political opponents of the regime. Consequently, in these quarters, we are urged to look for our salvation beyond our borders.

Nothing could be further from the truth.

It is true that world opinion against the policies of the South African government has hardened considerably in recent years. The All African People's Conference held in Accra in 1958, the Positive Action Conference for Peace and Security in Africa, also held in Accra in April 1960, the Conference of Independent African States held in this famous capital in June of the same year, and the conferences at Casablanca and Monrovia last year, as well as the Lagos Conference this month, passed militant resolutions in which they sharply condemned and rejected the racial policies of the South African government.

It has become clear to us that the whole of Africa is unanimously behind the move to ensure effective economic and diplomatic sanctions against the South African government.

At the international level, concrete action against South Africa found expression in the expulsion of South Africa from the Commonwealth, which was achieved with the active initiative and collaboration of the African members of the Commonwealth. These were Ghana, Nigeria, and Tanganyika (although the latter had not yet achieved its independence). Nigeria also took the initiative in moving for the expulsion of South Africa from the International Labor Organisation.

But most significant was the draft resolution tabled at the fifteenth session of the United Nations which called for sanctions against South Africa. This resolution had the support of all the African members of the United Nations, with only one exception. The significance of the draft was not minimized by the fact that a milder resolution was finally adopted calling for individual or collective sanctions by member states. At the sixteenth session of the United Nations last year, the African states played a marvelous role in successfully carrying through the General Assembly a resolution against the address delivered by the South African Minister of Foreign Affairs, Mr. Eric Louw, and subsequently in the moves calling for the expulsion of South Africa from the United Nations and for sanctions against her.

Although the United Nations itself has neither expelled nor adopted sanctions against South Africa, many independent African states are in varying degrees enforcing economic and other sanctions against her. This increasing world pressure on South Africa has greatly weakened her international position and given a tremendous impetus to the freedom struggle inside the country.

No less a danger to White minority rule and a guarantee of ultimate victory for us is the freedom struggle that is raging furiously beyond the borders of the South

African territory; the rapid progress of Kenya, Uganda, and Zanzibar towards independence; the victories gained by the Nyasaland Malawi Congress; the unabated determination of Kenneth Kaunda's United National Independence Party (UNIP); the courage displayed by the freedom fighters of the Zimbabwe African People's Union (ZAPU), successor to the now banned National Democratic Party (NDP); the gallantry of the African crusaders in the Angolan war of liberation and the storm clouds forming around the excesses of Portuguese repression in Mozambique; the growing power of the independence movements in South-West Africa and the emergence of powerful political organizations in the High Commission territories - all these are forces which cannot compromise with White domination anywhere.

But we believe it would be fatal to create the illusion that external pressures render it unnecessary for us to tackle the enemy from within. The centre and cornerstone of the struggle for freedom and democracy in South Africa lies inside South Africa itself. Apart from those required for essential work outside the country, freedom fighters are in great demand for work inside the country.

We owe it as a duty to ourselves and to the freedom-loving peoples of the world to build and maintain in South Africa itself a powerful, solid movement, capable of surviving any attack by the government and sufficiently militant to fight back with a determination that comes from the knowledge and conviction that it is first and foremost by our own struggle and sacrifice inside South Africa itself that victory over White domination and apartheid can be won.

The struggle in the areas still subject to imperialist rule can be delayed and even defeated if it is uncoordinated. Only by our combined efforts and united action can we repulse the multiple onslaughts of the imperialists and fight our way to victory. Our enemies fight collectively and combine to exploit our people.

The clear examples of collective imperialism have made themselves felt more and more in our region by the formation of an unholy alliance between the governments of South Africa, Portugal, and the so-called Central African Federation. Hence these governments openly and shamelessly gave military assistance consisting of personnel and equipment to the traitorous Tshombe regime in Katanga.

At this very moment it has been widely reported that a secret defence agreement has been signed between Portugal, South Africa, and the Federation, following visits of Federation and South African defence ministers to Lisbon, the Federation defence minister to Luanda, and South African Defence Ministry delegations to Mozambique. Dr Salazar was quoted in the Johannesburg Star of 8 July 1961 as saying: 'Our relations - Mozambique's and Angola's on the one hand and the Federation and South Africa on the other - arise from the existence of our common borders and our traditional friendships that unite our Governments and our people. Our mutual interests are manifold and we are conscious of the need to cooperate to fulfill our common needs.'

Last year, Southern Rhodesian troops were training in South Africa and so were Rhodesian Air Force units. A military mission from South Africa and another from the Central African Federation visited Lourenzo Marques in Mozambique, at the invitation of the Mozambique Army Command, and took part in training exercises in which several units totaling 2,600 men participated. These operations included dropping exercises for paratroopers.

A report in a South African aviation magazine, wings (December 1961), states: 'The Portuguese are hastily building nine new aerodromes in Portuguese East Africa (Mozambique) following their troubles in Angola. The new 'dromes are all capable of taking jet fighters and are situated along or near the borders of Tanganyika and Nyasaland'; and gives full details.

Can anyone, therefore, doubt the role that the freedom movements should play in view of this hideous conspiracy?

As we have stated earlier, the freedom movement in South Africa believes that hard and swift blows should be delivered with the full weight of the masses of the people, who alone furnish us with one absolute guarantee that the freedom flames now burning in the country shall never be extinguished.

During the last ten years the African people in South Africa have fought many freedom battles, involving civil disobedience, strikes, protest marches, boycotts and demonstrations of all kinds. In all these campaigns we repeatedly stressed the importance of discipline, peaceful and non-violent struggle. We did so, firstly because we felt that there were still opportunities for peaceful struggle and we sincerely worked for peaceful changes. Secondly, we did not want to expose our people to situations where they might become easy targets for the trigger-happy police of South Africa. But the situation has now radically altered.

South Africa is now a land ruled by the gun. The government is increasing the size of its army, of the navy, of its air force, and the police. Pill-boxes and road blocks are being built up all over the country. Armament factories are being set up in Johannesburg and other cities. Officers of the South African army have visited Algeria and Angola where they were briefed exclusively on methods of suppressing popular struggles.

All opportunities for peaceful agitation and struggle have been closed. Africans no longer have the freedom even to stay peacefully in their houses in protest against the oppressive policies of the government. During the strike in May last year the police went from house to house, beating up Africans and driving them to work.

Hence it is understandable why today many of our people are turning their faces away from the path of peace and non-violence. They feel that peace in our country must

165

be considered already broken when a minority government maintains its authority over the majority by force and violence.

A crisis is developing in earnest in South Africa. However, no high command ever announces beforehand what its strategy and tactics will be to meet a situation. Certainly, the days of civil disobedience, of strikes, and mass demonstrations are not over and we will resort to them over and over again.

But a leadership commits a crime against its own people if it hesitates to sharpen its political weapons which have become less effective.

Regarding the actual situation pertaining today in South Africa I should mention that I have just come out of South Africa, having for the last ten months lived in my own country as an outlaw, away from family and friends. When I was compelled to lead this sort of life, I made a public statement in which I announced that I would not leave the country but would continue working underground. I meant it and I have honored that undertaking. But when my organisation received the invitation to this conference it was decided that I should attempt to come out and attend the conference to furnish the various African leaders, leading sons of our continent, with the most up-to-date information about the situation.

During the past ten months I moved up and down my country and spoke to peasants in the countryside, to workers in the cities, to students and professional people. It dawned on me quite clearly that the situation had become explosive. It was not surprising therefore when one morning in October last year we woke up to read press reports of widespread sabotage involving the cutting of telephone wires and the blowing up of power pylons. The government remained unshaken and White South Africa tried to dismiss it as the work of criminals.

Then on the night of 16 December last year the whole of South Africa vibrated under the heavy blows of

Umkhonto we Sizwe (The Spear of the Nation). Government buildings were blasted with explosives in Johannesburg, the industrial heart of South Africa, in Port Elizabeth, and in Durban. It was now clear that this was a political demonstration of a formidable kind, and the press announced the beginning of planned acts of sabotage in the country.

It was still a small beginning because a government as strong and as aggressive as that of South Africa can never be induced to part with political power by bomb explosions in one night and in three cities only. But in a country where freedom fighters frequently pay with their very lives and at a time when the most elaborate military preparations are being made to crush the people's struggles, planned acts of sabotage against government installations introduce a new phase in the political situation and are a demonstration of the people's unshakeable determination to win freedom whatever the cost may be.

The government is preparing to strike viciously at political leaders and freedom fighters. But the people will not take these blows sitting down.

In such a grave situation it is fit and proper that this conference of PAFMECA should sound a clarion call to the struggling peoples in South Africa and other dependent areas, to close ranks, to stand firm as a rock and not allow themselves to be divided by petty political rivalries whilst their countries burn. At this critical moment in the history of struggle, unity amongst our people in South Africa and in the other territories has become as vital as the air we breathe and it should be preserved at all costs.

Finally, dear friends, I should assure you that the African people of South Africa, notwithstanding fierce persecution and untold suffering, in their ever increasing courage will not for one single moment be diverted from the historic mission of liberating their country and winning freedom, lasting peace, and happiness.

We are confident that in the decisive struggles ahead, our liberation movement will receive the fullest support of PAFMECA and of all freedom-loving people throughout the world."[20]

After the Addis Ababa conference, PAFMECA was transformed into a larger organization, PAFMECSA. And it was not long before an even larger organization came into being, replacing PAFMECSA which existed until 1963. It was replaced by the Organization of African Unity (OAU) formed in May the same year in Addis Ababa, embracing the whole continent.

Right from the beginning, PAFMECSA was unique in one respect in the sense that it was composed of nationalist political parties from both colonial and independent countries, while PAFMECA was at first an umbrella organization composed of political parties only from colonial territories, until December 1961 when Tanganyika became independent and the only independent country represented in the organization before its demise in February 1962.

Uganda would have become another independent country as a member of the organization but it did not win independence until October that year when PAFMECA had already been replaced by PAFMECSA.

In the case of some of the independent countries, such as Tanganyika after she won independence in 1961, it was actually the government rather than the local political party or parties which were represented in PAFMECSA. And in independent countries which had a one-party system, the party was in fact the government.

At the PAFMECSA meeting held in December 1962 in Leopoldville, capital of the former Belgian Congo, the following independent countries were represented: Burundi, Congo-Leopoldville, Ethiopia, Rwanda, Tanganyika, and Uganda. Also delegates from the following colonial territories attended the conference: Northern Rhodesia, Southern Rhodesia, Kenya, Zanzibar, Mozambique, and Angola. The meeting was also attended by representatives of the nationalist movements of the African National Congress (ANC) and the Pan-Africanist Congress (PAC) from apartheid South Africa which was an independent country but under white minority rule.

Earlier on 21 March 1960, the Pan-Africanist Congress (PAC) of South Africa under the leadership of Robert Mangaliso Sobukwe, organized a demonstration against the pass laws which led to the massacre of 69 Africans in the township of Sharpeville. More than 180 were injured.

Most of those killed and injured were women and children after a group of black protesters converged on the local police station, offering themselves up for arrest for not carrying their pass books. Police opened fire on the crowd, triggering international outrage and condemnation of the apartheid regime for the massacre. It was a turning point in the history of South Africa and the massacre helped galvanize the struggle against apartheid.

The pivotal role PAFMECSA played in the establishment of the Organization of African Unity (OAU) as we have just seen was also acknowledged by Nelson Mandela in his book *Long Walk to Freedom*:

"In December (1961), the ANC received an invitation from the Pan-African Freedom Movement for East, Central, and Southern Africa (PAFMECSA) to attend its conference in Addis Ababa in February 1962. PAFMECSA, which later became the Organization of African Unity, aimed to draw together the independent states of Africa and promote the liberation movements on the continent....

The underground executive asked me to lead the ANC delegation to the conference....The ANC had to arrange for me to travel to Dar es Salaam in Tanganyika. The flight to Addis Ababa would originate in Dar es Salaam....

Early the next morning we left for Mbeya, a Tanganyikan town near the Rhodesian border....We booked in a local motel (in Mbeya)....We were waiting for Mr. John Mwakangale of the Tanganyika African National Union, a member of parliament....

We arrived in Dar es Salaam the next day and I met with Julius Nyerere, the newly independent country's first president. We talked at his house, which was not at all grand, and I recall that he drove himself in a simple car, a little Austin. This impressed me, for it suggested that he was a man of the people. Class, Nyerere always insisted, was alien to Africa; socialism indigenous.

I reviewed our situation for him, ending with an appeal for help. He was a shrewd, soft-spoken man who was well-disposed to our mission....He suggested I seek the favor of Emperor Haile Selassie and promised to arrange an introduction....

Because I did not have a passport, I carried with me a rudimentary document from Tanganyika that merely said, 'This is Nelson Mandela, a citizen of the Republic of South Africa. He has permission to leave Tanganyika and return here.'"[21]

Although PAFMECSA led to the establishment of the Organization of African Unity (OAU), as did the efforts by the Casablanca and Monrovia Groups, African countries did not – as a step towards African unity – retain the federal structures instituted by the colonial powers to consolidate their rule the way they had agreed to maintain the territorial boundaries they inherited at independence in order to avoid chaos. There were not many federations which had been established by the colonial rulers during their reign. But there were some and were big enough to have made an impact on the international scene had they emerged from colonial rule, intact, as supra-national states each under its own federal government. Only one did, as we will learn shortly.

The French colonial rulers formed two large federations on the continent. There was French Equatorial Africa in West-central Africa comprising Chad, the Central African Republic, French Congo – what is now Congo-Brazzaville – and Gabon. Its capital was Brazzaville. But the federation was dissolved in 1959 when the constituent territories voted to become autonomous republics.

In 1959, the same countries formed a loose federation called the Union of Central African Republics. However, it was a union in name only. In 1960 they became fully "independent" as members of the French Community controlled and dominated by France as her neo-colonial umbrella for her former colonies.

The other federation established by France was French West Africa comprising twice as many colonies: Dahomey, French Guinea, French Soudan (Mali), Ivory Coast, Mauritania, Niger, Senegal, and Upper Volta. Its capital was Dakar, Senegal. Guinea pulled out of the French Community in 1958 when it became independent, the same year the constituent territories became autonomous republics within the French Community. But, like its sister federation of French Equatorial Africa, it, too, was dissolved in 1959.

In the same year, 1959, the colony of French Soudan, renamed the Sudanese Republic, joined Senegal to form the Mali Federation which became independent on 20 June 1960. But political differences shattered the federation. Senegal, led by Senghor, a Francophile, was conservative; Mali, led by Modibo Keita, an ardent Pan-Africanist, was a militant.

On 20 August 1960, Senegal declared itself independent and pulled out of the federation, dissolving it on the same day. The former French Soudan proclaimed itself the Republic of Mali on 22 September 1960 and withdrew from the French Community.

Therefore, none of the federations in Francophone Africa survived to form a basis for union of the member-countries under one government after they won independence. And prospects for unity got dimmer and dimmer through the years as the newly independent states jealously guarded their sovereign status. In fact, the sixties saw no concerted effort among the French-speaking African countries to form any kind of union, except for Guinea and Mali which formed a symbolic union with Ghana that was made impractical by geographical separation and other factors including lack of institutional mechanisms to make the union functional.

But even among Senegalese, who precipitated the dissolution of the Mali Federation when they pulled out, there were those who believed that there was an imperative need for unity transcending territorial boundaries. As Mamadou Dia, who before he became prime minister of Senegal served as vice premier of the short-lived Mali Federation, states in his book *The African Nations and World Solidarity*:

"It would be a fatal error for the nations of the *Tiers-Monde*, especially those just recovering their freedom, to think that the struggle ends with the proclamation of independence....

Narrow nationalisms reflect a lack of historical perspective and surely ill-advised when they hope to guarantee the development of the economies they want to liberate by suddenly reversing their policies, by skillful maneuvering, or by changing partners.

The road to real African independence, constructed on a solid rock of a strong economy, lies not so much in neutralism as in large groupings that permit the concentration of poles, centers, and axes of development. That is why Mali (the Federation) will be an open nation that must expand to fulfill its role."[22]

The Mali Federation was the third and last one to

collapse in Francophone Africa. However, the collapse of those federations was lauded even by the imperial Charles de Gaulle when he took a strong stand on the Nigerian civil war and eventually recognized the breakaway region of Eastern Nigeria as the independent Republic of Biafra. As Kaye Whiteman points out:

"De Gaulle based his argument on self-determination, and on hostility to federations in general. All those he mentioned were British creations, including Canada, – where he equally applies the self-determination principle in Quebec – but the real analogy he is making is the two federations the French had created in West and Central Africa, which were systematically dismantled in the late 1950's as independence approached.

France at the time was accused of balkanization – of creating a host of unviable mini-states in order to maintain a neo-colonial influence over them, but of late the French have been emphasizing that their decolonization did at least avoid a Nigerian war. It is significant that wealthy Ivory Coast and Gabon were the 'Biafras' of these failed federations, and it has been claimed that De Gaulle may have been influenced by President Houphouet-Boigny towards Biafra rather than the other way round."[23]

As for the British, they left an enduring legacy in the continued existence of the Federation of Nigeria which is also the only federation on the entire continent formed during colonial times that has survived. But they also formed another one: the Federation of Rhodesia and Nyasaland comprising three territories – Northern Rhodesia, Southern Rhodesia, and Nyasaland. It was formed in 1953 and its capital was Salisbury in Southern Rhodesia.

The British wanted to maintain the federation. But black Africans, fearing perpetuation of white domination as in South Africa without any hope of getting independence soon, were vigorously opposed to it. The federation was already dominated by the white settlers of Southern Rhodesia to whom the British transferred control, ostensibly to facilitate administration but in reality to perpetuate white domination over blacks.

The beginning of the end of the federation started in 1953 – the same year in which it was formed – when Nyasaland, which was almost all-black and hardly had any white settlers unlike Southern Rhodesia and Northern Rhodesia, was forced by the British into the federation. The Nyasaland African Congress founded in 1944 was resolutely opposed to the federation. Opposition continued through the years until the federation was dissolved on 31 December 1963.

However, one African leader with impeccable pan-African credentials was opposed to the dissolution of the Central African Federation as the Federation of Rhodesia and Nyasaland was popularly known. He was Dr. Milton Obote. As Professor Ali Mazrui states:

"Obote's stand on the Federation of Rhodesia and Nyasaland was the more interesting because, while he refused to recognize the present government of the Federation, he was nevertheless against the Federation's dissolution – a stand which put him almost in a class by himself among African nationalists."[24]

Given his pan-African inclinations, it is understandable why he was opposed to the federation's dissolution for the same reason many Nigerians – by no means all – and other Africans were opposed to the dissolution of the Nigerian Federation before and after independence. That is because it was possible to build a strong African macro-nation on the foundations laid by and inherited from the colonialists.

Had the Nigerian Federation been dissolved, there would be no Nigeria today, potentially one of the most powerful and richest black nations in the world. And had the Central African Federation of Rhodesia and Nyasaland survived and emerged from colonial rule as a single political entity under one government, it would have been one of the most powerful and richest black nations in the world together with South Africa and Nigeria; the kind of potential the former Belgian Congo also has.

And had Kenya, Uganda and Tanganyika formed an East African federation – taking advantage of the strong ties which already existed among those countries including a common currency and a common market facilitating the free flow of trade among them as members of the East African Common Services Organisation (EACSO) created by the British colonial rulers – the new supra-nation would have been "a power house," as Nyerere put it, as would have been any other macro-nations formed across the continent.

In fact, Nyerere was such a firm believer in the functional utility of an East African federation that he offered to delay the independence of Tanganyika if that would help facilitate unification of the three East African countries. He said Tanganyika would wait so that all the three countries would win independence on the same day and form a federation under one government.

In one of his last interviews with the *New Internationalist* in December 1998, almost one year before he died in October 1999, Nyerere said that after independence, he and Ugandan President Milton Obote went to see Jomo Kenyatta and told him they should unite and asked him to be the president of the federation. But Kenyatta refused:

"I respected Jomo (Kenyatta) immensely.

It has probably never happened before in history. Two heads of state, Milton Obote and I, went to Jomo and said to him: 'Let's unite our countries and you be our head of state.' He said no.

175

I think he said no because it would have put him out of his element as a Kikuyu Elder." - ("The Heart of Africa: Interview with Julius Nyerere on Anti-Colonialism" in the *New Internationalist*, Issue 309, January-February 1999).

Therefore there has always been a strong sentiment for unity among many Africans especially Pan-Africanist leaders such as Nyerere and Nkrumah. And with regard to the Federation of Rhodesia and Nyasaland, a case could indeed be made that an opportunity which could have been exploited by Africans, if the federation survived and emerged from colonial rule as a single political entity, was lost when it was dissolved. And that is probably what Dr. Milton Obote had in mind when he opposed its dissolution.

He saw a giant African nation emerging out of that if the three British colonies of Northern Rhodesia, Southern Rhodesia and Nyasaland won independence as a collective entity under one government similar to what was envisaged in East Africa had Kenya, Uganda and Tanganyika followed that path. And Africa would have benefited enormously, an achievement which also would have speeded up the collapse of the apartheid regime in South Africa which would have come face-to-face with a powerful and rich black independent nation as a neighbour; as opposed to Nigeria which is so far away, and Congo whose enormous potential – exceeding South Africa's wealth – was wasted during 32 years of Mobutu's kleptocratic rule.

Yet, there was also a perfectly legitimate reason against formation or perpetuation of such large federations by colonial powers: consolidation of white minority rule over vast expanses of territory inhabited by tens of millions of Africans left at the mercy of their imperial rulers. It was a fear the three East African leaders – Nyerere, Obote and Kenyatta – forcefully articulated in their declaration of intent to form an East African Federation which they signed in Nairobi on 5 June 1963:

"In the past century the hand of imperialism grasped the whole continent and in this part of Africa our people found themselves included together in what colonialists styled 'The British sphere of influence.' Now that we are once again free or are on the point of regaining our freedom we believe the time has come to consolidate our unity and provide it with a constitutional basis (for an East African federation).

For some years we have worked together in PAFMECA (Pan-African Freedom Movement for East and Central Africa – later expanded to PAFMECSA to include Southern Africa) where we have accepted common objectives and ideas and created the essential spirit of unity between ourselves and among our people....For forty years the imperialists and local settler minorities tried to impose a political federation upon us. Our people rightly resisted these attempts. Federation at that time would quickly have led to one thing – a vast white-dominated dominion."[26]

Their fears were well-founded. The British imperial government even considered creating, not only an East African federation dominated by white settlers, but also a vast federation stretching from Kenya all the way to South Africa to include all their colonial territories in the region: Kenya, Uganda, Tanganyika, Zanzibar, Nyasaland, Northern Rhodesia, Southern Rhodesia, Bechuanaland, Swaziland, Basutoland, South Africa, and South West Africa which was ruled by apartheid South Africa. As George Bennett stated in "Settlers and Politics in Kenya":

"(There) was an announcement that a commission of the Imperial Government...would visit East Africa to consider federation....

177

If federation was a 'forced card' as Lord Olivier said, it was forced by two influences of which those in Britain who desired to create a Dominion in East Africa were the prime movers.

In Kenya Lord Delamere had opposed the idea in the 1920 elections, believing that Kenya should stand alone until it was self-governing and that its own problems should be digested first. By 1925, however, he was ready for Grigg's federation plans, and supported the idea of building a Government House at Nairobi to be a worthy centre for the newly established Governors's Conference.

He provided an unofficial background to the Governors' first meeting at Nairobi in 1926 by calling a conference, at Tukuyu in southern Tanganyika...in October 1925, of settler leaders from the whole area from Kenya to Nyasaland and Northern Rhodesia."[27]

Thus, while Africans opposed the imperial federation for good reasons, they failed to form their own – in this case an East African federation – purely for their own selfish reasons.

Not all of them were opposed to federation. In the case of Tanganyika, Nyerere was ready to make a sacrifice. Tanganyika was to be the first East African colony to win independence from Britain. Independence was scheduled for 9 December 1961, but Nyerere offered to postpone it for the sake of federation.

Obote also was in favour of federation but was thwarted in his efforts by separatist threats from Uganda's provinces. The biggest threat which almost plunged the country into civil war during the sixties came from the Buganda kingdom. But other provinces constituted enough threat, as well, to warrant serious attention from the central government. As Colin Legum and John Drysdale state in *Africa Contemporary Record*:

"Although Buganda offered the toughest problem to

the mordenising nationalists, it was by no means the only difficulty they had to face. Each of the other three kingdoms – Toro, Ankole and Bunyoro – and the princedom of Busoga had their own well-structured political systems; each was suspicious of the modern political centre at Entebbe. Also they had traditional rivalries – especially between Buganda and Bunyoro."[28]

Kenya, the most economically advanced of the three countries since it was favoured by the colonialists with its capital Nairobi virtually serving as the capital of East Africa, simply did not want to sacrifice her privileged status and lose many of her benefits – which she enjoyed at the expense of Uganda and Tanganyika – for the sake of federation with her poorer sister-countries.

And nationalism, of course, triumphed over the spirit of Pan-Africanism embodied in the declaration of intent for an East African federation signed by Nyerere, Kenyatta and Obote. Had it not been for the nationalist sentiments and separatist tendencies which prevailed over the leadership in Kenya and Uganda, the federation would have been consummated. Among all the three East African countries, Tanganyika was the only country which strongly advocated federation.

Ten years after Nyerere stepped down as president of Tanzania, ending 24 years of his stewardship of the nation, he stated that failure to form an East African federation was his biggest disappointment. According to James McKinley of *The New York Times* who interviewed Nyerere for an hour in his home village of Butiama in northern Tanzania near the shores of Lake Victoria on 2 September 1996:

"Mr. Nyerere said his greatest failure was that although he managed to form a federation with Zanzibar in 1964 to create Tanzania, he never managed to persuade neighboring countries to form a larger federation, a move

179

he believes would have made the region a powerhouse. 'I felt that these little countries in Africa were really too small, they would not be viable – the Tanganyikas, the Rwandas, the Burundis, the Kenyas,' he said. 'My ambition in East Africa was really never to build a Tanganyika. I wanted an East African federation. So what did I succeed in doing?' he asked. 'My success is building a nation out of this collection of tribes.'"[29]

The failure of the three East African countries to form a federation during the sixties was even more tragic because the three countries had some of the best institutional structures linking them together which could have provided a strong foundation for the establishment of a federation. They had been linked together in a common services organisation for years. And they emerged from colonial rule with the East African Common Services still intact.

The constituent parts of the Common Services includes a transport network known as the East African Railways and Harbours Corporation; communication links collectively identified as the East African Posts and Telecommunications Services; a common airline under the aegis of the East African Airways Corporation; and the East African Scientific Research Institute.

In addition to the Common Services, the three East African countries also had a Common Market with a more or less uniform external tariff, "revenue sharing" rather than "protective" in intent. There was virtually a free flow of trade among the three countries both in goods imported from abroad and in goods produced within East Africa. They also had a common currency issued by the East African Currency Board, and no restrictions at all on the flow of money across territorial boundaries within the region.

After winning independence, they also established a single university system with each of the constituent colleges specializing in some areas to serve the manpower needs of East Africa.

The University College of Dar es Salaam in Tanzania had the largest faculty of law, in addition to other departments in various academic disciplines. Nairobi University College in Kenya was noted for its faculty of engineering and department of commerce, in addition to others. And Makerere University College in Uganda founded in 1922, one of the oldest and best on the continent and regarded as the "Harvard" or "Oxford" of Africa, had the school of medicine and other highly regarded departments including political science and economics among others.

The chancellor of the University of East Africa was Julius Nyerere, the president of Tanzania, himself a leading intellectual. Professor Ali Mazrui described him as the most intellectual leader among the East African presidents and the most original thinker among all the leaders in Anglophone Africa.

The three East African countries also established a common parliament, known as the East African Legislative Assembly, to deal with matters relating to the Common Market and Common Services. The legislators held their sessions on rotational basis in the three capitals of Nairobi, Kampala and Dar es Salaam. Most of the people in East Africa were also, as they still are, united by a common language, Kiswahili, known mostly to outsiders as Swahili.

Yet in spite of all those ties, the three countries failed to form a federation. However, the quest for unity was not a total failure in the region. After the three countries of Kenya, Uganda and Tanganyika failed to form a federation in 1963, Tanganyika and Zanzibar united the following year, on 26 April, and formed one country called Tanzania.

But the union of Tanganyika and Zanzibar was not well-received by everybody, including prominent politicians in East Africa, ostensibly because Zanzibar was said to be under "Communist influence." As Ronald Ngala, Kenya's opposition leader in parliament who led the Kenya African Democratic Union (KADU) which was opposed to a unitary state and favoured a federal structure for Kenya's provinces to protect the interests of smaller ethnic groups, stated upon hearing the news of the impending union:

"I hope...that the overseas influence infiltrated into Zanzibar will not spread to Tanganyika in any malicious way."[30]

But probably Ngala himself and others in East Africa and elsewhere who were not well-disposed towards the union of Tanganyika and Zanzibar would admit that the advantages of unity including regional integration even if not under a single government outweigh its disadvantages. That is why in East Africa itself, the leaders – including those opposed to federation under one government – went on to form the East African Community (EAC) as a vehicle for effective regional cooperation especially in the economic arena despite their political differences.

The EAC was formed in 1967 and superseded the East African Common Services Organisation (EACSO) and restructured the Common Market to accommodate regional differences.

The three countries no longer had a common currency – each went on to establish its own; they also instituted tariffs according to EAC guidelines to protect infant industries in Uganda and Tanganyika and restructure the imbalance in the flow of trade which favoured Kenya at the expense of her partners; and went their own separate ways in other areas but were united in their common desire to maintain economic links and facilitate regional cooperation through their membership in the East African Community (EAC) which they joined voluntarily.

The rationale for such regional cooperation and unification movements elsewhere across Africa is simple. As a developing continent, it is Africa itself which offers the best and safest market for African producers. And it is only regional integration or continental union which can stimulate and facilitate rapid economic growth.

Overseas markets can not absorb all African exports even if they wanted to; other countries have their own products to sell or consume. They are also protectionist, erecting tariff barriers to insulate their own industries and producers from outside competition. And some of them are hostile to African countries including what they produce for different reasons such as political differences and outright prejudice. There could be no stronger reasons for African countries to forge links among themselves in order to establish a common market and trade among themselves.

Formation of the East African Community as an intergovernmental organisation underscored the need for such regional cooperation the three East African leaders – Nyerere, Obote and Kenyatta – had emphasized three years earlier in June 1963 when they signed the "Declaration of Federation by the Governments of East Africa":

"Economic planning, maximum utilization of manpower and our other resources, the establishment of a Central Bank and common defence programme, and foreign and diplomatic representation are areas in which we need to work together.

Such approach would provide greater coordination and savings in both scarce capital, facilities for training and manpower. What is more we would have a total population of some 25 million people – a formidable force and a vast market to influence economic development at home, attract greater investment and enhance our prestige and influence abroad."[31]

The failure of the three East African countries to form a federation demonstrated the great difficulty even countries which have so much in common – for example in terms of economic ties and history as well as a common language as we have shown – are bound to face when they try to submerge their national identities in a supra-national body for the sake of unity under one government.

Even the Arab countries of North Africa which are racially, culturally and linguistically homogeneous and are virtually all-Muslim, failed to unite during the sixties around the same time the East African Federation failed.

Political differences and differences in territorial size contributed to the failure of federation or union government among the North African Arab states which tried to unite: the Maghreb states of Algeria, Tunisia and Morocco.

Algeria was militant, the other two conservative. Algeria was also seen as a threat because it is much bigger and richer than Tunisia and Morocco. And as a nation born in war and bloodshed during its struggle for independence in which one million Algerians died in seven years of guerrilla warfare against the French, Algeria's militancy even before the country won independence was viewed with apprehension by the other two Maghreb states of Tunisia and Morocco.

In spite of all that, the three countries agreed to form a union. But when Algeria won independence in July 1962, Morocco quickly claimed some border regions as hers and threatened annexation of Algerian territory. In October 1963, the two countries fought a brief but intense and bitter war over those claims, dashing any hopes of unity between the two countries in the near future.

Morocco alienated Algerians even further because of her neo-colonial image as a client state of the West, especially the United States and France. By contrast, the Algerian leadership took a very strong stand against neo-colonial penetration of Africa, a position articulated by only a handful of countries on the continent during that pperiod: Egypt, Ghana, Guinea, Mali, Tanzania, Uganda, and Algeria itself. As Algerian President Ahmed Ben Bella said in an interview with Maria Macciochi, a correspondent of *L'Unita*, an Italian daily newspaper, on 13 August 1962, in Algiers:

"I have declared that neocolonialism is our great scourge....Colonialism has been modernized. It has become more progressive, less crude. It understands that people can no longer be dominated by force, by machine guns, and by bloody repression. It seeks new ways of domination – an enlightened colonialism, so to speak – although based on a fictitious equality, a new form of slavery controlling the key positions in our society.

Either there is a revolution under way in the country and we will be able to pursue this course under our own power, or else Algeria will become a revised and improved version of other African governments which have accepted neocolonialism."[32]

Morocco's provocation of Algeria and her attempt to seize Algerian territory may have been interpreted in some quarters as part of a neo-colonialist plot by the West to subvert the Algerian revolution. And it was. King Hussein of Morocco invaded Algeria on his own, but he was also encouraged and "pushed" by the French and American intelligence agencies to attack her neighbour. The Algerian revolution and Ben Bella's ideological orientation were considered anathema to the West. In September 1963, Moroccan troops captured several Algerian border posts, triggering the so-called War of the Desert.

However, the conflict between the two countries was

not atypical on the continent. Although the sixties were euphoric times as Africans celebrated independence every year – until 1968 hardly a year passed without at least one African country winning independence – the decade was also one of crises in different areas, forcing the young African nations to face harsh realities of nationhood. The problems were political and economic as well as military.

At independence, the new African nations lacked many attributes of social cohesion and political stability critical to tackling the arduous task of national development and forging political unity among diverse groups living within the same territorial boundaries. Ethnic diversity presented one of the daunting problems demanding political acumen and statesmanship of the highest calibre. African countries were and still are no more than a collection of different ethnic groups, many of them hostile to each other. Few are well-integrated.

Also, the young African nations lacked trained manpower practically in all areas, resulting in poor performance. In almost all the countries, administrative and technical skills remained at a very low level all the way through the sixties. For example, the former Belgian Congo had only 16 university graduates at independence in 1960; Nyasaland, renamed Malawi, had 34 at independence in 1964; Zambia, formerly Northern Rhodesia, had 109 when it won independence in 1966; and Tanganyika had 120 at independence in 1961.

African countries won independence promising their people not only political freedom but also economic salvation and freedom from disease and ignorance. As Nyerere said in September 1963, although Tanganyikans had won the right to international equality when the country achieved independence, such equality was more apparent than real because a person who was ignorant and could not produce enough food for himself and suffered from disfiguring diseases could not really stand on terms of equality with all the others who were not in his condition.[33]

None of those problems can be solved without economic development. And economic development is impossible without modernization. Unfortunately even today, a modern industrial economy is beyond the reach of most African countries just as it was during the sixties. Yet, there is no alternative to economic development except perpetual misery.

So the fundamental question which was asked then and is still being asked today is, "Which Way Africa?" especially for an underdeveloped and predominantly agricultural continent.

Many economists contend that Africans can develop more rapidly and with less strain if development programmes first emphasize agriculture which is the mainstay of African economies, extractive industry, roads, power plants and light manufactures. Many African countries tried that during the sixties. But they also realized that development of heavy industry seemed to be the *sine qua non* for economic independence. And it is one of the great features which separate developed countries from underdeveloped ones collectively known as the Third World.

Countries such as Ghana and Tanzania also adopted central planning in the quest for rapid economic development and socialist transformation of their societies. And there was a historical precedent for that, China and the Soviet Union.

In the case of the Soviet Union, the country made spectacular achievement and became a super power within 40 years after the Bolshevik Revolution because of its emphasis on heavy industry and education, especially in science, under central planning. It would not have become a super power in so short a time without central planning which enabled the state to channel the nation's resources into specific fields to achieve specific targets within a specified period.

187

Dr. Nkrumah was one of the African leaders who wanted and tried to take that route towards rapid economic development, placing great emphasis on industrialization including the acquisition of nuclear technology. As he stated at a ceremony launching the construction of Ghana's Atomic Reactor Centre at Kwabenya near Accra on 16 December 1964:

"We must ourselves take part in the pursuit of scientific and technological research as a means of providing the basis of our socialist society. Socialism without science is void....We have therefore been compelled to enter the field of atomic energy because this already promises to yield the greatest economic resource of power since the beginning of man."[34]

Had he been able to achieve his goal, he would have paved the way towards industrialization for other African countries the same way he blazed the trail towards African independence when he led Ghana to become the first black African country to emerge from colonial rule. Unfortunately, shortly after he launched the construction of Ghana's Atomic Reactor Centre, he was overthrown about a year later on 24 February 1966 in a military coup engineered and masterminded by the CIA.

The ouster of Nkrumah was one of the most tragic events in the history of post-colonial Africa.

Nkrumah was the strongest advocate of immediate continental unification, a stand that put him in a class almost by himself. He was also, together with leaders such as Nyerere, Sekou Toure, Obote and Modibo Keita, one of the strongest supporters of African unity in general and of the African liberation movements and an uncompromising opponent of interference in African affairs by world powers and other external forces. And that made him an enemy of the West. He became prime target for the CIA:

"Declassified National Security Council and Central Intelligence Agency documents provide compelling, new evidence of United States government involvement in the 1966 overthrow of Ghanaian President Kwame Nkrumah.

The coup d'etat, organized by dissident army officers, toppled the Nkrumah government on Feb. 24, 1966 and was promptly hailed by Western governments, including the U.S.

The documents appear in a collection of diplomatic and intelligence memos, telegrams, and reports on Africa in Foreign Relations of the United States, the government's ongoing official history of American foreign policy.

Prepared by the State Department's Office of the Historian, the latest volumes reflect the overt diplomacy and covert actions of President Lyndon B. Johnson's administration from 1964-68. Though published in November 1999, what they reveal about U.S. complicity in the Ghana coup was only recently noted.

Allegations of American involvement in the *putsche* arose almost immediately because of the well-known hostility of the U.S. to Nkrumah's socialist orientation and pan-African activism.

Nkrumah, himself, implicated the U.S. in his overthrow, and warned other African nations about what he saw as an emerging pattern.

'An all-out offensive is being waged against the progressive, independent states,' he wrote in *Dark Days* in Ghana, his 1969 account of the Ghana coup. 'All that has been needed was a small force of disciplined men to seize the key points of the capital city and to arrest the existing political leadership.'

'It has been one of the tasks of the C.I.A. and other similar organisations,' he noted, 'to discover these potential quislings and traitors in our midst, and to encourage them, by bribery and the promise of political power, to destroy

189

the constitutional government of their countries.'

A Spook's Story

While charges of U.S. involvement are not new, support for them was lacking until 1978, when anecdotal evidence was provided from an unlikely source - a former CIA case officer, John Stockwell, who reported first-hand testimony in his memoir, *In Search of Enemies: A CIA Story.*

'The inside story came to me,' Stockwell wrote, 'from an egotistical friend, who had been chief of the [CIA] station in Accra [Ghana] at the time.' (Stockwell was stationed one country away in the Ivory Coast.)

Subsequent investigations by *The New York Times* and *Covert Action Information Bulletin* identified the station chief as Howard T. Banes, who operated undercover as a political officer in the U.S. Embassy.

This is how the ouster of Nkrumah was handled as Stockwell related. The Accra station was encouraged by headquarters to maintain contact with dissidents of the Ghanaian army for the purpose of gathering intelligence on their activities. It was given a generous budget, and maintained intimate contact with the plotters as a coup was hatched. So close was the station's involvement that it was able to coordinate the recovery of some classified Soviet military equipment by the United States as the coup took place.

According to Stockwell, Banes' sense of initiative knew no bounds. The station even proposed to headquarters through back channels that a squad be on hand at the moment of the coup to storm the [Communist] Chinese embassy, kill everyone inside, steal their secret records, and blow up the building to cover the facts.

Though the proposal was quashed, inside the CIA headquarters the Accra station was given full, if unofficial credit for the eventual coup, in which eight Soviet advisors were killed. None of this was adequately reflected in the agency's records, Stockwell wrote.

Confirmation and Revelation

While the newly-released documents, written by a National Security Council staffer and unnamed CIA officers, confirm the essential outlines set forth by Nkrumah and Stockwell, they also provide additional, and chilling, details about what the U.S. government knew about the plot, when, and what it was prepared to do and did do to assist it.

On March 11, 1965, almost a year before the coup, William P. Mahoney, the U.S. ambassador to Ghana, participated in a candid discussion in Washington, D.C., with CIA Director John A. McCone and the deputy chief of the CIA's Africa division, whose name has been withheld.

Significantly, the Africa division was part of the CIA's directorate of plans, or dirty tricks component, through which the government pursued its covert policies.

According to the record of their meeting (Document 251), topic one was the "Coup d'etat Plot, Ghana." While Mahoney was satisfied that popular opinion was running strongly against Nkrumah and the economy of the country was in a precarious state, he was not convinced that the coup d'etat, now being planned by Acting Police Commissioner Harlley and Generals Otu and Ankrah, would necessarily take place.

Nevertheless, he confidently - and accurately, as it turned out -predicted that one way or another Nkrumah would be out within a year. Revealing the depth of embassy knowledge of the plot, Mahoney referred to a recent report which mentioned that the top coup conspirators were scheduled to meet on 10 March at which time they would determine the timing of the coup.

However, he warned, because of a tendency to

191

procrastinate, any specific date they set should be accepted with reservations. In a reversal of what some would assume were the traditional roles of an ambassador and the CIA director, McCone asked Mahoney who would most likely succeed Nkrumah in the event of a coup.

Mahoney again correctly forecast the future: Ambassador Mahoney stated that initially, at least, a military junta would take over.

Making it Happen

But Mahoney was not a prophet. Rather, he represented the commitment of the U.S. government, in coordination with other Western governments, to bring about Nkrumah's downfall.

Firstly, Mahoney recommended denying Ghana's forthcoming aid request in the interests of further weakening Nkrumah. He felt that there was little chance that either the Chinese Communists or the Soviets would in adequate measure come to Nkrumah's financial rescue and the British would continue to adopt a hard nose attitude toward providing further assistance to Ghana.

At the same time, it appears that Mahoney encouraged Nkrumah in the mistaken belief that both the U.S. and the U.K. would come to his financial rescue and proposed maintaining current U.S. aid levels and programs because they will endure and be remembered long after Nkrumah goes.

Secondly, Mahoney seems to have assumed the responsibility of increasing the pressure on Nkrumah and exploiting the probable results. This can be seen in his 50-minute meeting with Nkrumah three weeks later.

According to Mahoney's account of their April 2 discussion (Document 252), 'at one point Nkrumah, who had been holding face in hands, looked up and I saw he was crying. With difficulty he said I could not understand the ordeal he had been through during last month.

Recalling that there had been seven attempts on his life.'

Mahoney did not attempt to discourage Nkrumah's fears, nor did he characterize them as unfounded in his report to his superiors.

'While Nkrumah apparently continues to have personal affection for me,' he noted, 'he seems as convinced as ever that the US is out to get him. From what he said about assassination attempts in March, it appears he still suspects US involvement.'

Of course, the U.S. was out to get him. Moreover, Nkrumah was keenly aware of a recent African precedent that made the notion of a U.S.-organized or sanctioned assassination plot plausible – namely, the fate of the Congo and its first prime minister, his friend Patrice Lumumba.

Nkrumah believed that the destabilization of the Congolese government in 1960 and Lumumba's assassination in 1961 were the work of the 'Invisible Government of the U.S.,' as he wrote in *Neocolonialism: The Last Stage of Imperialism*, later in 1965.

When Lumumba's murder was announced, Nkrumah told students at the inauguration of an ideological institute that bore his name that this brutal murder should teach them the diabolical depths of degradation to which these twin-monsters of imperialism and colonialism can descend.

In his conclusion, Mahoney observed: 'Nkrumah gave me the impression of being a badly frightened man. His emotional resources seem be running out. As pressures increase, we may expect more hysterical outbursts, many directed against US.'

It was not necessary to add that he was helping to apply the pressure, nor that any hysterical outbursts by Nkrumah played into the West's projection of him as an unstable dictator, thus justifying his removal.

Smoking Gun

On May 27, 1965, Robert W. Komer, a National Security Council staffer, briefed his boss, McGeorge Bundy, President Johnson's special assistant for national security affairs, on the anti-Nkrumah campaign (Document 253).

Komer, who first joined the White House as a member of President Kennedy's NSC staff, had worked as a CIA analyst for 15 years. In 1967, Johnson tapped him to head his hearts-and-minds pacification program in Vietnam.

Komer's report establishes that the effort was not only interagency, sanctioned by the White House and supervised by the State Department and CIA, but also intergovernmental, being supported by America's Western allies.

'FYI,' he advised, 'we may have a pro-Western coup in Ghana soon. Certain key military and police figures have been planning one for some time, and Ghana's deteriorating economic condition may provide the spark.'

'The plotters are keeping us briefed,' he noted, 'and the State Department thinks we're more on the inside than the British. While we're not directly involved (I'm told), we and other Western countries (including France) have been helping to set up the situation by ignoring Nkrumah's pleas for economic aid. All in all, it looks good.'

Komer's reference to not being told if the U.S. was directly involved in the coup plot is revealing and quite likely a wry nod to his CIA past.

Among the most deeply ingrained aspects of intelligence tradecraft and culture is plausible deniability, the habit of mind and practice designed to insulate the U.S., and particularly the president, from responsibility for particularly sensitive covert operations.

Komer would have known that orders such as the overthrow of Nkrumah would have been communicated in a deliberately vague, opaque, allusive, and indirect fashion, as Thomas Powers noted in *The Man Who Kept the Secrets: Richard Helms and the CIA*.

It would be unreasonable to argue that the U.S. was not directly involved when it created or exacerbated the conditions that favored a coup, and did so for the express purpose of bringing one about.

Truth and Consequences

As it turned out, the coup did not occur for another nine months. After it did, Komer, now acting special assistant for national security affairs, wrote a congratulatory assessment to the President on March 12, 1966 (Document 260). His assessment of Nkrumah and his successors was telling.

'The coup in Ghana,' he crowed, 'is another example of a fortuitous windfall. Nkrumah was doing more to undermine our interests than any other black African. In reaction to his strongly pro-Communist leanings, the new military regime is almost pathetically pro-Western.'

In this, Komer and Nkrumah were in agreement. 'Where the more subtle methods of economic pressure and political subversion have failed to achieve the desired result,' Nkrumah wrote from exile in Guinea three years later, 'there has been resort to violence in order to promote a change of regime and prepare the way for the establishment of a puppet government.'"[35]

Although he was overthrown, his influence and continental stature did not diminish. His ideas continued to have a major impact on political discourse on the future of Africa. And his advocacy of industrialization including development of heavy industry won him followers in different parts of Africa, and for good reason.

There is empirical evidence showing that heavy

industry has given countries a quantum leap over others towards economic development and independence. It is true, as the advocates of the heavy-industry approach claim, that emphasis on capital goods production allows a greater rate of reinvestment and therefore fosters a rate of growth that is higher than a more balanced approach between heavy and light industry combined with agriculture.

Moreover, without their own industries, especially heavy industry, African countries can not develop the other sectors of their economies, especially raw materials on which they heavily depend and will continue to be economic plantations for the West and the rest of the industrialized world including China which is destined to become another economic and military super power.

In addition to their underdeveloped status due to lack of manpower and industry, the young African nations were handicapped by their dependence on foreign aid soon after they won independence. And their demand that aid should be channelled through international agencies to avoid strings did not make much sense. All those agencies were and still are dominated by the very same countries, mainly Western, which offered aid. That was one of the harsh realities of nationhood Africans faced when their countries won independence.

Their demand made little sense for another reason. Only about 10 per cent of economic aid was funnelled through multilateral institutions, a negligible amount. The bulk of it came directly from the donor countries themselves. And they called the tune. The only alternative was to reject aid as Tanzania did in 1964 when West Germany tried to dictate policy to her over East German diplomatic representation on Tanzanian soil. Otherwise donor countries have the final say.

But even Tanzania itself was still heavily dependent on foreign aid from other countries besides West Germany, as were all the other newly independent countries on the continent. As Adebayo Adedeji, the Nigerian economist who served as executive secretary of the UN Economic Commission for Africa (ECA) stated:

"We entered the international economy at a time when, in spite of the rhetoric, the rich countries were not as selfless as they pretended to be. Even in the 1960s and early 1970s, when aid was generous, it was usually tied, and because it was tied, it tended to distort the priorities of developing countries and delayed the implementation process.

The donor countries and institutions have the last word, rather than the (African) governments themselves, such as in the recent controversy between the IMF and Tanzania (in 1983). I think, in the final analysis, that the IMF won. This is the grueling reality of poverty. When you are poor, you can never be right. It is the rich country that is right, because it is the only one that can help you out."[36]

As African countries were contending with poverty and tackling the formidable task of economic development without sufficient capital and skills, they also had to deal with political and military conflicts which erupted in different parts of the continent during the sixties. Some of those conflicts were within the countries themselves. A look at some of the important milestones illustrates this point.

The year 1960, probably the most important milestone on the road towards African independence, saw not only the emergence in a single year of the largest number of African countries from colonial rule; it was also a turning point in the history of the Portuguese African colonies, the oldest on the continent.

African nationalists in those colonies, seeing the victory of fellow Africans who had just won their freedom,

197

also felt that their time had come although, as events turned out, they were years off the mark. But they nonetheless drew great inspiration from their brethren who had just won independence in 1960 and thereafter in different parts of the continent.

In 1961, bloody uprisings erupted in Angola, the largest and richest of the Portuguese colonies on the continent. Guerrilla warfare had officially begun.

It was also in the same year, 1961, that Tanganyika became independent, the first country in the region close to southern Africa to win independence.

Soon after independence, Tanganyika became a haven for refugees and training ground for freedom fighters from the white-ruled territories in southern Africa, the bastion of white minority rule on the continent.

When the Organization of African Unity (OAU) was formed in Addis Ababa, Ethiopia, in May 1963, it chose Tanganyika to be the headquarters of all the African liberation movements under the auspices of the OAU Liberation Committee which was also based in the capital Dar es Salaam.

1962 was another important milestone in the history of African liberation when Algeria won independence from France after waging the bloodiest war on the continent which lasted for seven years at a cost of one million Algerian lives.

In 1963, African freedom fighters succeeded in seizing control of parts of Portuguese Guinea, now Guinea Bissau, in West Africa in what came to be one of the most successful wars in the history of African liberation. The war went on for ten years.

The year 1963 also turned out to be an important milestone in another respect in the history of African independence. That was the year in which President Sylvanus Olympio of Togo was assassinated in the first military coup in black Africa.

The assassination of President Olympio started a trend

of assassinations and military coups in Africa, as did Lumumba's in the Congo although in a somewhat different context since the Congo crisis was engineered by Western political and financial interests and turned the country into a theatre of rivalry between the East and the West during the Cold War.

Olympio's assassination showed not only how vulnerable African leaders were but also how precarious the existing order was, and how dangerous a recourse to violence could become to the continued stability of the modern African state.

The early sixties also witnessed some of the most successful campaigns against ethnic centres of power and traditional rulers who were reluctant to submit to central authority.

In Ghana, President Nkrumah subdued the Ewe, members of an ethnic group who live on both sides of the border between Ghana and Togo. He also neutralized the power of the Ashanti kingdom in central Ghana and other traditional centres of power in the northern part of the country to maintain national unity under a unitary state.

In Uganda, Dr. Obote achieved the same goal in the kingdoms of Buganda, Bunyoro and Ankole and in the princedom of Busoga. And in Zambia, Dr. Kaunda was also able to contain separatist tendencies in Barotse Province, also known as Barotseland, in the west, and among the Tonga and Ilunga ethnic groups in the south which supported their native son, opposition leader Harry Nkumbula of the African National Congress (ANC).

In both Rwanda and Burundi, the Hutu and the Tutsi were virtually in a state of war all the way through the sixties. The tension between them even erupted into open warfare now and then through the decade costing thousands of lives.

Other conflicts on the continent had also been going on for years. Besides the Algerian war of independence which started in 1954, there was also the Sudanese civil war which began in 1955, a racial and religious conflict between predominantly Christian blacks in the south and Muslim Arabs in the north. Fighting between the two sides went on throughout the sixties.

And the conflict in the Congo which had been internationalized by the intervention of outside powers went on until 1965. About 100,000 Congolese died in the conflict. It was one of the bloodiest in post-colonial Africa up to that time.

The bloodiest conflict in the sixties besides the Algerian war of independence was the Nigerian civil war.

At least one million people died; some estimates go up to two million. Most of those who died were Igbos in the secessionist Eastern Region of Biafra. A very large number of them were killed by Nigerian federal troops during the war itself. But the majority died from starvation which the federal military government deliberately used as a weapon to starve the secessionists into submission. It amounted to a policy of genocide. Federal Nigerian leaders, especially Obafemi Awolowo and Anthony Enahoro, explicitly stated that starvation was an instrument of war.

There were also, during the sixties, tensions and border conflicts between Kenya and Somalia, Ethiopia and Somalia, Ethiopia and Sudan, Chad and Sudan, and between Chad and Libya; tensions between Malawi and Tanzania over political differences and Malawi's claims to parts of Tanzanian territory; territorial disputes between Malawi and Zambia arising from Malawi's claim to Zambia's entire Eastern Province; disputes between Rwanda and Burundi, Gabon and Congo-Brazzaville, and Congo with her neighbours when Tshombe briefly served as prime minister.

Tensions in varying degrees also strained relations and led to conflict in some cases between Morocco and Algeria, Morocco and Mauritania, and between Egypt and Sudan. But the only conflict of a military nature was between Algeria and Morocco when Morocco invaded

Algeria and tried to annex some territory along the border between the two countries.

Political differences between Ghana and Nigeria also led to strained relations between the two countries because of Nkrumah's Pan-African militancy which led to the denunciation of the Ghanaian leader – and of Nasser – as power-hungry politicians who wanted to dominate Africa. As Ali Mazrui states:

"Nkrumah and Nasser were sometimes regarded as rivals for leadership in Africa. This, at any rate, was the assessment of the *West African Pilot* of Nigeria in one of its attacks against Nkrumah.

On the question of leadership in Africa, the newspaper taunted Nkrumah in the following terms: 'Until recently it was a tournament between Nasser and Nkrumah but Africa today contains many stars and meteorites, all of them seeking positions of eminence.'"[37]

The taunt was published in *The West African Pilot* edition of 18 May 1961. A similar jab at Nkrumah was published in an edition of *West Africa* on 6 May 1961. Yet, in spite of the hostility to Dr. Nkrumah by the Nigerian leadership, many younger Nigerians highly admired him:

"A strong, radically nationalist trend has existed within at least the younger generation of Nigerians.

Following the 1962 Commonwealth Prime Ministers' Conference speculation in Britain started as to why the Nigerian Government, with all its pragmatism, rejected out of hand a proposal for associate membership in the EEC (European Economic Community). Walter Schwartz, speaking on the European Service of the British Broadcasting Corporation (BBC) in October 1962, suggested that 'Nigeria's Government, always open to attack from its own youth for being too lukewarm about its nationalism, simply finds it politically impossible to lag behind Ghana on this issue.'

Visiting newsmen to Nigeria once discovered at a special meeting with young Nigerians at Nsukka that most of the youth were strongly in favour of Nkrumah's brand of militant African nationalism, without by any means necessarily coupling it with hero-worship for Nkrumah. One reference to this meeting appeared in the *The New York Times*, 3 March 1962."[38]

In addition to the tense relations between Dr. Nkrumah and the Nigerian leadership, there were also territorial disputes between Ghana and Togo; political conflicts between Ghana and the West African French-speaking countries all of which, with the exception of Guinea under Sekou Toure and Mali under Modibo Keita who were also Nkrumah's ideological compatriots, accused Nkrumah of trying to overthrow them. Nkrumah denied the charge and even wrote a "letter to President Hamani Diori of Niger denying any link with the attempt to assassinate Diori."[39]

But there is no question that Nkrumah scornfully described all the former French African colonies as "client states" of the former colonial power and of the West in general. The only exceptions were Guinea and Mali which he believed were genuinely independent and pursued uncompromising Pan-Africanist policies.

And some opponents of the Francophile regimes in West Africa, for example in neighbouring Ivory Coast, found sanctuary in Ghana where Nkrumah was sympathetic to their cause. And he helped them try to undermine those regimes which themselves were highly critical of Nkrumah and his policies including his pursuit of socialism; he also interfered in East Africa to thwart attempts to form an East African federation, although that is not why the federation was not formed.

In Francophone Africa, the Ivory Coast under

Houphouet-Boigny was Nkrumah's biggest challenge in the economic arena and also his biggest political adversary.

Senegal and the Ivory Coast also denounced Guinean leader Sekou Toure for his "subversive' activities against their governments. Sekou Toure returned the charge and was vindicated a few years later when the people who invaded Guinea in 1970 in an attempt to overthrow his government included citizens of Senegal and the Ivory Coast. Both countries harboured Guinean dissidents and attempts to topple Sekou Toure dated back to the sixties. Both, Senegal and the Ivory Coast, were deeply implicated in the plot. According to *Africa Contemporary Record*:

"Relations between the two countries (Guinea and Senegal) had deteriorated abruptly after a plot in 1966 to overthrow President Sekou Toure, in which he suspected Senegal of being implicated. The Ivory Coast was also accused of complicity in the plot; but signs of possible *detente* with President Houphouet-Boigny in late 1967 did not lead to any concrete improvement in relations during 1968."[40]

There were also, during the early sixties, tensions between moderates – the Brazzaville and Monrovia Groups – and radicals of the Casablanca Group over the Congo crisis, the Algerian war of independence, and over ideological differences. But after the Organization of African Unity (OAU) was formed in 1963, the Casablanca Group disbanded. The Monrovia Group followed suit.

However, the Brazzaville Group of Francophone countries refused to disband and said it would eventually fuse with the OAU. And tense relations between the moderate states (which included conservative states such as the Ivory Coast and Malawi) and the militant states continued within the OAU. Outside powers skillfully exploited those differences.

But it was the Congo crisis which thrust Africa into the international spotlight and attracted the largest number of outsiders into African affairs.

It was also the Congo crisis which proved to be the most frustrating without the slightest hope of ever being resolved by the Africans themselves; unlike the Rhodesian crisis and the Nigerian civil war both of which drew direct involvement of the independent African countries leading to some positive results strictly from African initiatives.

The Congo crisis was also an exasperating experience for the African countries which showed greater interest in it than others on the continent because their assistance was squandered, and their political input largely ignored, by the very same groups they were trying to help and which claimed to embody the ideals of the country's independence hero Patrice Lumumba.

The Congolese groups also fostered and thrived on one of Africa's worst nightmares: tribalism. And the Congo crisis itself ended up being the worst nightmare for Africa's most progressive states – Algeria, Egypt, Ghana, Guinea, Mali, Tanzania and Uganda – which, after Lumumba's assassination, tried to turn back the tide more than any other African countries which were less involved or did not want to get involved in the crisis.

Probably more than anything else, the Congo crisis demonstrated the weakness and fragility of the modern African state not only against external forces but also against its own internal weaknesses. As Nyerere stated in his speech to the Second Pan-African Seminar in Dar es Salaam, Tanganyika, in August 1961, about four months before he led Tanganyika to independence from Britain:

"There were obvious weaknesses in the Congo situation, but those weaknesses were deliberately used in a scramble for the control of the Congo.

There are obvious weaknesses on the African

continent. We have artificial 'nations' carved out at the Berlin Conference; we are struggling to build these nations into stable units of human society. And these weaknesses, too, are being exploited.

We are being reminded daily of these weaknesses. We are told tribalism will not allow us to build nations. But when we try to take measures to deal with tribalism, we are accused of dictatorship. Whenever we try to talk in terms of larger units on the African continent, we are told that it can't be done; we are told that the units we would so create would be 'artificial.' As if they could be any more artificial than the 'national' units on which we are now building!....Many (people) are deliberately emphasizing the difficulties on our continent for the express purpose of maintaining them and sabotaging any move to unite Africa....

So I believe that the second scramble for Africa has begun in real earnest. And it is going to be a much more dangerous scramble than the first one."[41]

That is what happened in the Congo. One of Africa's biggest and richest countries became a prime target for the big powers right in the heart of the continent. They wreaked havoc at will and the Congo crisis became a test case for Africa. It showed in a very painful and humiliating way how weak Africa was, unable not only to impose peace on herself but to resist foreign intrusion into the continent.

Even collectively, African countries were impotent against external intervention by outside powers from both sides of the iron curtain during the Cold War. And they failed to redeem the honour of Africa in the Congo because of their weakness.

Not long after that, African countries were again humiliated during the Rhodesian crisis when they failed to intervene and oust the white minority regime which had unilaterally declared independence against the wishes of the African majority in Rhodesia and in defiance of the rest of the Africans across the continent who, together with the black majority in that British colony, demanded independence on the basis of majority rule.

The stubborn resistance of the white minority settlers in Rhodesia and their declaration of independence in November 1965 clearly showed that the independent African countries in the sixties were not in a position to help fellow Africans achieve their freedom in that British colonial outpost in spite of the successes they had in uprooting some of the last vestiges of imperial rule on the continent.

Thus, while the sixties was a decade of triumph over colonial rule, it was also a decade of trials and tribulations for Africans in a number of areas including internal conflicts, the worst of which was the Nigerian civil war. It was the bloodiest conflict on the African continent in that decade of independence.

There are still many lessons to be learned from those years. Many of the problems African countries have faced through the years have their origin in the wrong policies African leaders have pursued since independence in the sixties.

Part II:

Africa in Crisis: Lost Years

Chapter Four

Failure of Leadership

Africa has faced a leadership crisis for decades since independence. Does that mean colonial rule was better than independence for Africans? Should Africa be recolonised?

The very idea itself, of recolonising the continent, is abhorrent, especially for people who are despised probably more than anybody else on Earth and who are considered to be intellectually inferior to members of others races, with the backwardness of Africa being cited as compelling evidence of that. And *The Bell Curve*,[1] a book written by Charles Murray and Richard Herrnstein in which the authors contend that blacks have lower IQs than whites, Asians and others, with blacks in Africa having the lowest scores on IQ tests because they have weak genes, has only "fortified" this incendiary thesis.

Yet, the two academics were unable to explain why many blacks, including those in Africa, have higher IQs than millions of whites and members of other races if blacks are indeed less intelligent than whites and other people. They, thus, inadvertently undermined their own thesis, although their book has continued to fuel debate on race and intelligence since it was first published in the United States in March 1994.

Still, the truth about Africa, all the misery and suffering because of bad leadership, is compelling enough to make some people, including many Africans themselves, think the unthinkable: Africa should probably be recolonised to end its misery. Let Europeans, our former colonial masters, come back and rule us again and end all these civil wars and corruption, revive the economy, maintain law and order, and develop Africa. "We have had it with our leaders, enough is enough," is the sentiment articulated and shared by millions across this beleaguered continent.

The call for recolonisation is also made by some of the most educated Africans, all of whom can not easily be dismissed as educated fools, brainwashed and whitewashed by their former colonial masters. Theirs is a desperate plea for help, shared by their brethren across the continent, to save Africa before it descends into the abyss.

Some believe it is already there; hence the designation, "The Lost Continent," a term used by a number of Africans themselves including former UN secretary-general Bhoutros Bhoutros-Ghali from Egypt as cited by George Ayittey, a Ghanaian professor of economics at The American University in Washington, D.C., in his highly controversial book *Africa in Chaos*[2] which has been described by some people as anti-African; so has Keith Richburg's equally inflammatory work, *Out of America: A Black Man Confronts Africa.*[3]

Since independence in the sixties, Africa has performed poorly in most areas because of bad leadership and bad policies, not because of weak genes.

Most countries on the continent won independence by 1968. Yet, more than an entire generation later, they have little to show for all those years they have ruled themselves. No one expects a country to develop in 30 or 40 years. But no one expects it to do nothing either. There is no excuse for the kind of economic retardation that has taken place in most countries across Africa since independence. A generation is not a week. When compared with other parts of the developing world, Africa has performed miserably in every conceivable way. And statistics tell the story, a sad story.

In 1965, Nigeria was richer than Indonesia, and Ghana richer than Thailand. Today Indonesia is three times richer than Nigeria, and Thailand five times richer than Ghana.

In 1965, Uganda was richer than South Korea. And in 1967, Zambia also was richer than South Korea. Zambia had a per capita income of $200, and South Korea, $120. After 30 years, South Korea's gross domestic product per person was more than $10,000 in 1998, and Zambia's $400.[4] Yet, by African standards, Zambia is considered to be one of the richest countries on the continent in spite of all the misery, hunger and starvation ravaging the country endowed with abundant minerals and arable land more than enough to feed its entire population.

And all African countries combined have a smaller gross domestic product than that of Belgium, a country of only 10 million people, and one of the smallest in the world. By contrast, Africa's population is more than one billion on a continent endowed with abundant natural resources. In terms of minerals and other resources including arable land, Africa is the richest continent; it is also the poorest, a paradox that does not require a genius to explain.

The gross domestic product of African countries is not only smaller but a mere fraction of Belgium's. What is even more depressing is that Indonesia, a developing country which in 1965 was poorer than Nigeria, has a bigger gross domestic product than that of all the black African countries combined. Yet, Indonesia itself was a colony like the African countries and won independence roughly around the same time that African countries did during the post-World War II era.

It is just as sad, probably even more so, when we look at the dismal performance of black Africa from another perspective. There are 41 black African countries out of 54 on the entire continent which includes the island nations of Madagascar, Mauritius, the Comoros, and the Seychelles, all in the Indian Ocean; Cape Verde, and Sao Tome & Principe in the Atlantic.

More than half of the gross domestic product of the black African countries is contributed by only two: South Africa and Nigeria. That means a total of 39 black African countries – almost the entire sub-Saharan region – have a combined gross domestic product that is only about a third of Indonesia's.

And the devastating impact of AIDS, civil wars and corruption makes things worse, much worse, with no relief in sight. Now, an increasing number of people across Africa are turning to churches calling for divine intervention to alleviate their plight.

Something is wrong, terribly wrong. But unlike in the past when it was fashionable for many Africans to blame colonialism and imperialism for almost all the problems our countries faced after we won independence, an increasing number of them today, especially those of the younger generation, insist on accountability within Africa itself as they apportion guilt accordingly; instead of blaming colonialists and imperialists for the perpetual misery – thanks to tyranny, corruption, poverty and disease – hundreds of millions of Africans have to endure all their lives.

To these millions, independence has remained an abstract ideal without any concrete benefits in their lives as they remain trapped in poverty and continue to be ravaged by disease while billions of dollars in foreign aid and taxes paid by the toiling masses are being stolen and squandered by unscrupulous politicians and bureaucrats together with their cronies and mistresses. It is clear where the problem lies. It lies within, not without. And the people are fed up. They are speaking up more and more against corrupt leaders, even risking their lives by doing so. As Ernest Aning wrote in an influential monthly news magazine, the *New African*:

"Millions of dollars are stashed away by corrupt leaders, their families and cronies....The message is the same in Zaire, Tanzania, Kenya, Nigeria, Sierra Leone, Burkina Faso, Gambia, Ghana, etc. Development in Africa has stagnated over the years due to turncoat politicians and soldiers who have perpetuated themselves in office by manipulating the system.

We find ourselves asking: Where did all the good people in Africa go?....What happened to the foreign exchange and the loans given for development projects?

Some of these funds find their way right back in donor countries, stashed in coded accounts.

Who do you call in Africa when you see waste and embezzlement? Nobody! Our courts are under the thumbs of the leaders. So what is the solution? Maybe we should all start to look around and ask questions about why there have been no additional hospitals, clinics, schools, roads, jobs or any change in our economic lives over the last two or three decades.

We should look at Thailand, South Korea, Indonesia, Singapore, Malaysia and all these countries that were just like us not too long ago. What are they doing, or better put, what did they do, to change things? What did their governments do to achieve all these successes?....

In Africa, the average Joe goes into politics by any means possible to steal as much as he can. We've reached a point where the people can no longer be aloof....(But) today, well-meaning citizens stand and watch because intimidation has become too real and life-threatening."[5]

And as Maxwell Oteng, another African, also states:

"A greater part of the blame on the present economic woes in our various countries should be apportioned to internal causes, especially bad political leadership. The Mobutus had a very good chance to push us away from being perpetual producers of raw materials to producers of value-added goods which would have given us control over our products. Instead, what did they do?....Until recent years, Malaysia was an agriculture-dependent primary producer like us, but it diversified the economy and encouraged local production of goods."[6]

And in the words of yet another African, Simbowe Benson:

"Mobutu's hour of reckoning has finally come. And he deserves no sympathy! For three decades, he has run Zaire as his personal fiefdom, culminating in mismanagement and institutional corruption. Zaire is a rich country....Now this rich nation has been reduced to penury while Mobutu and the Western business interests he fronts for have grown rich at the expense of the people. Laurent Kabila and his Alliance for Democratic Forces deserve our full support in their effort to unseat Mobutu and his sick regime."[7]

Initially, Kabila was seen and hailed as a liberator of his fellow countrymen from the clutches of Mobutu's kleptocratic regime. But he turned out to be no better than his predecessor and in some respects even surpassed him in outright incompetence.

It was the same cycle all over again, and the same collective sentiment echoed across the continent about rotten African leadership. It is rotten to the core.

Things are so bad that many people remember with nostalgia "the good old days" of colonial rule when they could at least afford basic necessities and even freely express their views without fear of being locked up for simply speaking up.

Colonial rule was oppressive and exploitative. There is no question about that. And it did not allow Africans to have the kind of freedom they normally would have under democracy. But when a leader like Archbishop Desmond Tutu says he had more freedom of speech under apartheid than other Africans do in independent African countries under the leadership of fellow Africans, as he said in Nairobi, Kenya, in the early nineties; then one gets a pretty good idea of what kind of mess we are in as a people across the continent.

Many older people also remember that during colonial rule, in spite of its curtailed freedom, they were allowed a degree of freedom they don't enjoy today in most countries even in this era of democratisation that was introduced across Africa in the early nineties following the collapse of communism and the end of the Cold War.

Whether we like to admit it or not, it is true that there was a degree of freedom during colonial rule. That is why African nationalist leaders were able to organise and form political parties and campaign for independence right under the noses of our colonial masters. It is the colonial rulers who allowed them to do that, although within prescribed limits to stifle nationalist aspirations. But they did allow our leaders to continue mobilising the masses for the nationalist cause. Yet, after we won independence, many of our leaders went on to deny us this very basic human right, freedom of expression, they claimed to cherish so much.

Sometimes curtailment of freedom was justified to keep countries united and from splitting along tribal (ethnic) and regional lines; a dreadful prospect which would have become a reality had the people been allowed to form opposition parties most of which would have been tribal and regional in character, a danger that was avoided when the one-party system was established in most African countries. But more often than not, it was sheer abuse of power by our leaders which resulted in the denial of basic human rights to the vast majority of the people across Africa. And it still goes on today.

Offensive as the idea of recolonising Africa may be, it pales into insignificance when compared to the horrors of wars and chopped limbs, massive starvation and diseases millions of Africans have to endure everyday for the rest of their lives – nothing but hell on Earth!

It is not a popular idea even in Africa itself, a continent mangled by war and disfigured by disease. But it resonates well among the victims as demonstrated by the people of Sierra Leone who were jubilant when the British returned to their former colony virtually to run the government and end the civil war which devastated the country for ten years.

The former Belgian Congo which has earned the unenviable distinction as the bleeding heart of Africa because of chaos and civil wars since the sixties, has had similar experience. Henry Louis Gates Jr., chairman of the African-American studies department at Harvard University, recalls one memorable incident during his visit to Congo and other African countries in the late nineties which illustrates this point.

During the same trip, he also visited my home country, Tanzania, where he first went in 1970 when he was an undergraduate student at Yale University and worked for one year at an Anglican hospital in Kilimatinde in the central region.

During his visit to Congo, someone had spread a rumour that the Belgians were coming back to rule the country again. He said many people were so excited when they heard the Belgians were returning that when the ship

214

in which he was a passenger arrived in Kisangani, formerly Stanleyville, on the banks of the Congo River, they formed a crowd waving tree branches to welcome the Belgians who were supposedly aboard the same vessel.

To their disappointment, *utter* disappointment, there were no Belgians on the ship who had come back to rule them again. It was no more than a rumour.

But it demonstrates, in a very tragic way, the utter futility of life in this heart of Africa under the oppressive and kleptocratic regime of President Mobutu Sese Seko who virtually bled his country to death during his 32 years of rotten leadership. It also demonstrates the degree of desperation among the Congolese who were so desperate that they remembered with nostalgia "the good old days" of Belgian rule and wished the Belgians had never left. Independence meant nothing to them.

Yet, this is also worth remembering, it was the same people, the Belgians, who killed Patrice Lumumba with the help of the CIA. It was also the same people, together with other Western powers including the United States, who installed Mobutu in power and plundered the country for decades leaving it an empty shell, with the help of this arch-traitor who was as treacherous as Moise Tshombe.

Still, these are the very same people some Congolese wanted back to rule them again. Yes, things had gone that bad. And that is not the end of it on this embattled continent which is so ravaged by disease and emaciated by hunger that the acronym AIDS also now stands for Africa Is Dying Slowly.

In Gabon, the small oil-rich country not far from the former Belgian Congo, there was even a political party whose leaders and supporters campaigned in the 1990s to turn their country into a province of France, the former colonial power. The French refused for obvious reasons. They knew what their former subjects wanted, economic benefits from France more than anything else, at any cost, including selling their country – and even their souls.

215

In fact, a precedent had been set much earlier elsewhere in Africa. In 1974 and 1976, the people of Mayotte voted against independence from France, the only island in the archipelago of the Comoros to do so. It remains virtually an integral part of France and is economically better off than the other islands.

The same sentiment for a return to the status quo ante of colonial days, as articulated by some Gabonese, is echoed in other parts of the continent by a significant number of people. They say, yes, tragic and humiliating as the idea is, colonial rule was better than what they have to endure today under the leadership of their own people, fellow Africans.

But was colonial rule really better? It is highly debatable. And both sides continue to maintain their positions on this inflammatory subject.

The tragedy of all this is that, to many people, the misery and suffering hundreds of millions have endured for decades under their own black governments since independence provides a clear-cut answer which does not even have to be articulated. Facts speak for themselves. Just come to Africa and see for yourself, they say. You don't even need to stay long. And compare what you see today with what we had during colonial rule. The answer is written on the wall for everybody to see. That is the tragedy of Africa.

Here is a continent where brother is killing brother, his fellow African brother, in senseless civil wars. It is also a continent where the leaders, at least most of them, don't have the slightest concern for the well-being of their people living in misery, everyday, seven days a week, for the rest of their lives. Not only is it a life of misery, it is living hell.

And it is a continent where millions have simply given up on their lives and have to depend on handouts from international relief agencies and other donors to get a simple meal now and then; sometimes once a day, and sometimes once a week, or never. But the reality is the same. Life is hard, very hard. And if Europeans and other foreigners can provide them with at least something, many Africans feel that these good Samaritans might as well stay. Our governments are doing nothing for us, they say. And it is a fact.

That is the harsh reality. And we have to be brutally frank about it. Such governments can not justify their existence. They thrive at the expense of their people who already live miserable lives. And their countries are no better off than Somalia which dissolved in anarchy and has had no government since 1991. President Siad Barre's oppressive and corrupt regime led to the collapse of Somalia, the first African country to "disappear" from the map.

Since independence, most African leaders have raided national coffers, bankrupted their economies; jailed, tortured and killed their opponents, real and imagined, including innocent civilians, to perpetuate themselves in office. They are among the world's richest people in the poorest countries in the world. They are also among the most brutal. And they continue to bleed their people to death in more than one way: ruined economies, shattered lives, summary executions and much more.

African countries have become international beggars. They have been begging since independence in the sixties. Yet, some of these very same countries had the potential to develop and outstrip their southeastern Asian counterparts which are now known as the Asian tigers because of their brilliant economic performance. And the contrast is glaring.

In the sixties, the southeast Asian countries were as poor as or poorer than some African countries which are now on international welfare, dependent on donors for their very survival. They include "prosperous" ones today such as Uganda. As Ugandan President Yoweri Museveni said in a speech to the United National General Assembly

217

in February 1997, in 1965 Uganda was "more prosperous than South Korea and Nigeria more prosperous than Indonesia."[8]

So what happened?

It is also worth remembering that the year 1965 when Nigeria was richer than Indonesia, Ghana richer than Thailand, and Uganda and Zambia richer than South Korea, was around the same time when all those African countries had just won independence from Britain; which means it was *not* the African governments which made those countries prosperous when compared to their southeast Asian counterparts. It was the British colonial governments which did that.

Ghana won independence in March 1957, Nigeria in October 1960, Uganda in October 1962, and Zambia, formerly Northern Rhodesia, in October 1964; hardly enough time – by 1965 – for the new African governments to have made any appreciable impact on their countries' economies to achieve significant progress within so few years and outstrip the southeast Asian nations.

The claim, if it is indeed ever made, that it is the black African governments which were responsible for this progress by 1965 – may be with the exception of Ghana under Nkrumah who ruled the longest among them from 1957 to 1966 – is further, in fact even more strongly, refuted by the fact that during the next 30 years after independence, economic ruin and political chaos became the norm rather than the exception in all those countries and the rest across the continent. They all ended up being the poorest in the world as they still are today.

Some African leaders have been frank about Africa's dismal performance through the decades, a rare admission among them. One of them is John Mahama, the president of Ghana, who states in his book, *My First Coup D'etat and Other True Stories from the Lost Decades of Africa*:

"There is a period of time often referred to as the 'lost

218

decades' of Africa. That description speaks to the dismal post-independence performance of African countries during the 1970s and 1980s into the early part of the 1990s. The median per capita growth of developing African countries during those 'lost decades' was 0.0 percent.

It was a period of crippling stagnation, especially when compared with the era of liberation that preceded it, within which is also included the initial post-colonial period that began in the late 1950s and continued throughout the 1960s and the early 1970s.

The description of 'lost decades' is used primarily to address matters of economy and development, but during those years, other aspects of life in Africa were undergoing an equally marked period of stagnation....The continent...devolved into what would ultimately become a lengthy cycle of political unrest and, by the mid-1970s, made a rapid plunge into poverty.

During the 'lost decades,' Ghana – and in fact all of Africa – experienced a 'brain drain,' a mass exodus that found many of our artists, intellectuals, professionals, and politicians living abroad in either a forced or a self-imposed exile. As a result, that period of time and the direct impact it had on the cultural, educational and political lives of those who remained has not been heavily documented, especially not from a personal perspective. They are years that are rarely discussed, years of untold difficulty and hardship, of ever-present hunger and fear. They are years that many have, understandably, tried to forget, to erase entirely from memory." – (John Dramani Mahama, *My First Coup D'etat and Other True Stories from the Lost Decades of Africa*, New York: Bloomsbury Publishing, USA, 2013).

Fortunately, some of us have not tried to forget those years. We will always remember them because of what our continent went through. It was a tragic period. And it's not quite over yet, despite some successes here and there through the years, especially since the late 1990s.

One of the strange paradoxes about Africa is that some of the richest countries on the continent are also among the poorest. Therefore most of the poverty in those countries can not be attributed to a lack of natural resources but to bad leadership, wrong economic policies, rampant corruption, and sheer waste and mismanagement including well-meaning incompetence.

No case better illustrates the utter waste of such potential than that of Zaire, now the Democratic Republic of Congo, under Mobutu Sese Seko, one of the most brutal, and most corrupt, dictators on the entire continent. He ruled a vast country endowed with an abundance of minerals and other natural resources including enormous agricultural potential, making it potentially one of the richest countries in the world.

In fact, in terms of mineral wealth, it is the richest country in Africa, richer than South Africa. But the government did nothing with all that enormous wealth through the decades to help its own people when it was led by Mobutu who inspired coinage of the term "kleptocrat"; an indictment equally applicable to most of the other African countries. As economics editor Thierry Naudin stated in November 1996 in a leading newspaper *The European*:

"In much of Africa, if a country is poor it seems bound to remain so indefinitely, and if it is rich, as Zaire is, it seems destined to be systematically plundered by a ruling minority....

Zaire, which is about as large as the European Union, sits on some of the world's richest reserves of gold, diamonds, copper, cobalt and another dozen metals. The state's water resources are adequate to generate the energy required to exploit those minerals, and could also support an agricultural sector big enough to feed Zaire's population of 44 million. Nearly four decades after independence, the country might have been expected to have developed some manufacturing sector of its own.

But something is very wrong, and none of this potential has been realized. In terms of overall production and income, Zaire is back to its 1958 pre-independence levels - and now has a population three times as great. Its per capita output - under $120 per year today, against $377 in 1960 - is one of the lowest in the world. Like many countries in the region, since the 1960s it has swung from being an exporter to an importer of foodstuffs."[9]

The country also has the potential, like Angola, to feed much of Africa. And the Congo River has enough potential to generate electricity for the entire continent. Yet all that has gone down the drain since independence under some of the most corrupt leaders on Earth. One of the richest countries in the world has become one of the poorest, and an international beggar, unable even to feed itself, because of corrupt leadership.

During 32 years of kleptocratic rule, Mobutu bled the country to death, and Zaire ended up being one of the poorest countries even in Africa itself. And the continent, of course, has the distinction of having the largest number of the poorest countries in the world. Almost all African countries are poor, desperately poor. They are all in sub-Saharan Africa.

Mobutu's personal wealth equalled the national debt, at the very least. He amassed a fortune estimated to be between $5 billion and $10 billion and was said to be one of the five richest men in the world.

Some reports say he had at least $8 billion. He owned properties not only in Zaire but also in Belgium, France, Switzerland, Portugal, Spain and other countries.

When he was asked on "Sixty Minutes," an American documentary programme on CBS television, how rich he was, he arrogantly responded by saying he didn't even know how rich he was, because he was so rich. He was an embodiment of everything that was wrong with African leadership and he died that way:

"Mobutu Sese Seko, who ruled Zaire for nearly 32 years with a combination of brutal repression and unbridled greed that impoverished his citizens while earning him millions, died in Morocco on Sunday, less than four months after being driven into exile by leaders of a popular rebellion.

Mobutu, who died at 66 after a long battle with prostate cancer, was for years the epitome of the African strongman. More than a dictatorship, his regime was often called a 'kleptocracy.'

He strode the African and world stages dressed in a trademark leopard-skin hat and carrying an ebony, ivory-tipped walking stick. He looted the treasury of his mineral-rich country, spending some of it on European homes and fine champagne and, reportedly, socking much of it away in Swiss bank accounts. Stern and imperious, he was little loved and mostly feared. When he was deposed in May by the onrushing troops of an old foe, Laurent Kabila, Mobutu was so ill that he could barely walk. And yet only one country, Morocco, agreed to accept him.

Mobutu once bragged in an interview on CBS-TV's "60 Minutes" that he was one of the world's richest men-- this as Zaire's infrastructure crumbled. Many of the country's paved roads had been swallowed up by the encroaching jungle, hospital patients were forced to provide their own medicine, and almost every police officer, regular army soldier and civil servant had resorted to banditry as a means to survive.

Joseph-Desire Mobutu was born Oct. 14, 1930, in Lisala, in what was then known as the Belgian Congo. The son of a cook and hotel maid, he first pursued a career in journalism before becoming a soldier. In 1960, shortly after independence from Belgium, he was named army chief of staff. When the Belgians pulled out, Mobutu was one of the country's few literate, high-school-educated non-Europeans. Recognizing that the United States was locked in a Cold War with the Soviet Union, Mobutu sewed up a relationship with the Central Intelligence Agency.

The first prime minister, Patrice Lumumba, whom the CIA suspected of Marxist tendencies, was quickly killed, and the U.S.-backed Mobutu spent the next few years maneuvering himself into position to become dictator.

On Nov. 24, 1965, he brought down the first post-colonial government--of Joseph Kasavubu--and declared himself president of the Second Republic. His hold on power remained unchallenged until the early 1990s, when the fall of communism in Eastern Europe stirred winds of democracy in Africa.

He Africanized his name to Mobutu Sese Seko Kuku Ngbendu wa za Banga--meaning 'the all-powerful warrior who because of his endurance and inflexible will to win will go from conquest to conquest leaving fire in his wake.'

A pro-democracy movement led by the Roman Catholic Church began pressing for multi-party elections in Zaire, but the shrewd Mobutu easily sowed divisions among his opponents.

The country Mobutu had renamed Zaire was never an African Arcadia. Hundreds of thousands (millions) of Congolese were worked to death by Belgian colonizers who gained international approval to create a despotic and exploitative 'Free State' in the watershed of the mighty Congo River and for the next century milked it for everything it was worth.

Although the country--renamed the Democratic Republic of Congo with Mobutu's ouster--is still considered to be fabulously wealthy, with vast timber reserves and hydroelectric potential and some of the world's richest mineral deposits, it is in shambles politically, economically and socially.

'Mobutuism' amounted to a one-party totalitarian system melded with African symbols and calls for self-reliance and self-sufficiency. Eventually, the word simply was a synonym for graft.

Besides what Mobutu siphoned off and stole, he paid himself generously. His personal salary was 17% of the state budget. By 1989, he officially received $100 million a year to spend as he wished, more than the government spent on education, health and social services combined.

Besides his French Riviera villa and the immense palace--known as 'Versailles in the Jungle'--that he built in his ancestral village, Mobutu's properties included a 15-acre beach resort, a plantation of orchards and a huge vineyard in Portugal, a 32-room mansion in Switzerland and a 16th century castle in Spain.

In the end, it was not only Mobutu's greed but his lifelong habit of meddling in the internal affairs of his neighbors that finally brought him down.

Mobutu had been friendly with the Hutu-led regime in Rwanda that in April 1994 unleashed a genocide against its ethnic Tutsi minority. Tutsi troops marching in from Uganda eventually drove out the Hutu government, but not before at least 800,000 Tutsis and moderate Hutus had been slaughtered. The genocide regime decamped *en masse* into eastern Zaire.

Sustained by international aid agencies and rearmed with Mobutu's help, the Hutus gained in strength and bravado until they began renewing massacres of Tutsis in Rwanda and eastern Zaire. This prompted Uganda and Rwanda to team up with Kabila, a onetime Maoist anti-Mobutu guerrilla and gold smuggler.

With the help of Rwandan arms and soldiers, Kabila's rebel forces routed the Hutus from their camps and then turned their guns on Mobutu. In a remarkable 1,000-mile campaign that lasted from November 1996 until Mobutu's downfall on May 16, they walked the breadth of Zaire to

224

take the capital, Kinshasa.

By now, Mobutu was deathly ill with prostate cancer. Only a heavy regimen of painkillers made it possible for him to hold meetings with Bill Richardson, the U.S. ambassador to the United Nations, and South African President Nelson Mandela, who had hopes of brokering a deal to ease Mobutu out of power.

Mobutu, meanwhile, was still under the illusion that his faithful army would rise up and beat the rebels when they got to Kinshasa. Finally, when his army chief of staff told him that his troops would not allow a blood bath in Kinshasha to save one man, Mobutu realized it was time for him to go. He spent the last months of his life in Morocco, living in seclusion in different luxury hotels and villas accompanied by a huge entourage of family members, servants, bodyguards and assorted hangers-on and undergoing various operations intended to slow the relentless progress of his cancer.

The treatment failed. Racked by illness, detested by the country that once treated him as a demigod and dependent on strangers in his final hours, Africa's last Big Man died bereft." – (John Daniszewski and Ann M. Simmons, "mobutu, Zairian Dictator for 32 Years, dies in Exile, *Los Angeles Times*, September 8, 1997).

His brutal dictatorship plunged his country into chaos, igniting a civil war which not only led to his ouster in May 1997 but also affected the entire Great lakes region comprising many countries.

The country was still torn by war for many years after his ouster.

Zaire, renamed the Democratic Republic of Congo (DRC) after his downfall, is just one example of a rich African country ruined by rotten leadership.

Neighbouring Congo-Brazzaville, also known as the Congo Republic or Republic of Congo, is another country endowed with an abundance of natural resources and fertile land. It is potentially one of the richest countries in Africa and in the entire Third World like a number of Africa countries are. They include South Africa, Nigeria, Angola, and Zimbabwe, besides the Democratic Republic of Congo.

Relatively speaking, the people of Congo-Brazzaville enjoy a higher standard of living than their fellow Africans do in many other countries on the continent. Yet, most of the country's wealth goes to only a few people, distributed on tribal or ethnic basis depending on whose tribe or ethnic group is in power.

If the president is a member of the Bakongo ethnic group from the south – which is also the largest in the country – like Pascal Lissouba, a former professor, his people get the largest piece of the pie. If he is a member of the Mbochi tribe, like Denis Sassou Nguesso, from the north or from any of the other northern tribes including the Sanga, his people grab the largest share.

Even the struggle for power is fought along tribal and regional lines, tragically demonstrated by the civil war which devastated the capital Brazzaville in a four-month civil war from July to October in 1997 at a cost of more than 10,000 lives. The country was still torn by civil war after that, a conflict ignited and fuelled by ethno-regional rivalries. As one senior West African diplomat in Abidjan, Ivory Coast, stated:

"What you have in Congo is a very rich state in deep decay. Unfortunately, there are no saints in this picture. The name of the game in Congo is being in charge so that you and a few people from your ethnic group profit from the country's huge oil earnings."[10]

Neighbouring Gabon is another fabulously rich country. It has a lot of oil and other natural resources more than enough for its small population of about 1.6 million to enjoy one of the highest standards of living in

Africa and in the entire Third World. And some of them do, the elite. Because of the country's abundant wealth, large numbers of immigrants from other French-speaking African countries, and from English-speaking Nigeria especially from the east, work in Gabon, mostly harvesting cash crops.

In fact, for many years, the people of Gabon had the highest per capita income in black Africa and second only to Libya's on the entire continent. But those were just numbers on paper.

After 42 years of autocratic rule and rampant corruption under President Omar Bongo who ruled the country from November 1967 (soon after his predecessor President Léon M'ba died on November 27th) until his death in June 2009, the Gabonese were still mired in poverty, as they still are, in spite of all that wealth.

After his son Ali Bongo Ondimba took over in October 2009, nothing changed. And because of disease and malnutrition, the people of Gabon also had one of the lowest life expectancies in the world, with an average man dying by the age of 25, even when the country was enjoying an economic boom from oil production during the 1970s.

This is also the same country where in the 1990s a political party with significant support across the nation actively campaigned to make Gabon an integral part of France, out of sheer desperation, because of misery and suffering inflicted on the people by rotten leadership since independence. To many of these people, French colonial rule was better, and they would rather be under the French again. Their own leaders, fellow Africans, have failed them miserably. It is that bad, and sad.

Other rich African countries notorious for squandering wealth include Cameroon where President Paul Biya has muzzled the opposition while enormously enriching himself; and Nigeria where military dictator General Ibrahim Babangida amassed a fortune estimated to be more than $30 billion, siphoned from petrodollars, making him one of the richest men in history. His successor General Sani Abacha, another despot, stole an estimated $4 billion within five years since he seized power in 1993 from Babangida who ruled from 1983.

In neighbouring Equatorial Guinea, the family of President Teodoro Obiang Nguema and their cronies stole billions of dollars from oil money in only a short time since the tiny west-central African country became oil-rich in the the late 1990s. They are still stealing.

Further west in the Ivory Coast, a civil war which erupted in 2002 because of ethno-regional and religious differences and rivalries split the country in half and devastated what once was the richest country in West Africa and one of the most stable on the entire continent since independence from France in 1960.

In southern Africa, three potentially rich countries were also devastated by conflicts.

Angola was devastated by civil war which lasted for more than 25 years. During all those years, the elite stole billions of petrodollars while doing nothing for their people. They used war as an excuse, saying the money from oil and other natural resources including abundant minerals such as diamonds, was being used to fight UNITA rebels. After the war ended, they could no longer use it as an excuse to explain where the money was going. Yet, billions of dollars continued to disappear from national coffers, raided and drained by government leaders and their cronies.

The other country was Mozambique, also torn by civil war from 1986 to 1992, with millions of its people displaced, and its economy in tatters. Countless sought refuge in neighbouring countries.

Another one, Zimbabwe, was also plunged into chaos because of expropriation of white-owned farms under the government's fast-track land reform programme which started in 2000 to seize land from whites and give it to blacks. Even if well-intentioned to correct colonial injustices when blacks were forcibly removed from their ancestral land by the colonial rulers to give the land to white settlers, the programme was ill-conceived. The economy went into a tailspin.

Kenya was also one of the most prosperous countries in Africa. But after 24 years of corruption, mismanagement, and dictatorship under President Daniel arap Moi who also ignited and fanned ethnic conflicts to perpetuate himself and his cronies in power, the economy was utterly ruined. The country became one of the poorest and most unstable on the entire continent.

The mess started under Jomo Kenyatta, the country's first president, who and his fellow Kikuyus seized vast tracts of land for themselves, leaving countless poor Kenyans hardly with anything. He also favoured members of his tribe, the Kikuyu, and instituted an ethnocracy which virtually excluded other Kenyans – who were *not* Kikuyu – from meaningful participation in government.

Those are only a few examples of the devastation wrought, and the potential wasted, across Africa since independence in the sixties.

Now, tell all those suffering millions that, by comparison, colonial rule was not better than what they have today under the leadership of their own people, fellow Africans. It is a tough proposition. Tell the hundreds of thousands in refugee camps who have fled from civil wars and who are now being fed, not by fellow Africans, but by the Europeans, the Americans and international relief agencies that, don't worry, your own people, your own leaders, will take care of you.

Put yourself in their position, starving and dying of hunger and disease without any relief in sight from African leaders and governments, and yet continue to wait for help, from them, that will never come; and honestly say, you are now better off than you were under colonial rule in terms of getting basic necessities just to survive. Then you

229

will understand why tens of millions of Africans are disgusted with their leaders; and why even some of them are nostalgic about the good old days of colonial rule.

It is tragic, and it is humiliating to us. But the logic behind such sentiments is unassailable in its own limited context, however offensive it may be to our nationalist sensibilities; which it is. As one starving elderly Kenyan, quoted by *The Washington Post* in the late nineties, put it: "It is only you white people who can save us."

Now, argue with him about that; a desperate man who is simply saying we are begging because we are starving. We don't want to die. Our governments, our people, are doing nothing for us.

Many people in the Democratic Republic of Congo, ravaged by war, hunger and disease, articulated the same sentiment. Ted Koppel, an American television journalist working for ABC (American Broadcasting Corporation), visited eastern Congo in 2001 and produced a documentary showing women who had been raped, beaten and starved by the rebels, pleading for help. It was a poignant report. They made it clear, abundantly clear, in that documentary that it was only white people who could save them from misery and suffering.

Once you see and hear all that, then you may begin to understand why some Congolese felt it would have been better if the Belgians had gone back to rule them again and maintain law and order.

Older ones remember that there was no such chaos, at least not on the scale they have now, when the Belgians ruled Congo. Chaos ensued right away when they left after independence; a tragedy they themselves were largely responsible for, of course, when they tried to split the country by supporting the secession of Katanga province. But relatively speaking, many people remember that they could at least get some food and other basic necessities, and some jobs, in the fifties when the Belgians were still in power. And there was law and order, even if it was for the purpose of maintaining colonial rule and securing the interests of the Belgians and other Westerners living in the Congo; which it was.

And let me make it clear, abundantly clear. I am *not* an apologist for colonial rule. I have never been and never will be. Nor do I advocate a return to the status quo ante, with colonial flags fluttering under the tropical sun on our continent.

I would rather die than see the British back in my home country Tanzania to rule us again even if they don't hoist the Union Jack. And I feel the same way about the rest of Africa.

Like most Africans, I don't want to see the Union Jack flying over Nigeria, Ghana, Gambia, Kenya, Uganda, Zambia, Zimbabwe, and Sierra Leone where the British are virtually back in power, or in any of the former British colonies in Africa. And I don't want to see the Tricolore back in Mali, Guinea, Senegal, Niger or in any of the former French colonies on the continent.

I don't want to see any of the colonial flags defying the African sky again, or any of our former colonial masters back to rule us again, with or without the flag.

It is, of course, easier said than done if you are not the one who is starving or whose limbs have been chopped off by the rebels as in Sierra Leone because your government has ruined the country's economy, failed to create jobs and provide security. Still, the idea of recolonisation is as reprehensible, and as abhorrent, as it is despicable; however irresistible it may be to the victims of utter neglect. And it is millions of them in every country, although not all of them, not even the majority, subscribe to this highly offensive notion which is also deeply humiliating to us.

But it is appealing to some people, if not to many of them. That is because something is wrong, terribly wrong, with our countries for some of our people to even entertain such an idea.

What it amounts to is this: It is a plea for help borne out of desperation and utter destitution our leaders have failed or refused to address adequately, if at all, since independence. In terms of development, post-colonial Africa is characterised by suffocation of dissent – neutralising the people who may have better ideas to develop our countries – and by infrastructural and institutional decay more than anything else instead of the reverse being the case.

Most of our leaders have even failed to build and maintain simple roads. They don't even pay the people wages and salaries because of neglect and corruption. They don't help the poor because they don't care. And they don't want to build anything to develop our countries. They only talk about it. It's all rhetoric. As Moeletsi Mbeki, the brother of South African President Thabo Mbeki, said about the failure of our governments to develop our countries, Africa was better off in colonial times than it is today. At least roads and other infrastructure were in good shape during colonial rule. And colonial governments did much better than post-colonial rulers have in terms of economic development. He was quoted by BBC Africa, 22 September 2004:

"The average African is worse off now than during the colonial era, the brother f South Africa's President Thabo Mbeki has said.
Moeletsi Mbeki accused African elites of stealing money and keeping it abroad, while colonial rulers planted crops and built roads and cities. 'This is one of the depressing features of Africa,' he said....

Downward Spiral

He said that while China had lifted some 400,000 people out of poverty in the past 20 years, Nigeria had pushed 71 million people below the poverty line.

'The average African is poorer than during the age of colonialism. In the 1960s African elites/rulers, instead of focusing on development, took surplus for their own enormous entourages of civil servants without ploughing anything back into the country,' he said.

In July, a United Nations said that Africa was the only continent where poverty had increased in the past 20 years.

Moeletsi Mbeki was addressing a meeting of the South African Institute of International Affairs, which he heads."[11]

Outside intervention to help resolve Africa's crises, including alleviating hunger and ending civil wars, digging water wells, building schools and even latrines, is sought and welcomed even by the African leaders themselves. And it amounts to a form of recolonisation when the intervening powers, "our saviours" – yes, that's what they are even if we don't want to admit that – have the final say on what should be done since they are the ones who provide us with the assistance we so desperately need.

So, it's really not a question of whether or not Africa should be "recolonised" – but what form this "recolonisation" should take, and what it should be called.

We asked for it. Shame on us. What did we do before Europeans came? Whom did we depend on?

Our dependence on other countries including a number of Third World countries such as those in Asia makes a mockery of our independence.

Camouflaging the phenomenon under the guise of humanitarian assistance or partnership for development – including NEPAD which is really masterminded by the West, not by us – may help blunt the humiliation we suffer when we beg outsiders to help us solve our problems as if we don't have enough sense to do for ourselves what other people have done and continue to do for themselves. So, terminology is important. Yet, the reality remains the same

233

in spite of the use of such clever semantics.

And let us also face this, much as we don't like it. We have lost our sovereignty to international donors, especially to multinational corporations in this era of globalisation. Aid comes with strings. Donors pull the strings, we dance to the tune. Some of the biggest donors are our former colonial masters themselves in the West. And all the major multinational corporations doing business in Africa and plundering our resources are also owned by Westerners.

We have, in a way, abdicated responsibility, have been re-conquered and recolonised; our perpetual dependence on other countries being the most searing indictment against our claim that we are genuinely independent – we have never been! We hate to admit it, but we know it is true. As Julius Nyerere said in one of his farewell speeches not long before he died:

"What sovereignty do you have? Many of these debt-ridden countries in Africa now have no sovereignty, they've lost it. It's in the hands of the IMF and the World Bank."[12]

But that does not mean that Nyerere wanted us to be ruled again by our former colonial masters or by anybody else. He was simply facing reality. And the reality is that we don't have control over our own lives and our own destiny as much as we would like to – if we continue to beg and depend on outsiders for survival and for development. Even if he was the last African on Earth, Nyerere would never have said it would be a good idea for our former colonial masters to come back and rule us again.

That is why he angrily described the IMF as the International Ministry of Finance and asked one famous question which underscored his frustration with this Western-dominated financial institution: "Who elected the

IMF to be the ministry of finance for every country in the world?" Except the big powers, of course, led by the United States, who literally own and control it.

In one of his last interviews not long before he died, Nyerere talked about the arrogance of power the industrialised nations are notorious for, especially in their dealings with us and other people in the rest of the underdeveloped – or developing – countries of the Third World. He had this to say in the interview which was published in the *New Internationalist*, December 1998:

"I was in Washington last year (1997). At the World Bank the first question they asked me was 'how did you fail?'

I responded that we took over a country with 85 per cent of its adult population illiterate. The British ruled us for 43 years. When they left, there were 2 trained engineers and 12 doctors. This is the country we inherited.

When I stepped down there was 91-per-cent literacy and nearly every child was in school. We trained thousands of engineers and doctors and teachers.

In 1988 Tanzania's per-capita income was $280. Now, in 1998, it is $140. So I asked the World Bank people what went wrong. Because for the last ten years Tanzania has been signing on the dotted line and doing everything the IMF and the World Bank wanted. Enrolment in school has plummeted to 63 per cent and conditions in health and other social services have deteriorated. I asked them again: 'what went wrong?'

These people just sat there looking at me. Then they asked what could they do? I told them have some humility. Humility – they are so arrogant!"[13]

Although he conceded the loss of African sovereignty to international financial institutions and other agencies controlled by the industrialised nations, he still believed until his last days that Africa's salvation and survival depends on unity and self-reliance among us more than anything else. As he said in one of his last speeches at the University of Dar Salaam, Tanzania – the speech was more conversational than formal in tone and delivery – attended by African diplomats and others:

"Africa south of the Sahara is fragmented. From the very beginning of independence 40 years ago, we were against that idea, that the continent is so fragmented. We called it the Balkanisation of Africa. Today, I think the Balkans are talking about the Africanisation of Europe. Africa's states are too many, too small, some make no logic, whether political logic or ethnic logic or anything. They are non-viable. It is not a confession....

Throw away all our ideas about socialism. Throw them away, give them away to the Americans, give them to the Japanese, give them, so that they can, I don't know, they can do whatever they like with them. *Embrace* capitalism, fine! But you *have* to be self-reliant....

Africa south of the Sahara is isolated. Therefore, to develop, it will have to depend upon its own resources basically. Internal resources, nationally; and Africa will have to depend upon Africa.

The leadership of the future will have to devise, try to carry out policies of *maximum* national self-reliance and *maximum* collective self-reliance. They have no other choice....

The small countries in Africa must move towards either unity or co-operation, unity of Africa. The leadership of the future, of the 21st century, should have less respect, less respect for this thing called 'national sovereignty.' I'm not saying take up arms and destroy the state, no! This idea that we must *preserve* the Tanganyika, then *preserve* the Kenya as they *are*, is nonsensical! The nation-states we have in Africa, we inherited them from Europe. They are the builders of the nation-states par excellence.

For centuries they fought wars! The history of Europe,

236

the history of the *building* of Europe, is a history of war. And sometimes their wars, when they get hotter although they're European wars, they call them *world wars*. And we all get involved. We fought even in Tanganyika here, we *fought* here, one world war (World War I).

These Europeans, powerful, where little Belgium is more powerful than the whole of Africa south of the Sahara put together; these *powerful* European states are moving towards unity, and you people are talking about the atavism of the tribe, this is nonsense! I am telling *you* people. How can anybody think of the tribe as the unity of the future?....

Europe now, you can take it almost as God-given, Europe is not going to fight with Europe anymore. The Europeans are not going to take up arms against Europeans. They are moving towards unity - even the little, the little countries of the Balkans which are breaking up, Yugoslavia breaking up, but they are breaking up at the same time the building up is taking place. They break up and say we want to come into the *bigger* unity.

So, there's a *building* movement, there's a *building* of Europe. These countries which have old, old sovereignties, countries of hundreds of years old; they are forgetting this, they are *moving* towards unity. And you people, you think Tanzania is sacred? What is Tanzania!

You *have* to move towards unity. If these powerful countries (of Europe) see that they have no future in the nation-states - what future do you think you have?

So, if we can't *move*, if our leadership, our future leadership cannot move us to bigger nation-states, which I *hope* they are going to try; we tried and failed. I tried and failed. One of my biggest failures was actually that. I tried in East Africa and failed. But don't give up because we, the first leadership, failed, no! You try again! We failed, but the idea is a good idea. That these countries should come together. Don't leave Rwanda and Burundi on their own. They cannot survive. They can't. They're locked up into a form of prejudice. If we can't move towards bigger nation-states, at least let's move towards greater co-operation....

I want to say only one or two things about what is happening in southern Africa.

Please accept the logic of coming together....South Africa, and I am talking about post-apartheid South Africa. Post-apartheid South Africa has the most developed and the most dynamic private sector on the continent. It is white, so what? So forget it is white. It is South African, dynamic, highly developed. If the investors of South Africa begin a new form of trekking, you *have* to accept it.

It will be ridiculous, absolutely ridiculous, for Africans to go out seeking investment from North America, from Japan, from Europe, from Russia, and then, when these investors come from South Africa to invest in your own country, you say, 'a! a! These fellows now want to take over our economy' - this is nonsense. You can't have it both ways. You want foreign investors or you don't want foreign investors. Now, the most available foreign investors for you are those from South Africa.

And let me tell you, when Europe think in terms of investing, they *might* go to South Africa. When North America think in terms of investing, they *might* go to South Africa. Even Asia, if they want to invest, the first country they may think of in Africa *may* be South Africa. So, if *your* South Africa is going to be *your* engine of development, accept the reality, accept the reality. Don't accept this sovereignty, South Africa will reduce your sovereignty. What sovereignty do you have?....

West Africa. Another bloc is developing there, but that depends very much upon Nigeria my brother (looking at the Nigerian High Commissioner - Ambassador), very much so. Without Nigeria, the future of West Africa is a problem.

West Africa is more balkanised than Eastern Africa. More balkanised, tiny little states. The leadership will have to come from Nigeria. It came from Nigeria in Liberia; it has come from Nigeria in the case of Sierra Leone; it will have to come from Nigeria in galvanising ECOWAS. But the military in Nigeria must allow the Nigerians to exercise that vitality in freedom. And it is my hope that they will do it."[14]

While Nigeria played a major role in ending civil wars in Liberia and Sierra Leone and in helping restore some kind of stability to these war-torn countries, it has failed to live up to its potential within Nigeria itself.

It is the richest black nation in the world, second only to predominantly black but multiracial South Africa; yet its people are among the poorest because of corruption and waste. As Ken Saro-Wiwa, the Nigerian writer and activist who was hanged by Nigerian putative military dictator Sani Abacha in November 1985, lamented: while other oil-rich countries used their money for development, Nigeria squandered hers, with the leaders enriching themselves.[15]

Although Saro-Wiwa came from Eastern Nigeria, he supported the federal military government during the Nigerian civil war against the secession of Biafra, fearing that the Igbos would dominate his ethnic group, the Ogoni, and seize for themselves the oil coming from Ogoniland.

Yet, he was not optimistic about the future after federal forces won the war and wrote bitterly: "the resources of the Ogoni and other ethnic minorities in the Niger Delta could be more easily purloined while paying lip service to Nigerian federalism and unity."[16] And as he said not long before he died: "My only regret is that I was ever born a minority in Nigeria."[17] His fears were confirmed.

He was afraid that ethnic minorities in the Niger Delta would be ruthlessly exploited by Nigerian leaders and by the oil companies. And that is exactly what happened.

Nigerian leaders have been looting the national treasury for decades. Most of the leaders have come from the country's three main ethnic groups: the Hausa-Fulani, the Igbo, and the Yoruba. But most of the stealing has been done by military rulers and politicians from Northern Nigeria, mostly the Hausa-Fulani who have dominated Nigeria for more than 50 years since independence in 1960 and even after Olusegun Obasanjo, a Yoruba from the south-west, became president in May 1999; and after Goodluck Jonathan from the Niger Delta also became president in May 2010. Most of the nation's wealth flows from oil in the Niger Delta inhabited by minority groups. Yet they get nothing or very little in return.

There has been some development in Nigeria, but hardly any in the areas of the ethnic minorities in the Niger Delta. And it has not benefited the vast majority of the people across the country. Billions of dollars have been stolen and continue to be stolen by the leaders. They are the taproot of the problem and the main cause of the mess Nigeria is in today.

The same applies to other African countries. But Nigeria, like South Africa, also has a unique role to play on the continent because of its wealth and size, and demonstrated ability to do so, however limited.

Both Nigeria and South Africa have the potential to serve as anchors of stability in their respective regions and in the entire sub-Saharan Africa; while North Africa is left to Egypt.

In East Africa, it may be Kenya or Tanzania or both, with an an even greater potential for stability and development if the East African countries including Uganda – as well as Rwanda and Burundi as Nyerere strongly suggested not long before he died – form a federation which has eluded them since the sixties when they talked about establishing one. And in the Horn of Africa, there is Ethiopia as the regional power.

But there is also resentment, especially in the case of Nigeria and South Africa, that the regional powers want to dominate other countries, playing an "imperial" role similar to what the colonial powers did when they dominated the continent.

Therefore, even this kind of "internal colonisation," however benevolent, is deeply resented by the weaker countries in their respective regions.

Resentment is even more bitter in the case of the former colonial powers trying to recolonise Africa, if they indeed were to be determined to re-impose imperial rule on the continent even if not in a brazen way as before and without invitation.

The idea of recolonising Africa is highly inflammatory because it implies that Africans, especially black Africans, are nothing but a bunch of idiots incapable of managing their own affairs. Sadly, it is partly true.

Since independence, African governments have terribly misruled our countries and ruined our economies, turning us, black Africans, not only into international beggars but the laughing-stock of the world. Just as tragic is the fact that it is the same stereotype about Africans as stupid people that was used to justify colonialism and the conquest of Africa.

When Africa was described as "the Dark Continent," the implication was that we also had "dark minds." We were unable to think. We were not creative and innovative as other people were, especially Europeans. Colonialism was a form of enlightenment, not an evil system of subjugation, oppression and exploitation that was imposed on us by our conquerors.

Therefore, recolonisation schemes are either racist or paternalistic or both. Few, if any, are altruistic. And they all provoke furious responses, especially being labelled racist. That was the case when Gordon Frisch, an American geopolitical analyst, wrote an article bluntly stating that it was time to recolonise Africa. The article was, depending on one's judgment, appropriately or inappropriately entitled, "Africa – Staring Into the Abyss: Send in the Mercenaries and Re-Colonize":

"Looking at Africa today, one can't help but think of a

line from Dante's Inferno: 'All hope abandon, ye who enter here!'

AIDS is devastating sub-Saharan Africa on a scale rivaling the worst plagues to ever besiege mankind. Annually, AIDS kills more people in sub-Saharan Africa than all of the continent's wars combined – 2 million in 1999, 85 percent of the world's total AIDS deaths, on top of 13.7 million Africans who've already died of AIDS. 70 percent of the world's HIV-positive people live in sub-Saharan Africa, and most will die in the next 10 years, leaving shattered families and economic devastation in their wake.

AIDS by itself is bad enough. Throw in rotten dictatorships, Marxism, corruption, illiteracy, racism, genocide, tribal and national wars, and the term 'utter hopelessness' is inadequate to describe Black Africa's plight. For years we've counseled investors to avoid sub-Saharan Africa, saying it was headed down a corrupt one-way road to collapse. It's arrived. Black Africa teeters on the edge of a yawning abyss, and at the bottom lies total anarchy and chaos. Many say it can't get much worse. We say: it can and it will.

Twenty years of failed Marxist policies have caught up with President Robert Mugabe. Zimbabwe is in economic and political meltdown due to rampant corruption, Marxism's fatal flaws, 25 percent HIV positive AIDS test rates, runaway inflation, etc. The crowning blow to this once vibrant economy was Mugabe himself; he emptied the treasury at the rate of $1 million per day to support 11,000 troops he sent to support fellow traveler Laurent Kabila, Congo's Marxist leader.

In a last ditch attempt at survival, Mugabe is lambasting every scapegoat on the planet – foreign media, the British government, the IMF, opposition political parties, white Zimbabweans, etc.

But Zimbabwe's white farmers, among Zimbabwe's most valuable assets, are bearing the brunt of Mugabe's misplaced wrath. They own 30 percent of the farmland, produce the bulk of agricultural products, employ 350,000 Blacks, and bring vital export income. Mugabe has sent state-supported thugs to attack white farmers, brutalize their black workers and grab their land 'to right colonial injustices of the past.'

At the end of April, Emmerson Mnangagwa, Zimbabwe's justice (?) minister said: 'Within 10 days the legal framework to take land and redistribute it to the people [without compensation to white owners] will be in place and we will immediately proceed.'

About the same time, an unregistered Ilyushin 76 former Soviet cargo plane arrived in Harare from Marxist Angola carrying a shipment of 21,000 AK-47's for Mugabe. They were promptly distributed to police and land-grabbing squatters. Chenjerai 'Hitler' Hunzvi, Mugabe's farm invasion organizer said: 'All those with British passports must go back to Britain. If they don't, they will go into the ground.'

Mugabe's land-grabbing contagion is spreading more rapidly than AIDS. Fear that South African Blacks could go on a similar rampage has caused the rand to plummet. It doesn't help that South Africa's President Thabo Mbeki recently joined ranks with Mugabe at a trade fair and Nelson Mandela avoids direct criticism of Mugabe. And it seems no one buys the assurances of KGB Joe Slovo's widow, Helena Dolny, that South Africa won't follow Zimbabwe into a black land-grab. Namibian Blacks are now chanting Zimbabwe's land-grab rhetoric.

In North [northeast] Africa, Ethiopia and Eritrea are in a needless, stupid war, fueled by recent Russian arms deliveries to both sides. In West Africa, the UN's feckless peacekeepers got caught in the middle of Sierra Leone's civil war and taken hostage by murderous RUF rebels, led by Foday Sankoh. It's noteworthy that in 1997, mercenaries captured Sankoh and turned him over to Sierra Leone's democratically elected president and peace ensued. Sankoh was saved from certain execution and released last year under terms of a peace process godfathered by none other than Reverend Jesse Jackson and the United States.

We never cease to be appalled at the incredible ignorance and denial displayed by the supposedly "civlized" world toward resolution of Africa's problems. Africa has immense economic potential, but is its own worst enemy and needs help. All the best intentions, trade negotiations, debt forgiveness, and blue helmets, are wasted efforts and ineffective. What is the solution?

Before any political solution can work, law and order, almost totally lacking in sub-Saharan Africa, must prevail. To accomplish this, as history has proven time and again in Africa, the most effective means is by the use of mercenaries. Neither the UN nor 'civilized' governments have the mandate or the will to do the job.

Once peace has been 'made,' then perhaps the UN could participate in 'keeping' it. Then, African governments should invite former colonists back as partners in running their countries, developing their economies and educating their people. The 'politically correct' hacks of the world will bristle at these proposals, but millions of Africans are dying while the 'politically correct' civilized world looks on in ignorant smugness. When all ivory tower theories fail, try something that has proved workable."[18]

Hysterical hyperbole aside, such as the outlandish claim that land-grabbing by black Africans is spreading faster than AIDS, this highly inflammatory article still raises fundamental questions and underscores the need to come up with practical solutions to Africa's plight *now*.

The author also makes another hyperbolic statement that Africa's plight will definitely get worse, implying that nothing can be done about it by the Africans themselves short of external or divine intervention; a loaded statement indeed whose racial implications can be easily understood even by some of the most hopeless mental weaklings across the racial divide.

None of this, however, can change the fact that Africa is indeed in a mess because of the failure of the Africans themselves to deal with it and help themselves as other people do. And the fact that such articles are written at all, about Africa's predicament, and in such a tone, clearly demonstrates the gravity and magnitude of the continent's misery and suffering and the utter futility in trying to solve these perennial problems the way African leaders have tried to do, if at all, since independence. The biggest failure has been in the economic arena.

Socialism proved to be a disastrous failure in many areas even in my home country, Tanzania, despite some successes – especially in the provision of social services including free education and free medical services, in the establishment of light industries for the manufacture of import-substitution items such as textiles, in food processing and so on – under the leadership of President Julius Nyerere.

The expulsion of non-indigenous Africans such as Ugandans of Asian origin – not just non-citizens who had British passports – by Idi Amin from Uganda, and of Zimbabweans of British origin from Zimbabwe which President Robert Mugabe tried to justifying by publicly stating that "Europeans are not indigenous to Africa," has only compounded the problem.

Yet, other Africans have either applauded these leaders or simply looked the other way; although there is definitely a need to address the land question in Zimbabwe, South Africa, Namibia and other parts of the continent, but in an orderly way; nor will Africa's problems be solved by anti-foreign sentiments or hostility towards anyone who is considered to be an outsider and therefore "does not belong here."

Hostility towards Africans of Asian origin in Kenya,

and even in Tanzania although to a smaller degree, through the years has also forced a large number of them to leave the only countries they have always known as home.

Even among the indigenous tribes themselves, there is intense hostility towards each other in many countries across the continent, leading to ethnic conflicts, political instability, chaos, and retarded economic growth as many leaders fan the flames of tribal hatred to perpetuate themselves in power and favour members of their own tribes.

That is just the tip of the iceberg of Africa's myriad problems.

Non-Africans who boldly suggest that Africa should be recolonised to end its misery are automatically denounced as racist. And Africans who do so commit the unpardonable sin of being traitors. Yet, both raise the same fundamental issue: African governments have failed to solve the continent's problems and millions of our people continue to suffer and die as a result of such incompetence and utter neglect.

Compared to our former colonial masters, African leaders have not only been a total failure but a disaster. Therefore our former masters should come back and rule us again. Colonial rulers were bad, but our leaders are worse, much worse. That is the argument made by some people who risk the danger of being ostracised and even of being lynched as traitors but who, out of desperation, see it as the only solution to their miserable condition.

Many people dismissed the article by Gordon Frisch as racist. But there were others who saw it as a blunt assessment of Africa's harsh reality and not as racist filth spewed by someone who hates black people and Africa. In response to his critics, Frisch had this to say:

"I have lived internationally for many years, on several continents, including Africa. I met and developed many friendships in all those places, including Blacks....Many remain good friends to this day and it has never occurred to me to differentiate between them on the basis of race....

The article I wrote on Recolonizing Africa derived its inspiration from several directions. Yes, I saw Frederick Forsythe's article having a similar theme, and I mostly agreed with it.

Also, a few years ago I spent a few hours - off the record - talking with two Black Africans, who had quite lofty positions with the UN in Geneva. They had PhD's, were highly educated, and they were greatly concerned about the future of sub-Saharan Africa. One was from the Ivory Coast, the other from Nigeria, and we had a totally frank talk about the mess that is Black Africa.

Astoundingly, and with no prompting from me, they said sub-Saharan Africa's only hope was a return of colonialism in some form. We all agreed that apartheid-like attitudes should never play any part in any recolonization. But there were many good aspects to the era of colonization in Africa, I saw it firsthand when I worked there. The positive aspects should be welcomed and encouraged, the negative discouraged and prohibited, simple as that.

Most of my views and inspiration for the article were derived from personal experience. I lived in Africa for a number of years and worked with Black, White and Arab Africans on a daily basis. My firsthand observations led me to suggest recolonization as a possible constructive solution to sub-Saharan Africa's problems. I was directly involved in training Blacks in Africa and there is no question that most are extremely eager and willing to learn and work. They just need the opportunity and they are not receiving it under the utterly corrupt leadership they must endure. Their own leaders are their downfall. This is not racism, this is fact, it couldn't matter less what color the leaders are. There are similar faults in White-ruled countries too, it's just that it's worst in Africa. The reasons are bound up in Marxism, corruption, nepotism, etc., the many things we talk about on a daily basis.

There is much negativism in today's world against multi-national corporations, and some of the criticism is indeed well-founded. But the flip side is that multi-national corporations also probably offer the last best hope many Third World countries have to conquer poverty, disease and corruption. Multi-nationals bring money, expertise, opportunity, jobs and build infrastructures. No alphabet agency in the world - IMF, World Bank, UN - can offer a fraction as much....

I certainly left a part of my soul in Africa. It is a wonderful continent with many wonderful people and I have mostly very fond memories of it. Regrettably, it is deteriorating beyond anything imaginable and I am immensely saddened to see it. I do what I can to help the situation, through talks, articles, correspondence, etc. But until Africa gets its politics sorted out, no amount of external help will accomplish anything significant."[19]

It may be easy to dismiss the author of the article as a racist in disguise, at best, even if he's not a racist at all. But it is not easy to dismiss as fiction the facts he presents; facts which are shared by millions of Africans themselves who know the harsh reality of our continent as a miserable place even if it's not necessarily living hell on Earth. There are pockets of tranquility and stability, even prosperity, across the continent, but not many. For tens of millions, it is utter destitution.

Dismissing all these people as liars is a tough proposition. And it defies common sense.

Africa's utter desperation assumes another dimension when some of the African leaders themselves including diplomats, even if grudgingly and privately, concede the imperative need for the restoration of the imperial order under the Union Jack, the Tricolore, or whatever, in one benign form or another, as the only hope of salvation for Africa with no other practical solution to the continent's plight in sight. Some have bluntly said so, even in public, especially in the most traumatised countries.

Sierra Leone provides a classic example of such national trauma which has compelled many people in that country to remember with nostalgia "the good ol' days" of imperial rule and wish the British had never left.

One of them was the country's prime minister himself, of all people, who publicly and in front of news reporters suggested, without blinking an eye, that Sierra Leone should return to the status quo ante and become a part of the British imperial order; for all practical purposes assume the status of a colony or a protectorate and may be even become an integral part of Britain itself.

Such is the desperation that pervades the land, however dim the prospects of integration with the former colonial power. But even the utter futility of such a dream could not constrain the honourable prime minister from making the bold assertion that Sierra Leone was better and safer during colonial rule and should indeed become a part of Britain:

"There was a vivid moment a couple of years ago during the first stage of the British intervention to support the struggling government of Sierra Leone.

Its prime minister asked a visiting British politician, in the presence of journalists, if it might be possible for his country to become part of the British Empire again. Most of those present believed the Sierra Leonese leader was serious.

The problems of African societies are so huge, so deep-rooted, that the few honest and decent politicians despair. They grasp at any straw to rescue their countries."[20]

In a very tragic way, Sierra Leone is Africa, and Africa is Sierra Leone; so is Somalia, Congo-Brazzaville, Chad, the Central African Republic, Kenya, and Angola; and so is Rwanda, Burundi, Congo-Kinshasa – the so-called

Democratic Republic of Congo, Nigeria, Ivory Coast, Zimbabwe, and South Sudan.

Each of them, at one time or another, has been or still is a microcosm of what Africa has failed to be. The words of President Henri Konan Bedie of Ivory Coast, although meant to convey exactly the opposite message, are appropriate in this context:

"For the image of Africa, the omnipresent media coverage of violence carries risks.

The danger, in effect, is that Congo, like Zaire before it, will appear as a condensed representation of Africa, and that by optical illusion, the image of one destabilized subregion replaces the image of an entire continent, which is come to be seen as bloody and burning."[21]

We may object to generalisation, as President Bedie does. We can point out the fact that Africa is a continent of 54 countries. All of them have not collapsed. And all of them are not burning and bleeding. All that is true. But it is also true that several of them *are* burning and bleeding. And many others are in imminent danger of collapse because of corruption, tyranny, tribalism, nepotism, waste, mismanagement, institutional decay, wrong policies and outright incompetence.

President Henri Konan Bedie himself was overthrown in December 1999 because of the despotic nature of his regime and discrimination against northerners and Muslims, stripping some of them of their citizenship in a xenophobic campaign that threatened to plunge the country into chaos.

One of the victims of this vicious campaign was Alasane Ouattara, the most prominent northern politician and former prime minister under the country's first president, Felix Houphouet-Boigny, who ruled the country for 33 years since independence in 1960. He died in December 1993.

A Muslim and born in the Ivory Coast, Ouattara was barred from running for president in the 2000 general election on dubious grounds that he was not a citizen because his father supposedly came from neighbouring Burkina Faso. It didn't matter that the former prime minister was born in Ivory Coast and had all along been accepted as a citizen just like the rest of his fellow countrymen, until President Henri Konan Bedie launched a xenophobic campaign against northerners, the vast majority of whom are Muslim.

Discrimination by southern Christians, who have dominated the government in the Ivory Coast since independence, against northern Muslim ethnic groups was one of the main causes of the civil war which erupted towards the end of 2002 and almost destroyed the country. It split the country in half, north against south, and claimed thousands of lives in only four months. The conflict continued in 2003 and beyond in varying degrees.

Yet, Ivory Coast was one of the most stable countries on the entire continent. It was also one of the most prosperous. It had the most dynamic and vibrant economy in West Africa, attracting tens of thousands of workers from all the countries in the region including Nigeria, the continent's giant and one of its richest.

But in only three months, it was almost consumed in a conflagration of ethnic and religious hatred that could have been avoided had President Laurent Gbagbo, a former history professor, had used just a little common sense to treat all Ivorians as equal citizens and upheld democratic rights; instead of pursuing xenophobic policies against northerners which pushed the country to the brink of disaster.

He won a rigged election in 2000, with less than 50 per cent of the vote and therefore had no mandate to rule. France, the former colonial power, intervened and averted a catastrophe. The government in Paris sent troops to help the Ivorian army in its campaign against the rebels –

mostly northerners – despite the claim that they would play a neutral role as observers to oversee the implementation of a shaky peace accord signed by the two sides.

Sierra Leone was not so lucky. Britain, the former colonial power, did not intervene early to neutralise the rebels of the Revolutionary United Front (RUF) who plunged the country into anarchy.

But it was also in Sierra Leone where the script was being written – of the unfolding drama in the quest for a renewed imperial role by the former colonial powers to restore peace and stability, and good governance, in their former colonies in Africa.

Britain did just that in Sierra Leone, setting a precedent, as much as Sierra Leone itself also set a precedent other African countries may follow in seeking salvation from their former imperial masters through partial renunciation of their sovereignty; if the former colonial rulers and technocrats from other industrialised nations assume an increasingly prominent role in running the economies and the civil services of the countries in sub-Saharan Africa as a mandatory condition for aid. Otherwise they get nothing.

It's tough love corrupt African leaders and bureaucrats hate. But they must accept it if our countries continue to depend on foreign aid just to survive, let alone thrive.

Now, the question is whether or not the former colonial powers really want to play such a role if they are invited, given the kind of mess Africa is in today. As Charles Onyango-Obbo, managing editor of the Ugandan daily *Monitor*, stated in the weekly *East African*:

"I have a friend who has given up on the Kampala government. Nothing new there. What is striking are the reasons for his despair.

He says he can understand why the Uganda government is so corrupt. What he can't comprehend is that it lacks even the vision of a 'good' corrupt government, because it is not doing anything to help people produce more and create more wealth so that it has something more to steal tomorrow.

Last week in London, I encountered this same despair in several reports in the British press on the murderous rebellion in Sierra Leone. These reports quoted local people begging the British to return and recolonise the country.

It was for the usual reasons. Unlike the British colonialists, past and present Sierra Leonean leaders and rebels had raped the wealth of the country and put nothing back. In between bouts of looting, they passed the time chopping off the hands and legs of the people they had robbed.

The British rulers at their worst as colonialists were still better than past and present Sierra Leonean rulers at their best, some people reasoned, obviously driven to that extreme position by desperation.

The fact that Britain sent troops who salvaged the beleaguered UN peacekeeping operation in Sierra Leone – and in the bargain organised the rag-tag bands that passed for the government army and its allied militia into a force which rolled back the advances of the dreaded RUF rebels on the capital, Freetown – helped British reputations quite a bit too.

One can understand where some of that nostalgia was coming from, since the British were once overlords in Sierra Leone. However, across the Atlantic in the US, I encountered similar arguments.

Last Wednesday (May 31, 2000), in an opinion piece carried by *The Wall Street Journal*, the marvellously acerbic George B.N. Ayittey argued for making Sierra Leone a UN colony. The only effective long-term solution to what he called the 'disaster in Sierra Leone,' he argued, 'is to declare a UN trusteeship or protectorate over [it], just as a bankrupt company is placed in receivership. Like

Somalia, Sierra Leone is a failed state, its government hijacked long ago by gangsters.'

However, all is not lost. Striking a more positive note, *The Washington Post* on the same day, in an editorial entitled 'Africa's Hidden Hope,' began by noting the problems.

Whereas malaria has been defeated in many parts of the world, in Africa it has increased by around 60 per cent in the past 30 years. Because conditions are so bad, they discourage investment, and so up to 20,000 African professionals leave the continent every year in search of greener pastures in the West. About 250 million Africans live on less than $1 a day, and more than two million of the continent's children die before their first birthday each year.

The Post nevertheless found hope in a new World Bank report, which notes that since the early 1990s, 42 of the 48 sub-Saharan states have held multiparty presidential and parliamentary elections. Growth averaged 4 per cent in the second half of the 1990s, compared with slightly higher than 2 per cent for 1981 – 94.

These numbers are, of course, meaningless in most of Africa, because they are cooked up. *The Post* found the usual suspect, Botswana – which, it opined, had 'shown that remarkable success is possible; Botswana's economy is among the fastest-growing in the world.'

So, will an Africa broken by suffering and all manner of miseries submit to colonialism? I have my doubts.

Even if it did, the reason Africans can be sure that they will continue to be the rulers of the continent, and have the freedom to fight wars and starve their people, is that I doubt that any of the old European colonial powers or USA, would actually want to run the place the way it is today. Our curse, in that sense, is also our saviour."[22]

Our saviour is also our curse. As we continue to run the place the way it is today as a dilapidated, mangled continent under inept leadership, because our former colonial masters don't want to come back to rule us again, we also continue to descend into the bottomless pit unless we rescue ourselves with good leadership.

That is where the problem lies: bad, incompetent, rotten leadership we have endured in most countries across the continent since independence.

Although it is a blessing in disguise that most of Africa is a ruined place and has therefore scared even some of the most daring former colonial masters and adventurers away from us and from even thinking about recolonising the continent, thus sparing us the agony and humiliation of imperial domination once again; nothing, absolutely nothing, is going to stop millions of desperate Africans from remembering with nostalgia "the good ol' days" of colonial rule when there was at least law and oder, peace and stability, without which life becomes living hell on Earth.

They wish happy days were here again. Those were the days, the halcyon days, when the imperial flag fluttered under the African sun. I remember the Union Jack when I was growing up in colonial Tanganyika in the fifties – I was under ten years old then – but can hardly recall those "good ol' days," if they indeed were. Although I was too young to know everything, I do remember that colonial rule was a system of racial inequality.

I have even written about it in some of my books, *Life in Tanganyika in The Fifties, Tanzania under Mwalimu Nyerere: Reflections on an African Statesman*, and *My Life as an African: Autobiographical Writings*. As I have stated in *Tanzana under Mwalimu Nyerere*:

"It's very interesting to know how the European settlers felt about their new life in the colonies they had established under the tropical sun far away from Europe. In spite of the difficulties they faced living in underdeveloped regions of the world, they were still very much satisfied with their new life. That is why they did not want to leave or relinquish power to Africans until they were forced to do so. In fact, life couldn't have been better, since many of our colonial masters would not have been able to get in their own countries – in Britain and elsewhere in Europe – the kind of jobs they had in colonial Africa. Since I focus on Tanganyika in this chapter, the examples I cite come from East Africa to illustrate my point. As Erika Johnson, writing about the 1950s in colonial Tanganyika, stated in *The Other Side of Kilimanjaro*:

'Robin [Robin Johnson was a District Commissioner, simply known as D.C. throughout British colonial Africa] maintains that there was no better life for a man in those days than that of a District Commissioner. It was a marvellous combination of an active open air life, coupled with a wide, varied and interesting amount of office work. You did long walking safaris through your area and slept under canvas, and in this way you got to know your parishioners and their problems.

Responsible for a vast area, you were father, mentor and disciplinarian to everyone, sorting out family and tribal disputes. You had to do anything and everything: build roads, dams and bridges, dig wells and be a magistrate and administrator of law and order. Your problems could vary from shooting a rogue elephant despoiling villagers' crops to trying a stock thief in court.

In later years, [Julius] Nyerere once said to a silent Robin that the D.C's had made little contribution other than collecting taxes!'

The colonial rulers did, of course, have a tendency to exaggerate their own importance because of their condescending and paternalistic attitude towards Africans, called 'natives,' a derogatory term as it was always used in this context. For example, it is obvious who built the roads, dams and bridges, and who dug the water wells: Africans. Yet Robin Johnson, typical of the clonialists' attitude, claims credit for all that without even mentioning the African labourers who did all the hard work; what the colonialists called 'dirty work' since it was beneath them to soil their hands or stoop to scoop up soil or make bricks or do whatever was required to be done. That is what prompted Nyerere to say they did nothing except collect taxes. And all that money, collected from the 'natives,' went to the colonial masters. Hardly any was used to help Africans, the very same people who worked so hard and paid taxes to maintain the colonial system that was oppressing and exploiting them.

In fact, I personally remember seeing African men doing 'dirty,' hard work, building roads, in the town and on the outskirts of Mbeya and also working on the road from Mbeya to Chunya, a district north of Mbeya; and in Rungwe District working on the road from Tukuyu to Kyela, 30 miles south of Tukuyu close to the Tanganyika-Nyasaland (now Malawi) border, when I was a little boy under 10 in the 1950s. They worked for the colonial Public Works Department, what was simply known as PWD, and rode in the back of Bedford lorries; they were British lorries imported from Britain. The lorries also were simply called PWD. I even remember their colour. They were painted green on the sides and white on top. The African laborers worked hard, all day long, often in scorching sun, for a mere pittance.

That was in the Southern Highlands Province. The province was under a British provincial commissioner called P.C. The town of Mbeya was the provincial capital where my parents and I, together with my siblings, lived in the early and mid-fifties before we moved to Rungwe District about four miles south of the town of Tukuyu. The town of Tukuyu is the district headquarters of Rungwe and is 45 miles south of Mbeya.

During those days of colonial rule, Tanganyika was

divided into seven provinces: The Southern Highlands Province, the Southern Province, the Central Province, the Western Province, the Lake Province, the Coast Province, and the Northern Province.

After independence, the Southern Highlands was divided into Mbeya Region and Iringa Region; so were the rest, also broken down into smaller regional administrative units. All were formally proclaimed as regions on 1 May 1963; coincidentally in the same month the Organisation of African Unity (OAU) was formed in Addis Ababa, Ethiopia. The OAU was formally established on May 25th.

Life was good for the colonial rulers. I also remember British men and women playing golf and tennis in Tukuyu. They used to give us tennis balls now and then when we passed through the golf course. Many of them came from Mbeya and even from neighboring Northern Rhodesia, now Zambia.

I was too young then to know what was going on in terms of colonial domination or what it meant to be ruled by the British or Europeans in general. But I do remember that whenever we saw them, they seemed to be very happy and satisfied with their lives which were made much easier by African servants in almost every European household. It was unthinkable not to have one since they all could afford to pay a pittance to the 'native' servants. And remember, Africans had no say in those days in our own countries. They could not go against our colonial masters until they started to mobilise forces to campaign for independence.

That was the last thing the colonialists wanted to see since they were not ready to give up power. They did everything they could to delay independence or stifle nationalist aspirations. In Tanganyika, the British settlers formed the United Tanganyika Party, known as UTP, to stem the nationalist tide that started to sweep across the country during the same time when British colonial rulers such as Robin Johnson felt that they were doing a wonderful job to help Africans while they were really helping themselves and enjoying themselves in the tropical climate.

One of the areas in which British settlers in East Africa became deeply involved was commercial farming. It happens that for us in East Africa, our blessing has also been our curse. East Africa is endowed with an abundance of fertile land, much of it at high altitude with a cooler climate, although still tropical. But it somewhat reminded the Europeans of the temperate climate back home in Europe, at temperatures they were comfortable with.

Much of East Africa is, of course, also hot, in fact very hot; for example along the coast, in the lowlands and in other parts of the region. But it also has more arable land, at higher altitudes, than West Africa does. For example, in an area where I come from called Kyimbila, there is a large tea estate called Kyimbila Tea Estate stretching for miles. We also grow a lot of coffee in our district.

It is one of the largest tea estates in Tanzania, indeed in the whole of East Africa, and was originally established by the Germans. In fact, there was a German settlement at Kyimbila, about a mile and a half from our house, when the Germans ruled Tanganyika as German East Africa (Deutsch-Ostafrika), and built a large church there, called Kyimbila Moravian Church. There is also a large grave yard at Kyimbila where Germans are buried. I remember reading the headstones showing the deceased were born in the 1800s; they were born in Germany. After the Germans lost World War I, the British took over the tea estate and continued to reap benefits, as the Germans had done before them, using cheap African labour.

When the British ran the tea estate when I was growing up, they always had a British manager who lived on the premises. I also remember vividly one tragic incident that happened in 1956 when I was in standard one, what Americans call the first grade. I was six years old then, and my schoolmates and I used to take a short-cut, walking past the manager's residence, going to Kyimbila Primary School about two miles from our house. I was the youngest in the group.

Everyday we went by, his dogs, a German shephered and a Dalmatian, used to bark at us. They were not always tied, or chained, so quite often they used to chase us before being called back by their master or by his African servant who washed clothes and cooked for the British couple and cleaned up the house. He wasn't very friendly, either, with us, anymore than his master and wife were; typical of the attitude of a 'house nigger' fawning and crawling before his master: 'Yes, boss; whatever you say, mister white man. You are the boss. Yes, Sir!' That kind of talk and attitude.

One morning on our way to school, both dogs were loose and they started chasing us. Although I was a fast runner, in fact a sprinter even at my tender age, my friends outran me that day. As the dogs kept on chasing us, I turned and looked back and knew I was not going to make it. So I dove under the tea shrubs, to my right, to take cover. The German shepherd went past me and kept on chasing the other children. But the Dalmatian saw me where I was hiding and came right under the bush and bit me on my right knee. I still bear a large scar on my knee almost 60 years later, a bitter reminder of the little regard our European conquerors had for us, even children.

The British manager of the tea plantation, and his wife, knew full well that school children went by their house every morning on the way to school, and every evening on their way home from school. But they didn't care to have their dogs tied or chained simply because we were black children. Had we been white kids, the story, and the outcome, would have been entirely different.

And nothing could be done about it. We were still under colonial rule, as British colonial subjects. We were not even citizens, in terms of rights, even in our own country since it was owned by our colonial masters, as *their* colony, and not by us. Therefore we had no rights, none whatsoever, a white person was bound to respect. We complained about it, but our teachers and our parents couldn't do anything about it.

At such a young age, we didn't know the British couple deliberately turned the dogs loose on us simply because we were African and black. It was not until years later when I was a teenager that I realised why this happened to us, and why I almost lost my leg, and my life, on that day and came perilously closing to meeting the same fate on many other occasions when were being chased by the dogs.

Our subordinate position as a conquered people was demonstrated on another occasion, and again in a very personal way, when my father was told by the British manager of a Shell BP petrol station in the town of Tukuyu that he could not put his lunch on the table used by the manager; it was *chapati* my mother made for him on that day. I remember that very well.

My father was very bitter about the incident and told us what happened when he came back home that evening. That was around 1958 or 1959. My father, having secondary school education, was one of the few people in the area who knew English and was hired as the assistant manager at the petrol station. He went to Malangali Secondary School in Iringa District in the Southern Highlands Province, one of the best schools in colonial Tanganyika and even after independence. He was also appointed head prefect at the school, by the headmaster, to discipline fellow students.

Earlier, he had worked as a medical assistant in many parts of Tanganyika – in Muheza, Tanga, Handeni, Amani, Kilosa, Morogoro – including the town of Kigoma, in western Tanganyika, where I was born on 4 October 1949, before returning to our home district of Rungwe from Mbeya in the mid-1950s. He was trained as a medical assistant in the mid-1940s at Muhimbili National Hospital in Dar es Salaam during British colonial rule; it was then known as Sewa Haji Hospital and was renamed Princess Margaret Hospital in 1956, the same year Princess Margaret visited our country. She came in October. She also visited Mbeya, among other places. I also wrote about her visit in my book, *Life in Tanganyika in The Fifties*.

The hospital was renamed Muhimbili after independence.

My father excelled in school and was supposed to go to Tabora Secondary School for further education in standard 11 and standard 12 after completing standard 10 at Malangali Secondary School but couldn't go any further because of family obligations, forcing him to seek employment early.

One of his classmates at Muhimbili National Hospital was Austin Shaba who, after completing his studies, went to Tukuyu to work as a medical assistant. He later became minister of local government in the first independence cabinet under Prime minister – later President – Nyerere. I remember my father saying Austin Shaba – they knew each other well – encouraged him to go into politics but he refused to do so. Both, like other Africans in Tanganyika, had been subjected to indignities of colour bar – another term for racial discrimination here in East and southern Africa – which probably played a major role in encouraging people like Austin Shaba to go into politics and campaign for independence.

Another classmate of my father at Malangali Secondary School who also went into politics was Jeremiah Kasambala. A son of a chief, he also became a cabinet member under Nyerere and served as minister of agriculture and cooperatives in the first independence cabinet. He came from Rungwe District, like my parents did, and he and my father had known each other for years. He also encouraged my father to pursue a career in politics but, again, he refused to do so.

Considering my father's experience with the British

colonial rulers and the indignities he was subjected to, such as the incident at the Shell BP petrol station in Tukuyu in the late fifties, it is a miracle he did not go into politics right away. But that was not his calling.

Still, those are the kind of incidents, and insults, which turn people into militants and revolutionaries, as would have the dog incident in my case had I been a grown-up when I was bitten by that Dalmatian back in 1956. Had there been a Mau Mau in Tanganyika, I definitely would have supported it, fully, at the very least." – (Godfrey Mwakikagile, *Tanzania under Mwalimu Nyerere: Reflections on an African Statesman*, Second Edition, Pretoria, South Africa, Dar es Salaam, Tanzania: New Africa Press, 2006, pp. 11 – 18).

There were vestiges of racial segregation – colour bar – even after we won independence. I remember when I was a teenager, there were still signs on toilets and other facilities including hotels in the town of Mbeya, clearly showing racial distinctions. Whoever was responsible was slow in taking them down.

But we definitely could not use some of those facilities during colonial rule. They were marked, "Europeans," "Asians," and "Africans." Ours were the worst. Arabs who did not neatly fit into any of the three racial categories used facilities marked, "Asians."

I remember one sign very well. It was at the bus station in Mbeya. It was on the toilet we used, marked "Africans," exclusively for blacks.

There were even those who deliberately wanted to maintain racial segregation after we won independence. Andrew Nyerere, President Nyerere's eldest son who was once my schoolmate (1960 – 1970) in the nation's capital Dar es Salaam, told me about an incident at a hotel in the city which infuriated the leaders of the newly independent nation because of the blatant racism practised by the hotel owner. I was in touch with Andrew years later when I was writing a book about his father and Africa as a whole entitled *Nyerere and Africa: End of an Era*. He stated the following:

"As you remember, Sheikh Amri Abeid was the first mayor of Dar es Salaam. Soon after independence, the mayor went to Palm Beach Hotel (near our high school, Tambaza, in Upanga). There was a sign at the hotel which clearly stated: 'No Africans and dogs allowed inside.' He was blocked from entering the hotel, and said in protest, 'But I am the Mayor.' Still he was told, 'You will not get in.' Shortly thereafter, the owner of the hotel was given 48 hours to leave the country. When the nationalization exercise began, that hotel was the first to be nationalized." – (Andrew Nyerere, in Godfrey Mwakikagile, *Nyerere and Africa: End of an Era*, Fifth Edition, Pretoria, South Africa: New Africa Press, 2010, p. 499).

We won independence on 9 December 1961. Years earlier in 1953, Andrew's father, Julius Nyerere, who in the following year was elected president of the Tanganyika African National Union (TANU), the party which led the struggle for independence, had a similar experience at another hotel in Dar es salaam. As Colin Legum, a South African writer and journalist, stated:

"I was privileged to meet Nyerere while he was still a young teacher in short trousers at the very beginning of his political career, and to engage in private conversations with him since the early 1950s.
My very first encounter in 1953 taught me something about his calm authority in the face of racism in colonial Tanganyika. I had arranged a meeting with four leaders of the nascent nationalist movement at the Old Africa Hotel in Dar es Salaam. We sat at a table on the pavement and ordered five beers, but before we could lift our glasses an African waiter rushed up and whipped away all the glasses

264

except mine.

I rose to protest to the white manager, but Nyerere restrained me. 'I am glad it happened,' he said, 'now you can go and tell your friend Sir Edward Twining [the governor at the time] how things are in this country.' His manner was light and amusing, with no hint of anger." – (Colin Legum, in Colin Legum and Geoffrey Mmari, eds., *Mwalimu: The Influence of Nyerere*,Trenton, New Jersey: Africa World Press, 1995, p. 187).

Therefore, colonial rule was not good for us. As Walter Rodney stated in his book *How Europe Underdeveloped Africa*:

"The only positive development in colonialism was when it ended." – (Walter Rodney, *How Europe Underdeveloped Africa*, Dar es Salaam, Tanzania: Tanzania Publishing House, 1973, p. 414).

But it *does* provide a contrast to the deterioration across the spectrum – poor living conditions, lack of security, law and order, rampant corruption, low quality of education and medical care, infrastructural decay including bad roads and bridges and so on – that has taken place in African countries since independence under own own leaders, not under foreign rulers. Older people, especially, remember those days and see the contrast. It is glaring.

But while a significant number of Africans continue to plead, beg, and even pray for the return of our former colonial masters to restore the imperial order, thousands of others are fleeing in the opposite direction, away from Africa, to Europe, to America, and to other parts of the world in search of better life. They are saying, "Any place but here."

They even flee to other Third World countries which themselves are not much better off than we are. That is how desperate our people are. You find them in Asia. You find them in Latin America and elsewhere. And they are all over Europe, of course.

They risk their lives to go to places where they are not even welcome – because things are so bad in Africa.

They even vote with their feet, risking their lives walking for one year across the Sahara desert under scorching sun, sailing in overcrowded rickety boats from West Africa to the Canary Islands in the Atlantic Ocean, and swimming across the Mediterranean Sea to get to Europe; which to them is paradise on Earth after leaving "hell" that Africa has become. They include pregnant women as well as children accompanying their parents and relatives.

Millions, not just thousands or tens of thousands, have already left Africa for good, no apologies.

Countless have perished at sea in their desperate attempt to seek better life elsewhere. Here is one tragic example: Bodies of some West Africans who died in the Atlantic Ocean were found as far away as Barbados, washed ashore, about 3,000 miles away from the coast of Senegal:

"The white ghost ship rolled in the Atlantic swell as the rescue boats approached it 70 nautical miles off Ragged Point, one of the most easterly places on the Caribbean island of Barbados.

The yacht was unmarked, 6 metres (20ft) long, and when Barbadian coastguard officers boarded it, they made a gruesome find. The boat's phantom crew was made up of the desiccated corpses of 11 young men, huddled in two separate piles in the small cabin. Dressed in shorts and colourful jerseys, they had been partially petrified by the salt water, sun and sea breezes of the Atlantic Ocean. They appeared to have come from far away.

The sea-battered yacht, identified by one local ship's captain as of French design, was towed into the port at

266

Willoughy Fort, Bridgetown, and the bodies, by now wrapped in plastic bags, were heaved on to the quay.

In a part of the world where legends and myths have often been furnished by the sea, the mystery of the dead men soon provoked curious speculation.

An air ticket from Senegal Airlines and a tragic note written by one of the men as he was preparing to die have, however, helped investigators from several countries set about unravelling the mystery.

For, although the floating coffin appeared off the coast of the Americas, those on board had set off four months earlier from the Cape Verde islands, off the African coast, and had been heading for the European soil of the Canary Islands.

The evidence reportedly points to them having been cut adrift in the Atlantic and left to drift off to a slow, painful end. Barbados police have said the cause of the deaths was starvation and dehydration.

'Please excuse me'

'I would like to send to my family in Bassada [a town in the interior of Senegal] a sum of money. Please excuse me and goodbye. This is the end of my life in this big Moroccan sea,' the note said, according to a Barbados paper, the *Daily Nation*.

Relatives of those aboard have been contacting the Barbadian authorities from as far afield as Senegal, Spain and Portugal. They have added pieces to the puzzle – based on telephone calls with relatives before they boarded, and with people who stayed in contact with the boat during the first stage of the voyage.

The story of the 11 dead and some 40 other would-be immigrants from Guinea Bissau, Senegal and Gambia starts on Christmas Day last year at Praia, a port in the former Portuguese colony of Cape Verde. There, for €1,300 (£890) each, they were promised a trip to the

Canary Islands by a mysterious Spaniard.

Their boat was to be a motorised yacht, recently repaired but bearing no name and no flag. They paid to make the voyage, assuming that the Spaniard – a mechanic based in the Canaries – would be skippering the boat. At the last moment, however, a Senegalese man took over and the Spaniard disappeared. Several then refused to make the journey. One, according to the *El Pais* newspaper yesterday, jumped from the yacht as it set sail. It is by no means clear what happened next.

Somewhere near the Mauritanian port of Nouadhibou the yacht ran into trouble. Another boat was sent to its aid, apparently after the skipper had contacted the Spaniard. The yacht was towed but, at some stage, the line was severed. *El Pais* reported that it had been hacked with a machete. With no fuel left and food and water running out, the migrants' fate was left in the hands of the sea, the weather, and luck. The latter soon ran out.

The yacht drifted into the stormy Atlantic and, it is assumed, people were tossed or washed overboard as they died.

The 11 last survivors, huddled together against the elements, were reported to have died by the end of January. At that stage their yacht became a ghost ship, battered by storms or winds until it appeared, 2,800 miles away, on the other side of the Atlantic. A Barbados fishing boat was the first to sight it on April 29, 135 days after it had set sail. The coastguard vessel HMBS Trident was sent to discover its awful secrets.

Anxious phone calls from relatives to the *Daily Nation* have turned up some of the names of those on the boat. They include a Gambian, Bouba Cisse, whose cousin Abdou Karime, now in Portugal, saw the case reported on TV. 'We've been watching it [the story of the 11 bodies found] on Spanish TV and a lot of family members I know would have wished for the bodies discovered to be returned to our country,' he told the newspaper.

268

Immigrant route

The 11 bodies now in a Barbados morgue, along with those presumed dead, add to a growing death toll on the newest immigrant route into Europe from Africa.

This route, from the west African coast to Cape Verde, opened up late last year. By March Spanish authorities claimed more than 1,000 had drowned.

That has not stopped the flow. Three vessels carrying 188 African migrants reached Tenerife yesterday. The number of immigrants to have reached the Canaries this year is close to 7,000.

Interpol, meanwhile, has asked police around the world to locate the mysterious Spaniard who took some €50,000 from the immigrants before they sailed to their death.

Last letter

'I am from Senegal but have been living in Cape Verde for a year. Things are bad. I don't think I will come out of this alive. I need whoever finds me to send this money to my family. Please telephone my friend Ibrahima Drame.

Signed Diaw Sounkar Diemi.'

***El Pais*'s account of note found on boat**." – (Giles Tremlett in Madrid, "After Four Months at Sea, Ghost Ship with 11 Petrified Corpses Washes Up in Barbados," *The Guardian*, London, Sunday 28 May 2006).

Yet, in spite of all the mess that Africa finds itself in, for which Africans themselves, especially the leaders, are largely responsible, there are always those who try to find excuses for Africa's tragic and despicable failure. They include Westerners, as we learn next.

269

Chapter Five

Western Apologists
for Africa's Failure

AFRICA has some of its strongest apologists in the West. Paradoxically, it is also the West that provides the largest amount of aid to Africa which is stolen and wasted by corrupt leaders and bureaucrats in this continent.

Many people in Western countries don't want to criticise Africa even when such criticism is justified because they are afraid that they will be accused of being racist. And many others, especially in the former imperial nations which once had colonies in Africa, feel guilty because their countries conquered, colonised and exploited Africa.

Other Europeans including white Americans feel guilty by association. They are members of the same race of the people who conquered, enslaved, colonised and exploited Africans and members of others races.

But it is Africans who probably suffered the most, with the outright enslavement of millions of their people for centuries being one of the worst crimes ever committed against humanity. As Indian Prime Minister Jawaharlal Nehru stated:

"Reading throughout history I think the agony of the African continent...has not been equaled anywhere."[1]

Yet it was the same Western countries which were also the first to launch a crusade against slavery they themselves started as an international traffic across the Atlantic from Africa to the Americas and Europe; and which they carried on for hundreds of years since the late 1400s when the Portuguese first took African slaves to Portugal and later to their colony of Brazil. Spanish slave traders were, of course, the first to take African slaves to the Americas, while the British had the biggest market for slaves in the West Indies and in the United States, with fewer going to Canada.

And it is their involvement in this diabolical traffic which is the main cause of Western guilt over Africa probably more than anything else.

Paradoxically, refusal by many Westerners to criticise Africans, especially the leaders and their governments, for their failures helps perpetuate the very condition they attempt to alleviate with economic aid to African countries.

Most of the aid provided by their countries simply goes down the drain, stolen or squandered by African leaders and bureaucrats. The people for whom the aid is intended get nothing, or very little.

Therefore, instead of helping the people, the poor masses who need help the most, Western nations end up helping corrupt African leaders and bureaucrats to steal even more. And the silence by many people in the West where most of the aid comes from and where African leaders hide their loot, compounds the problem.

But there is another dimension to all this. Compounding the felony is the fact that African leaders

272

work in collusion with many Westerners themselves and other donors to steal the money and exploit our countries – minerals and other natural resources. Western countries and corporations don't only contribute to Africa's plight; they are, in fact, the cause of many of the problems we face in Africa today.

They are deeply involved in the exploitation of Africa as they have been for many years. And, besides being the cause of many of the problems we face in our countries across the continent, they are also not really interested in helping us solve our problems.

They are only interested in securing and promoting their own political and economic interests. Nothing else. So are the Chinese and others – Japanese, Indians, Malaysians, Koreans – who are also now deeply involved in Africa, drawn to our continent by the abundant natural resources we have. They come to Africa to help themselves, *not* to help us. But by doing business with them, we may also end up getting some benefits if we plan and act accordingly and protect our interests.

Westerners have, of course, been the biggest culprits for historical reasons since they colonised us and have been involved in Africa the longest. And the problems they have caused us through the years cover almost everything. They have caused a lot of damage – more than just dumping toxic waste as they did in Ivory Coast in 2006 and as they have done and continue to do elsewhere in our countries including Nigeria where environmental damage by oil companies in Ogoniland and other parts of the Niger Delta has had a profound impact on the lives of the people in the region. They are not even being paid for the oil that is being pumped from under their feet. Their land is polluted. Even the fish they eat is polluted.

Still, we need to work with Western countries because we need each other. But there has to be a reciprocal understanding that this is for mutual benefit.

Unfortunately, African leaders help perpetuate the

asymmetrical relationship that exists between Africa and the West to our detriment because they have not made any concerted effort or genuine attempts on sustained basis to restructure the existing arrangements which continue to benefit the West and others far more than they benefit us. For example, we are not fairly paid for our minerals and other natural resources. And whatever is paid to us is stolen by many of our leaders across the continent.

Also, many of our leaders take bribes from multinational corporations and foreigners doing business in our countries and help them to exploit us. And in many cases, they deliberately sign contracts which favour foreigners at our expense, resulting in stunted economic growth.

Yet, African countries themselves have the potential, enormous potential, to end their misery and poverty, and develop, just like other countries have done and continue to do. The role model for Africa's development, if there is any, are the southeast Asian nations which were once colonies just like ours but which are now an economic success.

How do you develop a country? Create a climate conducive to investment, domestic and foreign. Civil wars, corruption, bad leadership and bad policies, don't do that. We can not count on the sympathy of Europeans, Americans and others to develop Africa. They are not coming. They come only to get what they want, what we have, as if it belongs to nobody – not even us, the rightful owners! And they are not going to invest in unstable countries torn by civil wars and riddled with corruption and which have no infrastructure. So we are on our own.

They are not even coming to colonise us again and run our countries as they did before. They know why some of our people want them to come back. Millions of our people are hungry. They are starving. They are dying in wars. They want food and medicine. They are sick and tired of corruption. Our governments have done nothing for them.

Most of our leaders have no respect for law and order, except when it affects them. They have no respect for property rights, except when their property is involved. They have no respect for human rights – none. They simply don't care about the well-being of the masses. They even steal and sell donated food from international relief agencies and donor countries intended for the poor, leaving the people starving. That's enough to scare anybody, including missionaries and relief workers, let alone investors.

Our people who want our former colonial masters to come back and rule us again want economic benefits they don't get from our governments which are busy exploiting them and pursuing wrong policies and thriving on corruption. They want our former masters to straighten things out and get us out of the mess we are in. And our former rulers know that very well.

But it's just too much for them. And it's too much for anybody, even for us. That's why we are so desperate for help. Yet, we can do a lot for ourselves. But we have failed to do so because of bad leadership; a point underscored in one of my books, *The Modern African State: Quest for Transformation*:

"It is a tragedy that the world's richest continent is, paradoxically, also the poorest. We have not exploited our full potential. That is why we always beg for help from other countries while other people laugh at us behind our backs; our lack of progress being attributed to our 'meager' intellect. And we help reinforce those stereotypes. We beg too much.

But we do have the potential to reverse that regardless of what our detractors say, some of whom are the very same people who exploited us ruthlessly and continue to do so under the new international economic order – globalization – over which we have no control.

275

But our failure to help ourselves – we can't even feed fellow Africans who are starving – and develop our countries in spite of the enormous potential we have to do that does not make us look very good before the rest of the world where we are already despised probably more than anybody else. And much of that potential, the labour and the resources, has been stifled or squandered under black governments since independence in the sixties.

What's wrong with Africa? Bad leadership probably more than anything else. It explains our stunted economic growth. If the leaders would only listen to what the people have to say, and let them manage their own affairs in the best way they know how; and if they would also listen to their critics who might have better alternative policies and solutions to our problems, things would be much different and our countries would be much better off than they are today. But they are too arrogant to listen.

The result is what we have today: nothing to show for our 40 years of independence in terms of development.

Jut look at how the rest of the world sees us. We don't have a single developed black nation on Earth – not one; a dismal performance with serious racial implications, reinforcing stereotypes about our innate inability to do for ourselves what others have done and continue to do for themselves.

Nigeria, once black Africa's great hope, has proved to be a great disappointment despite her great potential in terms of manpower and natural resources which would have been more than enough to make her a middle power in the international arena in the same league with countries such as Canada and Italy.

In the early seventies, Nigerian leaders and the elite even talked about the country's potential capacity to build an atomic bomb within a decade or so. Tragically, all that potential went down the drain under corrupt military dictators who siphoned billions of petrodollars into their pockets through the decades, earning this African giant the

276

unenviable distinction as one of the poorest countries in the world.

Another giant nation, the Congo, potentially the richest country in Africa, has been a monumental disaster since independence in 1960, pulverized from within. In fact, it ceased to be state under Mobutu Sese Seko who bled it to death. And it may continue to exist as an empty shell for many years to come if it does not disintegrate into fiefdoms dominated and exploited by warlords and other strongmen.

South Africa is, indisputably, the most developed country on the continent. But it is not a typical black nation; there are millions of whites, as well as Indians and Coloureds. And it was developed under white rule. Most of its scientific achievements and industrial progress requiring high-level manpower are attributed to white scientists and skilled workers for obvious reasons. Blacks were denied equal opportunity, education and skilled training during apartheid. Therefore they did not contribute to South Africa's scientific and technological advancement as much as whites did.

Angola is another country with enormous potential, endowed with abundant natural resources including oil, a dazzling array of minerals and extremely fertile land. But it has been devastated by civil war for almost 30 years, reducing it to rubble. It will take several decades, probably two generations, to rebuild.

The list of failed states across the continent goes on and on. And nothing is going to change without radical transformation.

The transformation must entail the complete overhaul of the institutions and power structures we inherited at independence. And it must take place across the entire spectrum, economic and political as well as social, to reflect African realities; accommodate and harmonize conflicting ethnoregional interests through extensive devolution of power to prevent secession and national disintegration; and harness the full potential of the people across the continent to develop our countries.

The quest for transformation of the modern African state requires bold initiatives and compromises. But, unfortunately, in most countries across the continent, it is a task that has hardly begun."[2]

As expected, not everybody likes or agrees with what I wrote in that book. And that includes some Westerners. As one white American critic stated:

"Sounds like another author making a name for himself among Europeans and Anglo-Americans (and other whites) who want to dehumanize and sustain the common stereotypical view of Africans and African inferiority. Back in the twenties, and even now we have some like that in America. Conservative Americans will practically jump on to any of their words and take them as if written right out of the New Testament.

It's a shame fewer and fewer people can capture the beauty in Africa, but then again that may be for the best. If Africa became one cool spot, you would have foreign bankers and investors, not to mention ravaging tourism and foreign corruption – which is much worse than local corruption – raping Africa of all it has.

Since Africa is the last 'un-europeanized' place on the planet, you already have mining, lumber and resortists salivating and waiting for enough people to die and the government to collapse enough for them to walk in and loot. Ask Mexico, or Jamaica or Trinidad or Nicaragua, they'll tell you."[3]

On my criticism of African leaders and African countries for their failure to achieve significant progress since independence in the sixties, despite their great potential do so, the American critic responded by saying:

"You're missing out SEVERAL important things about Africa's development. Keep in mind Africa was the LAST continent to get rid of its colonial powers, and all of the governments there are relatively young, while in Asia, and even the Americas the governments are around 150 – 400 years old.

If you look at any young country, you see harsh times. In Latin America, as well as the United States, the first hundred years of their governments' existences they were little more than Third World nations, or below. Many Latin American countries are the same now.

Also, Africa is NOT as fertile as you may think. The fertile areas, rain forest places, are not good for planting because they get depleted very quickly of minerals, and then desertification sets in. Ask the Brazilians about that, because that's exactly what's happening there as well. Much of far-southern and near-Saharan Africa, as well as far-eastern Africa, is pretty much desolate and incapable of farming as well.

The dictatorships are the result of young nations attempting to westernize too fast just after colonial dictatorships. The reason why there are so many is because most African countries gained independence at around the same time, hence they are about the same age, and in the same stage of growth. Eventually, when the people get too tired of it, they will grow out of it."[4]

His criticism, however well-intentioned, is misguided. Telling the truth is not a promotional campaign for a writer or anybody else.

Many people in Africa have gone to prison and have even died for telling the truth about the rotten leadership we have in this continent. Some of the lucky ones who came out alive even wrote books about their prison experiences. They include Wole Soyinka, known through the decades for his bitter condemnation of corrupt leaders and governments in Africa, who wrote *The Man Died*[5]

279

about the two years he spent in prison for criticising the Nigerian federal government during the Nigerian civil war; and Ngugi wa Thiong'o, locked up by the Kenyan government under Mzee Jomo Kenyatta and Daniel arap Moi, whose bitter experience in prison is chronicled in his book, *Detained: A Writer's Prison Diary*[6].

Even some African leaders have told the truth about Africa, however bitter. They include Julius Nyerere, acclaimed as "The Conscience of Africa"; Nelson Mandela, Archbishop Desmond Tutu, Kenneth Kaunda, Jerry Rawlings, and John Dramani Mahama.

Blanket condemnation that all writers write books just to promote themselves and even attempt to do so by denigrating Africa is unwarranted.

It is true that many American conservatives, even liberals, stereotype Africa. But many of them also tell the truth even if they are racist, as indeed many of them are, across the ideological spectrum. And many among us, Africans, also tell the truth. Those who don't are not helping Africa. And that includes sympathetic Westerners and others who simply don't want to tell the ugly truth about Africa because they don't want to hurt our feelings or don't want to be seen as racist. But that does not change the harsh reality about our condition. We just have to face reality, however painful it is.

As a people, black people, we have not achieved much like other people have. And we have not done for ourselves what other people have done for themselves even when we have had the opportunity to do so; especially in African countries since independence, raising serious questions about our mental capacity not only as an African people but as members of the black race which is also the most "backward" among all races.

And our failure to achieve what others have is ruthlessly public because the contrast is so glaring. It is the difference between day and night.

It may be a stereotype about us. And it is in terms of

mental capacity. There is no scientific evidence showing that we are genetically and intellectually inferior to members of other races. But it is disturbing, nonetheless, unless we prove otherwise with remarkable achievements in all fields of human endeavour, not just in some, or in only a few. I mean all.

And that includes developing our countries, instead of begging all the time. It also includes producing scientists who are truly innovative, not just parrots or those who simply regurgitate what they have swallowed from others, in order to help industrialise Africa the way, for example, Japan has after learning from the West as much as we are trying to do.

Every continent boasts of eminent scientists who have blazed the trail in a number of fields, except Africa. And every continent has universities and other institutions of higher learning and research laboratories which are among the best in the world, except Africa. The only exception on the continent is South Africa, about which we must also be brutally frank. It was whites, not blacks, who developed the country as the most industrialised on the continent, and who are responsible for most of the country's scientific achievements which rank among the best in the world.

We have not done enough for ourselves the way we should. And liberal sympathy for us by many Westerners is not going to change that if they refuse to tell the truth or simply sweep the dirt under the rug.

Conservatives may be harsh and even racist in their judgment or condemnation of Africa. But they sometimes tell the truth that needs to be told even if our dignity is wounded. We have even tried to salvage our dignity by re-inventing the past, a past that is not even ours. Many Afrocentric scholars are notorious for that. And they know it. They have enough sense to know the difference between fact and fiction even if they pretend that they don't.

Saying we built the pyramids or the ancient Egyptian

civilisation is *not* going to solve our problems. Even if we did indeed do all that, anyone with an ounce of common sense would still wonder why no civilisation of comparable stature, a product of the same mind and genius, and the same people, is not found or has not been unearthed *anywhere* in sub-Saharan Africa.

There is not even any convincing evidence, even if manufactured, showing that members of black African tribes or ethnic groups – the so-called Negroes, Bantus and others – south of the Sahara were indeed the ones who went all the way up north and produced the architectural wonders and magnificent splendour of ancient Egypt while they chose to remain in huts in their region; and when nothing of the sort, not even remotely close to the achievements of Egypt, is found in our part of the continent.

Why we thought it was such a wonderful idea to build a majestic civilisation far away in North Africa, in Egypt, while deliberately ignoring our region where we ourselves live in sub-Saharan Africa, still eludes me, and I'm sure many others. And it's definitely not very convincing, if at all, to the Egyptians themselves who not only don't even remotely resemble "Negroes" and "Bantus" who claim to have built the pyramids and the ancient Egyptian civilisation; they don't even have a common ancestry with the black tribes south of the Sahara. And frankly speaking, every mummy that has been found in Egypt, providing us with a sample of how the people of ancient Egypt looked like, does not have "Negro" or "Bantu" features including 'kinky" hair.

And if – as some Afrocentrists claim – our knowledge and inventions were stolen from us by non-blacks, which would perhaps account for our "backwardness," there is still no evidence, none whatsoever, showing that whoever stole all that, also stole our brains and inventive genius, preventing us from duplicating our achievements of the past and even charting out new territories in the scientific realm to develop our societies and contribute to the advancement of human knowledge.

We have given so many excuses for our failure to develop and make significant contributions to science and human development that we have run out of excuses. And nothing is going to change unless we harness our creative potential to the maximum and use our intellectual abilities in all fields of human endeavour, even during the worst of times, to be the best we can be like the rest of mankind who despise us more than anybody else because of our backwardness which has earned us the unenviable distinction as the most backward and least creative race on Earth.

If telling the truth about Africa is a way of dehumanising Africa as the liberal American critic contended in his critique of my work, and I consider myself to be an independent-minded liberal, not a conservative, then we need this kind of shock therapy to galvanise us into action to develop our continent and catch up with members of other races whose countries are far ahead of ours for reasons which have nothing to do with genes. Shame can be very therapeutic. It has galvanised even some of the most lethargic members of society, making them productive.

We can't even feed ourselves. Yet every African in Africa has, on average, four acres of arable land more than enough to feed an entire family; poor agricultural methods being one of the biggest obstacles to increased productivity in most countries across the continent.

We have countless rivers and lakes across the continent with more than enough water to irrigate our lands and farms. Yet we hardly use them. Can't we build canals to channel the water into arid regions or other parts where it is needed?

Can't we learn from the Egyptians – right there in Africa – who have turned barren land into productive land by using water from the Nile?

283

Can't we learn from others on the continent who use better or more advanced farming methods and techniques than we do so that we can at least grow enough food to feed ourselves instead of begging all over the world?

Is it not a shame that the United States, for example, has to send maize and beans to starving Africans on a continent where we can grow more than enough maize and beans for ourselves?

Don't we have any pride as a people? Is begging others to feed us something to be proud of?

Do we have any right to complain when other people laugh at us when we can't take care of ourselves?

Are we proud to have children so that they can be fed by other people from other countries?

If we can't feed ourselves well, and in many cases not at all but instead have to rely on international relief agencies to bring us beans and maize which we ourselves can grow in this predominantly agricultural continent, then we are in extremely bad condition which may require divine intervention to alleviate our plight. God helps. But He helps those who help themselves. So, praying alone is not enough.

It takes more than just praying for rain and begging for food.

We also have to wrack our brains instead of praying for rain, and begging all the time, more than anything else. And our liberal sympathisers and other apologists for our failures in the West and elsewhere should be kind enough, and bold enough, to remind us of that, lest some of us forget the imperative need for what we shouldn't even be reminded of: self-reliance.

We can't count on foreigners to feed us or solve our problems. The world just doesn't work that way. It never has, it never did, and it never will.

Some of our Western sympathisers are so guilt-ridden, so timid, or just so paternalistic, that they even refuse to agree with us when we ourselves tell the truth about our deplorable condition and pathetic performance in terms of development. Some of us have even written books about Africa's plight – to the delight of our detractors, of course – out of genuine commitment to the wellbeing of our continent, not to humiliate or insult ourselves and other Africans.

It is true that many non-Africans harshly criticise Africa because they are racist – they think they are better than we are. And they couldn't care less if we vanished from the face of the Earth today or got wiped out by hunger and disease.

But if what they say is true, it is true, regardless of who says it. If we don't want our enemies and detractors to say bad things about us and about Africa, then we should deny them the opportunity to do so by excelling in all fields of human endeavour to be equal to the best among the best among men across the colour line.

They are not going to like us anymore than they do now simply because we have excelled in all fields across the spectrum like other people have. But it will be much more difficult for them to write or talk about a condition that no longer exists if we work hard enough and collectively to end our misery.

Tragically, we are in the international spotlight precisely because we have failed to do so. And some of us, for example Ghanaian writer and economics professor George Ayittey, have been brutally frank about our condition. So have many others across the ideological spectrum round the globe. As one critic stated in his article, "African Nightmare":

"'Fears of famine in Ethiopia,' says the *New York Times*; 'Mugabe's 'surreal' policies ravage Zimbabwe's economy,' add the *Washington Post*--and those headlines are just from the past two weeks. Meanwhile, a civil war rages in the Ivory Coast, and generalized famine threatens most of Southern Africa---Zimbabwe, Zambia,

285

Mozambique, and Malawi.

And in the continent's most populous country, Nigeria, fundamentalist Islam, complete with the stoning to death of adulterers and the chopping off of thieves' hands, is on the march.

All that in countries which still have governments, because places---one cannot call them states in any meaningful sense---like Somalia, Sierra Leone, or 'The Democratic Republic of Congo' – formerly known as Zaire – do not enjoy even that dubious advantage. And then there are the civil wars: in the Sudan, between Arab Muslims and black Christians; and in Zaire, between Ugandans and Rwandans on the one side – or are there two? – and Zimbabwe, Angola, Namibia on the other.

Al Qaeda has a presence in Somalia, Kenya, Sierra Leone, Burkina Faso, and Liberia, and Libyan troops operate in Central Africa and run interference in West Africa. And last, but far from least, up to 40 percent of the adult population in countries like Lesotho and Zambia, to name but a few, are suffering from HIV/AIDS.

The more recent AIDS pandemic aside, and with a few names changed, similarly depressing headlines could have been read twenty years ago: let us remember Idi Amin, the cannibal ruler of Uganda; Jean-Bedel Bokassa, the convicted cannibal and emperor of Central Africa; Francisco Macias Nguema, the self-described 'sole miracle' of Equatorial Guinea, who publicly shot most of his ministers as the band played 'Happy Days are Here Again' -- all prior to 1979.

It would seem that sub-Saharan Africa today, as yesterday, remains behind all other areas of the world -- in economic, political and social terms. There are many reasons for this, and, one must say, there are a few flickerings of light at the end of the tunnel.

To begin with, most of the continent's problems today are inherited from the time of independence. With the exceptions of Liberia, Ethiopia and South Africa, not one of the contemporary sub-Saharan countries has any history of independent statehood. They are all creations of European rivalries and European bureaucrats in London, Paris or Lisbon. Nor, again with a few exceptions – Botswana, Somalia, and the island states – do they have any pre-independence sentiment of statehood, divided as they were and are along ethnic and linguistic lines. Declaring the former colonial language the official one is recognition of this reality: only a foreign language could provide a minimum of internal unity.

Once independent, in many cases without any popular demand for independence, country after country fell under the control of European-educated – at the Sorbonne or the London School of Economics – and influenced (naturally enough, by the leftist ideas prevailing there) elites. Socialism, occasionally Marxism-Leninism, was the favorite among the various ideologies that failed in richer countries but devastated Africa.

All this was encouraged by Western intellectuals and often paid for by Western taxpayers.

Thus, for decades, Tanzania's ruinous experiment with socialism was subsidized – at the highest per capita rate in Africa – by the Scandinavian countries. Julius Nyerere, the country's first president and 'father' of African socialism, admitted upon retirement that 'We failed.'

And then there was the Cold War. The countries under Soviet rule aside, no other region has lost more during it than Africa. Non-viable country after non-viable country had muddled through for four decades because outside support kept them together: Western economic and military aid; East German, Cuban, or Soviet arms, secret police advisers, and political support. Fear of some marginal state going to the other side attracted attention and support out of proportion, in many cases, to the state's importance in the larger scheme of things.

By 1989 it all came crashing down, and Africa was faced with the unpleasant reality of its actual status in the world. It turned out that the emperor had no clothes. Their vision no longer clouded by perceived geopolitical or strategic interests, outsiders began to see Africa in its real dimensions.

In fact, with some 650 million people, sub-Saharan Africa's combined GNP is somewhat smaller than that of Belgium (population: 10 million). As for per capita income – $474 in 2000 – it had a negative growth rate of 0.6 percent over the years 1988 - 2000, or 0.3 excluding the region's economic super power, South Africa. All this despite the fact that a few, usually small countries – Sao Tome & Principe, Equatorial Guinea – are experiencing a major oil boom, and a handful – Botswana, Uganda and Mauritius, e.g. – have competent and successful economic policies and healthy growth rates. Simply put, in the new world of globalization, a few commodities aside, Africa isn't a significant market, competitor or exporter.

Nor has Africa's longstanding ability to exploit Western guilt over colonialism retained its potency. Increasingly, taxpayers in the West, if not many intellectuals and the Left, find it harder and harder to attribute 40 years of post-independence decay to 80 years of colonialism--- especially since in many countries the statistics suggest that majority were worse off in 1990 than at the end of the colonial era.

The fiasco of the 2001 UN Conference on Racism in Durban was both significant, and in some ways, encouraging. It was significant because it demonstrated that attempts to mine Western guilt, at the cost of insulting both history and common sense, are still popular in some quarters; encouraging because the most vocal advocates of the most preposterous ideas advanced – 'reparations for slavery' and open anti-Semitism – were American racial demagogues and Arabs, rather than Africans.

This is not to say that Africans did not engage in racism, often with economically suicidal consequences. In the 1970s Idi Amin expelled the prosperous Indian

288

community of Uganda and stole their property; Lebanese in West Africa have occasionally been expelled and their property confiscated; and today Comrade Mugabe in Zimbabwe is engaged in a massive ethnic cleansing of whites and Asians and stealing their property, with dire consequences for most black Zimbabweans.

A case could be made that Mugabe is a Stalinist dinosaur and Idi Amin was certifiably unhinged, but the fact remains that there was no pan-African condemnation of their actions.

All of which should bring to light the obvious fact, avoided for decades by both African elites and well-intentioned Westerners, that outside the conceptual framework of racism there is no such thing as 'Africa.' Yes, there is the creation in 2002, through Muammar Qaddaffi's brainstorm and oil dollars, of the African Union, successor to the famously irrelevant organization of African Unity, likely to make the latter an example of effectiveness. But to understand how shallow the concept of African unity is in the real world, one only has to look at the post-1994 events in the Great Lakes region of Central Africa.

In 1994 the ruling Hutu regime in Rwanda engaged in the world's most obvious case of genocide since the Holocaust, with as many as 750,000 Tutsis murdered in a matter of weeks. An invading force of Uganda-based Tutsis then took power and the defeated perpetrators fled to Zaire. The Rwandans pursued them, and the result was an all-African free-for-all war that, for once, involved only African armies – at least six of them – and their local proxies.

It would be hard indeed to blame that war, fought over diamonds, titanium, manganese and copper as much as over territory, on Belgian colonialism. Nor is it easier to blame the recent Ethiopia-Eritrea war over a few patches of bush, with up to a million casualties, on Mussolini's Italy.

All of these are tragedies, but they are strictly African-made tragedies, and the good news is that Africans and outsiders alike are coming to see them as such. After decades of lies, blaming others, and irresponsible elites and outsider interveners, today Africa is forced to live in a global environment in which responsibility is what matters.

In economic terms, some African states are fighting to erase their well-deserved reputation of corruption and bureaucratic red tape and attract foreign investment. Many are oil-producing countries, but Uganda and Mauritius are succeeding even without oil. And West African oil needs not to be sneezed at: it is clean, offshore – thus minimizing frictions with the locals – and abundant.

Though hopelessly corrupt, divided and increasingly threatened by Islamic fundamentalism, Nigeria is for now the major producer. That will change in favor of small states with a need for protection against the likes of Nigeria – which is where U.S. technology, power projection capabilities and capital could come in.

If there is any positive political sign coming from Africa, it is that democracy is making some progress after decades of dictatorships and kleptocracies. A number of the continent's -big men' have lost elections – Kaunda in Zambia, Diouf in Senegal, Ratsiraka in Madagascar – or have retired voluntarily. Moi in Kenya, Rawlings in Ghana, soon Chissano in Mozambique. That does not a democratic march from Dakar to Khartoum or from Bamako to Harare make, but at least the signs are not all negative.

Because sub-Saharan Africa is, and is likely to remain, marginal in economic, political and strategic terms, regional self-sufficiency is the key to progress. To a decisive extent, that means South African supremacy. South Africa is the only country in the region with the capital, technological and professional resources and obvious interest – dictated by its location and experience – to help the entire region, or at least the southern and central areas of Africa.

It controls the transportation hubs – ports and railroads all the way to Zaire; it produces the bulk of manufactured goods and energy; and it has a still large – albeit diminishing due to massive emigration – professional and technical mass of qualified experts. If South Africa fails politically or economically, sub-Saharan Africa has no future outside a few isolated oil enclaves.

The problem is that South Africa does not play the role one would expect or hope. The case of Zimbabwe is a good example. While Mandela or Tutu pontificate about U.S. imperialism and cruelty in using the death penalty, their country's labor minister, Membathisi Mdladlana, just claimed that South Africa 'has a lot to learn' from Mugabe's Stalinist 'land reform,' which has destroyed the economy of one of Africa's few formerly prosperous countries. The minister's opinions may have been disavowed by his government, but the fact remains that it is Pretoria's tolerance and indeed active political and economic support that keeps Mugabe's criminal regime afloat.

Nor is Pretoria the only one at fault. The African Union itself had nothing to say about Zimbabwe's self-immolation – naturally enough, since Mugabe's financial sponsor, Muammar Qaddaffi, is also the Union's promoter. And African members of the Commonwealth blocked efforts to suspend Zimbabwe's membership.

Racial solidarity, once again, as in the cases of Bokassa, Idi Amin, etc., trumped decency and indeed rational self-interest.

If there is any problem that attracts the same old tired and demonstrably ineffective calls for more aid, more sympathy and more misguided and indiscriminate outside interference in Africa, it is the issue of AIDS. Since the pandemic originated in Africa, the continent has suffered longer than any other part of the world from its impact. Today, although sub-Saharan Africa represents only 10 percent of the world's population, it has 67 percent of known AIDS/HIV cases.

There are many reasons for this, and objective causes why it is so difficult to cope with the problem, some independent of whatever African governments could do. A very young population – in some cases 50 percent under the age of 20 – means that the most irresponsible group is unusually large; mass illiteracy and poor infrastructure make education and prevention difficult; and poor health services make treatment almost impossible. More important, however, is the attitude of African governments.

With the laudable exception of Uganda, for years they have denied the very existence of an AIDS problem. Even today, the president of South Africa, Thabo Mbeki, denies that AIDS is the result of a virus, and thus provides the worst possible example to other, far less developed, countries in the region.

Western pharmaceutical companies have given up their patents for AIDS medication, and relatively cheap generics exist---enriching Indian and Brazilian manufacturers. Massive Western infusions of medicines, medical personnel and funds are now available, but, as is the case with aid in general, these only lead to waste, corruption and demands for more.

Massive amounts of free U.S. food aid to southern African countries afflicted by famine are being rejected by Zambia and Malawi because they are genetically modified types of corn or wheat. Suddenly, starving people are denied food because, under the influence of paranoiac European Greens, their governments have decided to be politically correct.

All of this raises the question, is Africa going anywhere? The answer is unclear, and it all depends on how African states and Western partners treat each others. If African states finally decide that they have distinct interests, rather than pretending to belong to a non-existent

'Africa,' they could enjoy the fruits of their sound decisions---where those decisions are sound. If not, they should pay the price of failure, just like any other country, whether Bolivia, Nepal or Romania.

As for the West, it should finally stop its irresponsibly paternalistic treatment of 'Africa' as a perennial victim of everyone except its own rulers, reward the successful and leave the failed to pay the price."[7]

It could have been written by anybody: a liberal, a conservative, a racist, an African like George Ayittey or anybody else.

But it makes no difference who wrote it because it is true, painfully true, except for a few remarks here and there; for example, the author's denial of the existence of Africa as a single entity transcending geography, a subject I have addressed in one of my books, *Africa and the West*;[8] his biased treatment of the land issue in Zimbabwe which goes beyond land in terms of racial and historical injustices, but which ultimately still is predicated on land itself as the basis of independence without which all talk of independence is meaningless; and his unabashed advocacy of American corporate imperialism and hegemonic control of Africa by the West when he talks about American 'power projection capabilities and capital' in African countries which have oil and other natural resources.

We differ on all that. But most of what he says is true.

The article I just quoted was written by a white American conservative, Michael Radu, director of the Center on Terrorism and Counter-terrorism of the Foreign Policy Research Institute in Philadelphia, who was also a contributing editor of the institute's *ORBIS* journal, and whose ideological compatriots have an instinctive aversion to Africa and Black America.

Yet most of what he says is what Professor George Ayittey says in his book *Africa in Chaos*[9] and other writings in an even more strident a tone; so have other African writers including Wole Soyinka, Chinua Achebe, Ngugi wa Thiong'o, the late Nigerian Professor Claude Ake who died in a mysterious plane crash in his home country in 1996; and Kenyan Professor Peter Anyang' Nyong'o, a fierce opponent of Africa's despotic and kleptocratic regimes who was elected member of parliament and later in 2003 became minister of economic planning under the newly elected president, Mwai Kibaki, whose election ended almost 40 years of domination by the Kenya African National Union (KANU) which had been in power since independence in December 1963.

And there are many others, known and unknown, who are just as outspoken and sometimes even more so. They are tired of excuses for Africa's failures and our leaders' incompetence to help our countries develop and earn their rightful place in the constellation of nations. And we *don't* want our Western sympathisers and others to continue doing that. They only make things worse. The American critic whom I quoted earlier and who vehemently disagreed with what I wrote about Africa in my book, *The Modern African State: Quest for Transformation*,[10] is one of them.

His contention that Africa is in the kind of mess it is in because its countries are relatively young has no merit. They are indeed young nations, having won independence mostly in the sixties. But that is not the main reason why our continent is in trouble.

Africa is drowning in a fetid swamp of misery because of inept leadership more than anything else; something many of our sympathisers in the West and elsewhere refuse to acknowledge, yet which we ourselves readily concede as an irrefutable fact. We know what's wrong with our continent. And no amount of clever sheet balancing, blaming our former colonial rulers and other imperial nations while glorifying ourselves, is going to change that.

Is that why we are starving? Is that why we have no

clean water, no schools, and no medical service for most of our people? Is that the reason why even many of our university graduates are functionally illiterate? Even colonial secondary schools, known for their rigorous intellectual discipline, produced better graduates than many of our colleges and universities across Africa do today. Many college students in Africa can not even spell let alone write a single sentence with lucidity.

It is a searing indictment against our leaders, including ivory tower intellectuals in the citadels of academia, more than anybody else. And excuses by our friends in the West and elsewhere glossing over Africa's catastrophic failures, because of bad leadership, are worse than blistering attacks on us by our enemies and detractors. While the former numb our senses, and may be even soothe us, the latter may jolt us into action despite the stereotypes they sometimes use to belittle us and separate us from the rest of humanity as if we are a sub-species of mankind, although they also tell the truth a lot of times.

It is better to be told the truth by an enemy than to be told a lie by a friend. But the responsibility to tell the truth about our condition is *our* responsibility. And we must be the first to do so. As Adebayo Adedeji, an internationally renowned Nigerian economist and former executive secretary of the UN Economic Commission for Africa (ECA), stated in an interview with *Africa Report*:

"Quite frankly, I think the African governments have to accept full responsibility for the state of the economies today. The time has passed when we should lay this blame at the doors of others. If we continue to do that, it means we are not responsible people."[11]

All that is caused by bad leadership. As Adedeji also stated in *The Economist*: "What we confront in Africa is primarily a political crisis, albeit with devastating economic consequences."[12]

A few African countries such as Botswana have made impressive strides in the economic arena, while the vast majority continue to lag behind, because they have pursued good economic policies under pragmatic leadership; not the misguided and idealistic kind, however well-intentioned, which promises its people a pie in the sky – as they wait till kingdom come – while they are starving here on Earth when they shouldn't be starving at all in the midst of plenty: fertile land, plenty of water to irrigate the land, and a wide variety of food crops which can be easily grown and harvested in a relatively short period in most countries across the continent.

All these are all African countries. They have the same people, mostly black; basically the same climate, the same soil, and the same water. If some of them can succeed, why not the rest?

The rest have not succeeded because of bad economic policies even when some of them have had good, dedicated leaders such as President Julius Nyerere of Tanzania and Kenneth Kaunda of Zambia who had the best of intentions and were deeply committed to the well-being of their people, especially the poorest of the poor, but pursued failed socialist policies which resulted in stunted economic growth for decades.

There is no earthly reason why Africa should import food when it can grow enough to feed itself and export the rest. This is an agricultural continent, with tens of millions of acres of fertile land most of which is not even used. So what's the problem? And there is no reason why African countries should continue to pursue wrong economic policies which have proved to be a failure, and a disaster, when they can learn from others and change course.

Dogmatic thinking of our leaders has been one of Africa's biggest problems since independence. All that has to change if we expect to make any progress. But such progress, even with the right policies, is impossible without transparency and accountability.

Tribalism is another major problem we have in Africa. It is a perennial problem even in the few countries which have good leadership. Tribalism also leads to dictatorship as leaders from some tribes run over others. Dictatorship is another curse on the continent even in this post-Cold War ra of democratization. And it leads to corruption.

Corruption thrives under dictatorship because there is no independent and efficient police force, no independent judiciary, and no independent press to expose it. And it may be Africa's biggest problem, leading to the total collapse of national institutions and entire economies as happened in the case of Zaire under Mobutu.

Other African countries are on the same critical list for the same reasons: tyranny, corruption, tribalism and nepotism.

Many of our leaders are so bad that they make our former colonial masters look like saints. And they were bad enough themselves. So, things must be really bad for some of our people to say they wish our former colonial rulers were back to rule us again. And they *are* bad, because of bad leadership. As Wole Soyinka, although he would never entertain such an idea that Africa should return to the "good ol' days" of imperial rule, stated in his vitriolic condemnation of rotten, corrupt African leaders and their governments in his lecture at Wellesley College in the United States:

"It is a stirring sight to witness an African leader addressing the United Nations. Never mind that he's just left a nation where millions are on the edge of starvation, where medical delivery no longer exists, where the educational system has collapsed and university students have become virtually illiterate. Never mind that either before or immediately after sounding off on the United Nations podium, he and his entourage detour to the most exclusive medical clinic in Wiesbaden for a routine medical check-up, then stop in London and Paris to pick

297

up new million-dollar knicknacks for their wives, cronies and mistresses.

Never mind that he returns home to sign a few death warrants for his alleged enemies, tried in secret with no more evidence against them than confessions wrung from "witnesses" who have been tortured so brutally that they cannot even be present in court, so that only their written depositions form the evidence against the condemned men."[13]

And that will continue to be the case as long as African governments remain corrupt and power is concentrated in the hands of only a few people.

Please, dear sympathisers of ours in the West and elsewhere, don't tell us that is democratic centralism when our leaders centralise power. It is an oxymoron, a contradiction in terms. It can't be democratic and despotic at the same time. That is what democratic centralism means, and that is what it's all about. We know it from experience in most parts of Africa.

We have lived under it. It is intolerable, and suffocating. It stifles individual initiative, stunts economic growth, and even compromises standards of excellence across the spectrum by ignoring merit in education and employment, and by insulating minds from cross-fertilisation of ideas in a pluralistic context. It has destroyed African countries, as many apologists for Africa's failures in the West continue to find excuses for our countries' poor performance in every conceivable way.

Our friends in the West must concede that the modern African state, the institutions of authority within our territorial borders, is too centralised, too corrupt, and too inefficient to be of any use to us except as an oppressive apparatus.

It is true that countries can develop and even achieve spectacular success under dictatorship, although that does not justify tyranny. Singapore, South Korea, Malaysia,

Indonesia, and Thailand, the so-called Asian tigers, are just some of the countries whose economic performance has been phenomenal under authoritarian rule. But that is because they were able to create conditions and pursued policies conducive to economic growth. They focused on creating human capital by investing heavily in health and education in order to have a healthy and trained work force. They also focused on attracting foreign investment, encouraged entrepreneurship, and built domestic capital through national savings and private-sector growth.

Few African countries have done that. Instead, most African leaders have been busy stealing, and simply let their countries rot. Asians also steal, of course. Americans and Europeans also steal; so do other people in all countries. But they also have laws and enforce them to fight corruption, although not in all cases.

By a glaring contrast, theft and corruption in African countries has become institutionalised.

Governments and people in other countries also invest in education, health, and national development far more than we do in Africa. That is why South Korea, for example, whose per capita income ($120) was lower than Zambia's ($200) in 1967 three years after Zambia won independence from Britain, had – in 2006 – a per capita income of more than $13,000, while Zambia's was a mere $400; a pathetically low figure after an entire generation since independence in 1964.

In fact, Zambia is far better off than some African countries which have even more natural resources; a sad commentary on Africa's condition today and which shows no signs of significant improvement in the coming years without radical transformation and complete overhaul of entire political and economic systems across the continent. As Peter Anyang' Nyong'o states:

"At the very bare minimum, a large number of African states cannot even maintain and reproduce their own bureaucracies: civil servants are often not paid for months, armies and policemen rely on highway extortion to obtain their monthly wages, government offices are falling apart, water and telephone systems do not work, and national airlines cannot even respect their own tickets....

The fiscal crisis begins to manifest itself more dramatically when heads of state accept as valid currency only those legal tenders emanating from the industrialized world, and treat with contempt banknotes bearing their own heads."[14]

That is on a continent already burdened with enormous problems including huge foreign debts accumulated by corrupt leaders who have some of their best defenders in the West where the mantra among a number of them including liberal academic intellectuals is, "Give them some time. They will change, they will develop," as they continue to bleed our economies and suffocate dissent.

Africa is drowning in debt. Yet the amount taken out of the continent every year by many leaders, which amounts to billions of dollars, and deposited in overseas personal and hidden bank accounts, far exceeds the amount of foreign aid African countries get within the same period. And this is a documented fact, unbelievable as it may seem to some people. As Professor George Ayittey states in his book *Africa Betrayed*:

"An estimated $15 billion - more than what Africa receives in foreign aid - flees Africa annually....Kenyans alone have stashed more than $5 billion abroad, an amount which is greater than their country's foreign debt of $4 billion....In Mali former head of state, Moussa Traore, looted the country to amass a personal fortune worth over $2 billion - an amount equal to the size of Mali's foreign debt....

Even socialist Tanzania suffered (and still, under capitalism, suffers) from corruption. Prime Minister (later

300

vice-president) Joseph Warioba was moved enough to speak out with scathing frankness: 'Everywhere you go even in hospitals and schools, corruption and corrupt people seem to rule the day'....And as *New African* (April 1990, p. 16) reported: 'Ordinary Tanzanians are complaining bitterly that they have been let down by their leadership. Even essential services such as education, hospitals, and police are up to their necks in corrupt practices. People who use government hospitals expect to have to bribe doctors and nurses before they can be treated.'"[15]

And in neighbouring Congo when it was Zaire, President Mobutu himself publicly congratulated fellow kleptocrats who were bleeding the economy, saying there was nothing wrong with stealing as long as they invested within the country the money they stole. His personal fortune, an estimated $10 billion, was legendary; so was that of his friend, President Gnassingbe Eyadema of Togo, one of the smallest and poorest countries in Africa and in the entire world. In 1991, Eyadema had a personal fortune of $2.8 billion[16] in such a poverty-stricken country. And most of his money was in foreign banks.[17]

Where is Western condemnation of such grand theft and corruption by African leaders? Corruption is destroying Africa.

Most of the criticism comes from conservatives, who really don't care about Africa and don't even want to help when such help is needed. Very little comes from liberals who are more interested in defending than in exposing African leaders for their venality, while blaming themselves and their countries for the mess Africa is in today.

And where is African accountability? Most of our problems are caused by us, especially by the leaders, not by foreigners. As Chinua Achebe, whose analysis is applicable in a continental context, states about his country

301

in his book *The Trouble with Nigeria*:

"The trouble with Nigeria is simply and squarely a failure of leadership. There is nothing basically wrong with the Nigerian character. There is nothing wrong with the Nigerian land or climate or water or air or anything else. The Nigerian problem is the unwillingness or inability of its leaders to rise to the responsibility, to the challenge of personal example which are the hallmarks of true leadership....We have lost the twentieth century; are we bent on seeing that our children also lose the twentiety-first? God forbid!"[18]

While African corrupt politicians and officials continue to drain the continent of its wealth in collusion with foreign interests mostly in the West where they hide their loot, hundreds of millions of Africans continue to suffer, living in hell on Earth. And statistics are grim, and heart-rending.

Poverty is everywhere; so are diseases, hunger and ignorance. Some people even faint in offices because they have not eaten in many, many days. They can't afford to buy food because they have not been paid in months. Others simply drop dead.

Almost half of all the people in sub-Saharan Africa live on less than one dollar per day. That's almost 500 million people. Just as many don't have clean water. More than a third have no health care; and those who do barely get the minimum essentials in terms of treatment unless they bribe nurses and doctors or pull some strings to get some treatment in clinics and hospitals which don't even have enough medicine if at all. Nearly half the adult population is illiterate. And in many countries, the situation is getting worse, not better. Because of illnesses, hunger and poor health, productivity in Africa is the lowest in the world.

Almost all of the world's poorest countries are African. And they all have people starving, dependent on international relief just to survive, in many cases on less than one meal per day because they don't get enough help – maize flour, beans, and whatever else they can get.

Per capita income is lower in black Africa than in any other region except parts of south Asia.

And almost all this has to do with corrupt and misguided leadership Africa has had to endure for more than a generation since independence in the sixties. Yet, some of our friends in the West have the audacity to blame everybody else for Africa's misery except our leaders who are responsible for the mess we are in more than anybody else. We don't need that kind of sympathy. We would be better off without it.

It is true that conservatives in the West, including black American conservatives such as Thomas Sowell and Walter Williams, both economics professors, are the strongest critics of Africa for its failure in many areas including its failure to develop. But there are also a number of people at the other end of the ideological spectrum who are sometimes equally blunt in their criticism of corrupt governments in Africa and the wrong policies they have pursued since independence. They include Professor Robert Rotberg who studied Africa for decades since his student days when he was a doctoral student at the University of Oxford and met African leaders such as Julius Nyerere, Milton Obote and Tom Mboya during the struggle for independence. As he stated in his book, *Ending Autocracy, Enabling Democracy: The Tribulations of Southern Africa 1960 – 2000*:

"In the post-imperial years from 1960, Africa and southern Africa experienced great wealth and abject poverty; frustrating modernization failures; cascades of interminable intrastate war; merciless and brutal genocides and other bitter massacres; state weakness and state collapse; many rejections of representative democracy and denials of fundamental human rights; the rise of despots

303

and predators....

Already at independence, some of the new entities boasted per capita gross domestic products higher than most of the developing countries in Asia. Reaching the point of economic takeoff was thus only a matter of time, of financial assistance from their former colonial masters and others, and (for most) the organizing of appropriate instruments of state control. Anything was possible now that Africans were arbiters of their own destinies. That was the heady aspiration of the 1960s....

But, as the decade progressed, inherited representative democracy increasingly became an anachronistic and beleaguered pursuit. Some of the early post-colonial governments became authoritarian and corrupt, leaders hijacked their states, and economic potential based on cautious older methods almost everywhere was sacrificed to the grandiose panaceas of import substitution, heavy industry, tight regulation, and merciless intervention. Military coups became commonplace. Good governance became rare. So did the observance of basic human rights and the four freedoms. Africa began to squander its political and financial legacies and, partly in consequence, to solicit new sources of support from the West or the Soviet Union and China.

Optimism about prospects for Africa was not easily converted into skepticism and despair. That took another decade of leadership failure and spectacular economic misjudgment. Nevertheless, there was an ebbing away of confidence in African statesmanship and integrity.

The process of nation-building that began with such excitement in Ghana in 1957, when Kwame Nkrumah gave his country an African name in place of its British designation and envisaged a United States of Africa, began to slow considerably only after his and his regime's excesses became too scandalous to be ignored. Ethnic antagonisms came to the surface in several African states. Adherence to participatory procedures ebbed. Even so, the

West and critics in the West continued to support African leaders and states well after they had started suspending constitutions and converting their states into autocracies. Creating and holding Cold War allies was the higher goal. Gradually, however, the enthusiasm for and tolerance of black Africa receded." – (Robert I. Rotberg, *Ending Autocracy, Enabling Democracy: The Tribulations of Southern Africa 1960 – 2000*, Washington, D.C.: Brookings Institution Press, pp. 3, 11, 12, 2002).

Lack of interest in the West in supporting dictatorships and rotten governments in Africa reached its peak after the end of the Cold War. Western countries no longer needed client states in Africa and in other parts of the Third World because there was no need for them as was the case during the East-West rivalry which had dominated the international scene since the end of World War II. But even today, there is some tolerance of African incompetence for reasons I gave earlier.

You don't find many critics of rotten African leadership among liberals; and they are not as outspoken as their conservative counterparts are. But they can no longer defend the indefensible: Africa's failure to do better than she does now. They include black Americans such as Keith Richburg who does not even want to be called an African-American just as most black American conservatives don't. They say they are just Americans, not Americans who are also African.

Richburg is supposed to be a liberal but his criticism of Africa gravitates towards the other end of the ideological spectrum both in terms of tone and content, as well as prescription for Africa's chronic ailments. He has also kindled the ire of many blacks in the United States and elsewhere for implying that he is glad his African ancestors were enslaved since their enslavement made it possible for him to be born an American.

Wole Soyinka says Richburg hates himself because of

his negative attitude towards Africa. As Malcolm X used to say, "By hating Africa, we ended up hating ousrselves." Whether Richburg really hates himself, and hates Africa or hates only bad governments in Africa, is an entirely different matter. But he has told the truth about Africa.

He was the *Washington Post* Africa bureau chief based in Nairobi, Kenya, from 1991 to 1994, and bluntly stated in his book, *Out of America: A Black Man Confronts Africa*:

"I'm leaving Africa now, so I don't care anymore about the turmoil in Rwanda and have no interest in this latest tragic development....From now on, I will be seeing it from afar, maybe watching it on television like millions of other Americans....I will also know that the problems are too intractable, that the outside world can do nothing, until Africa is ready to save itself. I'll also know that none of it affects me, because I feel no attachment to the place or the people.

And why should I feel anything more? Because my skin is black? Because some ancestor of mine, four centuries ago, was wrenched from this place and sent to America, and because I now look like those others whose ancestors were left behind? Does that make me still a part of this place? Should their suffering now somehow still be mine?

Maybe I would care more if I had never come here and never seen what Africa is today. But I have been here, and I have seen – and frankly, I want no part of it.

So am I a coldhearted cynic? An Africa hater? A racist, maybe, or perhaps a lost and lonely self-hating black man who has forgotten his African roots? Maybe I am, all that and more. But by an accident of birth, I am a black man born in America, and everything I am today – my culture and attitudes, my sensibilities, loves, and desires – derives from that one simple and irrefutable truth.....Thank God my ancestor got out, because, now, I am not one of them.

In short, thank God that I am an American."[19]

It is important to understand the context in which he articulated those sentiments. He left America for Africa with some kind of optimism and romantic feelings about the homeland of his African ancestors. He left the continent full of pessimism about its future. He also left this mangled continent, which has been devastated by war and disease and corruption, dazed.

But he also had an ambivalent attitude towards Africa before he left America for the "Dark Continent," as European imperialists called it, and as many other people still call it today, knowing full well what this derogatory term implies : Africa is called the "Dark Continent," not because its native people have a dark skin, although it sometimes also means that; it is called the "Dark Continent" mainly because black Africans also have "a dark mind." They are incapable of thinking. That's exactly what the term means.

Whether or not Richburg, in the deepest recesses of his mind, also subscribed to this racist and imperialist notion before he left for Africa, is highly questionable. I seriously doubt that he did.

But by implying in his book that slavery was indeed a blessing in disguise, since it gave him the golden opportunity to be born an American in the land of milk and honey which is also the only paradise on Earth, he has made himself vulnerable to all kinds of charges and attack by many fellow blacks who see him as utterly insensitive to the plight and immense suffering of his African ancestors who were taken to America in chains as slaves. I also share this perception. Perception is reality, but it may not be the reality in his case. He probably could have articulated his position in a better way.

Still, by implying that he is glad his ancestors were enslaved, he is saying he would never have been born in the best country on Earth, America, had slavery not taken place. Therefore the slave masters were right in what they did. "Find a better country," as the highly controversial and abusive black American conservative radio talk show host Ken Hamblin says. That is also the title of his book which is a devastating attack on black America for its failures and on those – including Africans – who criticise the United States for different reasons.

What Richburg says or implies, being grateful for slavery, is equivalent to Nelson Mandela thanking the apartheid regime for keeping him in prison for almost 30 years since his long-term imprisonment made him an icon of liberation and gave him the golden opportunity to become the first black president of South Africa.

It is also equivalent to Jews thanking Hitler and the Holocaust since by fleeing Nazi Germany where up to six million of their kinsmen were exterminated, they got the opportunity to settle in other countries where they and their children became very successful in many areas. For example, the extermination of the Jews and the Holocaust gave Henry Kissinger the opportunity to become an American secretary of state because he fled Germany with his parents as a teenager and settled in the United States when he was around 14 or 15 years old.

Had the Holocaust not taken place, he would never have had the opportunity to become an American citizen, and therefore secretary of state, and would have remained in Germany and may have ended up as a non-entity or dead under the Nazis.

There are many other people who would be equally grateful to Stalin, Idi Amin and other bloody tyrants for forcing them to flee their homelands and for killing their kinsmen, since the forced exodus made it possible for them to settle in other countries where they became successful in life in a way they never would have been in their native countries.

Yet, in spite of all the furour Richburg caused with his highly inflammatory statements about Africa in his book, we must also concede that he had the courage to tell the truth about our continent in a way many African-Americans, out of racial solidarity with us, don't and never intend to do lest they be branded "traitors" or help white racists reinforce their negative stereotypes about black people and the "Dark Continent."

But hiding the truth about us, simply because we are fellow blacks and share a common history of oppression at the hands of whites who conquered us, is not going to help us, or encourage us, to solve our problems. Truth may be a bitter pill to swallow, but it may be the best medicine for our debilitated condition; a point underscored by Richburg in his trenchant work, *Out of America: A Black Man Confronts Africa*:

"This analysis may sound too harsh, an exaggeration, But for that I can offer no excuses, because I've been there, and I'm trying to tell it straight, just like I've seen it. Because that's been one of Africa's biggest problems, the lack of any straight talk even from – or should I say *particularly* from – Africa's friends in the West who want to help.

And so I return to Kibassa Maliba's question (Kibassa Maliba was a key leader of Zaire's united opposition movement against President Mobutu Sese Seko): Why in the twentieth century? Why do Africa's leaders behave the way they do, plunder their national treasuries and allowing their countries to collapse around them? Why do they cling to power through all means, long after they have accumulated their billions? Why here, in black Africa?

Before my arrival in Africa, I had spent four years reporting from Southeast Asia....What I found in Asia was a region of amazing economic dynamism, a place largely defined by more than a decade of steady growth and development, vastly improved living standards, and expanded opportunities. Almost all of the Southeast Asian countries had risen from poverty to relative prosperity,

309

creating huge and stable middle classes and entering the first tier of newly industrialized economies.

Why has East Asia emerged as the model for economic success, while Africa has seen mostly poverty, hunger and economies propped up by foreign aid? Why are East Asians now expanding their telecommunications capabilities when in most of Africa it's still hard to make a phone call next door? What are East Asians now wrestling with ways to control access to the Internet, while African students still must use cardboard drawings of computer keyboards because they don't have real computers in their classrooms?

Why are East Asian airlines upgrading their long-haul fleets, while bankrupt African carriers let planes rust on weed-strewn runways because they can't afford fuel and repair costs? Why are the leaders of Southeast Asia negotiating ways to ease trade barriers and create a free-trade zone, while Africans still levy some of the most prohibitive tariffs on earth, even for interregional trade?

There was nothing inevitable about Asia's success and Africa's despair. Both regions emerged from colonialism at about the same time and faced many of the same obstacles. In 1957, when Ghana gained its independence from Britain, it was one of the brightest hopes of black Africa, with a higher gross national product than South Korea, which was itself still recovering from a destructive war, and before that, from thirty-five years as a Japanese colony.

Today South Korea is recognized as one of Asia's 'dragons,' an economic powerhouse expanding into new markets throughout the region and the world. Ghana, meanwhile, has slid backward. Its gross national product today is lower than it was at independence. World Bank economists like to point to Ghana as an example of an African country that is 'recovering' under a strict fiscal discipline program; what they don't tell you is that the economy today is propped up by foreign aid.

It's an ugly truth, but it needs to be laid out here, because for too long now Africa's failings have been hidden behind a veil of excuses and apologies. I realize that I'm on explosive ground here, and so I'll tread carefully. It's all too easy to stumble into the pitfall of old racial stereotypes – that Africans are lazy, that Asians are simply smarter, that blacks still possess a more savage, primitive side.

But I am black, though not an African, and so I am going to push ahead here, mindful of the dangers, knowing full well that some will say I am doing a disservice to my race by pointing out these painful realities. But we have come too far now to pull back; the greater disservice now, I think, would be to leave the rest unsaid.

First let's look at the statistics, the cold and hard realities, many of them depressingly familiar. According to the World Bank, Africa is home to the world's poorest nations - and that doesn't even really count places like Somalia, where there is no government around to collect them. Africa's children are the most likely on earth to die before the age of five. Its adults are least likely to live beyond the age of fifty. Africans are, on average, more malnourished, less educated, and more likely to be infected by fatal diseases than the inhabitants of any other place on earth.

Africa's economy has contracted. Its share of world markets has fallen by half since the 1970s, and the dollar value of the continent's global trade actually declined during the 1980s. African trade accounts for less than 0.1 percent of American imports. With the exception of South Africa, the African continent has been largely relegated to the economic sidelines, to the irrelevant margins of the world trading system.

Talk to me about Africa's legacy of European colonialism, and I'll give you Malaysia and Singapore, ruled by the British and occupied by Japan during World War II. Or Indonesia, exploited by the Dutch for over three

311

hundred years. And let's toss in Vietnam, A French colony later divided between North and South, with famously tragic consequences. Like Africa, most Asian countries only achieved true independence in the postwar years; unlike the Africans, the Asians knew what to do with it.

Talk to me about the problem of tribalism in Africa, about different ethnic and linguistic groups having been lumped together by Europeans inside artificial national borders. Then I'll throw back at you Indonesia, some 13,700 scattered islands comprising more than 360 distinct tribes and ethnic groups and a mix of languages and religions; Indonesia has had its own turbulent past, including a bloody 1965 army-led massacre that left as many as a million people dead. But it has also had thirty years since of relative stability and prosperity.

Now talk to me about some African countries' lack of natural resources, or their reliance on single commodities, and I'll ask you to account for tiny Singapore, an island city-state with absolutely no resources – with a population barely large enough to sustain an independent nation. Singapore today is one of the world's most successful economies.

I used to bring up the question of Asia's success wherever I traveled around Africa, to see how the Africans themselves – government officials, diplomats, academics – would explain their continent's predicament. What I got was defensiveness, followed by anger, and then accusations that I do not understand the history. And then I got a list of excuses.

I was told about the Cold War, how the United States and the Soviet Union played out their superpower rivalry through proxy wars in Africa, which prolonged the continent's suffering. And I would respond that the Cold War's longest-running and costliest conflicts took place not in Africa but in Korea and Vietnam; now tell me which continent was the biggest playing field for superpower rivalry.

312

When the talk turn to corruption – official, top-level plunder – then at last we are moving closer to brass tacks. Corruption is the cancer eating at the heart of the African state...Of course there's corruption in East Asia, too. Wide-scale corruption....Yet (South) Korea is an economic superpower, Indonesia has reduced poverty more per year for the last quarter century than any other developing country on earth, and Thailand, Vietnam, and China have all been posting annual growth rates of about 8 to 10 percent.

Contrast that now with Africa, where corruption is similarly rife, but the results quite different....So endemic is African corruption – and so much more destructive than its Asian counterpart – that the comparison has even spawned a common joke that goes like this:

An Asian and African become friends while they are both attending graduate school in the West. Years later, they each rise to become the finance minister of their respective countries. One day, the African ventures to Asia to visit his old friend, and is startled by the Asian's palatial home, the three Mercedes-Benzes in the circular drive, the swimming pool, the servants.

'My God!' the African exclaims. 'We were just poor students before! How on earth can you now afford all this?'

And the Asian takes his African friend to the window and points to a sparkling new elevated highway in the distance. 'You see that toll road?' says the Asian, and then he proudly taps himself on the chest. 'Ten percent.' And the African nods approvingly.

A few years later, the Asian ventures to Africa, to return the visit to his old friend. He finds the African living in a massive estate sprawling over several acres. There's a fleet of dozens of Mercedes-Benzes in the driveway, an indoor pool and tennis courts, an army of uniformed chauffeurs and servants. 'My God!' says the Asian. 'How on earth do you afford all this?'

This time the African takes his Asian friend to the window and points. 'You see that highway?' he asks. But the Asian looks and sees nothing, just an open field with a few cows grazing.

'I don't see any highway,' the Asian says, straining his eyes.

At this, the African smiles, taps himself on the chest, and boasts, 'One hundred percent!'

The joke was first told to me by an American diplomat in Nigeria who had also spent time in Indonesia. It carried a poignant message about the debilitating effects of corruption in Africa versus its more benign counterpart in Asia. 'In Indonesia, the president's daughter might get the contract to build the toll roads,' the diplomat told me, 'but the roads do get built and they do facilitate traffic flow.' In Africa, the roads never get built. It was the difference, he said, between 'productive corruption and malignant corruption'....

Candid assessment is rarer still among Africa's friends and boosters in the West. Instead of straight talk about Africa, you're more likely to get doublespeak, apologies, excuses – and above all, hypocrisy."[20]

The worst apologists for Africa are the Western governments and multilateral financial institutions, the World Bank and the International Monetary Fund (IMF), which help corrupt African leaders to stay in power. They sometimes condemn the corruption, and the waste, in African countries. They know most African leaders are responsible for this. Yet, they continue to support them while paying only lip service to democracy, transparency and accountability demanded of African leaders.

Therefore corrupt and despotic regimes on the continent have nothing to worry about, as they continue to be bankrolled by the West, stealing the money intended for the poor and for development projects. No one has really come down hard on them.

Freeze their foreign bank accounts, and force them to return to their countries the money they stole. And prosecute them. No one should be above the law. That is a democratic concept. There are no infallible aristocrats here. And we *don't* want them with their imperial presidencies running over us, and suffocating us.

There has, indeed, been some success in introducing democracy in some African countries, with dictators and life-presidents knuckling under pressure exerted by their own people and donor nations, especially those in the West, demanding democratic elections, transparency and accountability as a condition for aid to African countries. But it has not lasted long. Most African countries continue to be ruled by authoritarian or despotic regimes.

Elections continue to be rigged; government critics and opponents are constantly harassed, beaten, tortured, killed, and even stripped of their citizenship to silence them as happened in the case of Alasane Ouattara in Ivory Coast and elsewhere; social services, including education and medical care, are virtually non-existent or so poor that many people have given up on them; economies continue to deteriorate, leading to institutional and infrastructural collapse; and rampant corruption, a malignant cancer, ravaging African countries, has become such a venerable institution among the leaders and the elite that nothing is going to change without a complete overhaul of the power-structure and the system in all African countries.

One of the most tragic results of all this is human capital flight, a massive brain drain Africa has suffered since the sixties.

Hundreds of thousands of educated people and professionals have fled the continent in search of better life elsewhere, especially in the West, where our former colonial masters came from.

It is a tragic irony that these are the very same people who are now being asked to come back to rule us again because life under them was "better" than it is today under our own leaders, fellow Africans, as the brain drain continues.

Chapter Six

The Brain Drain

AFRICA is the least developed and "most backward" continent. It also suffers from a massive brain drain, losing tens of thousands of its highly trained professionals and other educated people to the industrialised nations of the West every year.

This has seriously affected development in what is also the poorest continent, ravaged by disease, and blinded by ignorance, with the vast majority of its people still being illiterate decades after independence.

But it not hard to understand why Africans are leaving their countries in such massive numbers whenever they get the opportunity to do so. Again, like almost everything else that bedevils the continent, it has to do with bad leadership which includes collusion with external forces – by many of our leaders and bureaucrats - to exploit Africa.

Those who emigrate are not traitors or people who just don't care about our countries. Most of them want to help develop our countries. They want to help our people. But they can't because of intolerable conditions in Africa.

Many educated Africans leave our countries because of lack of opportunities to use their talents to the maximum; because of repression, and lack of incentives. Their contribution to society is not appreciated by the leaders who don't even care to pay them well, let alone guarantee them the freedom they need to do what they are supposed to do.

These problems were once highlighted in a dramatic way at a conference in Switzerland in June 1999 in a confrontation between President Jerry Rawlings of Ghana and Professor Ali Mazrui, a Kenyan who has been teaching in the United States since the early 1970s.

Mazrui is one of Africa's most prominent academic and public intellectuals and probably the most renowned in Western countries. As Professor Francis Njubi, himself an immigrant from Kenya teaching at San Diego State University in California, stated in his paper, "African Intellectuals in the Belly of the Beast: Migration, Identity and the Politics of Exile":

"According to the United States Bureau of census, migrants born in Africa have the highest level of educational attainment in the United States when compared to other migrant groups like Asians, Europeans and Latin Americans.

Census figures for 1997 show that 48.9 percent (almost 50 percent) of African immigrants in the 25-year-and-over age bracket have a bachelor's degree or higher compared to Europeans, 28.7 percent, Asians, 44.6 percent, and Latin Americans, 5.6 percent....

The (African) immigrants also endure alienation from their countries of origin. Academic exiles are likely to be victims of government repression even before leaving their home countries. Many are pushed out of their countries after political disturbances at university campuses. Others are exiled because their political perspectives do not correspond with the dominant ideological dispensation of

318

the time.

Yet, these same forces that kept them from achieving their full potential at home demonize them for leaving instead of contributing to national development.

These tensions between intellectuals and politicians have boiled over frequently in the postcolonial world, most recently in a shouting match between Ghana's President Jerry Rawlings and eminent Kenyan scholar Ali Mazrui during a conference in Davos, Switzerland, in June 1999.

The Ghanaian president was extremely upset because medical doctors trained in Ghana at great expense were leaving for the West as soon as they completed their studies. He argued that it was not enough for the professionals to repay their student loans because it took at least 7 years to train another doctor, leaving thousands of patients without medical care.

Professor Mazrui's position, however, was that politicians like Jerry Rawlings were to blame for the exodus of professionals and academics from the continent. Mazrui himself had gone into exile in the early 1970s after being expelled from Uganda by Idi Amin and being denied a position at the University of Nairobi, Kenya, the country where he was born (and raised). Mazrui, therefore, argues that African politicians are partly to blame for the exodus because of the political and economic crises they create and the lack of recognition of the contributions of African intellectuals.

Even today, Mazrui is bitter about the fact that Kenyan broadcasting systems refused to air his television documentary 'The Africans: A Triple Heritage' which was produced by the BBC. The series is the only one on Africa by an African.

According to Mazrui, 'I sometimes feel a bit bitter about the fact that my own country has refused to televise the series, despite its fairly innocuous and barely radical political content, and I am convinced that ignoring it in

Kenya was a case of the authorities having a grudge with the singer rather than the song."[1]

On another occasion, Professor Mazrui also said that after he fled Uganda during Amin's reign of terror, he returned to Kenya where he was told by the vice-chancellor of the University of Nairobi that the school authorities – the Kenyan government, really, including President Jomo Kenyatta himself – would be willing to hire him to teach there only if he would be 'a good boy.' Known for his criticism of African leaders and governments, it was obvious that he was not prepared to become one.

Years later, he was asked in an interview with Philippe Wamba – a young journalist who grew up in Tanzania and died in a tragic car accident in Kenya in 2002 – if he thought of himself as being in exile in the United States where he had been teaching for 30 years:

"Well, yes,...you have to, I mean, in the sense that it's not been possible to get a job in my country. I mean, I don't think the regime would lock me up, although they could have decided that they would. Fortunately, they decided that it was prudent not to do that.

But when I left Makerere University in Uganda, the natural thing to do for me would have been to go to Kenya. I couldn't work in Uganda because of Idi Amin, so the next stop should have been Kenya. That would have been the sensible thing to do.

Do you know what happened? Kenya at that time only had the University of Nairobi, so the natural thing would have been to go to the University of Nairobi.

So the vice-chancellor at the time, the equivalent of the president of the university (in the United States), he took me to lunch, and said, 'You know, we would have hired you if we were sure you would be a good boy.' So, I told him, 'Look, I'm always a good boy, I don't know what you mean.' He said, 'Oh, you know.'

And really what he was referring to was when I lived in Uganda, under Obote number one [Prime Minister, later President Milton Obote's first term, from 1962 to 1970; he became president in 1966], whenever I was unhappy about the direction the country was taking, I would say so publicly. And then, Obote number one being what it was, sometimes the president would answer me, you see.

So the president turned my utterances into state issues. If he had just ignored them, nobody would have noticed. But he turned them into state issues. When he answered me, then people would discover, 'Ali Mazrui had said that,' because the president said, 'Ali Mazrui said that.'

So there is this notion that you couldn't have an academic who goes around making policy pronouncements, you see.

In Uganda, Obote occasionally was very irritated with me and once publicly said I should go and teach elsewhere, but I didn't pack my bags. I stayed put because this wasn't an official order, it was a speech in parliament. But in general, the image of a professor who dares to take on the president, you know, percolated to Kenya.

In the case of Kenya, the persecution of intellectuals is definitely a crisis of leadership. In some countries where you have a great deal of poverty, people may leave for economic reasons, you see. But that was not the case in Kenya, people were not leaving because they wanted bigger salaries. They were leaving because they were not getting enough elbow room to be themselves, you see. And until the 1990s there was considerable control of your movements as an academic. You needed the president's office's permission to go to a conference in Zambia....

You waste so much time dealing with the bureaucracy of doing your scholarship that it really becomes a chore. And then, when certain dignitaries may accost you and you end up being detained, which happened to the other Professor Mazrui, my nephew, El Amin Mazrui, who was locked up for thirteen months, definitely this is a leadership issue.

Countries which can support their people economically and where it is possible for people to, of course, have very satisfying jobs, when they leave it's because the leadership is seriously wrong."[2]

The interview was entitled, "An American African Scholar: An Interview with Professor Ali Mazrui," a titled that also highlighted Mazrui's dual identity as an African and as an immigrant in the United States where he has lived and taught in "self-imposed" exile as one of Africa's most prominent scholars. And because he was born and brought up in Africa, he calls himself an American African as opposed to an African American, the latter term being used to identify people of African descent born in the United States.

In fact, it was Mazrui himself who coined the term, "American African," to make a distinction between the two – African-American versus American African – in order to identify Africans born and brought up in Africa who have become naturalised American citizens.

The fact that he could no longer teach in Africa, and at the same time enjoy academic freedom as he normally would or would have liked to, demonstrates the cruel predicament African intellectuals find themselves in and which forces them to flee to other countries. Without freedom, scholarship is dull, and stale, sapped of its vitality by the state because of bad leadership which brooks no dissent. Yet, it is vital to development, to which it contributes very little when it is no longer the vibrant and dynamic force it is supposed to be.

Most African leaders are highly sensitive to criticism because they don't want to admit mistakes, let alone be held accountable for doing wrong. They therefore insulate themselves even from constructive criticism and good advice including innovative ideas which could be critical to national progress and the nation's wellbeing.

Neutralizing dissent and intellectuals who generate some of these ideas is one of the best weapons leaders use to protect themselves from criticism in order to perpetuate themselves in office as they continue to pursue policies which have proved to be counter-productive through the years. For example, when Ali Mazrui was a professor and chairman of the political science department, later dean of the faculty of arts and social sciences, at Makerere University, Dr. Milton Obote, the Ugandan president, once asked him if he knew the difference between being a political scientist and being a politician.

Obote felt that the criticism by Mazrui was unwarranted and came from someone who was no more than an academic – a political scientist – and who, not being a politician, did not know what it meant to lead a country.

President Obote may have had a valid point, as someone who was in the trenches and not in the ivory tower of academia. Yet, tragically, many of these same leaders have run our countries into the ground because they don't want to listen to anybody else but themselves; forcing tens of thousands of educated Africans to flee the continent, headed West more than any other destination. And once they leave, they usually don't intend to go back.

Academic intellectuals, some of whom are among the most ardent critics of African despotic and kleptocratic regimes, are just a part of the migratory wave comprising the elite leaving Africa, or living outside Africa.

Those already living abroad include many educated Africans who have decided not to return home after getting their degrees and other professional qualifications. For example, in Harris county alone, in Texas, there are more than 10,000 Nigerians. A disproportionately large number of them live in Houston, the fourth largest city in the United States after New York, Los Angeles, and Chicago in descending order. And one of the largest

African newspapers, *USAfrica*, published outside Africa, is based in Houston. It is run by Nigerians, mostly Igbo.

And the loss is staggering. By 2005, there were more than 5 million Africans in different professions living outside Africa. Also, tens of thousands of African students who go to school in Europe, North America and other parts of the world every year don't return to Africa after they finish their studies.

In 2005, about 50,000 Kenyan professionals lived and worked in the United States alone; that's without even counting those in the United Kingdom where, for historical reasons because of former colonial ties, they have in the past gone in larger numbers than they have anywhere else. And that's just example.

Now, add Nigerians, Ghanaians, Ugandans, Tanzanians, Zimbabweans, Zambians, Sierra Leoneans – all from former British colonies – and others who live and work in Britain, North America and other parts of the world including Australia. Also think about how many Africans from Senegal, Ivory Coast, Guinea, Mali and other former French African colonies live and work in France alone. And why.

Then you can see why our continent is in such a mess.

The tragedy of all this is that all these people would be in Africa helping to develop our countries had it not been for the rotten leadership and intolerable conditions in most parts of the continent.

In five years alone, between 1985 and 1990, Africa lost 60,000 of its highly educated people and other professionals who left the continent in search of better life in Europe, the United States, Canada, Australia and other countries. Probably the majority of them don't intend to return to Africa permanently, if at all; may be just to visit. As Philip Ochieng', one of Kenya's and Africa's most prominent journalists, stated in his article "How Africa Can Utilise its Intellectuals in 'Exile'" in *The East African*:

"Between 1985 and 1990, Africa lost 60,000 scientists, doctors, engineers, technicians and other experts to Western Europe, North America and other countries of the geopolitical North. I obtained this dismaying figure from a workshop which took place in Addis Ababa recently.

Organised by the United Nations Economic Commission for Africa (ECA), it sought to find ways of turning '...the net loss of skilled professionals into a net gain if we are not to be even further marginalised....' Those words were spoken by Joseph Ngu, an ECA economic analyst, at the start of the workshop.

The problem is well known. It is called the 'brain drain.' The causes are also well known. As long as we are either unable or unwilling to pay our professionals properly, as long as we, in our individualistic and tribal interests, persist in misplacing them and ignoring their advice, as long as the econo-political circumstances remain volatile as a consequence – so long will the brain drain and the refugee problem overwhelm us."[3]

I know Philip Ochieng'. We were on the same editorial staff at the *Daily News* in Dar es Salaam, Tanzania, in the early seventies. He was a columnist. I was a news reporter. I used to wear a necktie most of the time.

One afternoon in 1972, when we were in the editorial office, Ochieng' lifted my tie and shook it lightly and half-jokingly said, "Godfrey, you are tied to the West!"

He said that because a necktie was identified with Western attire. I wore a tie almost everyday when I was at work.

Ochieng' wore a dashiki or a short-sleeved shirt all the time. He was also an ardent Marxist-Leninist. He is still one.

When I left for United States in November 1972, he was still working at the *Daily News*. I have been gone since then and he probably would say to me: "I told you so! You are tied to the West." But, as he himself has stated, he also knows why most Africans have left Africa for the West – more than any other place.

In many countries across the continent, this exodus has been fuelled by political and civil unrest and outright civil wars, draining them of much-needed manpower and resources. The result is not only stunted economic growth but continued marginalisation of Africa in the global arena in which we remain spectators rather than active players, and thus unable to protect our interests. We play only a peripheral role and have never been a part of the mainstream.

Even those who want to return to Africa are discouraged from doing so because of civil strife, corruption, tribalism and nepotism, poverty, and many other problems which continue to dog the continent because of poor leadership.

It does not mean that they are unpatriotic and don't love their countries as much as their fellow countrymen who still live in Africa do. It's just a matter of being realistic; it's also a matter of survival. As Dr. Gichure wa Kanyugo, a Kenyan-born psychiatrist working in Boston, Massachusetts, who has lived in the United States since 1984 and became a naturalised citizen, bluntly stated:

"We would like to return home, but domestic conditions don't allow us to do so. You cannot eat patriotism, can you?"[4]

It is a sentiment articulated and shared even by those who still live and work in Africa. As Professor Wene Owino of the University of Nairobi in Kenya, himself a disgruntled academic, said:

"It would be absurd to expect optimal productivity out of people who do not have reliable amenities, like medical coverage, from their employer."

Academic standards across Africa have also been one of the biggest casualties of all this. As Owino explained, undergraduates are taught by inexperienced lecturers, while graduate students are left with no supervisors.

Many qualified Kenyan professors have left for other countries, mostly in Europe and North America and even Australia, increasing the brain drain; a point also underscored by Owino. As he put it:

"The brain drain is one thing this country can not afford."[5]

Nor can the rest of Africa.

What Africa can afford is create conditions and an environment conducive to sustained growth, and retention of its trained manpower – university graduates and others – by rewarding them accordingly. But nothing of the sort can be achieved in a climate of fear and intimidation where governments employ Gestapo tactics to silence and eliminate their opponents and critics; where they also encourage, and even thrive on, corruption; foster tribalism and provide jobs on the basis of ethnic ties and loyalties rather than merit; and foment civil unrest to weaken the opposition in order to perpetuate themselves in power.

In countries where genuine attempts have been made to tackle these problems, there has been some success in stemming the tide of the brain drain. Botswana provides one such example; a country which has pursued good economic policies and maintained democracy since independence in the sixties.

It is within the capacity of other African countries to reverse the migratory trend of their highly trained professionals to minimise its devastating impact on the continent as a whole. Tragically, there is little optimism that is indeed going to be the case. And if history is indicative of anything in this context, probably nothing will be done on a significant scale. Prospects are bleak that anything will be done soon, if at all, because of the kind of leadership we have on the continent, increasing the brain drain.

It is ironic, yet expected, that the richest and most advanced country in the world and in the history of mankind also attracts the largest number of some of the most highly educated immigrants whom it doesn't even need as much as their countries of origin do. Africa is one such big source, supplying the United States as well as other industrialised nations with a steady flow of highly trained professionals every year. And the loss is of staggering proportions for such an underdeveloped continent.

According to the United Nations, about 27,000 highly educated Africans and professionals emigrated to Western countries between 1960 and 1975. And the number rose in the following years. From 1975 to 1984, 40,000 well-educated Africans left Africa every year, further and rapidly draining the continent of one of its most important natural resources, highly trained manpower, without which development is impossible; this resource is now almost depleted, compared to the continent's needs, compounded by civil wars, failed economies and political unrest.

The number of highly educated African immigrants headed West and elsewhere reached 80,000 by 1987, as the migratory trend accelerated between 1985 and 1987.

The 1980s were some of the worst years in Africa in terms of lost opportunities, collapsing economies and civil strife. According to the same UN sources, the numbers went down thereafter, with an estimated 20,000 African professionals leaving Africa for the West every year since 1990.[6]

It was also during this period that African countries abandoned their failed socialist policies and one-party states, and introduced multiparty democracy – even if grudgingly by the leaders – after the end of the Cold War.

The decline in the number of educated Africans

seeking greener pastures elsewhere may partly be attributed to that, but the emigration continued to have a devastating impact on the continent, nonetheless. As Peter Da Costa of Gambia, a senior communication advisor with the United Nations Economic Commission for Africa (ECA), stated:

"We have 30,000 PhDs living outside Africa. It's an all-pervasive problem."[7]

That's a continent that needs about one million scientists and engineers in order to develop.

Where are they or where are they going to come from? Once they are trained, they are gone! Not all but many of them. And many of those who are trained abroad don't return to Africa. The same applies to other fields in which Africa does not have a critical mass to set things in motion and achieve progress.

In 1993, a UN Development Programme (UNDP) report also had some very disturbing statistics on this perennial problem. It said 21,000 Nigerian doctors worked in the United States alone.[8] That is a staggering figure, considering Nigeria's great need for doctors.

What is even more disturbing is that the numbers increased dramatically within only a few years. According to the *New Internationalist*, there were at least 30,000 Nigerian doctors working in the United States by the end of the 1990s. The numbers may not have risen so sharply within only seven years or so since 1993 when the UNDP issued its report. But the figure, of 30,000, was within the range of possibility and highlighted the seriousness of the problem as much as it did the intolerable conditions within Nigeria itself which forced many educated Nigerians to flee or stay away from their country.

What is certain is that there were a lot more Nigerian doctors – far more than the 21,000 cited by the UNDP in 1993 – working in the United States alone by the end of the 1990s. They include some of my schoolmates in the United States in the 1970s from Nigeria and other African countries such as Ghana.

While Nigeria has all these doctors working abroad, the country continues to suffer from a serious shortage of trained personnel in all medical-related fields; with the shortage of doctors being the most acute.

Other African countries are caught in the same predicament, with the flight of trained manpower compounding the problem in societies which already don't have enough trained people in almost all fields including primary school education. For instance, in Ghana, 60 per cent of the doctors who were trained there in the 1980s left the country.

And they were trained at government expense; a point underscored by President Jerry Rawlings and which was one of the reasons why he exploded at the conference in Switzerland in a heated exchange with Professor Ali Mazrui on why many educated Africans had left and continued to leave their countries for Europe, North America and other parts of the world.

The emigration of so many Ghanaian doctors has, like in Nigeria and other African countries, left the health care system – already in tatters – grossly understaffed, making it impossible to provide even the most minimal let alone adequate service to the people on a continent ravaged by disease and crippled by all kinds of health problems.

But there is an equally important and compelling reason, besides the ones mentioned earlier, why so many educated Africans are leaving their countries.

More than 80 per cent of the scientific research in all fields is conducted in industrialised countries. Therefore there is very little incentive for African scientists and other highly trained professionals to remain in Africa where there are hardly any research facilities; where also the pay is low, and working conditions, including bureaucratic interference, make it impossible for them to do research and use their talents to the maximum to help their countries.

Yet, Africa can not expect to develop without technological advancement. As President Yoweri Museveni of Uganda said during a visit to Tanzania towards the end of 2002, African countries are not going to develop by selling stones. They need to industrialise and become an integral part of the global economy.

That is true. But how can they industrialise when their scientists and other highly educated people are leaving the continent because of intolerable conditions at home, conditions which are created by the very same people – the leaders including Museveni himself – who blame them for leaving and accuse them of being traitors just because they can not work in their countries the way they should?

Museveni did not address that. So, for now, we will keep on selling stones – gold, diamonds and other minerals – and agricultural products until there is fundamental change in leadership and outlook across the continent to put our countries on the right course.

Africa can not continue to rely on extractive industries – mining, and so on – to develop her economies. Oil will run out; so will gold, diamonds and other minerals. They are not enough even now to develop our countries.

What are we going to do when we run out of minerals and we are left with nothing but holes?

We need a strong manufacturing sector in order to develop our economies, create jobs for our people, and effectively compete in the global arena. In most countries across the continent, the manufacturing sector is very weak or non-existent. We import almost everything in terms of manufactured goods. We even import clothes and shoes.

If we can not effectively compete in the global arena, we should, at the very least, be able to trade among ourselves and have a vibrant market on a continental scale, preferably with a common currency. We can also trade with other Third World countries on terms beneficial to all of us without being exploited by the industrialised nations whose terms of trade have never been favourable to us.

Industrialisation may not be easy for African countries – it has never been easy for any country – but it is something that must be done.

I was once ruefully reminded of our dire condition when I was a student at Wayne State University in Detroit in the United States in the early and mid-seventies. I was talking to one of my professors, R.V. Burks, who was also one of America's eminent scholars with international recognition, when he brought up the subject of underdevelopment and emphatically said: "What you need to do is industrialise!" Those were his exact words.

That was in early 1974, when I was 24 years old, but I vividly recall the conversation as if it was only yesterday.

Professor Burks taught Western civilisation and was one of America's foremost authorities on communism and the Soviet Union and its satellites. I also remember him telling our class that he talked to Leon Trotsky and was one of the last people who saw him not long before the former Soviet leader was killed with an axe by Stalin's agent in Mexico City in 1940.

Professor Burks knew that I was an African student; in fact, the only one in his class of more than 100. He also knew that many of our countries had adopted socialism in one form or another; an ideology renounced in the late eighties and early nineties because it failed to develop our economies.

I agreed with his prescription that African countries need to industrialise. Tragically, 40 years later after my conversation with him, and decades after failed socialist policies and one-party dictatorships across the continent compounded by corruption and inept leadership without transparency and accountability, our countries are no better off today than they were back then; in fact, they are worse off, in many respects, and with an increasing number of highly educated people fleeing to Europe and North America in search of better life.

One of the countries which has suffered the most from this kind of haemorrhage, because of civil conflict for decades caused by bad leadership, is Sudan. More than 30 percent of the engineers, 20 percent of the university lecturers, and 17 percent of the doctors and dentists who graduated in 1978 left the country through the years. Had it not been for civil war and political instability, probably most of them would have stayed in Sudan to help develop their country.

Other countries which have suffered just as much and sometimes even more so because of wars and other forms of civil strife include Sierra Leone, Liberia, the so-called Democratic Republic of Congo (formerly Zaire), Congo Republic (commonly known as Congo-Brazzaville), Angola, Rwanda, Burundi, Somalia (dead as a nation), Uganda, Mozambique, Ethiopia and Eritrea; all devastated by large-scale conflicts for years and in some cases for decades.

Even South Africa, an anchor of stability on this mangled continent, has also been losing more than 30,000 people, mostly white and highly educated, every year since the end of apartheid in 1994; much of the flight being attributed to a wave of crime sweeping across the country and to what whites perceive to be anti-white policies pursued by the government to correct racial disparities by implementing affirmative action and other corrective measures across the spectrum.

Unjust as they may seem, such policies should be looked at in their proper historical context. None of that would have been necessary had the apartheid regime never existed. It did because the majority of whites supported it to maintain their privileged status at the expense of blacks and other non-whites, making it necessary for the post-apartheid governments to adopt policies to rectify the situation especially for blacks who suffered the most under the diabolical regime as victims of deliberate and systematic exclusion and discrimination by the white rulers.

Yet, the situation is not very reassuring even for them under black majority rule. Some of the people leaving South Africa, in fact a significant number of them, are highly educated blacks. Some of the reasons they give for leaving are the high rate of crime and lack of opportunities even under non-white rule.

Zimbabwe, one of the jewels of Africa, is another country which has lost a very large number of educated people especially since the late 1990s when the government started to implement its fast-track land-reform programme by seizing white-owned land to correct historical injustices resulting from the seizure of land from blacks by whites when they conquered and colonised the territory in the 1890s.

Tragically, it is an approach that plunged the country into violence and chaos destroying the economy when government supporters invaded white-owned farms, attacked black farm-workers and some whites to forcibly evict them from the land. They also attacked members of the opposition. But the opposition itself started violence in a number of cases as a preemptive strike and to destabilise the government.

There was need for land reform in Zimbabwe. But the violence was unjustified. The tactics employed, including seizure of land, only exacerbated the situation. Even more tragically, the violence came from both sides, although the government, because of its power, unleashed its forces and perpetrated more violence than the opposition did, forcing an increasing number of highly educated people and to flee the country.

What was once one of Africa's most successful and most developed countries became a bankrupt nation and a pauper because of misguided policies by one of the continent's most illustrious and highly esteemed leaders who was an icon of African liberation; Robert Mugabe. The violence under his leadership tarnished not only Zimbabwe but the entire continent and his image.

Yet, such violence and political instability is nothing new in this turbulent continent. It is a continental phenomenon. And it has cost Africa a lot, not only in terms of lives lost and economies destroyed, but also in terms of high-level manpower as trained professionals continue to flee to other countries for safety and better life; far better than their war-torn and unstable countries and dilapidated economies can provide. As Dr. Patrick Seyon, former president of the University of Liberia and later director of the outreach programme at Boston University's African Studies Center, stated:

"The violence, the repression, the economy, those are the main issues. This situation has become even more critical since the 1970's and '80's when repressive regimes began springing up and the scholars fled the universities. They have not been able to return."[9]

Dr. Seyon went on to say that low university salaries often force professors and other faculty members to take other jobs to supplement their income:

"In Nairobi they drove cabs. The university lecturer has little time to spend on academic research or to help his students."[10]

It is the same problem throughout Africa. It also applies to doctors and other trained professionals who engage in different activities including owning a cow or two for milk, a garden for vegetables and even for extra income, as well as other income-generating schemes to make ends meet because they are not paid well.

Professors and lecturers also become private tutors, and doctors working in government hospitals go into private practice, with offices at home, to add to their meagre earnings.

All this has led to erosion of academic standards and provision of poor medical services even in countries which are relatively developed by African standards, as the professionals also continue to leave the continent, never to return.

The countries include South Africa, the most developed and most powerful on the continent. Yet it continues to suffer from a massive brain drain especially since the end of apartheid.[11]

Just as critical is lack of employment for many university graduates. For example, in my own country Tanzania, many university graduates in all fields, including those with master's degrees, remain unemployed for years. Some of the very lucky ones eventually end up getting jobs which don't even match their skills and educational qualifications, and at very low wages. It is not uncommon to find a law graduate working as a secretary or an economics graduate teaching history at a secondary school. Jobs for university graduates are so scarce that some of them have even been asked to teach in primary schools from standard one to standard four.

A survey by one of Tanzania's leading newspapers, *The Guardian*, in 2002 showed that many university graduates had not been able to find jobs five years or more after they graduated from the University of Dar es Salaam and other institutions of higher learning in and outside Tanzania.

In neighbouring Kenya, some accountants and other university graduates have been hauling bricks and sacks of maize or coffee to earn a living, the equivalent of one dollar to four dollars per day not enough even for basic necessities. During President Daniel arap Moi's tenure, Kenyan leaders including the president himself were daring enough to publicly tell university graduates that they should look for jobs in other countries.

They did not even think about creating jobs for them,

as the economy continued to shrink under rotten and corrupt leadership in spite of Africa's enormous economic potential and all the aid poured into Africa through the decades. Since the sixties, more than $500 billion in grants and soft loans have been pumped into Africa. That was according to 2006 statistics. More has been poured into Africa since then.

Yet we have nothing to show for it. Where did all that money go? Stolen and squandered by our kleptocratic and egomaniacal leaders who also want to perpetuate themselves in office or be succeeded by their sons and other relatives or family friends.

This is the kind of leadership we have in Africa, in most cases. Yet, you wonder why we are in such a mess?

Don't blame those who seek greener pastures elsewhere. Don't blame them when they want to improve their lives elsewhere and even help some of their family members to get out of Africa as well. Blame our leaders, most of whom have done nothing for our countries and for us since independence besides raiding national coffers to enrich themselves and keeping our pockets empty with exorbitant taxes, low pay or none at all. They are busy stealing and squandering money. And as they continue to do so, tens of thousands of Africans emigrate to other countries every year as the only way to make it in life or just to earn a simple living.

A significant number of professionals and university graduates including lawyers and some with Ph.Ds who have left Africa have even taken jobs as janitors, taxi drivers, security guards or manual labourers in the United States and elsewhere just to survive. But they also earn a lot more money than they would ever have dreamed of earning had they remained in Africa.

Had it not been for the conditions at home, deplorable and intolerable, most of them would probably not have left Africa. And most of those educated abroad would probably have returned home. Yet, they are blamed for doing what any sensible person caught in a predicament or who is faced with a potentially dangerous situation would do. That is – get out of it if you can. As James Shikwati stated in his article "Brain Drain versus Africa's Economic Woes":

"Do African intellectuals who migrate to developed countries betray their home? If you have ever attended a fundraising function in Kenya meant to assist a student going for further studies abroad, you will surely never miss to hear a politician give a piece of advice thus: 'Make sure you come back home to develop your nation, this country needs your expertise.'

After three years or so, a keen reader of the local daily newspapers may read in the mail section of the paper, 'A Kenyan residing abroad urging Kenyans to be democratic, accountable and pro-progress.' In the same paper, there may be a story about certain top-notch academicians who migrated to other countries citing harassment, low pay, poor academic freedom and inadequate funding for research initiatives.

The editorial too may be screaming betrayal: 'They waste tax payers money and then vanish in search of greener pastures.' Meanwhile, on the page on African news, a number of African heads of state would be quoted lambasting Western countries for Africa's political and economic instability. In the same breath, they would be heard in conferences and seminars appealing for assistance from experts in the West to advise them both on economic and political issues.

Interesting enough, the 'imported experts' tend to be people using ideas from the 'African experts' who were exported by unfavourable conditions in Africa. Who is to blame for Africa's political and economic problems? Brain drain?

Take Kenya for instance. How many leaders listen to our local experts? Who runs our universities – academics, or politicians? From primary schools, secondary schools, college to university level, academic institution leadership is controlled by political alliances. Political correctness is the key to success, so states political law. When serious academicians migrate, betrayal is the tag they receive.

Those who choose to remain and voice what their rationality dictates, are told, 'You've been paid by foreign masters.' The same political acrobats ask for aid from the very foreigners to 'develop their country.' If they miss aid, they opt to insult the developed countries for having robbed Africa.

Do we have such a thing as brain drain? If you dig a drainage channel outside your house to direct storm water away from your compound, are you to reproach the storm water for escaping? Will it be justified to import water when you allow your own to run off? If Kenya does not nurture an environment conducive to academic growth, holds intellectuals with conjecture; what effect does it expect from its actions?

How can Africans expect to escape the quagmire they are presently wallowing in by blowing bridges to their freedom, and economic prosperity? If you enslave men of ideas, if you discourage thinkers and murder reason – why pretend to be seeking solutions to African problems? How can a system that holds poverty as a virtue struggle for prosperity?

Revulsion against intellectuals in Africa is suicide to our economic and political stability. Free the academic world, and the spring of ideas to solve African problems will emerge.

People who oppose reason fill the void left by the migrant intellectuals. Haters of reason are quick to blame brain drain, 'unpatriotic' intelligentsia for their shortcomings. But one thing they fail to recognize is that the haters of reason provided the infrastructure of destruction. They polluted the intellectual world of reason by their strategy of 'carrots and sticks.'

Africa's woes are a result of reason held hostage by pseudo-intellectual leadership. They are further sustained by the robber ultimatum of 'your life, or your mind.'

The Western countries that are absorbing Africa's thinkers do so because they recognize the power of the mind. Africa fails to learn from its environment. For instance, it is a known fact that some plants are adjusted to the climate in such a way that they have deep taproots in areas with less water, and they also shed leaves during dry seasons.

Africa, unlike its characteristic vegetation mentioned above, does not make any effort to tap its intellectual potential. It has not learnt to adjust according to seasons – colonial, postcolonial and neocolonial seasons – it specializes in the 'blame industry.' The taproot of African governments is aimed at destructive military arsenals, destruction of reason, techniques of silencing dissenters and populist policies.

By failing to offer 'green pastures' for its own intelligentsia, Africa is committing suicide by slow poison.

In conclusion, African intellectuals who migrate to developed nations do not betray Africa. They simply illuminate the fact that priorities are misplaced in this continent. For example, why do African governments that claim to be poor, find it logical to pay expatriates hundred times more than local experts? The message to Africans is clear: go abroad to seek green pastures.

The African intellectuals have been betrayed by their mother countries. Their abilities were doubted before being put to a test. It would be better for a politician presiding over a fundraising in aid of a student jetting abroad to say: 'This country is in no urgent need for thinkers, go for a holiday and come back to sing praise songs.'"[12]

That is Africa's tragedy. Yet, human capital flight is not unique to Africa. Asia, Latin America and other parts of the world including former communist countries also suffer from the brain drain. But the problem is worst in Africa. Tragically, it is also the poorest and least developed continent which can ill-afford to lose such capital: its trained professionals and other highly educated people.

And statistics on the problem don't get any better no matter where you look. For example, another study by the World Bank says about 70,000 highly qualified African scholars and experts leave Africa every year to work in other countries, mostly in the industrialised West. This figure does not include the large number of students who also leave the continent every year to study overseas. A very large number of them don't return, either, after they finish their studies. And for good reason.

To replace those who left, African countries spend about $4 billion annually on hiring an estimated 100,000 expatriates without whom the continent would literally come to a grinding halt or degenerate into total chaos and even dissolve in anarchy in some cases.

Almost everything of an infrastructural and technical nature would shut down due to lack of a critical mass of highly skilled manpower needed to keep the countries functioning as socio-political and economic entities.

The problem is so serious that Africa is destined to remain on the periphery of the international mainstream unless something is done now, by our leaders, to reverse the trend. As the World Markets Research Centre stated in its 2002 report, "The Brain Drain – Africa's Achilles Heel":

"The brain drain problem has also contributed to Africa's growing marginalisation in the global economy. According to a study by the Geneva-based intergovernmental body, the International Organisation for Migration (IOM), there are currently just 20,000 scientists and engineers in Africa – or just 3.6 per cent of the world's

341

scientific population – serving a population of about 600 million.

Africa would need at least 1 million scientists and engineers to sustain the continent's development prospects. At least one-third of science and technology professionals from developing countries are currently working in Europe, the US, Canada and Australia."[13]

And as Katrin Cowan-Louw, assistant programme officer at the International Organisation for Migration (IOM), said:

"There are more African scientists and engineers working in the US than there are in Africa. Long-term economic growth cannot be achieved by primarily exporting natural resources."[14]

One tragic case after another demonstrates the utter futility of the efforts by African governments to keep educated Africans in their countries with empty rhetoric and with promises the leaders never intend to fulfill.

A few years ago, Zambia had 1,600 doctors. By 2002, only 400 remained in the country. The rest had emigrated, literally fled, to Europe, the United States, neighbouring Botswana and South Africa, lured by higher salaries and better working and living conditions.

Some African countries may have lost fewer doctors, but the impact is the same, nonetheless, in terms of diminished capacity to cope with Africa's enormous problems in the health sector, compounded by the flight of other professionals whose departure from Africa has ripple effect across the spectrum as much as that of any other highly trained personnel leaving our continent to work overseas.

So far, we have failed to reduce let alone stop this outflow of human capital from our continent; as much as we have failed to stop the financial haemorrhage of our countries caused by our leaders who are busy stealing billions of dollars from us every year, depositing the loot in foreign banks, mostly in the West. It is a loss we can't afford in either case.

But in spite of the mess we are in today, one also wonders if we can really afford to be colonised again as some of our people, desperate for help, have suggested.

We have come a long way since independence in the fifties and sixties. And we still have a long way to go. We are now at the crossroads.

Chapter Seven

What Went Wrong
and What Should Be Done

AFRICAN COUNTRIES are in a mess today because of bad leadership and the wrong policies they pursued for decades since independence.

And we are still on the wrong path because of the refusal by most of our leaders to change course despite claims to the contrary especially since the end of the Cold War. We have lost more than an entire generation to such wrongheaded leadership and, in a few cases, even well-meaning incompetence.

The record of African governments in the economic arena since the sixties is one of dismal performance at best, and tragic failure at worst.

They have failed to function as a dynamic force for fundamental change because of their poor economic performance. They have, more than anything else, served as instruments of oppression and exploitation, stifling

345

individual initiative by dominating the economy and neutralising dissent. They have also earned a well-deserved reputation as highly corrupt institutions whose failure is writ large on the African economic landscape telescoped into appalling statistics.

Even in this era of globalisation, many people don't want to invest in Africa because of corruption, civil wars and unrest, political instability, lack of law and order, utter disregard for individual freedom and property rights, unwarranted bureaucratic interference and intrusion, lack of infrastructure, and a myriad other problems.

Even local investors are scared to invest in Africa. As Herman Cohen, the American assistant secretary of state for African affairs under President George H. W. Bush, stated:

"(Africa) does not provide the climate for investment and economic growth.

Not only do foreign investors worry about the safety of what they're going to put in, but local people have the same problem.

When I went to Ghana recently (1989), they asked why American investors aren't coming in. And I said, how come Ghanaian investors aren't investing? They said they're waiting for the Americans to show that we have confidence."[1]

Since the mid-nineties, international trade, foreign investment and increasing technology have transformed the global economy and continue to improve the lives of tens – if not hundreds – of millions of people in the Third World. But this improvement has taken place mostly in Asia and in some parts of Latin America, alleviating poverty.

Africa is the only underdeveloped region that has been almost completely left out. Hundreds of millions of Africans have become poorer through the years; their poverty and misery compounded by the AIDS pandemic which claimed more than 20 million lives in Africa alone from the early eighties to the late 1990s and early 2000s and continued to kill about 2 million Africans every year. And there seems to be no way out of this vicious cycle of poverty and misery.

Political chaos, corruption, wrong economic policies, lack of infrastructure – poor transportation and communications and storage facilities – and a host of other problems including lack of skilled labour due to low levels of education and poor health services have all retarded economic growth in African countries. And diminution of the labour force because of frequent and long-term illnesses has been compounded by the AIDS pandemic ravaging the continent.

All those problems collectively are the reason why African countries are in such a deplorable condition more than an entire generation after independence.

In fact, most of the African countries were better off during the first decade of independence in the sixties than they are today.

Besides the former Belgian Congo and a few other hot spots, they had less chaos then than they do today. And they had more to eat then than they do now. Some of them even exported food three decades or so before the sixties. And they still had plenty left for the people to eat and sell on the domestic market. As Dr. Robert Gardiner, the internationally renowned Ghanaian economist who was the first Executive Secretary of the UN Economic Commission for Africa, stated at the 15th Session of the UN Economic and Social Council in Geneva, Switzerland, on July 12, 1968:

"Africa, Asia and Latin America were all net grain exporters thirty years ago, when the total grain outflow from these regions was taking place at an average annual rate of 11 million tons. In the 1940s, the developing

347

regions became net importers; and by 1965, developing Africa was importing 4 million tons of cereals more than it exported."[2]

Today, more than 40 after independence, almost all African countries not only import a substantial amount of food; many of them depend on food donations and other forms of assistance from other countries for sheer survival.

Even other developing countries sometimes donate food to Africa, although they are not rich themselves but painfully aware of Africa's plight. They feel sorry for us.

Yet they were just as poor as their African counterparts a generation ago. Some were even poorer. Not only are they richer today; they are also far more technologically advanced than almost all the African countries are. Even simple technology has bypassed Africa. And where such technology exists even if in rudimentary form, it can still be a battle to get things done, as this case illustrates:

"For years, customers could not call Kwabena Afari, a pineapple exporter, directly in Aburi, his hometown 65 miles north of here (Accra). His clients first had to call this city, Ghana's capital. Then someone here would call the Aburi post office. Then a post office messenger (from the Aburi post office) would go to Mr. Aburi's home (usually walking, or on a bicycle).

If anything went wrong, and it frequently did, he might not receive the message for days. 'Customers were complaining,' said Mr. Afari, 46, who recently bought a cellular telephone. 'My guy in Turin (Italy) got fed up. He said, 'I can't work with you anymore. It is hard to communicate."

Mr. Afari's struggles are an example of what ails sub-Saharan Africa....As a great wave of trade and foreign investment transforms the global economy...sub-Saharan Africa has been left behind."[3]

That is something most of us admit. In fact, things are worse than that. Africa has not even entered the race for a share of the global economic pie which goes to the swiftest: those who attract foreign investors and have the upper hand in technical skills Africans don't have, creating a climate conducive to investment. As Lucia Quachey, head of the Ghanaian Association of Women Entrepreneurs, put it: 'It's not that we have been left behind. It's that we haven't even started.'[4]

Africa has fallen so far behind that she really has nowhere to go but forward even if it's at a snail's pace while others are flying past her.

Statistics tell the story, and it's a sad one through the years. They paint a gloomy picture of Africa's socioeconomic status, yet a realistic one.

In its report entitled "ECA and Africa's Development, 1983 - 2008," the Economic Commission for Africa (ECA) stated the following:

"In 1980, the average per capita income of the African region was only $741 compared with a per capita GNP of $9,684 in the industrialized countries. But this crude measure says little about the sad realities of life in Africa."[5]

The report then went on to depict an even more appalling statistical profile of Africa's socioeconomic plight in stark terms:

- 70 out of every 100 Africans are either destitute or on the verge of poverty.
- Only 1 out of 4 Africans has access to clean water.
- Of the 33 million people added to the work force during the 1970s, only 15 percent found remunerative employment.
- Per capita income has risen more slowly in Africa

than in any other part of the world in the last 20 years.

- Africa's population is expanding at a rate of 2.8 percent annually, while food production is expanding at 1.5 percent.

- In 1980 Africa spent $5 billion importing 20.4 million tons of grain, excluding substantial freight costs.

- In 1980, the average African had 12 percent less home-grown food than in 1960.

- Africa's potential arable land is estimated at 4.2 acres per person, yet only 1.4 acres per person are currently being used.

- Africa's average food production per acre is about half of the world's average.[6]

In his introduction to the report, ECA Executive Secretary Adebayo Adedeji said if the current trends continue for 25 years, which means until 2008, Africa's socioeconomic situation would be 'horrendous.'

In many respects, Africa is no better off than she was back in 1983 when the ECA report was issued.

Nevertheless, to avert the catastrophe the ECA back then called upon massive reforms in Africa and in the international system.

To reverse the negative historical trends, the Commission called for the industrialised nations to live up to their commitment of devoting 0.7 per cent of their gross national product to development assistance for African countries, a pledge made to other Third World nations as well. It also exhorted African nations to manage their own resources better in order to fuel an "industrial takeoff."

Warning African countries about the devastating effects of their dependence on imported food, the ECA report recommended changes in agricultural pricing which discourages African peasants and farmers from producing a lot of food since they are not paid much for it when they sell it on the domestic market. It also recommended changes in land-tenure practices. Both of these changes were recommended as an incentive to increased food production.

But the ECA report proposed nothing new in terms of solutions, except emphasis. In emphasising the darker side of the continent's predicament, with grim statistics, the report left no doubt that Africa faces enormous problems just to be able to survive at the subsistence level, let alone develop.

In fact, ominous trends to where Africa was headed were evident as far back as the 1960s. During that decade in the initial euphoria of independence, economic growth in African countries was very slow and generally below the modest target established by the UN General Assembly for the newly independent nations.

Even back then, Africa had the largest number of the poorest and least-developed countries in the world as it still does today. Its economic growth was also the lowest compared with the other developing regions of the world, mainly Asia and Latin America. Computed in 1960 prices, African total output grew by 3.4 percent per year from 1960 to 1966; while per capita income grew by a mere 1 percent annually during the same period.[7]

As a result of such retarded economic growth, the poverty and misery which were so common across the continent at the beginning of the decade continued virtually unabated during the following years. Africa's poor economic performance during the sixties was also highlighted by stark contrast as it has been through the years since independence.

Higher growth rates in other developing regions have served to sharpen the contrast between Africa's plight and the relatively better conditions in many other parts of the Third World. For example, Mozambique is not Guyana nor is Niger the same as Trinidad & Tobago in terms of economic conditions, although they are all Third World countries.

There are poor countries, and there are those that are

351

the poorest of the poor. And that's where Africa comes into sharp focus.

Unfortunately, the strategy African countries – hence African governments – adopted to pursue economic development was more externally- than locally-based. They counted a lot on foreign aid to fuel their economies. And that was a tragic mistake, and failure, by the modern African state practically in every country across the continent. The reason is simple, although perhaps deceptively simple, which may explain why it eludes even some of our best minds.

We can not depend on the goodwill of the industrialised nations to develop Africa. To a very large degree, their very prosperity depends on perpetuating the status of African countries and other underdeveloped regions of the world as plantation economies for the provision of cheap raw materials to the industrialised world, and as a source of cheap labour for the manufacture of consumer goods for the metropolitan countries. It has now become common practice for companies in the industrialised world to transfer some of their operations or relocate to Third World countries to take advantage of the virtually unlimited reservoir of cheap labour.

This asymmetrical relationship between the industrialised and underdeveloped countries also guarantees markets in the Third World for manufactured goods from the metropolitan nations.

African countries through the years have been flooded with goods from other nations instead of encouraging the growth of their own industries to manufacture import-substitution items. African governments discouraged such entrepreneurship because they dominated the economies of their countries through nationalisation of most businesses, thus excluding local investors and entrepreneurs. They also squandered the nation's resources which could have been better spent to achieve economic growth and industrialisation.

And this served the industrialised nations well, since it meant African countries would remain primary producers of raw materials for the industrialised world and continue to be a dumping ground for its cheap manufactured goods.

That is what they still are today. And any talk of a new international economic order to redress the imbalance is sheer wishful thinking.

Rich nations dominate the world economy, hence the world market. They are not interested in changing terms of trade to their detriment in order to enable Africans and other Third Worlders have access to markets in metropolitan countries and sell their products to Western consumers on fair terms; nor are they going to allow them to have control over the prices of the goods they produce and sell on the global market.

That is not how the profit system works; not at the national level or at the international level. You can't reform the price system for the benefit of the underdog because the only way it is meant to work is to serve the interests of the rich and the powerful; be it the industrialised nations vis-a-vis the underdeveloped countries of Africa or the local retailer versus peasant customers who buy sugar and cooking oil from him.

There is no room for sentiment in business. Businessmen, individuals or nations, are not in the business of reducing their profits. They are in the business of making more and more, not less. And the international economic system, controlled and manipulated at will by rich powerful nations, is based on the exploitation of the weak raw-material producing countries. Therefore it can not be reformed to benefit the exploited.

The contradiction is obvious. For example, when African countries and other Third World nations called for a new international economic order to transfer some of the wealth from the rich to the poor nations, the former American ambassador to the United Nations, Daniel Patrick Moynihan, bluntly said: "That is looting." And he

353

said it on American national television which was as effective in transmitting his message across the world as if it were an international medium. That was in the late seventies.

So we are on our own. What African countries need to do is to be self-reliant by increasing trade among themselves and establish an African common market on which they can even sell their own manufactured goods to each other which may not be competitive on the world market. Without regional integration and a continental market, we are doomed. Africa's infant industries are simply not ready to compete on the world market flooded with manufactured goods from the industrialised nations.

Had this strategy been pursued from the beginning soon after independence, African countries would not be in the kind of mess they are in today.

But instead, they sought wider markets outside Africa for their primary commodities, and unimpeded access to customers in the industrialised nations to try and induce them to buy African semi-manufactured and even a few manufactured goods which, unfortunately, were no match for those produced in the developed countries. They are also sought the transfer of resources and technology to Africa which would have amounted to about 1 per cent of the gross national product of the developed nations per year.

To their dismay, they found out that the industrialised nations erected tariff barriers against African imports, except for those goods they really needed and could not produce themselves. The governments of the developed countries also subsidised exports from their own producers, farmers and manufacturers, giving them a competitive edge over African commodities. And in most cases, the industrialised nations did not honour their commitment to contribute 1 per cent of their gross national product to finance economic development in Third World countries; they still don't today.

Behind all these strategies and policies was the modern African state which since independence has been the fundamental dynamic in Africa's economic development; without any input from local entrepreneurs since the state discouraged the growth of the private sector; and without any input from the opposition, of which there was virtually none since the state tolerated no dissent, all of whom could have proposed alternative policies which could have saved Africa from economic ruin.

That is still the case today in most countries across the continent, as the state continues to muzzle the opposition while paying only lip service to democracy, and only grudgingly implementing free-market policies intended to dismantle state monopoly over the economy and replace it with the private sector as the engine for economic growth. The state still wants to maintain monopoly despite its tragic failure as a catalyst for economic growth.

The role the opposition could have played here – pointing in the opposite direction as the best route to economic development, and demanding transparency and accountability from those in office – can not be underestimated; even if such opposition had been allowed to flourish and present alternative policies within the ruling party itself, while maintaining the one-party system especially during the early years of independence for the sake of national unity which could have cracked along ethnic and regional lines under "multiparty" – read, multi-tribal – democracy many people were demanding soon after the young African nations emerged from colonial rule.

But that does not mean that the one-party state should have, as it did in most African countries, snuffed out the opposition, muzzled the press, and discouraged cross-fertilisation of ideas in public forums, just for the sake of "national unity."

Had the people been allowed to freely express their views without fear of retribution and instant justice from the nation's security forces, and to publicly challenge government policies and present alternative policies even without the existence of an official opposition in parliament, almost all African countries would have adopted free-market policies soon after independence, and their economies would not be in tatters today.

People want money and profit. They can't get that under socialism, or they get very little of it. They don't get paid or earn enough for their labour and skills – and sacrifices – under socialism. But they can do that under capitalism more than any other economic system, despite the predatory nature of capitalism which thrives on greed and competition.

African countries have now adopted free market policies and democracy – one generation too late.

The people should have been allowed to decide what they wanted to do with their lives and what kind of policies their countries should pursue. But they were denied that right and were scared to speak up. Freedom of speech is a natural right, and difference of opinion a part of human nature. As one Ugandan professor at the Makerere University in Kampala, Uganda, who for his own safety asked that his name not be used, said in an interview in 1998:

"Don't tell me democracy is a Western concept. It's a market concept. Don't tax me and say I should not question you."[8]

But there were also other problems during the sixties and later on through the decades which retarded Africa's economic growth; again, thanks to the ubiquitous presence of the modern African state, directing virtually everything instead of allowing the people to micro-manage their own affairs and letting the invisible hand of *laissez-faire* play a role in pursuit of economic development.

However, some of those problems also had their own

dynamics and momentum due to the underdeveloped nature of the African economies and would still have impeded progress even if the state had played a minimal or peripheral role in directing economic development. But the problems were also compounded by unwarranted intrusion by the state, misguided policies, and waste of resources through outright theft and mismanagement by government officials and their auxiliaries.

However, it is also very important to remember that although the modern African state failed to fuel economic growth through state enterprises, its failure should also be looked at in its proper historical context.

There would have been no economic development in Africa at all without state involvement and enterprise. In the absence of a vibrant indigenous private sector, and there was hardly any, it was only the state in the young African nations which had the money – from export commodities, taxes, and foreign aid and investments – to launch and finance development projects and invest in the economy.

Equally important to remember is the fact that when African countries won independence, the first thing they had in mind was the consolidation of the nation-state – no country can survive under a weak government and without national unity – and the provision of education and health services (training teachers, doctors and nurses; building schools, clinics and hospitals), as well as the building of infrastructure: mainly roads and bridges, railways and harbours, communications networks, power plants, storage facilities, and so on.

All those were all essential projects, as they still are today. But they were not productive right away. They absorbed more funds and other resources than they yielded benefits during the early years of independence. It was years before African countries could see the results, and not all positive.

Agriculture was, of course, the backbone of the

357

economy in all African countries, as it still is today and probably for decades to come. But unfortunately, between 1960 and 1966, agricultural production grew more slowly than the other sectors of the economy in most African countries. In 1960, the agricultural sector accounted for almost 40 per cent of the gross domestic product of Africa. And during the next six years, the value added to total output by agriculture increased at a dismal rate of 1.3 percent per year.[9]

The low level in agricultural production explains, more than anything else, why incomes grew so slowly in African countries during that period. And it is easy to understand why agricultural output was so low, as it still is today in this continent of a peasant economy.

In most parts of Africa, most of the food and export crops are produced in very old-fashioned ways; "primitive" is the word others use, but we don't because of its derogatory connotation in this context applicable to Africans and other non-Europeans.

But it is true that farming techniques in African villages, where most of the crops are grown, have remained relatively the same probably for hundreds of years, severely limiting agricultural production mostly to the subsistence level. Such low yield can guarantee only one thing: economic stagnation, even retardation, and poverty.

Also, such output has not kept pace with population growth and increasing urbanisation. Even the peasants themselves don't always have enough food for their own families, let alone for urban dwellers. One of the devastating consequences of such low production is hunger. Food shortage across Africa through the years since independence has forced African countries to import and even beg for food without which there would be mass starvation.

Yet, all these are primarily agricultural countries which should be exporting food instead. They have more than enough arable land for that. Even in some fertile areas, people still starve because they don't produce or work hard enough; they have large families they can't fully support; and they use poor farming methods without modern skills and equipment.

Income levels have equally stagnated or climbed very slowly through the decades, so that by the late 1990s, almost half the entire African population – and not all that half is a wage-less peasant population – was living on less than $1 per day. That was almost 400 million people back then; today it is 500 million. As Stephen Buckley reported from Africa in 1997 in the *International Herald Tribune*:

"About 40 percent of Africa's people live on less than $1 a day. From 1989 to 1992, nearly half of the continent's countries suffered negative economic growth rates.

Only in the last two years have there been signs of an upturn as such countries as Ghana, Mozambique, Tanzania and Uganda pursue free-market policies; regional growth may have reached 5 percent last year, according to the International Monetary Fund.

Still, in the last 20 years, per-capita income has crawled upward roughly $70 in Africa, compared with a $900 jump in East Asia."[10]

As Africa's population continues to grow at a phenomenal rate, at least 20 million more people every year, there is an imperative need for African countries to improve agricultural production and marketing in order to increase output and income especially for those living at the subsistence level. As you increase the purchasing power of the vast majority of the people, who are mostly peasants and workers, you also improve prospects for industrialisation which is impossible and meaningless without a large domestic market for manufactured goods.

An improvement of the agricultural economy will also increase the labour force for industry – by producing enough food for urban dwellers where factories and workers are – and expand other sectors of the economy whose growth depends on the existence of a vibrant agricultural sector in preindustrial societies like Africa.

Eevn today almost 50 after since independence, the industrial sector in most African countries is still very small and rudimentary, not very much different from what it was during the sixties, despite its steady growth in some parts of the continent through the years; for example, in Ivory Coast, Nigeria, Ghana, and Kenya, which are some of the most industrialised countries in black Africa, at least by African standards; by international standards, they are not industrialised at all – nothing but agrarian societies like the rest on the continent.

Between 1960 and 1966, the contribution of manufacturing production to total output in Africa as a whole grew at an annual rate of 4.2 per cent. However, by 1966, the manufacturing sector accounted for less than 12 per cent of Africa's gross domestic product.[11]

Some of the major obstacles which impede industrialisation in Africa are the very same ones which retard economic growth: lack of investments; a weak infrastructure; shortage of energy supplies in spite of the fact that Africa alone has 40 per cent of the world's hydroelectric potential, the largest of any continent, which unfortunately is underutilised; low levels of technical skills; poor health and rampant disease; and the limited scope of domestic markets. For example, in terms of market potential, 30 African countries in 1968 had a total population of less than 5 million each. Some even had less than 1 million. That was in a continent of 52 countries then; there are 54 today.

Compounding the problem was the fact that these small populations were spread over vast expanses of territory, called countries of course, whose per capita and aggregate purchasing power was almost negligible in terms of sustaining a large domestic market for both agricultural and industrial products.

But even if all these problems, besides small population, were eliminated overnight, most African countries simply did not have large domestic markets to justify large-scale investment in industrialisation without coordinating their activities to pursue industrial projects at the regional level. Today, they have larger populations, but still not large enough individually to achieve rapid economic growth and industrialisation. It is only through regional integration that they can do that.

A regional grouping is in a much stronger position to attract larger investments, especially from foreign investors who have the largest amount of capital, because of its large size for a domestic market and provision of raw materials. An integrated region is also in a much stronger position to form common services and taxation systems and build a solid infrastructure at the regional level, all of which are vital for rapid economic growth.

In the absence of massive foreign aid, such growth is possible only when the private sector is allowed to flourish and operate as the main engine of progress. And it is possible to achieve such progress on a continental scale because of Africa's enormous potential wealth. Tragically, the world's richest continent in terms of natural resources is also the poorest. It is a paradox that will continue to haunt us for a long time. But Africa's plight does not have to be permanent. We can end our poverty and misery.

The effort has to start in Africa itself on regional basis to integrate the continent as a whole, instead of being so dependent on outsiders in terms of trade and economic aid. We must be self-reliant and self-sufficient. One way to achieve this is through inter-territorial and inter-regional trade on a continental scale. Unfortunately, African countries do very little trade among themselves. They also have very few transportation and communication links between them.

Because of the continent's colonial past, the transport

361

system African countries inherited at independence was oriented towards export and import trade with countries outside the continent, and was also intended to serve the colonial powers in their own areas. There was no road, railway or telecommunications network linking several African countries as one region.

Where some of those links existed, it was mainly between countries under the same colonial power. For example, Kenya, Uganda, and Tanganyika had a common market, a common currency, and common services under the East African Common Services Organisation (EACSO) established by the British in 1921.

The common services were the East African Railways and Harbours Corporation (EAR&H) which also included the road network; the East African Posts and Telecommunications Services; and the East African Airways (EAA). The East African Currency Board issued a common currency. And there was the East African Common Market and joint research facilities. As Walter Elkan stated:

"The three mainland territories of East Africa, Kenya, Uganda and Tanganyika - all of them administered by Great Britain - were associated in three ways.

First they constituted a common market with more or less uniform external tariff, 'revenue raising' rather than 'protective' in intent. Within East Africa there was virtually free trade both in goods imported from abroad and in goods produced in the region.

Secondly, they were associated by a common currency issued by the E.A. (East African) Currency Board and freely convertible into sterling with which it stood at par. There were no restrictions whatever upon the movement of money and since the commercial banks were all - with one exception - subsidiaries or branches of banks whose headquarters were in London, the whole system could be viewed as in a sense part of the British system with its apex in the Bank of England rather than in East Africa.

Thirdly, they shared a number of common services which were jointly administered by the E.A. High Commission, later reorganised and renamed the East African Common Services Organisation (EACSO). Some of these, the railways, posts and airways, were described as 'self-contained' because they were financed from their own revenues.

The others, called the General Funds services, which included the collection of direct and indirect taxes and the provision of a number of agricultural, medical and other research services, were financed partly by the British CD&W funds and various overseas foundations, and partly by the three East African Governments. The High Commission also administered a number of other matters on which the three (colonial) territories tried to act in concert."[12]

In fact, East Africa was the most integrated region in British colonial Africa. Yet, it was not economically linked with the other neighbouring countries some of which were under different colonial powers. For example, when Tanganyika was under British rule, it had no commercial or transport and communication links with Portuguese Mozambique; very little with Belgian Congo, and only limited commercial ties with Burundi which, like neighbouring Rwanda, was also under Belgian rule. The ties with Burundi were due to the fact that most of that country's exports and imports went through Tanganyika, as they still do through today – through Tanzania.

But colonial Tanganyika hardly had any trade links with Rwanda; virtually none with Nyasaland (which is Malawi today), except some transport links through the shipping service on Lake Nyasa (a lake that belongs to Tanzania, Malawi, and Mozambique, not just to Malawi and Mozambique) in spite of the fact that both countries were under British rule. Tanganyika also hardly had any

363

commercial ties with neighbouring Northern Rhodesia (now Zambia), another British colony.

Instead, Nyasaland and Northern Rhodesia, together with Southern Rhodesia (Zimbabwe today), belonged to what was then called the Central African Federation which was established by the British in 1953 and dissolved in 1963. Yet, the federation had no formal or even informal links with the three British territories of East Africa: Kenya, Uganda, and Tanganyika. It was more oriented towards apartheid South Africa.

That was the nature of the relationship among African countries during colonial rule. The continent was fragmented in more than one way, although the colonial boundaries themselves were bad enough. And when the modern African state came into being at independence, it unfortunately did very little to facilitate regional cooperation let alone integration.

In fact, it was during the post-colonial era that Africa witnessed the collapse of the East African Community (resurrected in 2001) which could have fostered economic growth at the regional level for the benefit of the three countries involved – Kenya, Uganda, and Tanzania – and for Africa as a whole It would have been an economic powerhouse.

Therefore, as in all the other African countries, the task of economic development had to be carried out by individual states within their own boundaries after the Community collapsed; which proved to be an almost impossible task for such economically non-viable states without strong regional cooperation. Almost all African countries are non-viable economic and political entities.

Besides lack of regional cooperation, all African countries faced other major problems after independence. As Adebayo Adedeji, an internationally respected Nigerian economist who served as the Executive Secretary of the UN Economic Commission for Africa (ECA), stated in 1983 in an interview with *Africa Report*:

"These countries today are faced with major economic crises. We are now increasingly dependent on food imports. We have energy crises for the majority of the member states that are non-oil producing. We have balance of payments problems and debt burdens. We are in a way the victim of the international economic community because, as a result of colonialism, we inherited economies that were utterly dependent on the international economic community.

We made the mistake of not cutting the link as soon as we became independent. We continued with the same mix of policies that we inherited – producing for export and import substitution industry. But we now know that this has not only failed to help us, but it has aggravated our very poor position."[13]

Trade among ourselves to achieve self-sufficiency would have helped to alleviate our plight and solve the problem. Externally-oriented trade also had a devastating impact on Africa in another way. Undue emphasis on production of export crops – coffee, tea, sisal, tobacco and others – left Africa hungry through the years; in fact so much so that we turned to other countries for relief, begging for food we ourselves could have easily produced on this agricultural continent with plenty of arable land more than enough to feed everybody across Africa, and with plenty left to export.

African countries should have emphasised food production first, as soon as they won independence. Instead, they did exactly the opposite. It is true that they needed foreign exchange earned from export commodities as much as they do today. But what good does it do when they end up spending the foreign exchange they just earned to buy food from other countries – at an even much higher cost than what they earn from export crops – they themselves could have produced on their own soil?

It is the independent African countries themselves, not the colonialists who have long been gone, which are now responsible for their condition and for having their priorities in the wrong order: export crops first, food last, instead of the reverse being the case.

Even today, African economies are still oriented towards export production to serve outsiders instead of being geared towards food production to feed their own people. That's why we beg so much.

And unfortunately, African exports themselves have not done well on the world market. They are not in high demand, they fetch low prices, and are easily substituted in the industrialised countries by local products; a lot of them synthetic.

Yet these are the very same nations Africans expect to be their biggest customers. But they are not buying much from them. So Africans are stuck with their commodities or end up selling them at very low prices. That alone is a compelling argument for the establishment of an African common market on which Africans can sell their products to each other even for better prices instead of waiting for outsiders to buy their products and get paid very little for them.

Even Africa's industrialisation depends on outsiders, not only for capital investment and technical skills but also for provision of raw materials. With regard to the first two, Africa will probably have to depend on foreigners for a long time. They are the ones who have the capital to invest far more than Africans do. They are also the ones who have the technical skills Africans don't have.

But in terms of raw materials, African countries can do far better than what they do now. And African governments are the ones who are at fault because it is they who formulate policies and strategies for national development including industrialisation.

Why do they import raw materials when Africa produces all kinds of raw materials which can be used by

366

the industries on the continent? Most of the industries in Africa use imported raw materials. Yet their operations could be adapted to use local materials and produce goods from domestic resources.

Even in the petroleum sector, it's the same problem. For example, Nigeria is the world's fifth largest producer of oil; it is also Africa's largest producer. Yet it does not even have enough petrol for its own people.

That is the same contradiction Africans face with regard to food. Africa is an agricultural continent which can produce more than enough food to feed its own people. Yet African countries import food, and even beg for food, counting on donor nations and international relief agencies to send food to Africa.

Such dependence on imported food has even changed the eating habits of many Africans. They want to eat the kind of food their countries can not even produce because of the different climate. Food grown in America, Europe and Australia, continents which have a temperate climate, can not be grown in Africa's tropical climate.

Dependence on imported food has also affected agricultural production. Some people don't want to grow enough food because they are waiting and expect to be given food donations. And there are those who don't grow enough food because they don't want to eat African food anymore. They are tired of eating cassava and cassava leaves, for example, and want wheat, instead; they also want oats, powdered milk, and so on.

And it is the same situation with raw materials for African industries. Many Africans may be surprised to hear that most industries on the continent use imported raw materials which could very easily be replaced by local ones. But it's true. As Adebayo Adedeji pointed out:

"Eighty percent (which is really almost 100 percent) of the industries in Africa depend on imported raw materials and this is a raw material-producing continent. This is an agricultural continent. That is the greatest contradiction we face....

We have created enclaves of modernized sectors that really have no linkage with the rest of the economies. In the production of beer, for instance, every raw material except water is imported, because we do not produce malt, barley, etc. Again (like in the case of food) it is a question of adapting.

Why can't we adapt our own products? We must have industry based on the use of our own raw materials....

The result is that what should have been a savings of foreign exchange becomes instead a great demander of foreign exchange (to pay for imported raw materials, which Africa would not have to, if she used her own raw materials). And when you are short of foreign exchange, industries close down because you cannot purchase raw materials or spare parts."[14]

In spite of Africa's vast amount of natural resources, industrialisation on the continent has proceeded at a very slow pace through the years. Foreign investments, a vital component of Africa's industrialisation strategy, have not poured into the continent but have, instead, been diverted elsewhere; although Africa's potential as a highly lucrative market is beyond dispute considering the continent's immense resources and large population.

Not all foreign investors have ignored Africa, but a substantial number of them have. And if investment figures are a good statistical indicator of where the continent may be headed, it is highly probable that Africa will remain on the periphery of the global economy for many years; unless the continent moves *en masse* as an integrated whole into the mainstream of the world economy, and not as a fragmented region of dozens of non-viable states whose weakness and instability not only discourages but scares away investors. Investment figures tell the story, and it is a sad one.

From 1988 to the mid- and late nineties, foreign investors invested more than $400 billion in developing countries.[15] Yet only a trickle of that went to Africa. Trade in most parts of the world, including business transactions between developing nations in Asia and Latin America, has grown enormously since 1988. Yet African countries are still desperately struggling to find customers for their agricultural products and manufactured goods on the world market. Collectively, Africa receives only 3 percent of the total foreign investment directly invested in the Third World.[16] The rest of it, a staggering 97 percent, is poured into Asia and Latin America.

Africa's minuscule share could diminish even further. For example in 1995 alone, according to the United Nations, the amount invested in Africa dropped by 27 per cent, a frightening figure for a region that is already not getting much investment. In terms of dollars, the amount dropped down to $2.1 billion. That was the total amount invested in the whole continent, which was less than what China received in only two months.[17] And most of that money was invested in South Africa which always gets the lion's share of foreign direct investment (FDI) going to Africa.

And it is easy to understand why Africa does not attract many investors as I explained earlier. It is for the same reasons why the continent is not industrialised. And it is for the same reasons why it has not even started to develop.

They include shortage of high-level manpower and other skilled workers; and lack of infrastructure and a large domestic market which would justify large foreign investments. These are just some of the major reasons, including political instability, why foreigners don't want to invest in Africa in large numbers. For example, it does not make any sense for a foreign manufacturer to build a manufacturing firm in Malawi or Mali to make refrigerators when only very few people in those countries

369

can afford them.

And that applies to almost all African countries across the continent except South Africa. As John Koo, president and chief executive officer of the giant Korean manufacturer LG Electronics, said in 1997:

"With Africa, we have a problem making investment decisions and we don't have a solution at the moment."[18]

Africa's inability to find enough investment from foreign countries has been made even worse by the reduction in foreign aid African nations have depended on so much since independence. The end of the Cold War has aggravated the situation. The Soviet Union is dead. Therefore there is no more competition between the two former ideological foes – the capitalist West led by the United States and the communist East led by the Soviet Union – for client states in Africa they used to entice with money and other forms of assistance.

The amount of aid from donor countries and multilateral institutions to Africa dropped from $17 billion to $15 billion between 1990 and 1994. As President Henri Konan Bedie of Ivory Coast put it:

"We see certain countries going through budgetary difficulties that want to back away from offering development aid. They say everything ought to be referred to the private sector. If you wait until the private sector comes to build primary schools for children, I think you could wait a long time."[19]

He did not, of course, address the fundamental problem. As a leader himself, he knew he was a major part of the problem just like most of his colleagues across the continent are. In fact in most cases, they are the cause of the problem.

Schools, hospitals, roads and bridges, are not being

built in African countries, *not* because of the Americans, the British, the French, the Germans and others; they are not being built *because* most African leaders don't want to build them or do anything else for their people. They are busy stealing. That is why our countries don't have enough schools, hospitals and medicine. That is why the infrastructure is crumbling. That is why institutional decay has become a part of national life. And that is why some of our people want our former colonial masters to come back and rule us again. Life was better under them.

When nothing is done in our countries, don't blame donor nations for that. They can't keep on pouring money into Africa only to be stolen. So don't complain when they talk about donor fatigue. And don't complain when they are pulling out. Africa is *not* going to be developed by foreigners. It is going to be – and it must be – developed by us: Africans. But it has not because of bad leadership notorious for neglecting the continent's deplorable condition.

It is such neglect which has been used by soldiers to overthrow governments across the continent through the years. Tragically, they have not done any better than the leaders they overthrew. Military coups since the sixties soon after independence, and civil wars which have ravaged the continent for decades, have made the situation worse.

Since the first military coup in sub-Saharan Africa which took place in Togo on 13 January 1963, resulting in the assassination of President Sylvanus Olympio, more than 90 military coups have been carried out; an average of at least two coups almost every year since 1963.

In most of those years, more than one government was overthrown, sometimes within the same country. For example, two governments were overthrown in Nigeria in 1966; and three, including one civilian, were overthrown within the same month in Sierra Leone in April 1968.

In addition to military coups, more than 30 civil wars

have been fought on the African continent since the sixties. That is an average of one every year, but in reality more than one are being fought.

There are also separatist tendencies, some violent: in Casamance province in Senegal; in the Ogaden region and among the Oromo people in Ethiopia; in the Comoro Islands; Angola, Nigeria, Namibia, Sudan; Tanzania where secessionist sentiments in Zanzibar are becoming more widespread; and elsewhere on the continent although muted, compounded by other form of strife caused by neglect.

Not every African country is on fire. But the conflicts are unsettling enough for many potential investors to avoid Africa and invest elsewhere where there is less conflict or no fighting at all. There are many conflicts across the continent, and there are many countries which are politically unstable even if they have not exploded into full-scale civil war as happened in Rwanda, Burundi, Somalia, Liberia, and Sierra Leone. Perception matters even if it is not reality in all cases. Therefore, it is easy to understand why many investors are not very enthusiastic about investing in what is generally perceived to be a highly volatile continent.

Then there is the question of leadership even in the investment sector itself. Most leaders and other government officials across the continent are corrupt, demanding huge kickbacks from investors and stealing outright from their own people and whatever they can scoop out from foreign aid. They even steal donated food and clothes. They steal *anything*. And they steal from anybody, including the poorest of the poor.

Yet they have the audacity to blame foreigners for the kind of mess we are in today, the same kind of mess we have had since independence in most parts of Africa. As George Ayittey, a Ghanaian professor of economics at The American University, stated in 1997:

"(Africa's economies will remain crippled) as long as you have these mafia governments, these predatory states. In Nigeria, in Zaire, all over the continent, the people in government are just looters."[20]

They also perpetuate themselves in power so that they can continue to steal. Yet they are the very same people who constitute the modern African state which is the fundamental dynamic in Africa's economic performance. Unfortunately in most cases, they have achieved nothing or exactly the opposite. As Ayittey stated on another occasion a few months earlier in *The Wall Street Journal*:

"Africa's economic performance has lagged persistently behind that of other Third World regions, despite receiving more than $300 billion in foreign aid since 1960.

Crumbling infrastructure, senseless civil wars, political instability, high taxes, rampant inflation, runaway government expenditures, unstable currencies and high-level corruption have all conspired to stunt Africa's economic growth and render the continent unattractive to foreign investors. According to the World Bank, in 1995 a record $231 billion in foreign investment flowed into the Third World. But Africa's share was a paltry $2 billion or 1 percent.

Even Africa's own kleptocrats avoid the continent. The UN itself estimated that $200 billion – or 90 percent of sub-Saharan Africa's GDP – was shipped to foreign banks in 1991 alone.

The secrets of economic growth are known: rule of law, private property rights, pro-market and pro-trade policies, investment in human capital and creating an entrepreneurial environment. But Africa's problem is the predatory state itself – government hijacked by gangsters and con artists, who have turned the state sector, instead of the market, into the arena for private wealth accumulation.

The underlying ethic is self-aggrandizement and self-perpetuation in power. The richest people in Africa are heads of state and their ministers. Helping the poor, promoting competitive economic growth and reforming the state are anathema to the ruling elite.

If pressured, they adopt temporary, cosmetic 'reforms' that ensure a continued flow of Western aid. But most Africans understand this reform posturing as the 'Babangida boogie': one step forward, three steps back, a sidekick and a flip to land on a fat Swiss bank account."[21]

But how have southeast Asian countries which are also corrupt been able to develop and surpass Africa in every conceivable way within a generation since independence? The colonial experience does not explain the difference. Both regions were colonised. Both emerged from colonial rule around the same time. And both suffered or benefited from colonial rule.

If colonial suffering accounts for the disparity, then we Africans need to be reminded that southeast Asian countries suffered even longer, in fact much longer, than we did under colonialism. And they were devastated during World War II in a way our countries were not. Yet they were able to recover – and zoomed right past us.

How do we explain the difference in economic performance? Why have we performed so poorly? Some amongst us have even found clever ways to explain or justify our failure to develop. As the mayor of Congo's largest city Kisangani, Alauwa Lobela, stated in 1997:

"In Africa the climate is such that there's always fruit around, in the back of the house, and you just reach up and pick it when you're hungry. But in Europe and Asia, the climate forced people to get food, to protect themselves from the cold in the winter, to develop a spirit of battle."[22]

Yet we can not explain why millions of our people are

374

undernourished and starving on this continent of abundance. If we are satisfied with our condition, while napping under the tropical sun after eating some fruit easily plucked out of trees, then we will be sleeping for a long time while others sleep with their eyes wide awake, busy working. They include southeast Asians whom we have failed or simply refuse to emulate. And the contrast is glaring.

Since 1965, the per capita incomes of southeast Asia grew 11 times faster than those of sub-Saharan Africa. The question is why such a huge gap in economic performance between the two regions both of which emerged from colonial rule roughly around the same time during the post-World War II era.

There are several reasons. Economists point to a combination of factors associated with rapid economic growth in East Asia during the post-war period: countries like Japan, China, Taiwan and South Korea underwent land redistribution after World War II and became relatively egalitarian nations. That is one prime factor in the acceleration of their economic growth.

The other factors, besides land redistribution which helped transform those countries into egalitarian societies, cited by economists to explain Asian economic success include a well-educated and healthy population; a dramatic decline in birth rates; and open free-market policies emphasising exports which East Asian nations adopted relatively early, contrasted with Africa.

A combination of all those factors proved to be a potent formula which helped fuel spectacular economic growth in the southeast Asian countries.

They also emphasised fiscal responsibility, contained inflation, vigorously promoted export trade, and kept their currencies undervalued.

And they are still following the same combined strategy.

African countries did exactly the opposite. They did

375

nothing to reduce or contain skyrocketing inflation. They squandered money. They discouraged production of export commodities by controlling the economy and imposing very high taxes. And they did not devalue their currencies, a critical step towards rejuvenating weak economies.

Failure to do all those things paralysed African economies and made it impossible for their exports to compete on the world market.

Then there was socialism. Almost all African countries adopted socialist policies in one way or another. And a number of them – for example, Ghana under Nkrumah, Guinea under Sekou Toure, and Tanzania under Nyerere – were virulently anti-capitalist. As Professor Ali Mazrui stated in his book *Towards A Pax Africana* which was first published in 1967, the euphoric sixties when most African countries won independence:

"No ideology commands respect so widely in Africa as the ideology of 'socialism' – though, as in Europe, it is socialism of different shades.

In Guinea and Mali a Marxist framework of reasoning is evident. In Ghana Leninism was wedded to notions of traditional collectivism. In Tanzania the concept of *Ujamaa*, derived from the sense of community of tribal life, is being radicalized into an assertion of modern socialism.

In Kenya there is a dilemma between establishing socialism and Africanizing the capitalism which already exists. In Nigeria, Senegal and Uganda some kind of allegiance is being paid to the ideal of social justice in situations with a multi-party background.

There are places, of course, where no school of socialism is propagated at all. But outside the Ivory Coast there is little defiant rejection of the idea of 'socialism' in former colonial Africa." – (Ali Mazrui, *Towards A Pax Africana*, london: Weidenfeld & Nicolson, 1967, p. 97).

Capitalism was, and for good reason, identified with colonialism and the colonial powers, all of them capitalist, from whom African countries had just won independence, and was therefore seen as a system of exploitation whose continuation by the new African nations would only perpetuate their colonial bondage in a new form: neo-colonialism.

Nkrumah and Nyerere became some of the most vociferous and articulate exponents of the theory of neo-colonialism. And they were vindicated by history despite the failure of their socialist policies to develop their countries.

By remarkable contrast, East Asian nations, especially the most successful ones, avoided socialism. They were also vindicated by history.

Through the decades, socialism proved to be disastrous round the globe and African countries were among those which suffered the most.

Savings is another factor which has played a vital role in the rapid economic growth of East Asian nations.

Savings are needed to finance new factories and provide capital for investments that stimulate economic growth. Partly because of market incentives and government initiatives, national savings rates have been much higher in Asia, averaging more than 30 per cent of the gross domestic product, than in Africa whose savings rate on average is about only 12 per cent. For example, from 1981 to 1990 according to the World Bank, sub-Saharan Africa's savings rate was 12.6 per cent contrasted with 33.2 per cent for South Korea, Hong Kong, Singapore and Taiwan; and 31.9 per cent for Thailand, Indonesia and Malaysia.[23]

And many Africans are well aware of the problem. As Professor Samuel Ndomba of the University of Kisangani in the Democratic Republic of Congo (DRC), stated:

"Our problem is that we don't save. When people get a

bit of money, they just spend it to buy a beer."[24]

Congo became one of the poorest countries in the world under the kleptocratic regime of Mobutu. Yet it is potentially one of the world's richest even without a national culture of savings. As Nicholas Kristof stated in his report from the diamond-rich city of Kisangani, in *The New York Times*:

"The area around this river port city in eastern Congo (on the Congo River), is dilapidated and impoverished yet (fertile and) studded with diamonds, like a billionaire on Skid Row.

Back in the 1950's, when this country and several others in Africa were at the same income level as South Korea and while blessed with far more natural resources, it might have seemed reasonable that Africa would soon leave Asia in the dust. Now (resource-poor) South Korea has a per capita income of about $10,000 a year (1997 statistics), and (mineral-rich) Congo stands at $150 per person."[25]

Rotten leadership combined with Western greed ruined Congo. And failure to save only made things worse through the years. Like people in other African countries, many Congolese justify spending their money even on things they don't even need by saying that they don't have enough to save.

But besides the profligacy of some individuals, one of the main reasons why many Africans don't save is inflation and political instability compounded by corruption. Money saved ends up being stolen or simply confiscated in many cases in many countries.

There is no-one to take to court because government officials and the courts themselves are corrupt. And they work together. The judges are appointed by corrupt politicians, and politicians cannot be locked up by the judges they appointed. And the police who are supposed to be making the arrests are just as corrupt. Therefore they are not going to arrest the culprits who bribe them on regular basis and who are, in fact, more powerful than they are. It is a vicious cycle.

If a lot of money was saved, it would help fuel Africa's economic growth. And it can be done. Southeast nations, the Asian Tigers, have done it. And they continue to do it.

Japan also has done it, as have many other countries. And they continue to do so, except us. For example, during the nineteenth century, Japan had very low savings rates. But they went up dramatically because of sustained government campaigns encouraging the people to save. The savings also increased because of the establishment of savings institutions in different parts of the country where the people could save their money. Eventually, the large national savings were used to finance Japan's industrialisation, one of the most successful in history.

Japan also invested heavily in education to train a large number of people who then went on to play a critical role in the country's industrialisation and rapid economic growth.

Without a strong educational foundation, and a large educated work force, no country can develop regardless of how much foreign investment is poured into it, and regardless of how much natural resources – minerals, oil, gas, abundant arable land, lakes and rivers and so on – it has.

Before anything else, even natural resources, a country needs manpower. It comes first. Look at Singapore, a city state without natural resources. It is one of the most developed countries in the world.

It relied on brain power to develop. Its people are some of the most highly educated in the world, with a large number of scientists who have played a critical role in the country's spectacular economic and industrial growth – without minerals and other natural resources besides its people, the most important natural resource every country has.

Once a country has enough manpower including highly trained and skilled workers, it can then plan the next move, which includes absorbing technical information from the industrialised nations because it already has a critical mass of highly trained people and professionals who constitute the scientific community needed to digest and use that information for national development.

Many developing countries, including ours in Africa, demand technology transfer from the industrialised world without knowing exactly what they are going to do with it. Where are the people who are going to apply the technology? Do we have the scientists needed? There aren't even enough people who understand the technical journals coming from Europe, North America and other parts of the developed world. As Michael J. Moravcsik and J. Ziman, professors of physics at the University of Oregon and the University of Bristol, respectively, stated in their article, "Paradisia and Dominatia: Science and the Developing World," in *Foreign Affairs*:

"There are still those who seem unconvinced of the urgency of the need for an indigenous scientific community in a country such as Paradisia. With scientific knowledge and technological know-how available for all on the world market, would it not be easier to import and use whatever is needed, without building 'local production facilities' in these commodities?

This commercial metaphor is appropriate, since the essence of this argument is an appeal to the principles of classical liberal economics – the open market, free trade, economies of scale, and the division of labour. Let the great knowledge factories of the advanced countries export their great surpluses of information, fact and theory, in exchange for industrial products manufactured in the newly developed nations.

At the most elementary level, this analogy is entirely fallacious. Scientific knowledge lacks many of the necessary attributes of a commercial commodity, and cannot be fairly bartered for material goods and services. It is not possible simply to 'import' science and technology in the absence of an indigenous scientific and technical community....

(In) Japan, the large-scale importation of scientific techniques in recent times was preceded by decades of development of an indigenous scientific and technological community....Japan's industrial power is now matched by the intellectual resources of a first-class scientific community."[26]

In addition to Japan, each of the other East Asian nations that is developed also has a scientific community which is bigger and better trained than any found in black African countries with the exception of South Africa which inherited a lily-white first-class establishment built by the apartheid regime to perpetuate white supremacy.

But East Asia also has had another big advantage over Africa in terms of manpower in general, besides the large number of scientists and technicians it has. And that is something African countries can not achieve within a relatively few years, not even in a generation, as demonstrated by Africa's slow progress through the decades since independence in the sixties; although things could be better, in fact much better.

Countries such as South Korea started out on the road towards economic development with citizens who were already more educated, also more healthy and free of debilitating diseases and other health problems such as worm infestation, than those in Africa and other developing regions of the world. And they continued to improve their educational and health services through the decades when African countries were taking their first step on a parallel road towards the same destination.

Health problems are much more serious in Africa than they are in the Asian countries which have achieved rapid economic growth. Parasites, and microbes unheard of in other parts of the world, destroy people and the economy. They are common in Africa. As Nicholas Kristof stated in his report from Africa published in *The New York Times*:

"Health problems have also been a greater economic burden on Africa than is often realized. Most Africans, for example, have stomach worms, and as a result millions of people cannot study or work energetically, and some children have their intelligence permanently impaired because of anemia caused by parasites. 'From the age of two, most people here have worms,' shrugged Bakondagama Barandala, a 24-year-old nurse at a shabby clinic in Mambasa, in northeastern Congo.

The clinic is a metaphor for public health in Congo: it is the only clinic in the region, yet it has no doctor, no electricity, no drinking water, no instruments and no medicines."[27]

The Congolese government under Mobutu did nothing to help the people. Those who succeeded him have not done anything either. It is the same complaint across Africa.

Governments do nothing to help the people, prompting some to recall with nostalgia the "good old days" of colonial rule when things were much better than they are now.

And it is the same former colonial masters that we have now turned to, for solutions to our economic problems, in terms of adopting capitalism as the best means to achieve our goals. Foreign aid is not going to develop Africa. In fact, it has not worked. And nothing is going to work as long as corruption remains a major problem. It is endemic. And nothing is going to work if African countries don't integrate their economies at the regional level.

Even the money given to implement free-market reforms has not always worked, mainly because of rampant corruption and waste. As Michael Chege, a Kenyan professor in the United States, stated in *The Times Literary Supplement*:

"In the ostensible effort to kick-start self-sustaining and 'open' – as opposed to protectionist – capitalist economies in Africa, no region in the world has received as much external aid over the past two decades: $36 per capita in 1993, compared to $8 in Latin America and just $4 in South Asia.

On average, some 16 per cent of that gradually disappearing global share of the African gross domestic product was made up of concessional financial infusions from Western governments and multilateral organizations like the World Bank and the European Commission.

In equally poor Asia, economic recovery is already under way, even though foreign donations as a share of GDP were running at about a third of those of Africa up until the early 1990s."[28]

While Africa continues to lag behind other regions of the world, the continent's economic and political condition continues to deteriorate because of corruption and political instability. Where there has been some improvement, such improvement is either temporary or insignificant considering the enormous problems African countries face in all areas. Yet they expect foreigners to come and invest in those countries, knowing full well that our leaders have not done enough to create a climate conducive to investment.

Conditions must be suitable for investment in Africa, and must be constantly improved, to attract foreign investors and even local investors. And investors, especially foreigners who have the largest amount of capital to invest, must have confidence in Africa's economic prospects before risking their investments. But the primary emphasis by African countries must be on capital accumulation from national savings and domestic investments which is the only way they can fuel and guarantee sustained economic growth.

Foreign investments do help, when they are available, and in amounts African countries deem necessary to finance economic development. But that is not always the case. And they are no substitute for locally created wealth as the best source of capital for long-term economic growth. Dependence on foreign investments to develop a country is suicidal.

Foreigners invest to help themselves, not to help develop a country in which they invest. If it goes down the drain, they simply pull out and go elsewhere to invest.

It is only the citizens of that country who can develop it, with or without foreigners. That is one lesson we have not learned well in Africa as we continue to count on foreigners to develop our countries. And it partly explains why we are so marginalised in the global arena.

Although Africa is on the periphery of the mainstream in the global economy, it still is an integral part of the international system run along capitalist lines on terms dictated by the West where our conquerors came from. Capitalism itself is cruel by nature because it thrives on greed. Paradoxically, it is this very same vice, greed, which is its greatest virtue as an incentive to production many African governments failed to achieve under socialism with its redistributive ethic.

Other governments which did not pursue socialism also failed to develop their economies because of heavy-handed interference in the economy by the state just like their socialist counterparts did. As Tanzania's President Benjamin Mkapa said after free-market policies were adopted in the nineties:

"The Rubicon of reform has been crossed. Government

has no business doing business."[29]

Yet, it is the responsibility, hence the business, of the government – any government – to protect the weakest members of society from cruel market forces and other predators. Otherwise it can not justify its existence. It is this failure by African governments to help and protect their people which has prompted many of them to seek relief elsewhere, especially from the West, including an appeal by some Africans to our former colonial masters to come back and rule us again.

Globalisation itself, which is a form of penetration of Africa and other developing regions of the world on terms stipulated by the West, has caused a lot of misery and suffering in countries implementing structural adjustment programmes (SAPs) as a mandatory requirement for aid from the World Bank, the IMF and donor nations. But it has at the same also benefited many people adept at playing the capitalist game in the open field of market forces where the rules of the game are profit-making and self-aggrandisement, hoping for a ripple effect to spread the benefits of capitalism to the poor across society.

Whether or not globalisation will help Africa to develop in the long run is one of the most contentious issues of our time. But there are those who feel that, with or without golobalisation, Africa may be headed in another direction, and in fact should, because of the failure of African leaders to put our countries on the right track.

It is an idea that is terrifying and infuriating to many, if not the majority. But it is also a prospect, however bleak, whose compelling logic is derived from Africa's traumatic experience since independence.

One thing is certain. We are headed somewhere.

Chapter Eight

Which Way Africa?

RECOLONISATION of Africa has always been a distinct possibility since the end of colonial rule. But what form it may take, if it ever comes to that, is an entirely different matter.

It has also been a subject of discussion and continuing debate among politicians and intellectuals especially in pan-African circles within and outside the continent.

And there are those who contend that African countries are really not free, and have never been free. They only have what President Nyerere called "flag independence." Any country that is not economically independent can not claim to be truly independent.

In his book, *Neo-Colonialism: The Last Stage of Imperialism*,[1] Ghana's first president, Dr. Kwame Nkrumah, addressed the subject in a pan-African context warning of the danger the United States and other Western powers, especially the former colonial rulers, posed to Africa by trying to establish hegemonic control over the continent, using their economic muscles to impose a stranglehold on African countries in order to exploit the continent and promote Western geopolitical and strategic interests. He also accused the CIA of fomenting trouble on the continent, including overthrowing governments the United States did not like.

After the book was first published in 1965, the United States government sent Nkrumah a protest note and immediately cancelled a $35 million aid-programme to Ghana. A few months later, Nkrumah was overthrown in February 1966 in a military coup engineered and masterminded by the CIA.

Yet, what Nkrumah said was true. And it is still true today. He was vindicated by history, himself being a victim of CIA plots including assassination attempts; and his ouster being one of the most dramatic demonstrations of power projection capabilities by the United States in our continent.

The American government never stopped its subversive activities in Africa. For example, when I was a student at Wayne State University in Detroit in the state of Michigan in the United States in the early and mid-seventies, one of the country's leading newspapers, the *Detroit News*, published an article stating that the CIA was active on university campuses recruiting foreign students to work for the agency, targeting those it considered to be potential leaders when they returned to their home countries.

The paper named the University of Michigan and Michigan State University as the CIA's main recruiting grounds in the state because of the large number of foreign students attending those schools. It concluded by stating:

"The emphasis is on the emerging nations of Africa."[2]

The CIA's interest in Africa and African students was nothing new, going back to the fifties. In 1954, the United States government established the African-American Institute, based in New York City, to promote American interests in Africa. The institute was funded by the CIA and published an influential magazine *Africa Report*.[3] Coincidentally or not, publication of the magazine ended in 1989-1990, during the same time when the Soviet Union and other communist regimes collapsed in Eastern Europe.

The African-American Institute also had a scholarship programme, funded by the CIA, as a way of buying influence in Africa, especially with African governments. The CIA, hence the American federal government, hoped that after the students returned to Africa, they would help to advance or serve American interests on the continent, especially if they worked in the government as many of them were expected to.

American interest in Africa also included plans to invade Nigeria. In August 1975, a secret military plan for the invasion of oil-producing countries, including Nigeria which is one of the world's largest producers, was sent to Congress for approval in case a second oil embargo – after the first one in 1973 during the Arab-Israel conflict – was imposed by the oil-exporting countries, thus threatening vital Western interests.

Nigeria did not participate in the 1973 - 1974 embargo imposed by the Organization of Petroleum Exporting Countries (OPEC), of which it is a member, and launched an era of unprecedented economic growth during which this giant African nation had one of the highest per capita incomes in the world. It ranked 33rd during the oil boom of the seventies.

However, the American government did not want to take any chances and feared that the militant new Nigerian military ruler, Brigadier-General Murtala Muhammed would join a second oil boycott against the United States and other Western countries, "crippling" their economies.

Fears in Washington of a possible oil embargo by Nigeria increased when the Nigerian leader rejected a proposed visit to Nigeria by the US Secretary of State Henry Kissinger, which would have been the first by an

American secretary of state to black Africa's most powerful country and its largest in terms of population.

American officials also expressed deep concern about Nigeria's growing influence and the country's support for the liberation movements on the continent. They suggested that the United States can contain or neutralise Nigeria's rise to power only through sabotage.

In fact, on 2 February 1976, a secret despatch from the American embassy in Lagos, Nigeria, warned that Nigeria enjoyed a "very healthy current account balance as a result of booming oil sales," and advised that the country was moving towards having a modern, well-equipped army.

It was Donald Easum, former American ambassador to Nigeria at the time of Murtala Muhammed's assassination and later head of the African-American Institute, who recommended ways to contain Nigeria's growing military strength; a recommendation which was taken seriously by the CIA and top American government officials and other leaders including senators and congressmen.

American interest in Nigeria – including plans for clandestine operations in this major African country – has frightening parallels to what happened in the former Belgian Congo which became the bleeding heart of Africa because of American intervention since the sixties with the support of other Western powers in order to control and dominate the country and the rest of Africa. And it amounts to nothing less than attempts at recolonisation of Africa, best demonstrated in Congo, renamed Zaire, during Mubutu's reign.

In fact, the largest CIA station in Africa was in Kinshasa, capital of Zaire, when the country was ruled by Mobutu. And it was from Kinshasa that the CIA launched its missions to destabilise the MPLA government in Angola and support anti-government factions during the Angolan civil war which lasted for almost 30 years since seventies.

Therefore fears of recolonisation of Africa are not

paranoia or a figment of the imagination but reality grounded in history and validated by contemporary experience. One contemporary aspect of this is the deep penetration of Africa by Western business interests in this era of globalisation at the expense of the indigenous people.

Little is done to meet their needs or redress their grievances, as tragically demonstrated by the callousness of the oil companies operating in the Niger Delta in Nigeria where members of the local ethnic groups have been subjected to all kinds of abuse including environmental pollution, thus denying them basic human rights, including food and shelter.

Their water, fish, and land have been polluted, destroying their means of livelihood without getting compensation from the Western oil companies or from the Nigerian federal government itself. Their aspirations as a people have been stifled right in their homeland without the slightest concern for their future and wellbeing.

Yet all this is taking place in a country which is supposed to be free and independent, and under the leadership of Africans who are supposed to care about the wellbeing of their own people.

All they care about is themselves, as they work to serve the interests of their Western masters who never really left when we won independence in the sixties. As Nyerere said, they went out through the front door and returned through the back door. That is what neocolonialism is all about. And it is a reality in Africa today as much as it has been since independence.

Nyerere also warned of the danger of recolonisation as far back as the sixties. As he stated in August 1960, even before he led Tanganyika to independence the following year, at a conference in the capital of Tanganyika, Dar es Salaam:

"The phase through which we are emerging

391

successfully (from colonial rule) is the phase of the first scramble for Africa – and Africa's reaction to it. We are now entering a new phase. It is the phase of the second scramble for Africa....

So I believe that the second scramble has begun in real earnest. And it is going to be a much more dangerous scramble than the first one....

The phrase 'the second scramble for Africa' may sound far-fetched, in the context of the Africa of the 1960's....But anybody who thinks this is far-fetched has been completely blind to what is happening on the African continent. Take, for example, the Congo: There were obvious weaknesses in the Congo situation, but those weaknesses were deliberately used in a scramble for the control of the Congo."[4]

Throughout his presidency Nyerere continued to warn about the danger of neo-colonialism and did so even after he stepped down. As he stated in a speech in Atlanta, Georgia, in the United States, in 1998 not long before he died, multinational corporations were playing a leading role in the recolonisation of Africa. And they did not want civil wars and other conflicts to end in African countries because it was easier for them that way to exploit the continent; with the rebels also playing a critical role in looting the continent and selling the resources to foreigners at very low prices.

And there is a very simple explanation for that. Where there is no law and order, it is very easy to steal. Only the strongest survive. And it is multinational corporations and other foreign interests which benefit the most, while the people, the poor masses of Africa, get nothing.

Nyerere's warning is an enduring reality and will remain valid as long as Africa continues to be dominated and exploited by foreigners:

"On May 7, 1998, Mwalimu Nyerere spoke with

392

eloquence and prescience about Africa's recent past and its immediate future during the first National Summit on Africa Southeastern Regional Summit in Atlanta.

He warned of a second scramble for Africa, not unlike the one that partitioned Africa at the Berlin conference in 1884 (November 1884 - February 1885) in the interest of European political domination and free trade. He suggested that this time the scramble was led by multinational corporations aligned with rebel leaders, whose goal is to plunder the mineral resources of Africa with the result of introducing new political instability and even civil wars in several regions on the continent. This was the case in Liberia and Sierra Leone and it still prevails in Angola and the Democratic Republic of the Congo."[5]

Yet it is such instability which is invoked by the proponents of imperial order, including some Africans, for a return to the status quo ante – colonial rule – because of the failure by African governments to end conflicts, restore law and order, and even implement principles of elementary justice let alone help fight poverty, hunger and disease on the world's poorest and most disease-ridden continent.

So, should Africa be recolonised? My answer is "No," an emphatic "No."

We did not fight for independence only to be colonised again. Our struggle for independence was not for temporary relief from colonial oppression and exploitation. We did not intend to be recolonised in the future by our former colonial masters or by any other Western power or by anybody else. And it is the West which still poses the biggest threat to our independence despite its professed commitment to the principles of racial and human equality. It is also the citadel of arrogance because it conquered the world.

Tragically, among all the people in the world, it is we

393

Africans, black Africans, who are the most despised. Much of this denigration of Africa has its roots in the West, although Westerners did not invent racism. It is a universal phenomenon. But the attitude of many Westerners towards Africans and people of African descent is not very good; nor is that of Asians and others. It is patently racist, and condescending at best.

James Baldwin's remarks about the attitude of many white Americans towards black Americans, descendants of Africa, is appropriate in this context in terms of analogy. As he stated in his essay, "Fifth Avenue, Uptown":

"Negroes want to be treated like men: a perfectly straightforward statement containing seven words. People who have mastered Kant, Hegel, Shakespeare, Marx, Freud and the Bible find this statement impenetrable."[6]

It has been that way since Europeans conquered Africa. Success by black Africans in all fields of human endeavour has not changed this attitude. It has become second nature to many whites; with the advancement of the West being cited as proof of their racial superiority even if many of them don't say so publicly. We may be poor and far less developed in terms of material success, but we are no less human and we know when we are being insulted and despised.

The West has, indeed, achieved a lot in terms of material civilisation unmatched anywhere else in the world. And there is a lot that we have learned from Europeans probably even more so than we did when we were under colonial tutelage. And we continue to learn a lot from the West.

But there is nothing intrinsically virtuous, or intrinsically evil, about the West. I have lived in the West for many years and I have seen both. It has its virtues and vices just like any other part of mankind.

One of the worst things that came out of the West,

which was a product of Western material civilisation, was greed which led to imperial ambitions and ultimately the conquest of Africa and other parts of the world. As Immanuel Kant, one of the leading Western philosophers who is also acknowledged by many as one of the world's greatest thinkers, stated in one his works, *Eternal Peace and Other Essays*:

"If we compare the barbarian instances of inhospitality...with the inhuman behavior of the civilized, and especially the commercial states of our continent, the injustice practiced by them even in their first contact with foreign lands and peoples fills us with horror; the mere visiting of such peoples being regarded by them as equivalent to a conquest....

The Negro lands,..., the Cape of Good Hope, etc., on being discovered, were treated as countries that belonged to nobody; for the aboriginal inhabitants were reckoned as nothing....And all this has been done by nations who make a great ado about their piety, and who, while drinking up iniquity like water, would have themselves regarded as the very elect of orthodox faith."[7]

Yet he did not bat an eye in denigrating Africa. He was an unreconstructed racist who also bluntly stated:

"The Negroes of Africa have received from nature no intelligence that rises above the foolish. The difference between the two races (black and white) is thus a substantial one: it appears to be just as great in respect of the faculties of the mind as in color."[8]

So, the argument that black people are genetically – hence intellectually – inferior to members of other races is nothing new. It is a stereotype rooted in the Western intellectual tradition and has been given "credibility" by some of the most eminent thinkers of the Western world.

Besides Kant, other prominent Western philosophers who have ridiculed the African mind include Georg Hegel, David Hume, and Baron de Montesquieu.

Some of them did not even consider us to be full human beings. As Montesquieu stated in *The Spirit of the Laws*:

"These creatures are all over black, and with such a flat nose, that they can scarcely be pitied.

It is hardly to be believed that God, who is a wise Being, should place a soul, especially a good soul, in such a black, ugly body.

The Negroes prefer a glass necklace to that gold which polite nations so highly value: can there be greater proof of their wanting common sense? It is impossible for us to suppose these creatures to be men."[9]

Another great Western mind, David Hume, used his intellectual power to make this equally superstitious statement:

"I am apt to suspect the Negroes...to be naturally inferior to whites. There never was any civilized nation of any other complexion than white, nor even any individual eminent in action or speculation. No ingenious manufactures among them, no arts, no sciences....

Such a uniform and constant difference could not happen, in so many countries and ages, if nature had not made an original distinction betwixt these breeds of men."[10]

Hume was, of course, also an atheist and gave some of the strongest "proofs" of the "non-existence" of God. And he remains an icon in the pantheon of Western thinkers.

Equally irrational was Hegel whose great mind also led him to state:

"Africa...is no historical part of the world; it has no movement or development to exhibit."[11]

It is a sentiment echoed more than 100 years later in contemporary times by many people including one of the most prominent British historians, Arnold Toynbee, who died in 1975 when I was a student at Wayne State University where one of my professors extolled the virtues of Western civilisation and the achievements of the West that provided such a sharp contrast with those of Africa as if our continent belonged to another planet.

It was an empirical fact, and I was acutely aware of the difference in terms of material civilisation and technological advancement. After all, there I was, from Africa, at one of the great centres of learning in the Western world to be taught by Westerners simply because we did not and still don't have enough schools in our countries. And it makes us look bad, very bad. As Toynbee bluntly stated:

"The black races alone have not contributed positively to any civilization."[12]

No less condescending in his attitude towards us was that great humanitarian, physician, philosopher and theologian, Dr. Albert Schweitzer, who worked and died for us, the so-called members of the lesser breed. His work at the mission hospital he established in Lambarene, Gabon, in Equatorial Africa under French rule, is what legends are made of. He also wrote and spoke extensively about the works of Jesus and St. Paul and about the Bible in general as a true Christian who believed in the brotherhood of man and equality of all people here on Earth and before God.

Yet, he made one of the most racist and paternalistic statements about blacks ever made by anybody when, without the slightest doubt in his mind, he stated:

"The Negro is a child, and with children nothing can be done without the use of authority. We must, therefore, so arrange the circumstances of daily life that my natural authority can find expression.

With regard to the Negroes, then, I have coined the formula: 'I am your brother, it is true, but your elder brother.'" [13]

The implication is obvious. Whites have divine mandate to rule blacks. And younger brothers never catch up with their elder brothers, chronologically speaking; hence in terms of wisdom as well. The older are wiser; so are whites versus blacks.

That was the general attitude among Europeans before and after the conquest of Africa. The conquest of our continent only solidified this attitude, our defeat at the hands of our conquerors, because of our inferior technology, being cited as indisputable proof of our inferiority to them.

That was the technological theory of imperialism. They had guns. We had bows and arrows. And when we met on the battlefield, we were no match for them.

Then they also noticed that, besides lack of modern weapons, we had not achieved much in terms of material progress in other areas, thus further validating their belief in the hierarchy of the races as something ordained by God; or by nature with the black race being on the lowest rung of the evolutionary ladder, destined to stay at the bottom.

In terms of material progress, there is no question that we did benefit from the West in many ways. Our conquerors introduced us to many things. Colonisation, of which missionary penetration of Africa was an integral part, brought us material benefits such as schools and hospitals, roads and cars and even railways; and many other things we never had before Europeans came to

Africa. We must admit this to be true instead of lying to ourselves and to the rest of the world that this was not the case. Many of us lie that way. But we are only deluding ourselves.

So, there were some benefits from all that after Africa met Europe and the two became inextricably linked. And when our imperial rulers left, we did not ask them to take everything they brought to Africa.

Otherwise we would have told them to close down schools and hospitals, take back their typewriters and even pens and paper, cut off telephone lines and strip buildings of electrical wires and other installations as the French did in Guinea when the people under the leadership of Sekou Toure voted "No," in 1958, to a French proposal to keep their country within the French Community not as an equal partner but as a satellite in the French orbit just like the rest of the former French colonies in Africa were.

We asked them nothing of the sort. We would even have asked them to dismantle railways and demolish the rest of the infrastructure including buildings we never had before they came. The list goes on and on.

We didn't do that for obvious reasons. Therefore, whatever benefits we got from Western civilisation must be acknowledged by us. And we continue to enjoy them even today, frankly speaking, and probably even more so in this era of globalisation despite our denunciation of the West, most of which is justified especially in terms of exploitation of our continent and destruction of African civilisation by our conquerors in a number of areas, although much of it remains intact.

Still, much as we have benefited from the West in many ways, it remains a fact that it was also the same Western powers, our conquerors, who ruthlessly oppressed and exploited us for centuries since the era of slavery. They did not come to Africa to help us but to help themselves. And our labour and natural resources contributed significantly to the growth of Western civilisation far more than we benefited from the West. That is something that has never been fully acknowledged by the West.

Europeans also robbed us of our independence and dignity when they conquered us. As Kwame Nkrumah said, it is far better to misgovern ourselves than to be governed by anybody else. And in the words of Ghanaian philosopher Dr. Willie Abraham, independence is a state of nature.

It is a sentiment that still echoes across the continent, even if it has not resonated well everywhere. But it is an aspiration, this desire to be free and independent, every human being cherishes and which is an integral part of human nature. We are born free. And we are meant to live free; not to be ruled or dominated by others who, by virtue of their position among fellow men as defined by themselves, think they are better than us and other people.

That has been one of the biggest moral failures, and one of the worst vices, ever to come out of the West: the belief by our conquerors and imperial rulers and many other whites that it is their "divine right" to rule us because they are superior to us; and that as members of "the lesser breed," we have no right, absolutely none, to question their mandate or their wisdom. Thank God, not everyone of them shares this belief, although the majority of them probably do.

So, it is very humiliating to us when hear that some of our people are even thinking about inviting these very same people to come back to rule us again. It is the ultimate insult. But it must also be understood in its proper context.

Where does this sentiment, this agony and anguish, come from? We all know the answer. It comes from the failure of our leaders to do what they are supposed to do, instead of enriching themselves at our expense, denying us basic human rights sometimes in a way far worse than the colonialists did, and killing and persecuting those who are brave enough to complain about such rotten leadership. And it is rotten to the core.

That is what makes a large number of our people, although not the majority, remember with nostalgia the "good old days" of colonial rule. Compared to what they see today, those were golden days, far better in terms of individual freedom however limited it was; in terms of getting basic necessities and other things that are now totally out of reach; and in terms of law and order which has been replaced by anarchy, civil wars and other forms of strife and political instability fuelled by rampant corruption in most countries across the continent decades after independence.

This is also on a continent where in many cases the people can not even feed themselves but have to beg for food from other countries. Ironically, some of the food we get from abroad, such as maize, can be grown right on our own soil, right here in Africa. But we don't produce enough to feed ourselves.

It is also on a continent where we really don't care about each other. If we did, we would not have all these civil wars and other conflicts; tribalism would not be a major problem; and people fleeing from wars would not be left homeless. It is a shame that Africans are refugees in Africa, their homeland, of all places.

We claim Africa is one, yet deny them help, close borders when they beg to come in, refuse to give them citizenship, and even chase away those who are already in some of our countries, telling them to go back where they came from. Where is the African brotherhood we talk about so much? There is no respect for human life on our continent.

We are also talking about a continent where a deranged leader, Idi Amin, was applauded in all the countries as a hero for expelling Asians, including Ugandan citizens of Asian descent. Even fellow leaders, let alone many ordinary black Africans, quietly applauded him as a true black nationalist. Only one African leader, President Julius Nyerere of Tanzania, was vocal in his condemnation of Idi Amin. A few others, such as Kenneth Kaunda of Zambia and Samora Machel of Mozambique, also condemned Amin but not as strongly as Nyerere did.

That is why even fellow African heads of state, and many other people described Nyerere as "The Conscience of Africa."

Tragically, Africa has produced few leaders of such moral stature who also had the courage to admit our failures. As he once said about our continent's condition: "Africa is in a mess."

It is, indeed.

But something can be done about all that. And it can be done *only* by us. This is what we can and should do.

First of all, we must acknowledge, however painful, the fact that we don't have the kind of political and economic independence we would like to have as a people and as nations. We fought for it, and won part of it especially political independence. But we have lost most of it. As Julius Nyerere said in what amounted to a farewell speech to Africa a few months before he died, we have lost our sovereignty to the IMF and the World Bank.

We have also lost our sovereignty to donor nations on whose terms we formulate and implement economic policies especially in this era of globalisation, however painful this is, as has been tragically demonstrated by the enormous negative impact of structural adjustment programmes on the poor, forcing millions out of work, drastically reducing their incomes, and forcing African governments to spend less or nothing on education, health and other vital social services for the masses.

All this is because of capitalism which we have embraced as the best means to develop our countries. In fact, probably more than anything else, it is economic hardship – hunger, starvation, lack of money and jobs as well as basic necessities – which is the main reason why many Africans remember with nostalgia the "good old days" of colonial rule; and why some of them even wish the Europeans were back to rule us again.

And they did so under capitalism, a system which fuelled Western economic growth and industrial might despite its lack of concern for the poor. Under capitalism, the strongest survive and thrive. Each to his own.

There is no doubt that capitalism is highly productive. But it is also ruthless by nature. It thrives on greed. And most people are greedy, of course. They care only about themselves. That is what makes capitalism so successful, unlike socialism, its antithesis.

But although socialism failed to develop our economies, it did create and foster an egalitarian disposition among the people, especially in Tanzania under Nyerere, which helped to spread equality across-the-board. It is these egalitarian ideals that are worth preserving if we are going to implement policies which benefit everybody.

Development requires lifting everybody up from the bottom. Capitalism alone is not going to do that. It is not even part of its nature to care about the poor. Therefore there must be a concerted effort by the government to curb its predatory instincts and protect the weakest members of society. They can not be left at the mercy of ruthless market forces. If you do that, be prepared for war, more than just minor civil unrest.

Who is going to protect the poor if the government does not intervene on their behalf? Good economic policy must translate into good social policy. And that entails fostering and implementing egalitarian ideals to guarantee economic justice and equality for all. Development statistics and other indices of economic growth may be impressive to economists and government officials but they mean absolutely nothing to people who don't have jobs, food, medical care, clean water or other basic necessities they need to live as decent human beings. People come first.

And much as we have lost our sovereignty to the World Bank, the IMF and donor nations which help us to develop our countries and sustain economic growth, we can try to regain and retain some of that independence by having a controlling share or interest in all the investment ventures started by foreigners in our countries.

No country worth its name if is going to allow foreigners to control its economy and own its assets and natural resources. The American economy is the most successful capitalist economy in history. Yet the United States has not allowed foreigners to own or control most of the country's businesses and assets; and it is not going to. So why should we?

Our weakness does not justify injustice we suffer under powerful nations who dictate terms to us simply because they dominate the international system of which we are an integral part despite the peripheral role we play in the global arena. But we can still develop because we are human beings, endowed with the same mental faculties like everybody else. Intelligence based on race has no basis in science. Empirical evidence demonstrates otherwise. And intellectual achievements by Africans in all fields is part of this proof, although we are dwarfed by others but for reasons which have nothing to do with genes.

The question is how can we develop?

African countries can develop and attain a degree of independence without being recolonised. Southeast Asian countries – South Korea, Malaysia, Indonesia, Singapore, Thailand – did not ask Europeans to go back and rule them again in order to develop. They developed without being recolonised. So why not us? We can do the same.

Therefore, instead of saying Africa should be recolonised – which is a minority view, anyway, but with a powerful emotional appeal because of our desperate situation – the following should be done:

Because of rampant corruption, donor nations and aid

agencies must insist on administering aid programmes in our countries to make sure that the money they give us is not stolen or spent on irrelevant projects. It is humiliating but we asked for it. We have to suffer the consequences including wounded dignity because of lack of concern for us by our leaders. They are just cruel.

If our leaders don't agree to that, our countries should get nothing from the donors. Then it is for the leaders to explain to the people why they are rejecting economic assistance and refusing to allow donors to administer aid programmes to make sure that the money is well-spent; when it is common knowledge that whenever these programmes have been administered by local experts and bureaucrats, the money has always been stolen or spent on irrelevant projects.

They should also explain why they are blocking foreign aid when they themselves do nothing for us. Appeal to nationalist sentiment, contending that they are maintaining our independence and preserving national honour, is nothing but a diversionary tactic used by our leaders to soothe the masses and numb their sense, and cover up their failures, while they are busy stealing.

They have failed to develop our countries. They have even failed to formulate the right policies and come up with practical solutions to our problems. Therefore, there is no reason why they should refuse to allow donors to administer aid programmes to help develop our countries. They refuse to do so, not because they want to protect us from foreign intruders and maintain our independence as free nations. They refuse to do so because they want to administer aid programmes themselves so that they can steal the money. And if that is the case, here is some good advice to donor nations and agencies: Give us nothing.

Another thing that needs to be done is this: African governments should form a new partnership and strengthen ties with the former colonial powers to draw on the reservouir of highly skilled manpower those countries have in many areas. The partnership should include hiring these experts and placing them in key positions in an advisory capacity in different ministries – except foreign affairs, defence, and national security – to help fight corruption, which is destroying Africa, and provide efficient administration. As long as we continue to rely on foreign aid, we should be prepared to suffer the consequences – lost sovereignties, wounded dignity, loss of national pride and so on.

Dependence on other countries is highly offensive to our nationalist sensibilities. We are insulting ourselves. But that is probably what we need to galvanise us into action and stop begging.

We have failed to make maximum sacrifice to be self-reliant. We don't need foreign aid if we pull our resources together and if use those resources constructively. Africa has far more resources than it gets from donors. What it does not have is good leadership. That is why it is imperative to decentralise power all the way down to the grassroots level. That is where real power should be. Let the people decide. They know what is best for them.

We should also learn from fellow Africans to find out how and why countries such as Botswana, Ivory Coast and Mauritius have achieved significant progress through the years, having robust economies – even if by African standards – while the rest across the continent have either stagnated, deteriorated, or collapsed.

Much as we may hate it out of nationalist pride, the kind of relationship Ivory Coast has had with the former colonial power, France, through the years since independence in 1960, has proved to be economically beneficial to this West African country. It has benefited Ivory Coast to such a degree that its economy became the most successful in West Africa and one of the most successful on the entire continent, and second only to Nigeria in size in that region, attracting millions of people from other West African countries including Nigeria itself which has the second-largest economy on the continent after South Africa; after some data manipulation, it is now said to be the largest on the continent, although in practical terms, it has not replaced South Africa.

Other African countries can learn from Ivory Coast how this country has been able to have a vibrant economy for decades since the sixties, but without mortgaging their independence the way the Ivory Coast has done by becoming a French satellite and remaining a virtual colony of this metropolitan power.

Our continent does not have to be recolonised or become a neocolonial appendage to Europe or the United States in order to develop. Southeast Asian countries, the Asian tigers, did not become colonies again in order to develop or build schools and hospitals and other infrastructure. They developed without being recolonised or by inviting their former colonial masters to rule them again.

Do they have innate qualities we don't have? No. But we can emulate them. They are probably the best role model we have since they once were colonial subjects like us; they were poor like us, and some were even poorer than us; and they won independence during the same period we did, that is after World War II.

African governments should also liberalise immigration laws and policies to attract highly skilled farmers from other parts of the world to help develop our agricultural sector which is the backbone of African economies and the biggest employer in our countries. They should also launch an aggressive campaign and offer incentives to other foreigners with needed skills and capital to become citizens – not just invite them to invest – the same way developed countries such as Canada and others provide incentives to attract highly skilled immigrants who play an important role in boosting the economies of those countries.

If industrialised nations such as the United States and

Canada have policies and programmes to attract high-skilled immigrants from around the world, why shouldn't African countries have similar policies, depending on their needs?

Africa is an agricultural continent. It has plenty of fertile land. It needs capital and technology. And it can greatly benefit from foreigners if they become citizens of our countries. Invite them. For example, in terms of agriculture, many of them have much-needed skills they can impart to local peasants and farmers to boost production.

And because they have large capital, they will also be able to provide employment and invest in the economy. For example, Mozambique, Zambia, and the Central African Republic invited white farmers, whose farms were seized in Zimbabwe, to settle in those countries; so did some state governors in Nigeria. They offered them some land and made it clear that highly skilled farmers would be a boost to the national economy whose mainstay is agriculture as much as it is in the rest of the countries across the continent.

South African white farmers who are also leaving their country because of conflict over land and the polarised racial situation should be encouraged to settle in other African countries. Some countries have offered them some land. They have also invited white South Africans in general and others to invest in the economy, although there has been some hostility and nationalist backlash among some people in those countries who complain that foreigners are taking over the economy. It can happen. So, there must be safeguards to protect the indigenous people. Foreigners have been acquiring huge tracts of land in African countries at throwaway prices mainly because of corruption which is a product of bad leadership.

But if we want foreigners – no matter where they come from – with skills and money to invest in our economies and help develop our countries, we should welcome them.

We are going to have investors or no investors.

We don't have enough local investors with enough capital to fuel our economies. Therefore, we need foreign investors. And we need highly skilled people to work and even settle in our countries permanently. All this will have multiplier effect and help to develop our economies and create jobs our governments have failed to create for our people. But local people including new citizens, and the government, must have a controlling share in all investment ventures in our countries. Otherwise our countries will be owned by foreigners.

One of the most critical areas where we face the danger of losing our continent to foreigners, and where conflicts between the indigenous people and foreign investors could destabilise our countries, is land ownership.

We have a phenomenon – land grab or land grabbing – that has evolved into what can rightly be called the second scramble for Africa. It involves foreign investors, including multinational corporations, who are acquiring land across Africa on a scale never seen before, often by dubious means, and dispossessing rightful owners of millions of acres in collusion with unscrupulous politicians and bureaucrats who are in every government, in every country, on the continent.

Tanzania's minister of foreign affairs and international cooperation, Bernard Membe, conceded in an interview with Voice of America (VOA) in 2011 that we have lost hundreds of millions of acres of land to foreigners. He went to say, collectively, the amount of land Africans have lost is equal to the size of Germany. The land does not belong to us anymore, he emphasised.

Yet, the government of Tanzania itself, his own government, signed a deal with Saudi Arabia which gave the Saudis 500,000 hectares of land to grow food crops for their own consumption in Saudi Arabia. And they are not the only people who have acquired vast tracts of land in Tanzania on long tenure to grow different kind of crops for human consumption and for industrial use such as biofuel production.

Other African governments have signed similar agreements, with many foreign countries and investors, depriving their own people of arable. This has led to food shortages and even starvation in many parts of Africa. Land which belongs to Africans is used to grow crops to feed foreigners while Africans themselves are starving or do not have enough to eat in their own countries.

Even a desperately poor and traumatised country like Sierra Leone which went through a horrendous tragedy during its 10-year civil war in the1900s can not justify its enormous sale of land to foreigners. The government has sold a fifth of the land to British, Indian, Chinese and Belgian companies, according to a report by Africa Today, PressTV, London, in April 2013.

According to the same report, Sudan has sold more than 700,000 hectares of land to South Korea. And Liberia has sold 30 per cent of its land to foreigners; some reports say it has sold 50 per cent of its land.

India is one of the biggest investors in Africa. It has acquired hundreds of thousands of hectares of land in Ethiopia, Kenya and Madagascar to grow food crops such as rice and maize to feed its people.

In the Democratic Republic of Congo (DRC), one of the largest, richest and most fertile countries in Africa and in the entire world, the government has sold 50 per cent of the land to foreigners. That land does not belong to the people of Congo anymore. When the land goes, so do the minerals underneath; everything goes to those who have bought the land: foreign investors.

And they hardly pay anything for it, compared to its value. For example, in Ethiopia, investors from India have leased some land for only one dollar per hectare. It's not much different in other countries on the continent where some investors have even acquired land for less than one dollar per hectare.

There is another very disturbing example of how Africans are losing their land on very "generous" terms. It has to do with South Sudan.

One Nigerian social activist, Nnimmo Bassey, former executive director of the Environmental Rights Action in Abuja, Nigeria, said in television interview with Henry Bonsu of Africa Today, PressTV, London, in April 2013, that there was an American company which, after speculating that South Sudan would become an independent country one day, bought 600,000 hectares of land there for only 25,000 US dollars. It is going to own the land for 50 years. The company bought the land not long before South Sudan won independence after seceding from Sudan on 9 July 2011.

There are similar and very disturbing reports from many parts of the continent on how Africans are losing their land to foreigners and at a very fast pace. African farmers, most of whom are poor peasants and whose only means of surviving is farming, virtually have no right to land ownership in their own countries if the government decides to taken land away from them.

Countless across Africa have been forcibly removed from their land, with many of them dying of starvation because they don't have arable anymore where they can grow food crops. Food security has not become a major concern across the continent because of land grabbing by corrupt and insensitive African governments working with foreign investors who are busy acquiring vast tracts of land at the expense of the indigenous people in this era of globalisation. This is the second scramble for Africa, a new invasion of Africa Julius Nyerere warned about more than 50 years ago, in 1960, even before Tanganyika became independent the following year under his leadership. As he stated at a conference on Dar es Salaam, Tanganyika, in August 1961:

"We are now entering a new phase. It is the phase of

411

the second scramble for Africa." – (Julius Nyerere, in a speech delivered to the Second Pan-African Seminar, World Assembly of Youth, Dar es Salaam, Tanganyika, August 1961, in *WAY* (World Assembly of Youth) *Forum*, No. 40, September 1961; reprinted in Paul E. Sigmund, Jr., editor, *The Ideologies of the Developing Nation*, New York: Frederick A. Praeger, 1963, p. 205. See also *Tanganyika Standard*, Dar es Salaam, Tanganyika, August and September 1961).

Multinational corporations and other foreign investors, in collusion with African leaders, are at the forefront of the second scramble for Africa. It is a new form of colonialism under the the guise of partnership for development, with Africans being at an enormous advantage in this partnership. Globalisation is the new imperialism.

Pleas by Africans who are losing their land have fallen on deaf ears. Even many who were most productive on their land before this new invasion have not been spared. As Justine Mutale, a Zambian social activist who was also involved in an international organisation to fight global hunger, stated in an interview with Henry Bonsu of Africa Today, PressTV, London, in April 2013:

"I am very concerned about land grabs and I do acknowledge that land grabs... some people might not be aware of this, but it is a wider segment of a wider policy by the international community starting all the way from the Washington Consensus that came into Africa and asked, or rather in a way imposed on Africa, to try and open their borders to international trade. It is part of the trade policy and it's a policy that benefits foreign investors.

Land grabs also started with colonization. Before that, Africans had a right to their land, we had customary land, land that we inherited from generation to generation for our own use.

To talk about trying to feed ourselves - there was a time in some parts of Africa up til today you don't need to have money to eat because we have wild fruits we have wild vegetables we have wild game, all you need is to just go out to get that food.

But the moment that a certain way of life was imposed on us where you have to exchange your labor in order to eat, where you have to work to earn money as in notes and coins in order to eat rather than your labor to labor to go and hunt, to go and harvest so that you can eat the food that you directly harvest...

Even today we have capable Africans.

My own grandmother more than 5 generations ago, she owned a coffee farm in Zambia and she used to export her coffee to all over the world. And this coffee farm, at the time that title deeds and foreign land ownership was introduced has been taken away from our family.

It is something that I could have carried on, or one of my children or even my nieces and nephews could have done, but we found that this coffee farm, this land that my grandmother used to farm coffee and export - she even came to England on a trade fair to display her coffee - That land has been taken away from our family because we didn't have title deeds.

Remember we had the right and access to use the land it was a customary or social contract.

I am totally against any foreigners coming into our land to take our land....

Even to do a deal I'm totally against that.

My Grandmother fifty years ago she managed to feed the country, we used to export her coffee, it's just that the land was customary inherited so she didn't own title deeds and when the title deeds were introduced to our countries and to Africa we found that our country lost out on that.

I could have done it, my children could have done it or even any of my cousins... could have carried on feeding the country with coffee.

We believe that this is a scandal and it's a scandal that needs to be stopped because land grabs render people refugees, they make people become refugees in their own God-given land.

They make people go hungry and making people go hungry is a violence against those people. You take away their rights of livelihood from the people; you take away their rights to shelter to food to clothing to anything they can do with the land that they have. You take that away from them and that is what the IF campaign is about is to stop land grab so that indigenous people can have their own dignity; can go back and use their land as they see fit.

All these generations we have been able to feed ourselves - until somebody comes and says you can't feed yourself. We know we can feed ourselves. If these people they come and purchase the land in which natural resources - underneath we've got copper or diamonds - they buy it and then they suddenly own the copper and diamonds, which should have belonged to my family or to the family that lived on that land."

The people are completely left out. They do not take part in any negotiations involving such sales because they are not even invited by the leaders. African governments do what they want to do. They are ones who negotiate with the foreign investors, and they are the ones who sell the land to them, ostensibly for the benefit of the indigenous people.

The problem is compounded by the terms, unfavourable to the indigenous people, under which land is acquired by foreign investors reminiscent of what happened during the colonial era when long leases – for example, the 99-year leases in colonial Kenya – were common, enabling white settlers to acquire tens of thousands of acres of land at the expense of the indigenes who were not only barred from those vast tracts of land leased to white settlers; countless were forcibly removed

414

from their ancestral lands which were then given to whites. Just remember the Kikuyu and the Mau Mau uprising against the white settlers in central Kenya, the homeland of the Kikuyu.

The land question was one of the most volatile issues – if not the most incendiary – not only in Kenya during Mau Mau but also during the liberation struggle in the countries of southern Africa under white minority rule.

It is still a major problem today, as the conflict over land in Zimbabwe, has clearly demonstrated, and as the ethnic conflicts in the Rift Valley Province and elsewhere in Kenya – ignited and fuelled by unfair acquisition of land by the ruling elite since independence – also clearly show.

The only way to avert such catastrophes is to redistribute land fairly. Otherwise expect more eruptions and conflagrations over the central question of land.

Also, long tenures of ownership – all this nonsense about half-century and 99-year land leases to foreigners and even to local investors – should never be given. Those already given should be renegotiated to take into account the interests of the indigenous inhabitants who have been victimised by the land grabbers in these nefarious schemes in collusion with government officials who take bribes from foreign investors to grab land from the local people.

Land should be leased for no more than 20 years. After that, the terms of the lease should be renegotiated, taking into account the interests of the local people, how the land has been used, and what benefits the indigenes have been able to get from the investments in their area during that period. Shorter land leases will make investors more accountable, unlike 50 – 99-year leases.

The indigenous people should never be expelled from their land, deprived of ownership, to give room to investors. Never. Otherwise foreign investors are going to take over the continent and we will become slaves in our own land, owning nothing.

There is also an imperative need to create larger markets to encourage inter-territorial trade – for example, between Kenya, Uganda and Tanzania in East Africa – to promote and foster regional integration. The objective should be to achieve self-sufficiency across the continent by creating an African common market which is a product of interlinked regional markets, with regional currencies, and finally a common currency for the whole continent.

Africa plays only a marginal role in the global market in this era of globalisation. And that will continue to be the case for many years, if not for decades, to come. We should just face it. But we can "globalise" Africa by integrating our economies and promoting inter-regional trade – between East and West Africa, central and southern Africa and so forth – in the African world which can then become an integral part of the global market by its sheer size and vibrancy.

Without self-sufficiency, and industrialisation, Africa is going to remain on the periphery of the international mainstream; and millions of Africans, drowning in the fetid swamp of poverty and misery, will yearn even louder in nostalgia for the "golden era" of colonial rule wishing our former colonial masters had never left.

African countries also need to invest heavily in health and education to have healthy and skilled workers to build strong economies and develop our countries.

But we must also be willing to critically analyse our condition, something our leaders refuse to do or allow others to. Without the right diagnosis, we can not provide the right prescription.

One of those prescriptions involves radical treatment of failed states which have dissolved in anarchy or are on the brink of collapse. When the leaders of those countries appeal to the United Nations and the international community for help, they must be told in no uncertain terms that assistance will be provided only if their countries are placed under effective UN administration in conjunction with the African Union for an indefinite period until law and order is restored and a competent local administration is established.

Call it recolonisation. Fine. It is of the most benign and best kind Africa can ever get. After all, who is paying for UN peacekeeping operations and for all the help we get from international relief agencies? African countries?

Somalia, Sierra Leone, Liberia, Rwanda, the so-called Democratic Republic of Congo, Central African Republic, South Sudan, have all at one time or another been prime candidates for such effective international administration under UN mandate; although Somalia defies solution after the whole country dissolved in anarchy and remains a stateless state after more than 20 years.

Probably the best solution in the case of Somalia is for the different clan-based authorities and territorial enclaves to remain as they are and form a confederation instead of a highly centralised state which stifled local aspirations in clan communities and destroyed individual freedom under President Siad Barre's despotic regime that instituted and institutionalised tyranny in the country of fiercely independent clans which even the colonial authorities never fully succeeded in taming into submission.

But Somaliland, which seceded from the rest of Somalia and succeeded in establishing an effective administration and is now a functional political and economic entity, should be recognised as an independent state. As a *de facto* state, it has functioned well for more than 20 years since 1991 as sovereign state, in fact far better than many failed states across the continent which enjoy international recognition despite their despicable record as independent entities. It has all the attributes of nationhood and should be recognised as an independent nation. Denying it recognition is a travesty.

Besides repression, one of the main reasons why Somalia collapsed as a state, and as a nation, was the weakness of its economy under failed socialist policies pursued by President Barre.

Even after his government was overthrown and different groups started fighting for power, the country would have been able to absorb the shock generated by the conflict if it had a strong economy able to meet the needs and desires of the people. Instead, the economy's weakness helped fuel the conflict and civil unrest, as the people fought for survival over whatever little was available in an economy that contracted through the years since the introduction of socialism under the Marxist-Leninist banner soon after Siad Barre seized power in a military coup in October 1969.

Socialist policies had the same devastating impact in other African countries despite their enormous potential to develop and escape poverty; in many cases far more potential than the southeast Asian nations have even today in terms of natural resources besides people. Yet within a few years, they surpassed us in terms of development, in fact so much so that we now beg from them. What did they do that we failed to do?

They pursued free-market policies and encouraged entrepreneurship. They promoted local and foreign investment. They also promoted and expanded international trade. They diversified their economies. They emphasised fiscal responsibility. They encouraged saving and domestic capital accumulation. They trained skilled workers. They invested heavily in health and education, creating a large reservouir of healthy and educated people to develop their economies.

And they emphasised discipline, making southeast Asian countries some of the most productive in modern times; sometimes far more productive than their level of technological development contrasted with the far more advanced nations of the industrial West.

African countries did none of that, or very little of it. And if we still can't do it, forget it. There's no hope for Africa.

But there is hope. There must be fundamental change in leadership.

We have lost an entire generation since independence. We can't afford to lose the next.

Part III

Conclusion

THE SIXTIES was a decade of excitement as Africans celebrated the end of colonial rule in most countries across the continent.

But the excitement did not last very long. In every country, when Africans woke up the next day after independence, they knew that little had changed.

The people had indeed regained their dignity and the right to rule themselves after years of colonial rule. And they were highly optimistic of the future, riding on a wave of high expectations for the fruits of independence although they did not see any tangible benefits right away.

The only major change they witnessed, or were aware of, was the transfer of power from Europeans to Africans. And the most obvious difference was in the race and skin colour of the rulers.

In most cases, white rulers relinquished power to blacks and in some cases to other non-whites.

They were the people who led the struggle for independence and were an integral part of the indigenous elite that assumed the leadership of the newly independent countries.

But in terms of power and institutional arrangements, and the relationship between the leaders and the led, things remained almost the same as they were under colonial rule.

The power structure instituted by the colonialists remained intact; only that this time it had new masters: the indigenous elite. To the new rulers, one of the most attractive features of the colonial power structure was centralization, or concentration of power in the hands of a few people at the centre, under a unitary state.

And in a way, the departing colonial rulers found many comfortable allies among the indigenous elite who admired European ways of life and institutions. It was clear where they got this influence.

Almost all the new African leaders were educated in schools which had been established by missionaries or by colonial governments. Like the colonial rulers, the missionaries themselves came from Western countries. The education they provided, as did the colonial authorities, was based on the Western intellectual tradition. And the values they instilled in their African students were also Western.

Many educated Africans became carbon copies of Europeans, although poor carbon copies. They could never be the same as the original.

Yet, in spite of all that, they still and quite often tried to be more European than the Europeans themselves. Among them were dedicated "nationalists" who led the struggle for independence.

Some of the best examples of this abjectly servile and despicable imitation of the imperial masters were the leaders of Francophone Africa who after independence remained beholden to France and were unabashedly

Francophile.

Another good example is Dr. Hastings Kamuzu Banda of Malawi who was very British in his manners, values and attire.

He even established a school in Malawi named after himself, Kamuzu Academy, where he allowed only whites to teach in order to produce a generation of African Anglophiles who would follow in his footsteps to spread Western education and "civilization" in Malawi and, hopefully, in other African countries as well.

And as *The New York Times*, 27 November 1997, stated in its report, "Kamuzu Banda Dies: 'Big Man' Among Anticolonialists":

"Hastings Kamuzu Banda, a founding father in postcolonial Africa who led Malawi to independence in 1964 and then ruled it with a combination of caustic wit, eccentricity and cruelty for 30 years, died on Tuesday (25 November) night in a hospital here (in Johannesburg)....

After a revolt within his cabinet, he declared himself President for Life in 1971 and said his opponents would become "food for crocodiles." Hundreds were killed, tortured or forced into exile....

Dr. Banda was perhaps the most idiosyncratic of the "big men" who led their countries out of colonialism. He held degrees from American and Scottish universities and his London medical offices became a sort of anticolonialist salon frequented by Jomo Kenyatta of Kenya and Kwame Nkrumah of the Gold Coast (now Ghana).

But once in power, Dr. Banda simultaneously affected the lion-tail fly whisk of an African king, the dark suits and homburgs of a British businessman and the arms of a Scottish baron. He refused to make speeches in African languages and established a school modeled on Eton in his birthplace, Mtunthama, where penniless students were taught Latin, Greek and African history from the British point of view. He hired only white foreigners to teach at the school and to run the ministries and businesses that built his personal fortune.

Under his rule, Malawi spurned black nationalist movements and was the only African nation with diplomatic ties to apartheid South Africa and to Israel. He was the darling of cold warriors and big business, and amassed power in his own hands, keeping the Ministries of Justice, Foreign Affairs, Agriculture and Public works to himself, as well as the trusteeship of the state monopolies in tobacco farming, factories, oil and banking....

Victorian in his demands on public morality, he banned women from wearing pants or miniskirts. Long-haired male tourists arriving in Malawi either submitted to shearing by the airport barber or went home.

He also banned television, though he watched it himself by satellite, and prevented the Simon and Garfunkel song "Cecelia" from being played on local radio, considering it an affront to his consort (Cecilia Kadzamira). He referred to Malawi's 10 million citizens as "my children" and was said to be deeply embittered when they turned him out in 1994....

His sleek capital, Lilongwe, was built with South African money and South Africa underwrote and trained the red-shirted Young Pioneers, a paramilitary youth group that spied on citizens and terrorized dissidents. And in one of the world's smallest and poorest nations, where the per-capita income was $200 a year, Dr. Banda kept five residences, a fleet of British luxury cars and a private jet....

His first education was at a Church of Scotland mission, but he left at a young age to run away to South Africa....After eight years as a clerk at a Johannesburg gold mine, studying at night, he won help from a Methodist bishop to come to the United States. He studied at the Wilberforce Institute in Xenia, Ohio, and at Indiana University before becoming the only black to graduate from the University of Chicago in 1931.

He received an M.D. from Meharry Medical College in Nashville, then moved to Britain to train at the Universities of Glasgow and Edinburgh and study tropical medicine in Liverpool.

He prospered as a physician in suburban London, but in 1953, furious that Britain had allowed the establishment of the Federation of Rhodesia and Nyasaland instead of taking power away from white expatriates, he moved to the Gold Coast, now Ghana, and railed against British treachery. Despite their fear of his firebrand tendencies, the colonial authorities let him return in 1958 to lead the Nyasaland African Congress.

He had apparently forgotten his native tongue, but got an uproarious welcome when he told his audience in English, borrowing from Patrick Henry, "In Nyasaland, we mean to be masters. And if that is treason, make the most of it."

Riots broke out, and he spent a year in prison in Rhodesia before being released to lead his new Malawi Congress party to victory in a 1961 election. He told white settlers to accept majority rule "or pack up"....

In 1994, under pressure from Western nations who cut off aid to enforce demands for democratic reforms, he called elections. He was defeated by Bakili Muluzi, a former protege who had resigned from the Cabinet in 1982 suspecting he was about to be killed. His replacement, Mr. Muluzi said, was murdered."[1]

Dr. Banda ended up being one of the worst dictators Africa has ever produced.

Soon after independence, he turned against his colleagues such as Kanyama Chiume and Henry Chipembere, the very same people who had invited him back to Nyasaland from Britain to help lead the struggle for independence.

By the time he was invited, he had lived in the United States and Britain for 40 years, mostly in Britain, and spent some time in Ghana after his friend Kwame Nkrumah became the leader of that country, only to become a tyrant soon after he led Nyasaland to independence.

His former compatriots were forced to flee their homeland and sought refuge in neighbouring countries, especially Tanzania and Zambia.

Banda was just one among many African leaders who went on to establish authoritarian or despotic regimes soon after independence.

Therefore, while independence was supposed to have ushered in a new era of freedom, the people soon learned that the freedom they had been promised was more apparent than real. Yet, one of the most attractive slogans African leaders used in their campaign for independence was that they would establish democracy the people had been denied under colonial rule. But when independence came, it was an entirely different story.

In almost all African countries, the new African rulers had little respect for freedom. They justified curtailment of freedom on grounds of nation unity and security, contending that they could not afford the luxury of freedom which entails the establishment of opposition parties in pursuit of partisan interests to the detriment of national well-being.

Therefore multiparty democracy was out of the question, not only for the sake of national unity but for other reasons as well: nation building and consolidation of independence which could not be achieved without mass regimentation, according to this rationale.

Freedom of speech was curtailed and opposition parties were strongly discouraged or banned, ushering in what became a new era of one-party rule and dictatorship on a continent where the people had been promised freedom during the struggle for independence.

There were only a few exceptions, in countries such as Nigeria with its regionally entrenched parties dominated by the country's three main ethnic groups – the Hausa-Fulani in the north, the Yoruba in the west and the Igbo in the east; Botswana, Gambia, and Senegal; also Zambia but where the ruling party (UNIP – United National Independence Party) remained dominant at the expense of two opposition parties which, unfortunately, thrived on ethnoregional loyalties in the western and southern regions.

Kenya is another example. The ruling party, KANU (Kenya African National Union), wanted a strong central government under a unitary state but virtually an ethnocracy dominated by the Kikuyu.

Soon after independence, it neutralized KADU (Kenya African Democratic Unity), the opposition party in parliament which wanted a federal constitution under which there would be devolution of power to the regions to safeguard the interests of smaller ethnic groups which were afraid of being dominated by the country's two main ones: the Kikuyu and the Luo.

The situation was basically the same in other countries on the continent which also had opposition parties. The opposition parties were neutralized or simply withered soon after independence. And in many cases they were banned.

But even in countries such as Tanganyika, where the opposition party, the African National Congress (ANC), was simply overwhelmed at the polls by the ruling party TANU (Tanganyika African National Union), and thus died a natural death in the early sixties, laws were passed to give legal status to one-party rule leading to the establishment of the one-party system.

Tanganyika became a *de jure* one-party state in 1965, within five years after independence in December 1961 when it was a *de facto* one-party state like most were, across the continent.

One-party states became the dominant feature of the African political landscape at the expense of freedom soon after independence. Tolerance of dissent was equated with weakness and abdication of responsibility by the leaders.

Some people still spoke up, but at their own risk. They knew that criticism of government was tantamount to treason. And the authorities left no doubt in any one's mind how they would respond. They were ruthless in their suppression of dissent.

Thus, paradoxically, the new era of freedom led to denial of freedom. If the new nations could not be built into cohesive units because the people had the freedom to disagree on how to build those nations, then freedom had to go.

Therefore in most African countries, freedom became the first casualty under the new African leaders who felt that it was only they who knew what was best for the people and not the people themselves. It was a betrayal of trust and the people became increasingly distrustful of their own leaders who not long ago had led them to independence.

But freedom was not the only casualty. Nation building, which the new leaders argued could not be achieved if opposition parties were allowed to exist and if criticism of government even by individuals was allowed as well, also suffered because the people – besides the leaders – were not given the opportunity to examine and challenge government decisions.

Had they been allowed to do so, and had opposition parties which were truly national in character been allowed to exist, African countries would have had the chance to pursue alternative policies which in some and may be even in many cases would have been better than those pursued by the government.

But the people were not allowed to do that. They couldn't even freely discuss government policies and offer constructive criticism even among themselves without fear of being arrested. They were muzzled.

All that led to apathy with dire consequences for the

new nations in terms of nation building and national development. For, without the people's involvement in decision making all the way down to the grassroots level, meaningful change including development is virtually impossible. It is the people themselves who know what is best for them. Yet the leaders turned a deaf ear to what they had to say except in a few cases. The result was pursuit of wrong policies, by the leaders, which led to stunted economic growth.

This was compounded by a lack of high-level manpower and necessary skills needed in many areas to implement development projects and provide efficient administration throughout the country.

At independence, almost all African countries lacked a critical mass of educated people and professionals as well as administrative skills not only in technical fields but in almost all the other areas as well. For example, when my home country, Tanganyika, won independence from Great Britain in December 1961, it had only two engineers and 12 doctors.

The situation was basically the same in most countries across the continent, except in countries such as Ghana and Nigeria which had a significant number of educated people compared with other African countries.

Without trained workers and needed skills, it was obvious that the young African nations would not be able to develop. The only place they could turn to for help to meet their needs was foreign countries including their former colonial rulers.

But foreign aid, which included financial and technical assistance, did not solve Africa's problems. In most cases, there were no trained people or well-established institutions to use the assistance effectively and on the right projects. In some cases, the wrong kind of aid was sought or provided, sadly demonstrated by rusted machinery which one could see in many countries on the continent. The equipment couldn't be used and was simply left out there to rust.

And in other cases, when the equipment arrived, there were no skilled people to use it. Or there were no spare parts or someone to fix it when it broke down. Sometimes it was the wrong kind of machinery that was sent; for example snow ploughs, instead of tractors, sent to Guinea from the Soviet Union.

Also, because the new governments lacked accountability since there was no organized or formal opposition to act as a watchdog over those in power, mismanagement of resources including outright theft became a major problem in the early days of independence.

Ethnic loyalties was also a major factor in the allocation of power and resources and, most of the time, those in power usually came from one or only a handful of ethnic groups, thus accentuating ethnic cleavages in multiethnic societies. People sought power to help themselves and "their people," members of their own "tribes," almost to the total exclusion of other ethnic groups.

Thus, while the leaders who led the struggle for independence also campaigned against tribalism, contending that the colonial rulers had used divide-and-rule tactics by keeping "tribes" separate from each other and sometimes even turning some against others, they did exactly the same thing themselves when they assumed power.

They used ethnic and regional loyalties to perpetuate themselves in office by keeping their opponents divided. They also outlawed opposition parties even if there were some prospects that some of those parties could have become truly national parties in character, transcending ethnic loyalties, regionalism and other forms of sectarianism militating against national unity.

Yet, there were some leaders who made genuine attempts to achieve national unity on the basis of equality for all regardless of race, class, ethnicity, national origin or religious affiliation: Nkrumah, Nyerere, Obote, and Kaunda among others.

They were also some of the most prominent Pan-Africanists and among the strongest advocates of African unity on a continental scale and on regional basis.

Nkrumah stood out alone among them as an opponent of regional federations or formation of any regional blocs which he described as "balkanization on a grand scale" and an obstacle to continental unification.

But in spite of the genuine attempts by a number of African leaders to create a sense of national unity and identity among their citizens, ethnoregional loyalties remained strong and an intractable problem in most African countries and one of the most devastating. And it was only one among many of the major problems the new African nations faced in their early days of independence in spite of the optimism the leaders and the people had for their future free from colonial rule.

Therefore, in the initial euphoria after independence, even the leaders themselves did not realize the scope and magnitude of the task that lay ahead especially in terms of nation building. And in many cases, it is a task that has yet to be accomplished. A large number of countries across the continent remain fractured along ethnic and regional lines, and most of them are still trapped in poverty, fifty years after independence.

The struggle for power among different ethnic and regional groups, mainly because many of them have been excluded from the decision-making process and allocation of resources, is a perennial problem. And it has been one of the major causes of conflict on the continent since independence.

Tragically, even after decades of independence, few African countries have seriously considered decentralisation, and devolution, as a viable alternative to concentration of power at the centre and as a practical solution to so many problems – including ethnic rivalries and conflicts – which plague the continent.

African countries, almost all of which are composed of diverse ethnic and racial groups, need to be innovative and devise means or formulate solutions relevant to African conditions in order to maintain unity in diversity without imposing uniformity in an attempt to create homogeneous societies and thereby risk civil conflicts and wars by members of different groups who don't want to be regimented into a monolithic whole under the oppressive machinery of the highly centralised state.

They must also redefine the concept of sovereignty – domestic and international legal sovereignty exercised by independent states – in order to reflect their own realities and without compromising their national identities. A number of countries around the world have done that and have survived and prospered without falling apart. There is no reason why African countries can not do the same thing to accommodate conflicting interests, defuse ethnic tensions, and neutralise secessionist tendencies and sentiments which are accentuated when different groups feel that they are excluded from the political process and from other areas of national life simply because of what they are.

Some of the most suitable candidates for this experiment in the reconfiguration of Africa include the so-called Democratic Republic of Congo (it is a mockery of democracy to call it democratic as is the case with most countries across the continent), Angola, and Rwanda and Burundi.

Somalia would be another prime candidate for such restructuring. But she is dead as a nation-state. However, the same approach may be tried in the case of Somalia as well, to see if the country can be put back together, although probably as a confederation – of Somaliland, Puntland, and the other components of the rest of Somalia – and may be as a loose federation.

A look around the world gives us a glimpse at what some countries have done to share sovereignty with their people instead of having power concentrated in the hands of a highly centralised authority only to risk explosion. Details will have to be worked out by the African countries themselves which may want to use some of these arrangements to suit local circumstances. It is the underlying principles – not the mechanics – of these political systems which are most relevant in terms of application in the African context.

There is no question that after what we have witnessed on our continent during the past decades since independence, African countries – especially those which are torn by conflict or those which face chaos and instability – need to establish autonomous, federal or confederal systems to replace the highly centralised unitary state which tends to fuel strife by muzzling dissent and denying the people the opportunity, *and the right*, to manage their own affairs.

In deeply divided countries such as Congo, Somalia, Rwanda and Burundi (although in the last two, especially in Rwanda, the Hutu and the Tutsi don't live in separate ethnic enclaves), restive provinces should be given maximum freedom to rule themselves as domestic sovereign states, but without the international legal authority exercised by *bona fide* independent nations. In other words, they will be independent domestically without being independent internationally.

That may be one of the best ways to discourage secession – an aspiration that is, more often than not, inspired by oppression and marginalisation of groups which want to secede – and end civil conflicts in African countries; for example, the separatist insurgency in Casamance Province in Senegal, as I have explained in one of my other books, *Military Coups in West Africa Since The Sixties*.[2]

Another example is the insurgency among the Tuaregs

in northern Mali who complain that they have been ignored by national leaders in the capital Bamako in the southern part of the country since independence. For decades, they have demanded autonomy for their homeland and even asked the French colonial rulers before independence to partition the country so that they could have their own independent state in the north.

Continuing to ignore them could radicalise them even further and rekindle secessionist demands in the future, backed by armed struggle as they did in 2012 until the French intervened in 2013 to neutralise them and keep Mali intact.

The uprising by the Tuaregs could have been defused – it could even have been avoided – had they been allowed to rule themselves as a *de facto* independent state while remaining an integral part of Mali. They have been fighting for their rights since 1916.

It is the same situation in neighbouring Niger where the Tuarges in the northern part of the country are marginalised and face the same fate as their brethren in Mali. Before the advent of colonial rule, the Tuarges in what is now northern Niger had their own form of government, confederation, that suited them well.

When the French colonised the region, they changed all that and centralised power. After independence, the new African leaders continued to rule the same way the French did, denying the people the right to make decisions for themselves as they had done in the past before they were conquered by Europeans.

But there is a way to avoid conflict. It's simple. Allow the people to rule themselves. Let them have their own form of government, their own "independent state." Devolution is not synonymous with national disintegration.

Such maximum freedom and capacity for self-rule is a form of self-determination which Biafra (Eastern Nigeria) could also have been accorded to keep it within Nigeria as a domestic sovereign entity or state without international recognition. It should have been done before the eruption of the conflict, but even in the midst of war to mitigate disaster.

Self-determination in a domestic context does not mean or imply independence in all cases, with full diplomatic recognition and all the attributes of sovereignty a legal sovereign entity such as Nigeria or Senegal has. It can be applied to *de facto* states such as Somaliland which seceded from the defunct state of Somalia in 1991. It can be applied to Casamance Province if the restive region is accorded such status – as a *de facto* state like Somaliland or even Puntland.

And it could have been applied to Biafra had the Nigerian federal government chosen to resolve the conflict peacefully, while keeping the federation intact, with the secessionist Eastern Region as an integral part of it – but without secessionist aspirations which would have been neutralised through compromise. Or the Nigerian federation could have been restructured and reconstituted to form a confederation to accommodate conflicting ethno-regional interests and loyalties and end domination of other ethnic groups by the three major ones: Hausa-Fulani, Igbo, and Yoruba.

There are many precedents for extensive devolution of power, although not necessarily based on the model presented above. The main point here is that maximum self-determination (which *must* include equitable revenue sharing to satisfy the demands of local communities where resources such as minerals are extracted by the state and whose income is channelled into national coffers) – synonymous with full domestic sovereign status – for constituent units of nation-states is a practical proposition with a lot of benefits including preservation of national integrity.

In Africa itself, post-apartheid South Africa has achieved a degree of devolution or decentralisation rare on the continent for a unitary state; and by doing so, has not only reduced the danger of national disintegration but also of civil war caused by provinces which may opt for violence to secede from the union as the predominantly KwaZulu-Natal Province threatened to do in the early nineties.

KwaZulu-Natal, the homeland of the country's 10 million Zulus who constitute the largest ethnic group in South Africa (the Xhosa in the Eastern Cape being the second-largest), enjoys a large degree of autonomy virtually as a *de facto* domestic sovereign entity – an ethnostate (overwhelmingly Zulu); so does the Western Cape dominated by whites and Coloureds.

In 1994 and 1998 the ruling African National Congress (ANC), which enjoys a high degree of popularity across the country because of its unrivalled status and credentials as a liberation movement which freed South Africa from white domination, lost elections in KwaZulu-Natal to the Zulu Inkatha Freedom Party (IFP) whose ethnic composition is reminiscent of the Kabaka Yekka, a party – led by Kabaka (King) Mutesa – composed of the Baganda of the Buganda kingdom in Uganda.

In both cases, ethnonationalism prevailed in the formation of those parties, and in the case of KwaZulu-Natal, even at the polls.

But ethnonationalism can be a threat to national unity if it is not properly managed as an expression of local aspirations and sentiments. Equally dangerous is suffocation of local dissent and aspirations which can lead to instability if the people are not allowed to ventilate their grievances and pursue their goals for the benefit of their own communities.

In Uganda, secessionist threats by the Buganda kingdom were neutralized by force when soldiers from the Ugandan army led by Idi Amin on orders from President Milton Obote stormed Kabaka's palace on Mengo Hill to oust him and preserve national unity under a unitary state.

In South Africa, KwaZulu-Natal remained an integral part of the nation, although at a cost of thousands of lives in the early nineties, after it achieved a high degree of autonomy and at the expense of the ruling African National Congress at the polls in the province which is overwhelmingly Zulu.

The African National Congress also lost in 1994 in Western Cape to the old apartheid National Party dominated by whites and supported by the vast majority of Coloureds who were apprehensive of black majority rule which became a reality after apartheid formally ended in May that year with the establishment of the first democratically elected government in the history of the country, with Nelson Mandela as the first black president.

In the 1998 general election, the ANC won in Western Cape but was frozen out of power in the province by a coalition of parties supported by whites and Coloureds.

But also in both provinces – KwaZulu-Natal and Western Cape – it was a case of self-determination and curtailment of national sovereignty in a domestic context, yet without compromising national unity and state authority and the essence of the democratic tradition.

Another example is Tanzania where Zanzibar enjoys a high degree of autonomy, although there are strong secessionist sentiments in the former island nation which need to be addressed and defused through dialogue, especially by granting more autonomy to the isles or by holding a referendum for the people of Zanzibar to decide whether or not they want to remain in the union and under what kind of political arrangement.

But a referendum should be the last resort. Before that, the two sides, the former nation of Tanganyika and the former nation of Zanzibar, should try to form a confederation in which both will regain their sovereignties but continue to be under one government with limited powers responsible for only a few things such as defence, national security, monetary policy and immigration.

A confederation may be the best system for Tanzania because the people of Zanzibar have been complaining since the union was formed in April 1964 that they have been "swallowed up" by Tanganyika; and that they are junior partners in the union and are not treated fairly by the union government ("dominated by Tanganyikans") which also serves as the government for the mainland. Zanzibar has its own government.

Zanzibaris are so conscious and so protective of their identity as Zanzibaris that nothing is going to stop them from identifying themselves as Zanzibaris and from saying they are different from the people of Tanzania mainland or what they like to call Tanganyika, although Tanganyika no longer exists as a country; it does not even exist as a geographical entity let alone as a political region.

Most Zanzibaris don't even call themselves Tanzanians. They call themselves Zanzibaris, mainly because that is what they are, but also as a protest against the union. It is also an assertion of their identity. They claim a separate identity which sets them apart from their counterparts on the mainland whom they continue to call Tanganyikans, deliberately, to make a point that the two peoples are different, have nothing in common, and have only been forced to be together in a union they don't like.

They even call the people on Tanzania mainland, the former Tanganyika, "Wadanganyika," instead of "Watanganyika."

"Watanganyika" is a Swahili term which means "Tanganyikans," and "Wadanganyika" is "Danganyikans" in English.

"Wadanganyika" is a derogatory term derived from Kiswahili meaning "gullible ones," deliberately coined to rhyme with "Watanganyika," implying the people on Tanzania mainland, or in Tanganyika (although the country no longer exists), are "gullible."

In Kiswahili or Swahili, "danganya" means "cheat, dupe or deceive."

438

"Amenidanganya" means "He or she has cheated me."

"Ametudanganya," singular form, means "He or she has cheated us."

"Umenidanganya," singular form, means "You (an individual) have cheated me."

"Mumenidanganya," plural form, means "You (as a people or as a group) have cheated me."

"Mumetudanganya," plural form, means "You (people) have cheated us."

"Wametudanganya," plural form, means "They have chaeated us."

"Umedanganywa," singular form, means "You have been cheated."

"Mumedanganywa," plural form, means "You (as a people or as a group) have been cheated"; for example, the people of Tanganyika or Zanzibar or both have been cheated.

"Wamedanganywa" means "They have been cheated."

"Tumedanganywa" means "We have been cheated."

I know all this because I am a native speaker of Swahili which we call Kiswahili.

Zanzibaris emphasise that it is "Tanganyikans" who are "gullible" because they are the ones who believe that President Julius Nyerere of Tanganyika was right when he united the two countries. Hence the designation "Wadanganyika": "gullible ones."

Nyerere was the driving force behind the unification of the two countries, together with Abeid Karume, the president of Zanzibar.

Although the union of Tanganyika and Zanzibar has survived, it also has come under a lot of strain through the decades. There are many people on Tanzania mainland who don't want the union just like many Zanzibaris don't. The main argument advanced by Tanzanians on the mainland is that Zanzibar is an economic burden on them; which it is. It is Tanzania mainland which pays for almost all the expenses incurred by Zanzibar.

439

The former island nation has virtually nothing in terms of natural resources besides cloves. Even one former cabinet member in the union government, Hassan Diria, a Zanzibari who also served as Tanzania's ambassador in a number of countries and as minister of information and broadcasting and as minister of foreign affairs at different times, among other posts, bluntly stated that Zanzibar can not survive and prosper without the union.

But ways must be found to allay the fears of Zanzibaris that they have been "swallowed up" by "Tanganyika" and that they are being dominated and exploited by "Tanganyikans" although there really is nothing for "Tanganyikans" to exploit in Zanzibar.

One of those ways has been to let Zanzibar continue to exist as a political entity with its own government, enjoying extensive autonomy, and to let Zanzibaris retain their identity as Zanzibaris, while denying former Tanganyikans the same right. There is no Tanganyika, and there are no Tanganyikans anymore. They are the ones who were swallowed up by the union when the two countries united in 1964.

Restructuring the union to form a confederation may allays the fears of many Zanzibaris and may help to contain or even neutralise secessionist sentiments.

If a confederation fails, dissolution of the union of Tanganyika and Zanzibar which led to the creation of Tanzania will be the only option left. But the dissolution must be confirmed by the people in a referendum to make sure that is what the majority of them – on both sides – want.

Technically, and constitutionally, Zanzibar is semi-autonomous. But for all practical purposes, it is really autonomous despite professions to the contrary by Zanzibaris.

There is also the case of Nigeria, a federation of 36 states whose federal constitution is being continually challenged by the people to achieve maximum self-rule; a challenge the government sees as a threat to its authority and national unity.

But if carefully managed, the result of such devolution of power will be exactly the opposite, instead of being the beginning of the end of the Nigerian federation. It will not lead to dissolution of the federation or to the disintegration of Nigeria as a nation or as a single political entity.

The conflict between the states or the people and the the federal government is best exemplified and clearly illustrated by the case of Zamfara, a state in the northern part of the country.

Located in northwestern Nigeria, Zamfara is an overwhelmingly Muslim state. It is mostly inhabited by the Hausa and by the Fulani, two ethnic groups which are close allies and which share the same culture including language (Hausa); hence the designation Hausa-Fulani, since they are identified as one group. They have so much in common that they are virtually the same people.

Members of smaller ethnic groups also are among the indigenous people of Zamfara. Like the Hausa-Fulani, they are also overwhelmingly Muslim.

But Zamfara also has some Christians, mostly Igbos and some Yorubas as well as others from the southern part of the country, especially in the state capital Gusau. There are also other people from other parts of Nigeria.

In October 1999, the newly-elected governor of Zamfara, Ahmed Sani (his whole name is Ahmed Rufai Sani Yerima but is simply called Ahmed Sani), an economist and former civil servant in the federal government, introduced *sharia*, or Islamic law. The announcement was significant in another respect because Sokoto, the country's Muslim spiritual centre, is also located in Zamfara.

Sokoto was also the home of the late Sir Ahmadu Bello who controlled the Nigerian federation in the sixties when he was the premier of Northern Nigeria. He controlled the federation because the largest number of the members of the Nigerian parliament were northerners who were under his rule since he was the the premier of the region they came from. The federal prime minister himself, Abubakar Tafawa Balewa, also came from the north and was controlled by the northern premier.

Also, the largest number of soldiers in the national army, the most powerful institution in the country, were northerners. A large number of the army officers were also northerners.

Almost all the Nigerian rulers since independence, including military heads of state, were northerners. The exceptions were Nnamdi Azikiwe who served as governor-general and then as the country's first president from October 1960 to January 1966 when the government was overthrown in a military coup.

Northerners dominated the Nigerian federation from independence in 1960 until 1999 when a southerner, Olusegun Obasanjo, was elected president. He became the second southerner, after Azikiwe, to serve as president.

Ahmadu Bello, also known the Sardauna of Sokoto, dominated the federation until he was assassinated on 15 January 1966 during the coup. And he was the unchallenged head of the northern Muslim aristocracy.

The introduction of *sharia* in Zamfara, a Muslim stronghold, amounted to a *de facto* declaration of independence from the federal government and to an assertion of domestic sovereignty as a Muslim state.

Nigerian President Olusegun Obasanjo declared the adoption of the rigid Islamic code to be unconstitutional. And the draconian nature of an Islamic fundamentalist theocracy – one is reminded of Saudi Arabia, Afghanistan under the Taliban, and Iran under the Ayatollah Khomeini and his fanatical successors – alarmed many Nigerians; the potential for the establishment of such a theocratic state in a country that was under a secular constitution could not be ignored. According to a report from Gusau, Zamfara, by *The Economist*:

"Mr. Sani says he intends to enforce the (Islamic) law strictly, as in Saudi Arabia, which means that thieves could have their hands amputated and people caught drinking could be flogged....Zamfara's Christians, he says, will not be affected, but will remain under the jurisdiction of the existing legal code.

The Christians do not agree. 'The *sharia* will surely affect us, because we are part and parcel of the state,' says...the Reverend Olu Joseph (of) a small Christian church in Gusau, the capital of Zamfara....

Zamfara, a rural and hitherto obscure state, is now at the centre of a controversy with much wider ramifications. Africa's religious fault-line, between a predominantly Muslim north and a more pluralist but largely Christian south, cuts across the Sahel, dividing several countries.

Sudan has suffered decades of religion-based civil war. In Nigeria, the massacre of thousands (at least 30,000) of Christian Igbos in Kano and other northern cities in 1966 was one of the factors that led to the Biafran civil war.

In recent years, relations between Nigeria's north and south have been relatively calm but, even so, they remain delicate, all the more so since religious and ethnic divisions tend to overlap."[3]

Governor-elect Ahmed Sani's announcement inflamed passions among Christian leaders across Nigeria who saw the introduction of Islamic law in Zamfara state as a violation of the country's secular constitution whose strict interpretation demands separation of church and state. Therefore adoption of *sharia* by a secular government – which, by doing so, is invoking religious authority and illegally transforming itself into a theocratic regime – upsets the uneasy religious balance in a country deeply divided along ethnoregional and religious lines between Muslims in the north and Christians in the south.

When Sani made the announcement, Muslim leaders,

443

especially in the north where they predominate, either supported the change or said nothing publicly. As one northern politician said: "People in the north can't come out and oppose this thing in public. If you do, you open yourself to the accusation that you are unIslamic."[4]

President Obasanjo himself said nothing at first in public. As a Christian, any public criticism of the introduction of Islamic law by him would have infuriated many Muslims. And as a southerner, from southwestern Nigeria, he was already being criticised by northerners who claimed – although without any credible evidence – that he was favouring his own people, the Yoruba, at the expense of other ethnic groups.

The new governor of Zamfara tried to exploit the situation to advance his Islamic cause. But he was wrong thinking that the Nigerian president would remain passive or silent on this highly volatile issue. And when he spoke, he made made it clear that the introduction of Islamic law in Zamfara state – or anywhere else – violated the Nigerian constitution.

However, Governor Ahmed Sani was adept at invoking and at manipulating the same constitution to promote his Islamic agenda. It is true that the Nigerian constitution – as a concession to the country's large Islamic population, which is probably the country's largest religious group – has a provision that allows the introduction of *sharia* but only in the area of family law dealing with divorce, inheritance and other related matters.

In response to that, Sani – and here, he was on solid ground – contended that the fundamental right to freedom of worship, which is also enshrined in the federal constitution, justifies the introduction of Islamic law, although he did not explicitly acknowledge the prescribed limits mandated by federal law. So, he proceeded to introduce the measure, with immediate impact:

"The new policies are already beginning to show. It is

444

now virtually impossible to buy alcohol in Gusau. Boys and girls are soon to be educated in separate schools, and men and women are starting to travel in separate buses. Mr. Sani has even said that only men with beards will be awarded government contracts."[5]

In December 1999, Kano state said, it too, like Zamfara, would adopt Islamic law.[6] By January 2000, three northern states had adopted *sharia* and three more were getting ready to do so. According to *The Economist*:

"Islamic law – *sharia* – came into force in Zamfara state in Nigeria. Two other state legislatures have passed laws adopting *sharia* and three have committees studying it."[7]

But the introduction of *sharia* did not proceed well. It sparked ethnoreligious violence between northern Muslims, mostly Hausa-Fulani, and southern Christians living in Northern Nigeria.

In February 2000, more than 100 people were killed in the city of Kaduna following clashes between the two sides as a result of protests by Christians opposed to the proposed introduction of Islamic law in the northern state of Kaduna, named after its major and capital city, which is also the second-largest in the north after Kano.

The city's population is equally divided between Muslims and Christians (mostly from the south), providing a potent mix of an ethnoreligious cauldron. According to a report from Kaduna:

"HUNDREDS of Christians burst into the offices of the governor of the northern Nigerian state of Kaduna this week to protest at the demand by local Muslims for the imposition of the *sharia*, or Islamic law. An office was smashed, several civil servants were beaten and slogans ranging from "Jesus is Lord" to "Sharia is not Y2K

445

compliant" were daubed on the wall....

Over 100 people were killed, shops and houses were destroyed, and cars and trucks set on fire, in a terrifying outbreak of communal and religious violence. On February 23rd, an indefinite curfew was declared in the city and surrounding towns. Troops and heavily armed paramilitary police struggled to separate the armed gangs of militant Christian and Muslim youths responsible for the killing."[8]

The conflict took another dimension when it became regionalised, with other Muslims in the north expressing solidarity with their Islamic brethren in the midst of crisis, and with more northern states adopting *sharia*:

"By unhappy coincidence, the authorities in two other states, Niger and Sokoto, chose this week to sign bills that declared the *sharia* to be the law in their states. Last month, Zamfara, which had announced its intention of imposing Islamic law in October, began implementing it with the public flogging of a man found guilty of drinking alcohol. At least three more states – Kaduna, Kano and Yobe – are now thinking of introducing the law.

Of all the states, Kaduna and Kano present the greatest potential for trouble. Unlike other cities in the Muslim-dominated north, Kaduna has a population that is split roughly equally between Muslims and Christians. Kano, by far the largest city in the region, has a sizeable Christian minority and a history of religious violence.

Muslims in northern Nigeria are drawn to the idea of the Islamic code, partly because they are disillusioned by years of corrupt military rule, but also because they are alarmed by ever-rising crime figures. The Muslim governors of the northern states that have introduced the *sharia* try to reassure Christians by saying repeatedly that it will not affect non-Muslims.

But Nigeria's Christians are not reassured. "They are

saying that anyone who is a Christian should act like a Muslim. They ban drink. They ban men seeing their wives," said Wajoba Bhaturi inaccurately. He is a blanket-maker in Kaduna, and he was sporting a bandage over a deep cut in his forehead after the fighting this week.

For many Nigerians, the issue is more political than religious. Islamic law has existed in Nigeria for centuries, but under British and military rule it was restricted (as in several Arab countries) to family matters. Now, in a new era of elective politics, it is seen as a winning policy for governors in states with strong Muslim majorities. Parliament this week said it would start to investigate whether imposing the *sharia* is legal under the 1999 constitution.

All this leaves President Olusegun Obasanjo, a committed Christian, in an extremely difficult position. All he could do, this week, was to appeal rather helplessly to all sides to settle their religious differences peacefully. His critics say his difficulties are partly of his own making: he has been too weak on the issue."[9]

But the introduction of *sharia* was not mainly for religious purposes. The religious issue was politicised because it resonated well among northern voters. Such deep resonance proved to be a powerful platform for northern politicians to articulate their grievances against the federal government and promote their agenda – which naturally took on a religious character – in states that are predominantly Muslim and where, because of the dominance of Islam as a way of life, many issues assume a religious dimension.

Leading Islamic candidates for gubernatorial office easily coasted to victory on a wave of religious sentiment, sending panic among minority Christians living in the north and even raising the spectre of a civil war between northerners and southerners which could split Nigeria along religious and ethnoregional lines. As Minabere

447

Ibelema, a Nigerian professor at the University of Alabama, Birmingham, in the United States, stated in his article, "Nigeria: The Politics of Marginalization," in *Current History: A Journal of Contemporary World Affairs*:

"These ethnoreligious tensions are reminiscent of the events in 1966 and 1967 that precipitated Nigeria's civil war in which more than 1 million Nigerians died when the Igbos created the secessionist state of Biafra.

Emeka Odumegwu Ojukwu, who led the 30-month secession, has been blamed by some northern leaders for fomenting this year's Kaduna crisis. Ojukwu has responded by calling the accusation a halluciation and by suggesting psychiatric examination for the accusers. But he has also said of the Igbos that 'we have to get prepared, be on our toes and wait.' Leaders used similar language directly preceding the declaration of secession in 1967."[10]

Nigerian President Olusegun Obasanjo who was elected in February 1999 and inaugurated in May the same year vowed to keep Nigeria one; the same vow he made during the Nigerian civil war (1967 – 1970) when he spearheaded the final military offensive against the secessionist Biafran forces as a senior officer in the Nigerian federal army, forcing the secessionist to surrender.

But northerners were equally adamant, determined to pursue their agenda of Islamisation of the northern states in the secular spheres of law and government to virtually separate themselves from other Nigerians. And some of them implemented the measures in a highly defiant manner to snub the president who remained resolute in his commitment to uphold a secular constitution:

"In a pointed snub, Sokoto has said it will start implementing Islamic law on May 29th, the first anniversary of the president's coming to power."[11]

Many northerners and other Nigerians also misinterpreted the president's initial response to the promulgation of *sharia* as indecisiveness in the midst of what could have escalated into a national crisis. He didn't say much about it at the beginning. However, what was perceived as a tepid response by Obasanjo was a calculated move on his part to seek a diplomatic solution to the crisis and avert escalation of the ethnoreligious conflict.

Those who had underestimated him or misconstrued his muted response also had a rude awakening when he responded forcefully with federal might. More than once, he sent federal troops to Kaduna to end the violence between Christians and Muslims and maintained that federal law was paramount. The president was also able to exert enough pressure on the governors of northern Nigeria, enabling the federal government to secure substantial concessions from them by the end of February 2000. According to a report from Nigeria by *The Christian Science Monitor*:

"Governors of northern Nigeria had the task of explaining to their mostly Muslim people why the decision had been made to abandon the idea of adopting strict Islamic law.

The agreement earlier this week with President Olusegun Obasanjo also calls for states that already have *sharia* to stop enforcing it. The deal followed three days of rioting between Muslims and resentful Christians that killed at least 400 people.

Analysts said the retreat from *sharia* could pose a problem for the governors, who made the strict code the basis of their platform in Nigeria's elections last year."[12]

Some reports said probably as many as 2,000 people

449

were killed in the violence in Kaduna in February.[13] And the suspension of *sharia* did not end the violence or the demand for the enforcement of Islamic law; nor did it stop the adoption of the rigid Islamic code in other parts of Northern Nigeria. It only fuelled discontent in the Islamic population whose members overwhelmingly voted for the adoption of the strict law based on the interpretation of the Koran by their fundamentalist clerics.

Enforcement of *sharia* brought even more publicity to the theocratic state authorities in Northern Nigeria when on 24 March 2000, a man in Zamfara who was sentenced under Islamic law for stealing cows had his right hand amputated in what was reportedly the first case to be adjudicated under *sharia* since the law was adopted by the predominantly Muslim state at the beginning of the year.[14]

There was widespread criticism of *sharia* and this kind of punishment, with many critics in other parts of Nigeria, especially in the south, invoking the sanctity of the country's secular constitution. One such critic was Steve U. Nwabuzor who stated in *Niger World*, 24 March 2000:

"Again, we are called upon to raise our voices, dip our pens and scrutinize the very basis of our existence as a nation. Zamfara state government, despite the recent undertaking to put on hold implementation of the Sharia penal code, has been quoted to amputate a man said to be notorious for stealing cows. In this pursuit of amputation, we are told that a medical professional was party to it.

One is forced to ask, when will this madness stop? Common sense has shown that sanity produces peace, while madness begets anarchy and intolerance. This latest show of insanity by the Zamfara State government should not go unchallenged. It was barely a month ago that President Obasanjo informed the whole world of the criminality of stoning and amputation of any individual, as these were against the provisions of the Nigerian constitution.

Sharia activists are not willing to abate their struggle, at least in Zamfara. What does Zamfara State government want? Why decimate Nigerian citizens in order to score cheap political points? This latest act occurring at a time when the constitutionality of the Sharia penal code is being challenged by some indigenes of Zamfara only points to one fact, that the Zamfara government is ready to bite the hand that feeds her and I hope that hand would smack the mouth, and if possible snuff the life out of it.

My hypothesis on Sharia being a tool for intermittently causing unrest for the Nigerian nation still holds. We should not forget that Zamfara is the arrowhead of the Sharia for testing the waters of the Federal government. Zamfara was the first state to declare Sharia criminal law, and now it has effected the first amputation.

Other sharianized states are watching if the federal government is just a toothless bulldog.

I hope our leaders are not going to say this is just a flash in the pan and wish this incident away.

Apparently, Zamfara government is determined to continuously generate controversy within the Nigerian polity.

Saddening to note that a state that is the poorest in Nigeria has decided to be the rate-determining step in our progress. While efforts should be geared in Zamfara to improve the lots of the numerous beggars and jobless charlatans roaming the streets, more handicaps are being manufactured for the system. There are right now enough beggars and physically disabled people in Nigeria. We do not need more of these.

This latest act was meted out to a Moslem and so we might be tempted to say who cares? After all, it is their Sharia. We are further told that the amputation received applause from a sizable crowd within the precincts of a government hospital where the amputation took place. If there is any way to define sadism, this latest incident is more than a perfect example.

451

The Federal government continues to palliate the proponents of the Sharia penal code by making ambiguous statements to the effect of seeking a political solution, rather than judicial. Why can't the federal government pursue the legal and political in tandem? One is disappointed at the Nigerian Bar Association for supporting only the political option. Are we being told that we do not have good cause to challenge this illegality and barbaric act that has further tarnished our image in the civilized world?

A trend is emerging in this unfolding drama, it is the game of the 'father of all lies,' which is to cause confusion in the minds of those opposed to the wiles of these agents of destabilization. When there appears to be a lull, the Sharia dragon is unleashed and goes berserk.

We need to put on our girdles, for this Sharia penal code is a spiritual battle. The plan has been made in the spiritual domain of darkness to obfuscate the progress of the Obasanjo regime. Now we (those opposed to the Sharia penal code) have to go back to the drawing board and invoke our spiritual armor in Christ. It is only then can we be assured of victory.

Meanwhile, let the Obasanjo government confront this dragon with all the might it can muster. It is only then will the true message cut deep into the 'Sardauna of Zamfara.'"[15]

If the criticism above is indicative of anything, it was a passionate plea to respect Nigeria's secular constitution which prohibits the establishment of a theocracy anywhere in the country. But by invoking the spiritual guidance of Jesus Christ, as Steve Nwabuzor did in his commentary above obviously because he was a Christian, his criticism also had a religious dimension and reflected a collective sentiment prevalent among southern Nigerians the majority of whom are Christian, thus showing that there is a very real divide between the north and the south that is defined along religious lines.

Although other northern states, all overwhelmingly Muslim, agreed (at least in theory) to suspend enforcement of *sharia* in criminal proceedings until the matter was resolved constitutionally by the federal authorities, the governor of Zamfara refused to do so until the Nigerian federal government agreed to settle the dispute without compromising the essence of Islamic law and the interests of his Muslim subjects who supported the measure.

Many people in Nigeria including the federal government wanted civil and criminal statutes – as stipulated by the constitution in what is essentially a secular nation – to take precedence over Islamic law invoked by the theocratic regimes in the northern states.

In May 2000, more violence erupted in Kaduna, claiming more lives and fuelled by religious intolerance:

"Renewed sectarian violence has killed more than 100 people in northern Nigeria, reports said. Heavily armed soldiers and police were patrolling the city of Kaduna after two days of fighting between Christians and Muslims, a revival of the clashes in February in which hundreds – and perhaps as many as 2,000 people – died. The violence was inspired by the proposed imposition of *sharia*, the rigid Islamic legal code, which prescribes such punishments as amputation."[16]

And that was not the last of it. Violence continued to erupt, now and then, here and there, between northern Muslims and southern Christians in Northern Nigeria. There was religious-inspired violence even in some parts of Southern Nigeria, for example, in Lagos in the heart of Yorubaland in the southwest, where the Hausa and other northerners lived in large numbers.

The Hausa have interacted with the Yoruba as traders for hundreds of years. But an increasing number of them also settled in southern Nigeria when the country was under military rule dominated by northern generals for almost 40 years since independence in 1960. The ethnoregional crisis in the north only exacerbated tensions between northerners and southerners in Southern Nigeria. As Minabere Ibelema pointed out:

"The recent institution of planned introduction of shariah – the Islamic penal code – by several Muslim-populated states in northern Nigeria has aggravated the already complex political atmosphere. Since October 1999, at least 5 northern states have passed laws in favor of implementing the code, and one – Zamfara – has signed it into law.

Tension over imposing shariah climaxed in February in a bloody clash in the northern city of Kaduna between northern Muslims and southern Christians residing in the north. As many as 400 people were killed, most of them southerners. Reprisal killings of resident northerners soon followed in the southeastern city of Aba.

The ensuing insecurity precipitated an exodus of southerners (reminiscent of the mass exodus of southerners from Northern Nigeria just before the outbreak of the Nigerian civil war, 1967 – 1970) – especially Igbos who are mainly Christian – from northern cities, and of northern Hausa-Fulani, who are mainly Muslim, from the south....

Radical members of the Yoruba group Oodua People's Congress have...attacked non-Yorubas in Lagos at the slightest pretext. In November 1999, a Yoruba and Hausa merchant skirmish over control of a food market spiraled into a conflict that killed nearly 100 people....

Following a February 29 meeting of the Council of States – attended by state governors and former heads of state – the federal government ordered the suspension of shariah as a criminal code. Its long-standing application to civil cases, which is acknowledged in the constitution, was allowed to continue.

The responses of the affected states have been mixed. A few, such as Jigawa and Zamfara, seem intent on defying the federal government; Zamfara demonstrated its resolve in late March by amputating a convicted thief's right hand, as required under shariah.

Other states, such as Niger and Yobe, have formally shelved the code, and Kwara has declared it will never implement it. Several states, including Kaduna and Plateau, appear ambivalent about their intent."[17]

But even such ambivalence was more than enough to send confusing signals to southern Christians and other southerners living in Northern Nigeria that they were not welcome in the north; which partly explains the departure of many of them from all parts of the region, their exit facilitated by the violence that erupted in Kaduna.

It was reminiscent of the sixties when more than 2 million Eastern Nigerians were forced to flee the north just before and after the outbreak of the civil war. It was one of the largest mass migrations in modern history precipitated by an ethnoregional conflict. Almost the same kind of conflict again threatened to split the country 30 years later in the nineties and beyond. Religion was one of the factors in the massacre of Igbos in the north in 1966; it was a factor again in the 1990s and beyond when southern Christians were forced to flee Northern Nigeria.

The prospect for such an outcome, fragmentation or dissolution of the federation, seemed real to many Nigerians in the 1990s – as much as it was in the 1960s during the civil war – especially after the military head of state, General Ibrahim Babangida, a northerner who seized power in 1985 from Major-General Muhammadu Buhari, a fellow northerner, annulled the results of the 1993 general elections to prevent a southerner, Moshood Abiola who had won the electoral contest, from becoming president. One of the Nigerians who felt that Nigeria could collapse anytime during that period was prominent author Wole

455

Soyinka. As he stated in his book, *The Open Sore of A Continent: A Personal Narrative of the Nigerian Crisis*:

"When I listen therefore to some pontificating voice declaring that the unity of Nigeria is non-negotiable, I detect only woolly or opportunistic thinking....There is absolutely no foundation in the absolute for such a declaration....

We did not shy from the probability of a civil war and the possible disintegration of the country as a consequence....With all the imponderables that confronted the nation, with all the variables of sectarian interests, some of them overlapping, others canceling one another, I frankly could not advance any invulnerable reason for my preference for a solution that did not involve disintegration.

I had been involved in discussions with countless numbers of people...businessmen, intellectuals, students, traders, professionals, clergymen. The mood for them was this: Let us prepare for the inevitable separation or, at best, the loosest arrangement possible, such as confederation.

During the most violent day of the anti-Babangida riots, trapped within the tumult of thousands that submerged my car, sat, drummed, or danced on it, voices would ring out with shouts of 'Lead us out of this mess called Nigeria!' 'I am ready, recruit me. Let's go our own way'....

All highly emotive, born out of deep frustration, but one must be careful not to dismiss such voices as products of an abnormal moment, of a temporary phase. They were outbursts that conveyed a summation of positions argued in offices, marketplaces, bus stops, factories, palace courtyards and more secretive recesses of traditional enclaves, classrooms and debating halls. They were a continuation of discourses begun in 1960, and even long before then.

We heard them during the various Leaders of Thought

456

meetings after the countercoup of July 1966, we heard the then head of state, Yakubu Gowon, declare loud and clear that there was no longer any basis for Nigerian unity.

We were deafened by the apotheothis of such sentiment in the roar of guns during the Biafran war....

Every day still reminds us that the factors that led to Biafra neither were ephemeral nor can be held to be permanently exorcised."[18]

While northern domination of the federation helped precipitate the Nigerian civil war during the sixties, it was the north again – the end of its domination of Nigeria – which threatened to destroy the country this time because northerners sill wanted to assert their dominance, at least in the north, without or with very little federal control over them.

The problem was compounded by complaints from other ethnic groups in different parts of Nigeria that they were marginalised in the federation, prompting some of them to threaten secession or seek a new political arrangement including confederation – which President Obasanjo flatly rejected, saying it was tantamount to treason. As Professor Ibelema states:

"That 36 smaller states rather than four powerful regions now constitute federal Nigeria would seem to militate against secession (Nigeria in 1966 was composed of the North, the East, the West, and the Midwest regions). Regional coordination among states has, however, created powerful alliances.

Since the shariah crisis, political and religious leaders from northern, western, eastern, and southern minority states have met as discrete blocs to formulate unified positions or to discuss Nigeria's political future. Youths from the middle-belt states have also called for a separate leadership meeting of their states. Still, differences among the states within each bloc makes regional cohesion and

457

secession unlikely.

As in 1967, claims have been made that some military personnel have supplied weapons to and otherwise aided civilians in the communal attacks....

In an address in the wake of the Kaduna riots, the chief of defense staff, Rear Admiral Ibrahim Ogohi, admonished them to eschew partisanship and to remain loyal to federal civilian authority. He pledged to defend Nigeria's nascent democracy.

Similar statements of commitment to a united and democratic Nigeria have been made by political and religious leaders on all sides. Yet these statements have been countered by others advocating confederation, dissolution, or even secession. Thus, the danger remains that Nigeria could splinter violently.

Although the present crisis is veiled in religious differences, it is at root political. The causes of tension and instability in Nigeria remain the same as in the (1967 – 1970) civil war: the fear of domination."[19]

The election of Olusegun Obasanjo in 1999 as president ended almost 40 years of northern domination of the Nigerian federation. And many northerners were painfully aware of that when power was transferred to a southerner, who was also a Christian, for the first time after an entire generation.

The campaign to introduce *sharia* in the northern states was a very important part of an effort by northern leaders to regain some of the power they had lost in the federation and reassert their authority as the only rulers at least of the northern states where they felt the federal government could be challenged and obstructed from exercising full control by introducing and enforcing Islamic law.

They used Islamic law in an attempt to "nullify" the federal constitution in their states by invoking religious freedom enshrined in the same secular constitution they did not want to uphold when it clashed with their interests, ignoring the fact that federal law is paramount: when state law conflicts with federal law, federal law must prevail.

It was obvious that northern Muslims were not going to abandon *sharia*. And the violence it spawned underscored the imperative need to forge a national consensus on the matter in order to balance – within constitutionally prescribed limits – the interests of the vast majority of the people in the northern states who supported Islamic law and the rest of the Nigerians who wanted to uphold a secular constitution as the paramount law of the land because of the country's religious and ethnic diversity.

We have had similar experiences in my home country, Tanzania, where for the sake of national unity and respect for the right of the Muslim majority in Zanzibar to live under Islamic law, the union constitution allows the enforcement of the Islamic legal code in well-defined areas involving civil matters without compromising the interests of Christians and other non-Muslim minorities in the isles (of Pemba and Unguja – the latter also known as Zanzibar – which together constitute the autonomous political entity known as Zanzibar); a subject I discuss in a chapter entitled, "Tanzania: Union of Two Independent States – Challenge to Unity and Ideology," in one of my books, *Economic Development in Africa*.[20]

The constitution unequivocally states that Tanzania is a secular state, a stipulation that acknowledges the country's religious and ethnic diversity in order to protect the rights of all of its citizens which would be impossible under a theocracy.

Similarly in Nigeria, there is a need for a secular constitution, which the country already has, in order to accommodate different religious and ethnic groups. And where there is a clash between state and federal law, the latter must prevail. Unity in diversity is possible only when federal law is paramount. And protection of the rights of all Nigerians is possible only when state law is superseded by federal law.

If the doctrine of nullification – prevalence of state law over federal law – is to be applied, it must be only when the majority of the states in the federation decide to nullify federal law in specific areas. It can not be nullified by unilateral action – taken by one state or by only a few states – or by violence.

However, what the violence that was sparked by the introduction of *sharia* helped to do, although in a very tragic way, was to highlight local grievances and the urgent need for devolution of power but without undermining federal authority. It also underscored the fragile nature of African countries, in general, which inherited the highly centralised state at independence without restructuring it to reflect African realities and accommodate conflicting interests.

One of those realities should have been, right after independence, a concerted effort to build unity in diversity under a strong central government necessary to maintain national unity and neutralise secessionist threats but without stifling dissent. And that would have entailed decentralisation and devolution of power to achieve true democracy all the way to the grassroots level.

The northern Nigerian states could not legitimately claim that they were denied freedom of expression by the federal government especially after the end of military rule. It was precisely because they had such freedom that they were able to openly campaign for the adoption of Islamic law and even succeeded in introducing it. But the violence that erupted as a result of those efforts to introduce and enforce *sharia* was not protected by the constitution and justified federal intervention. According to a report by *The Christian Science Monitor*:

"Nigerian security forces intensified efforts yesterday (25 May 2000) to halt renewed religious violence in the northern city of Kaduna, in which more than 200 people have died. Hundreds of buildings – including mosques and churches – have been burned to the ground since fighting broke out Monday (22 May)....

Since the turn of the 20th century, when the British conquered the Sokoto caliphate and extended colonial rule into what is now northern Nigeria, the application of *sharia* in Muslim communities has been restricted largely to civil and customary law. But popular demand for its extension into other areas of life – including criminal law – has spread rapidly across the mainly Muslim north of the country since October (1999). It was then that the governor of the rural state of Zamfara unilaterally declared it the governing legal system of his state."[21]

The escalation of violence continued to demand and provoked an even tougher response from the federal authorities. Also, opposition to Islamic law in the northern states by many Nigerians including some Muslims who wanted Nigeria to remain a secular state found forceful expression in the national media which articulated a collective sentiment that resonated across the country, especially among Christians who were some of the most vocal and ardent supporters of secularisation of authority at the state and federal levels.

Some people openly talked about the possibility of a civil war that could engulf the whole country if the matter was not resolved amicably and if Muslims continued to enforce or adopt Islamic law in the north. And there were those who said a civil war was already going on in Nigeria. As Joe Igbokwe, an author and social commentator, stated in an interview published in the weekly *Tempo*:

"We just had a war in Kaduna, a civil war....

Let nobody describe this as a religious upheaval. What is happening now has been designed because they [northern leaders] can no longer go to their friends in Saudi Arabia and Libya and tell them that Nigeria is an

461

Islamic state....They no longer have easy access to the national treasury...(and) government contracts."[22]

And in the same edition, *Tempo* stated in an editorial: "The proponents of Sharia are intent on implementing a political agenda."[23]

Another Nigerian newspaper, the *Guardian*, expressed similar sentiments:

"We recognize the right of Muslims to fulfill the tenets of Islam to the letter, but the carnage that the Sharia has brought is indefensible. Now Christians in Kaduna are demanding their own portion of the state."[24]

Such demands only fuelled the conflict in a country that already had to contend with secessionist threats especially in the Niger Delta. But similar rumblings calling for secession and dissolution of the federation during the 1990s and thereafter were heard in other parts of the country: among the Yoruba in the West, the Igbo in the East, and some groups in the North and in the mid-regions. For example, Ojukwu, who led Biafra's secession and who was still seen as an embodiment of the ideals and aspirations of his people, expressed a sentiment shared by many Igbos when he said:

"(The) problem is that we are in Nigeria and we are finding it extremely difficult to find accommodation in Nigeria."[25]

The introduction of Islamic law in the northern states, in addition to widespread discontent among Nigeria's different ethnic groups, is another potent force that can lead to serious political instability in the future and even fragmentation of Africa's largest nation. The adoption of *sharia* is, in fact, tantamount to *de facto* secession of the northern states from the federation since they are trying to evade and defy federal control. And it may be the biggest threat to the continued existence of Nigeria as a nation and as a single political entity unless a consensus is reached on how to maintain a delicate balance between the interests of the states and of the federation.

How Nigeria reacts to this challenge – which may trigger a chain reaction in the rest of the overwhelmingly Muslim northern states and in other predominantly Muslim communities elsewhere in the country which may follow suit and adopt Islamic law – will have profound implications for the future of Africa's largest federation. Clamping down on Islamic fundamentalists will not solve the problem of conflicting interests between secular authorities and theocratic elements. Algeria learned the hard way during the 1990s.

Nigerian leaders may say Nigeria is not Algeria. That is true. But Islamic fundamentalism is Islamic fundamentalism regardless of how distorted its image is, when refracted through secular lenses, and regardless of where it is practised – Algeria or Nigeria, Egypt or Somalia, Mali or Mauritania, Kenya or Tanzania. It is an enduring phenomenon. And it provides spiritual sustenance to a large number of people.

The key to conflict resolution lies in making maximum concessions to the states which constitute the Nigerian federation – virtually granting independence from the central government in all matters that can be administered and resolved locally – yet without compromising national sovereignty. Devolution of power does not mean dissolution of national sovereignty or national unity.

An autonomous state is still subject to central authority and national laws as long as the laws do not deny the state the right to choose and decide what is best for its people but without sacrificing the rights of minority groups living under its jurisdiction: for example, Christians in Zamfara, Kano or Kaduna, or the Hausa-Fulani in Oyo state of the Yoruba people in the southwest or in Imo state of the Igbo in the southeast.

If the majority of the people in a given state are denied – by the national government – the right to choose how they want to live and how they want to be governed, as long they don't violate the rights of the minorities amongst them, then the national government can not honestly say that it is protecting all its citizens. And the constitution it is invoking to exercise power over them would be unconstitutional since it does not embody the will of the governed even if a majority of the states conspired against a few states to deny them the right to choose. There is no stronger case for self-determination for the oppressed group, whether a state or states, or ethnic groups such as the oppressed Hutu majority in Rwanda and Burundi or the Tutsi minority who fear extermination at the hands of the Hutu.

Let's take Rwanda as an example.

The Tutsi-dominated government of Rwanda (of the Rwandan Patriotic Front – RPF), afraid of extermination of its Tutsi minority, can guarantee the safety of its people by allowing the oppressed Hutu majority to rule themselves. This form of self-determination may not amount to statehood – of domestic sovereign status – in the Rwandan context because the two groups do not live in separate ethnic enclaves. They live on same hills, in the same villages, share the same land as neighbours as much as they share deep mistrust of each other especially after the 1994 genocide.

But such self-determination will allow maximum self-rule for the Hutu which they have been denied throughout Rwanda's history, for hundreds of years, except for the 32 years they were in power since independence in 1962, a position they maintained with ruthlessness at the expense of the Tutsi minority until they were ousted in July 1994 by the predominantly Tutsi Rwandan Patriotic Front (RPF).

Unless such extensive devolution of power takes place

– short of complete separation of the two groups into fully sovereign ethnostates as some African leaders such as former Kenyan President Daniel arap Moi have suggested – there will be no peace in Rwanda. There will also be no peace in Rwanda if the Tutsi are not guaranteed security and if they continue to fear they are going to be exterminated by the Hutu.

A similar situation exists in Nigeria where the survival and stability of this large federation hinges on maximum devolution of power to the states to enable them to enjoy self-determination, not as independent states but as domestic sovereign entities whose sovereign status is superseded in only a few areas – such as national defence, foreign affairs, immigration, international trade, and monetary policy – by federal authority; which is not the case today.

Even if such extensive devolution of power leads to the establishment of a confederation – a move President Obasanjo equated with treason – and to more loss of power for the central government, it should be embraced as a positive change because it is better than the disintegration of Nigeria into independent tribal homelands. Such fragmentation would be a disaster for Nigeria and for Africa as a whole.

Decentralisation is not abdication of responsibility by the central government; nor is it encouragement of secession. It's simply sharing power with the people: allowing the people to rule themselves, allowing them to manage their own affairs.

Even the United States which has a strong central government at the federal level has a constitution which allows states to exercise a lot of freedom in many areas. States are allowed to enact their own laws. They are allowed to have their own judicial systems all the way up to the highest court in each state. They elect their own leaders, including governors who are the "heads of state" of those states. They even conduct trade with foreign countries as if they were independent states, but within prescribed limits restricted and guided by federal laws.

They even have their own legislatures, or parliaments, their own constitutions, their own flags, and their own anthems: official state songs.

That does not mean they are independent nations. It does not mean they are not integral parts of the United States of America; nor does it mean that they have been given or have been allowed that kind of freedom to rule themselves so that they can secede.

There is no reason why African countries can not do the same thing: allow their constituent parts – regions or provinces – to manage their own affairs without interference or guidance from the national government as long as they don't violate national laws which are vital to keep the regions and provinces united to maintain national unity and territorial integrity of the countries on the continent.

If the people don't want to have federations, because federations are too restrictive in some matters, they can have confederations of the constituent parts which collectively constitute African countries. It's not going to be the end of African countries as we know them.

Paradoxically, a confederation – despite its potential for encouraging secession – can neutralise separatist tendencies precisely because it allows its component units to enjoy maximum freedom in the management of their own affairs as if they were *de facto* sovereign states. And benefits of membership in a larger body, such as a confederation, will also discourage secession because the advantages of such membership far outweigh its disadvantages especially in terms of security and economic viability. Also, it can be a form of confederation with a strong central government that does not allow secession but more devolution of power to accommodate conflicting interests and contain secessionist sentiments.

Therefore a confederation could serve Nigeria well,

unless the current federation wants to avoid that by taking further steps to give more power and freedom to the states to manage their own affairs but without trampling on the rights of minority groups – in which case the central government would have the right to intervene to protect them. Any government that can not protect minority groups does not have the moral authority to rule even if it has the electoral mandate to do so.

Unfortunately, despite having a federal constitution which guarantees decentralisation – hence devolution of power to the states – Nigeria has, more often than not, functioned as a highly centralised state especially under military regimes which have no respect for the constitution. But even under civilian leadership, it has functioned the same way although without being draconian as is the case when soldiers are in power.

The objectives, for example maintaining national unity and stability under a highly centralised state, may be noble. But such concentration of power at the centre has had tragic consequences – oppression, suppression of freedom, exploitation which can not be challenged because people are muzzled – which could have been avoided had power been decentralised even under a unitary state. It has thus achieved exactly what it intended to avoid, including instability, chaos and even threats to national unity.

Zamfara's promulgation and enforcement of Islamic law – that of other northern states as well – may have been a quest for such extensive autonomy, but only if it was done within well-prescribed constitutional limits. It may also have been a major part of a hidden agenda by the northern Islamic rulers to destabilise and possibly destroy the Nigerian federation while invoking the constitution which allows devolution of power and implementation of Islamic law in some areas of life – because they resented the loss of power to southern leaders since Obasanjo was elected president in 1999.

After Zamfara adopted the rigid Islamic legal code, other northern states followed suit as if they had formulated a common strategy to pursue a common agenda for northern "salvation" from southern "domination."

Besides the quest for freedom and self-rule, equally important is diversity within African countries as a matter of paramount concern to the people who make up these heterogeneous societies. It is in the context of unity in diversity – and not unity in uniformity as if Africa's different ethnic groups constitute a monolithic whole – that the quest for devolution of power must be seen, including the introduction of Islamic law in Zamfara and other states in Northern Nigeria.

However, such unity – in diversity – is impossible if the people are not free to choose the kind of political system under which they they want to live. If they are allowed to choose, there is no question they are going to choose a system that allows them maximum freedom to manage their own affairs and which accommodates conflicting interests and loyalties without compromising national unity and identity.

That is the only way the people in different countries can work together to build and develop their multiethnic societies. Governments can force them to live together within the same national boundaries. But they can't force them to work together productively. They have a way of life they want to preserve, and they should be allowed to do so, as long as they don't impede national progress, and as long as they don't interfere with the lives of others who are equally entitled to theirs and to maximum local expression in all areas – social and cultural, economic and political, as well as religious.

What happened in Zamfara was an expression of collective will in the quest for maximum self-rule, hence domestic sovereignty, within constitutional limits critics of the state's theocratic regime contend the governor overstepped, as he probably did, by invoking a secular constitution – of the Federal Republic of Nigeria – to establish a theocracy. But what should not be overlooked is the will of the people of Zamfara – and of the other predominantly Muslim states in Northern Nigeria – regardless of how much one may disagree with them on the adoption and enforcement of Islamic law.

Yet the majority of the people of Zamfara and other northern states can not legitimately claim they have the right to enforce Islamic law while ignoring the rights of the minorities amongst them. That is a violation of the federal constitution which guarantees equal rights for all.

Still, since Muslims constitute the vast majority in each of those states, they are automatically entitled to majority rule (so are the Hutu, of course, in both Rwanda and Burundi). That is democracy. And you can't have peace and stability without them (the majority) even if you bring in tanks. There can be peace and stability, hence harmony and progress, only if they get what they are entitled to, as they did when they introduced *sharia*, although violation of the country's secular constitution – which supersedes state law – is a matter of concern for the entire nation.

But if the constitution does not accommodate the interests of the northern Islamic states (and there are several of them, with tens of millions of people), it losses its legitimacy which is derived from the consent of the governed who include probably no fewer than 70 million Muslims in Northern Nigeria. No one can pretend they don't exist; and there's no one who claims they don't. They are there. They are going nowhere. And they support Islamic law. As Tajudeen Suleiman stated about the support for sharia in Zamfara in his article, "The Man Behind Sharia," in the Nigerian independent weekly, *Tempo*:

"The official notice preceding the declaration of Islamic law, or Sharia, by the government of Zamfara, a state in northern Nigeria, came as a surprise only to people outside the area. The groundwork for the establishment of Islamic law was laid before the election of Governor Ahmed Sani.

Sani, as a secretary in the state's Ministry of Lands and Housing, promoted the renovation and construction of several mosques and Islamic schools in Zamfara. These were said to have prepared for him a fertile ground when he decided to go into politics.

The indigenous peoples of the predominantly Muslim state simply drooled over him, seeing him as a pious person who would promote the cause of Islam in the state....

With the support of moneybags such as All People's Party (APP) official Alhaji Ruwan Dorowa, he had enough resources to oil his political machine. He also had sufficient mass appeal with his Islamic bent. Sani's campaign rallies kicked off with vigorous shouts of 'Allahu Akbar,' three times before any speech. This, it was gathered, greatly endeared him to the masses, who thronged his rallies.

During the All People's Party primaries, Sani defeated Ezed Anka, who was regarded as a more cosmopolitan figure. While campaigning, Sani courted clerics and village heads whom he felt would have sympathy for his envisaged Islamic revolution. Wherever he went during his campaign, Sani visited imams and village heads before going to see the political leaders. He was said to have sought their support and that of the congregation with a promise of the adoption of the Sharia. Sani's campaign slogan was openly tilted toward his promise: '[Sani] Yerima for Islam' worked instant wonders, culminating in his electoral victory.

The governor has become both a political and spiritual hero among ordinary folk. According to Sambo Gusau, a local official, Sani 'is a God-sent man doing what we want. In fact, we are lucky to have him as governor'....Alhaji

Ahmed A. Ladan Gusau, an All People's Party chieftain in the state, agrees with this view....'Sani,' he says, 'is a boy who is blessed with foresight. We all know him. He did not enter politics to amass wealth. He is always thinking of the people.' Ladan further argues that since Christianity abhors prostitution, drunkenness, and other vile practices which the Sharia would eliminate, there was no reason for Christians to fear.

Sani was born 40 years ago, is married to four wives, and has many children. He holds a master's degree in economics and has been a civil servant all his life. Sani began his career at the (Federal) Ministry of Finance and Economic Planning, where he rose to become the director of budget. He worked with the National Directorate of Employment in Lagos (the former federal capital) and the Central Bank of Nigeria. He later returned to Sokoto. On the creation of Zamfara state, Sani was named permanent secretary in the Ministry of Land and Housing, from where he resigned to join politics."[26]

Ahmed Sani will go down in Nigerian history as the first elected governor of a state to seriously challenge the constitutionality of the country's secular constitution, one of whose bedrock principles is the separation of church and state. However, his theocratic agenda was equally challenged on constitutional grounds by invoking the same principle: there shall be no state religion. Yet, by introducing Islamic law, he also attempted to achieve maximum self-rule within constitutionally prescribed limits by citing a constitutional provision that allows the adoption of such a law, although only in a few areas unlike the mandate he sought from the Islamic electorate in Zamfara to institute a theocratic state.

Zamfara became Nigeria's first theocracy, although without explicitly saying so, and pushed the federal constitution to the limit as a blueprint for extensive devolution of power to the states. Cameron Duodu, a

471

Ghanaian and one of Africa's most seasoned journalists, expressed some concern over the adoption of *sharia*:

"Ahmed Sani's declaration to adopt Islamic law, or Sharia, in his state is a frontal attack on the Nigerian constitution, which designates Nigeria as a secular state. Scores of alarmed organizations and prominent citizens called on President Obasanjo to intervene and prevent Nigeria from becoming a country in which there is one law for some citizens and a different law for others....

Apart from ethnicity, religion is the most explosive issue in Nigerian politics....Some areas of the north already practice the Sharia through traditional rulers, known as emirs, and their underlings. But the emirs' courts are restricted in what they can do.

Governor Sani and other advocates of Sharia have tried to explain that it will be applied only to Muslims. But this has not reassured non-Muslims, who know from experience that Sharia, in practice, will also affect them. Advocates of the Islamic law argue that Nigeria's 'superior' courts, which operate under secular laws, can protect individuals. In practice, however, these superior courts may not be able to intervene to help non-Muslims enforce their rights under the Nigerian constitution, because once an establishment has been marked 'sinful,' every Muslim will feel obliged to ensure that it ceases to operate.

Another bone of contention, which even Muslims are worried about, is the severity of Sharia punishments....The (federal) constitution forbids the imposition of inhuman or barbaric punishment, which may leave some Sharia punishments (such as amputations) open to challenge. Many fear that the clash of laws can bring about a nasty constitutional confrontation between the state governments of the north and the federal government.

Nigeria has already experienced one extremely costly attempt at secession (Biafra's)....Clearly, Obasanjo does not want any such eventuality."[27]

Compromise solutions should be found to resolve the conflict between Islamic law and Nigeria's secular constitution while enabling Muslims in the predominantly Islamic states of Northern Nigeria to live under *sharia*. They should include the following:

Cases involving only Muslims should be adjudicated under Islamic law. Those involving Christians and Muslims should be tried in secular courts under state and federal. No Christian should appear in any Islamic court to testify for the prosecution or for the defence. If his or her testimony is needed, the case – even if it involves only Muslims – must be tried in federal court or in a secular state court under state and federal law.

Cruel punishments such as amputations and flogging imposed by Islamic courts should be challenged in secular courts under federal law. Islamic courts should also, under federal law, be compelled to take into account mitigating factors – and accept plea bargains – to reduce the severity of cruel punishments and to temper the rigidity of the Islamic code with pragmatic considerations. Anybody convicted in an Islamic court should have the right to appeal the decision in a federal court.

There should be no discrimination against Christians and other non-Muslims in areas of employment which have nothing to do with Islamic law or the Islamic way of life involving only Muslims. And all establishments owned by non-Muslims, including bars and businesses which sell pork and other items offensive to Muslims, should be exclusively under federal law.

Probably one of the best things to come out of this controversy over *sharia* is the constitutional debate on the clash between state and federal laws which may clarify matters and increase, rather than reduce, prospects for extensive devolution of power currently severely limited by the Nigerian federal government which functions as a highly centralised unitary state.

It is a debate that will resonate across the continent and may contribute to conflict resolution in different contexts; for example, the war in Sudan – between the south which is predominantly black and Christian and the north which is mostly Arab and Muslim – that was routinely described by pundits as just another political conflict in spite of its racial overtones and religious nature even after the south seceded in July 2011 following a referendum in which more than 98 per cent southerners voted to secede.

Another major example is the conflict between the Hutu and the Tutsi in Rwanda and Burundi that also calls for dynamic compromise between the two groups to achieve peace, enable the Hutu enjoy their rights commensurate with their status as the democratic majority, and guarantee security for the dominant Tutsi minority if the Hutu come to power.

There are many other examples. Almost in every African country where violence has erupted – in the quest for power, fighting over resources – ethnicity has always played a role. Politicians stir up and fuel ethnic conflicts and exploit ethnic differences, loyalties and rivalries in the quest for power. The people themselves compete on ethnic basis. And in many cases, there is always the desire to exclude members of other ethnic groups in favour of one's own, and for personal gain, even if there is no threat from other groups. It is raw-naked tribalism.

Conflict in the quest for power with tribal or ethnic overtones has been a prominent feature of African politics since independence. And complaints by smaller or weaker groups is a perennial problem in every African country where there are dominant groups which routinely discriminate against other groups.

In Kenya, there are complaints against the Kikuyu and the Luo by smaller ethnic groups. As far back as the sixties even before independence, members of other groups feared they would be dominated by the Kikuyu and the Luo after the country attained sovereign status. They

474

formed political parties to protect the interests of smaller tribes. One of those parties was the Kenya African National Union (KADU), formed in 1960. It was led by Ronald Ngala, a former teacher from the Coast Province and one of Kenya's most prominent politicians.

KADU called for the establishment of a federation, instead of a unitary state, as a safeguard against domination of the smaller tribes by the larger ones. It advocated devolution of power to the regions, enabling smaller tribes in those regions to rule themselves under a federal system – granting regional autonomy – which would have circumscribed the powers of the central government, something that could not be done under a unitary state.

Bloody ethnic conflicts have also been an integral part of political campaigns in Kenya, as happened in the 1990s in the Rift Valley Province where many Kikuyus and other people were killed by the Kalenjins. Their property including land was confiscated and they were forced to flee the region. The Luo and the Luhya were also expelled from the province. But the primary target were the Kikuyu.

Those who survived the attacks were forced to return to their original tribal homelands, making a mockery of their common Kenyan citizenship which gives them the right to live anywhere they want to live. It was a case of ethnic cleansing. As Professor Michael Chege, a Kenyan who was teaching at Harvard University during that time, stated:

"As in Rwanda (in 1994), Kenya in 1992 – 93 witnessed state-sponsored violence directed against ethnic Kikuyu, Luo and Luhya farmers who had migrated to the Rift Valley – President Moi's home province – and then voted for parties opposed to his KANU (Kenya African National Union) Party, which is associated in the main with Moi's own Kalenjin tribe and its allies.

475

The perpetrators of the violence – window-dressed as 'Kalenjin warriors' – attacked wearing uniform T-shirts and shorts. They conducted Klan-style night rallies and vowed to cleanse the Rift Valley of the baleful 'Kukes' (Kikuyus). Use of guns, bows and arrows, and nighttime firebombing of homestead, Christian churches, and Kikuyu businesses were standard procedures....Some fifteen hundred people – mainly Kikuyus – perished in these pogroms, while about three hundred thousand others became, and remain, internal refugees."[28]

Only a few years later before the presidential election in 1997, the Coast Province was the scene of the same kind of violence: ethnic cleansing. The people who were targeted and killed were mostly "outsiders" who came from other parts of Kenya and settled in the Coast Province.

The violence was indigenous in inspiration. It was also partly inspired by politicians who exploited and fuelled the animosity and visceral hatred some people in the Coast Province had for the non-indigenes from other parts of Kenya.

Leaflets written in Kiswahili were distributed in the Coast Province urging the people native to the region to drive out the "invaders" from other provinces. They were regarded as "foreigners" who had settled in the region to exploit the indigenes and deprive them of economic opportunities and take their land. According to the *International Herald* Tribune, 18 August 1997, some of the leaflets stated:

"The time has come for us original inhabitants of the coast to claim what is rightfully ours. We must remove these invaders from our land."[29]

The ruling Kenya African National Union (KANU) under President Moi – which was dominated by the

Kalenjins (who are a collection of different groups of people who speak the Nandi language) and their allies who were also mainly members of "smaller" groups like the Kalenjins themselves – was accused of instigating the violence.

The main target were members of tribes opposed to Moi's despotic rule. They were mostly Kikuyu, Luo, Luhya, and Kamba, Kenya's major and most influential ethnic groups. But others were targeted as well.

The attacks were reminiscent of what had taken place in other African countries where members of ethnic groups who were not considered to be original inhabitants of the regions they had migrated to were killed or expelled from those regions where many of them had lived for decades.

The attacks in the Rift Valley and Coast Provinces in Kenya and the inflammatory language used by the instigators of this kind of violence to inflame passions among the indigenous people in those areas had strong similarities to what happened in Nigeria in the sixties and in Zaire in the early nineties.

The language had striking parallels to what Northern Nigerian leaders said about the Igbo who had settled in their region. As Representative Mallam Mukhtar Bello stated in the Northern House of Assembly during the February-March 1964 session just two years before the massacre of the Igbos in that region:

"I would like to say something very important that the Minister should take my appeal to the Federal Government (controlled by Northerners) about the Igbos....I wish the number of these Igbos be reduced....There are too many of them in the North. They are just like sardines and I think they are just too dangerous to the Region."[30]

The rest of the representatives in the Northern Regional Assembly expressed the same sentiment, including the Northern Premier himself, Sir Ahmadu Bello.

The Premier, Alhaji The Honourable Sir Ahmadu Bello, K.B.E., Sardauna of Sokoto:

"It is my most earnest desire that every post in the Region, however small it is, be filled by a Northerner (Applause)."[31]

Representative Mallam Muhammadu Mustapha Maude Gyari:

"On the allocation of plots to the Ibos, or the allocation of stalls, I would like to advise the Minister that these people know how to make money and we do not know the way and manner of getting about this business.... We do not want Ibos to be allocated plots, I do not want them to be given plots."[32]

Mallam Bashari Umaru:

"I would like (you), as the Minister of Land and Survey, to revoke forthwith all Certificates of Occupancy from the hands of the Ibos resident in the Region (Applause)."[33]

Mr. A. A. Abogede (Representative of Igala East):

"I am very glad that we are in Moslem country, and the Government of Northern Nigeria allowed some few Christians in the Region to enjoy themselves according to the belief of their Religion, but building of hotels should be taken away from the Ibos and even if we find some Christians who are interested in building hotels and have no money to do so, the Government should aid them, instead of allowing Ibos to continue with the hotels."[34]

Dr. Iya Abubakar (Special Member: Lecturer, Ahmadu

478

Bello University, Zaria):

"I am one of the strong believers in Nigerian Unity and I have hoped for our having a United Nigeria, but certainly if the present trend of affairs continues, then I hope the Government will investigate first the desirability and secondly the possibility of extending Northernization policy to the petty traders (Applause)."[35]

Mallam Ibrahim Muse (Representative of Igala North-West):

"Mr. Chairman, Sir, well, first and foremost, what I have to say before this honourable House is that we should send a delegate to meet our honourable Premier to move a Motion in this very Budget Session that all Ibos working in the Civil Service of Northern Nigeria, including the Native Authorities, whether they are contractors, or not, should be repatriated at once."[36]

Mallam Bashari Umaru:

"There should be no contracts either from the Government, Native Authorities, or private enterprises given to Ibo Contractors. (Government Bench: 'Good talk' and shouts of 'Fire southerners'). Again, Mr. Chairman, the Foreign Firms too should be given time limit to replace all Ibos in their firms by some other people."[37]

Alhaji Usman Liman (Representative of Sarkin Musawa):

"What brought the Ibos into this Region? They were here since the Colonial days. Had it not been for the Colonial Rule there would hardly have been any Ibo in this Region. Now that there is no Colonial Rule the Ibos should go back to their Region. There should be no

479

hesitation about this matter. Mr. Chairman, North is for Northerners, East for Easterners, West for Westerners, and the Federation for us all (Applause)."[38]

The Minister of Land and Survey, Alhaji The Honourable Ibrahim Musa Gashash, O.B.E.:

"Mr. Chairman, Sir, I do not like to take up much of the time of this House in making explanations, but I would like to assure Members that having heard their demands about Ibos holding land in Northern Nigeria, my Ministry will do all it can to see that the demands of (the) members are met. How to do this, when to do it, all this should not be disclosed. In due course, you will see what will happen (Applause)."[39]

This hostility exploded into violence almost exactly two years later against the Igbos who had settled in Northern Nigeria. Most of them had lived there for decades.

And almost exactly 30 years later, the same thing happened in the Coast Province of Kenya against the people who came from the interior; and in Zaire (now the Democratic Republic of Congo) in 1993 when President Mobutu Sese Seko employed the same tactic against his opponents, igniting tribal violence which led to the massacre of thousands of people from Kasai Province who had settled in Shaba Province (formerly Katanga Province).

They also had lived there for decades. And their home province, Kasai, was also the home region of Mobutu's most powerful and influential rival, Etienne Tshisekedi.

Like the Igbos in Northern Nigeria, and the Kikuyu, the Luo, the Luhya, the Kamba and members of other tribes from inland who had settled in Kenya's Coast Province, the people from Kasai Province were also expelled *en masse* from Shaba Province.

And in all these cases, murder was the primary weapon used to facilitate the expulsion of these "outsiders" and "invaders."

Kenyan newspapers were quick to report the violence in the Coast Province and stated that the attacks in that region appeared to be similar to those which took place in the Rift Valley Province before and after the general election in 1992.

There was unmistakable evidence of ethnic hostility which ignited and fuelled the violence. At least 1,500 Kikuyus and members of other tribes – but mostly Kikuyus – who had settled in the Rift Valley Province were killed. Their property was also destroyed. As Gibson Kuria, a renowned human rights lawyer who was active in the movement for constitutional reforms, stated:

"This looks too much like 1992. The violence is aimed at certain ethnic communities, the government response has been lukewarm, and the violence we're seeing has had the same kind of brutality."[40]

When the attacks were launched, no one knew what the outcome would be. There were tens of thousands of Kikuyus, Luos, Kambas, Merus, Luhyas and members of other inland tribes who had lived in the Coast Province for decades and knew no other place as home. They were well-established in the region and no one would have expected them to pack up and leave just like that. And it seemed that the majority of them were going to stay. But that is not what happened in many cases.

Marauding gangs of between 200 and 500 indigenous people, native to the Coast, attacked these "foreigners" and "invaders" indiscriminately, determined to force them to go back where they came from. And they succeeded in driving them out of many areas.

They used all kinds of weapons including guns, clubs with nails, machetes, and bows and arrows. They also used arson as a major weapon. According to the *International Herald Tribune*:

"They burned homes and businesses and hacked off people's limbs....Signs of tension are everywhere. Trucks bounce along, stuffed with fleeing families' belongings (going back upcountry)."[41]

The government denied involvement but there was incontrovertible evidence showing that it was indeed behind the violence.

In fact, some of the irrefutable evidence came from the government itself and its ruling party officials based on what they said in public on different occasions before this politically motivated ethnic violence – fuelled by xenophobia – erupted. Even the police, to fool and impress the public, arrested one KANU activist involved in the violence – yet did nothing to stop it:

"Thus far, police have arrested at least one KANU activist in connection with the unrest....

In recent months several ruling party politicians have exhorted indigenous Mombasans to force outside groups back up country."[42]

The fears opponents of Moi's regime had expressed were now justified. They accused the ruling party, KANU, of using violence to consolidate the president's position just before the general election and burnish his image in the Coast Province by expelling from the region members of ethnic groups such as the Kikuyu and Luo opposed to his tribalistic and autocratic rule. As Richard Leakey, a Kenyan of British origin born in Kenya who was one of Moi's most vocal critics, bluntly stated:

"There is no doubt that there is a political agenda in scaring the hell out of the upcountry people."[43]

The Luo and the Kikuyu, who are main rivals, have also clashed at different times during Kenya's turbulent post-colonial history. They are the dominant groups in the country and have been rivals for decades since the sixties when they first dominated Kenyan politics.

When Tom Mboya, a prominent politician who was a Luo and who was considered to be Jomo Keyatta's heir apparent, was assassinated in July 1969, the Luo directed their wrath against the Kikuyu. Mboya's assassination was seen by many Luos and others as an effort by the Kikuyu to prevent a Luo from becoming the president of Kenya. He was said to have been killed by the Kiambu Mafia composed of Kenyatta himself and other Kikuyu leaders including cabinet members from Kiambu, Kenyatta's home district.

Another prominent Luo, Oginga Odinga, who once served as vice president under Jomo Kenyatta, had his political career ruined by Kenyatta who even detained him without trial. He differed with Kenyatta politically and resigned as vice president in 1966. He formed an opposition party in the same year and was arrested in 1969 following disturbances in the town of Kisumu, a Luo stronghold and Odinga's operational base in western Kenya, where President Kenyatta was almost killed by a mob of angry Luo men and women who blamed him for Mboya's assassination in July. Oginga Odinga was detained for two years after his arrest. The Kenyan authorities blamed him for the disturbances.

In fact, it was Oginga Odinga who was the most prominent African leader in Kenya during the struggle for independence when Kenyatta was in prison and even led the Kenyan delegation to the constitutional talks in London on the transfer of power from the colonial rulers to Africans. He also spearheaded the campaign to release Kenyatta from prison and would have become Kenya's first president had he wanted to. Some people encouraged him to seek the presidency and sideline Kenyatta but he refused to do so. Instead, he stepped aside to let Kenyatta lead Kenya to independence after Kenyatta was released. But only a few years after independence, Kenyatta undermined Odinga and went on to favour his fellow tribesmen, the Kikuyu, who became the dominant group in the government.

Relations between the Luo and the Kikuyu got worse after that. And inter-ethnic warfare between them remains a strong possibility as they continue to compete for power on the basis of ethnic loyalties, including mobilising support from their ethnic and regional allies with whom they can share power.

When Vice President Daniel arap Moi, a Kalenjin from the Rift Valley Province, succeeded Kenyatta in 1978 following Kenyatta's death, it was his fellow tribesmen who became the most powerful leaders in the country. They came to be known as the Kalenjin Mafia and went on to marginalise the Kikuyu and the Luo as well as other groups, thus fuelling tribal sentiments, and as Moi went on exploit ethnic rivalries to consolidate his political base, a tactic typical of most leaders across the continent who have not yet transcended ethnic loyalties for the sake of national unity.

Here are other examples:

In Uganda, rivalries and conflicts have assumed ethno-regional dimensions since the sixties, especially between the north and the south, and between Nilotic tribes in the north and Bantu tribes in the south.

In Guinea, the Fula (or Fulani) and other groups have complained about discrimination by the Mandinka, especially when Sekou Toure, a Mandinka, led Guinea for 26 years since independence in 1958 – until his death in 1984. He was a great-grandson of the legendary Samori Toure who resisted French colonisation of West Africa for about 16 years until he was captured in 1898 and sent into exile in Gabon where he died two years later in 1900.

In spite of their large numbers, the Fula feel they have been marginalised. No Fula has ever served as president of Guinea.

In Togo, members of the Kabye tribe have dominated the country since Gnassingbé Eyadéma (formerly Étienne Eyadéma) became president after seizing power in a military coup in 1967.

In Malawi under Dr. Hastings Kamuzu Banda, members of his tribe, the Chewa, dominated the country.

In most cases, members of the tribes which have produced presidents and other national leaders are the biggest beneficiaries, as those who have been left out continue to demand their share of the national cake usually through violence since there are no other ways for them to get what they are entitled to. And that is a continental phenomenon.

Opportunity in almost all countries across the continent is virtually synonymous with ethnicity. The result is conflict among ethnic groups most of which are on the periphery of the mainstream because of discrimination by the members of the tribes which are in control of the country or many areas of national life.

None of those conflicts can be resolved without providing equal opportunity to all. The alternative is to grant autonomous status to different groups so that they can control their own areas including resources on the basis of a formula that enables them to get a fair share of the resources while at the same time contributing to the national economy.

Autonomy in their home districts and regions or provinces must also be in well-defined areas such as local government, police control, taxation, revenue allocation, the judiciary, health and education.

The national government should exercise power only in areas which affect the whole country including enforcing the right of all citizens to live anywhere they want to live, not just in their home districts and provinces or regions.

None of these groups can work together, as a nation, to achieve unity and progress unless their concerns are addressed. And in most cases, they do have legitimate grievances.

There is no better way to address their grievances than to allow them maximum local expression through their own institutions without any interference by the national leaders in some distant capital who hardly know anything about local circumstances, problems, interests and needs. How such self-determination is achieved will depend on the history and circumstances – and demographic composition – of each country.

In Africa itself, there are examples of political entities – during precolonial times – in which the people made decisions on what to do with their lives, in their own communities, without interference by the "national" leaders. Power was decentralised. For example, in what is Ghana today, there was the Ashanti confederation formed in the 17th century. It was one of the most powerful on the continent and fought the British in one of the most bitter conflicts in the history of colonial Africa.

There was also the Fanti confederation. The Fanti, who are members of the Akan stock like the Ashanti, formed the confederation in the early 1700s primarily as a means of protection against Ashanti invasions but also, like the Ashanti, to allow a maximum degree of independence for component units of the union. It was, like the Ashanti confederation, one of the most well-known and most successful confederations in precolonial and colonial Africa.

The existence of these powerful confederacies in Ghana (even before it became a British colony known as the Gold Coast), as well as in other parts of Africa such as Zimbabwe and Congo, shows that Africans in different parts of the continent were able to forge unity in diversity, maintained the territorial integrity of their nations, and enjoyed maximum self-rule until colonial rulers came and imposed on them alien institutions which evolved into the highly centralised modern African state that we know today and which is notorious for its instinctive aversion to democracy and devolution of power.

African countries can do better than what they are doing now if they do one thing: return to roots for better governance. If they are ashamed of their traditional institutions (which can be modified to conform to modern realities) because they think these social and political structures are "primitive," then they should look elsewhere, for example, Switzerland, for inspiration; only to find out that "what you are trying to learn from others is already within you."

Even the political systems inherited from colonial rulers can be restructured to satisfy the demands of the people, maintain stable political entities, and provide an environment in which freedom – as perceived by the leaders – is no longer seen as a threat to national unity, peace and stability.

Look at the United Kingdom which had colonies in Africa. It has embraced devolution, prompted by Scottish nationalism and by a resurgence of the Welsh language and culture which has fostered a strong national identity among the Welsh.

In 1999, with strong support from Britain's prime minister, Tony Blair, Wales opened the Welsh National Assembly, the first real self-government Wales has had in more than 600 years. And in the same year, the people of Scotland elected their first separate parliament in 300 years.

Yet, such devolution of power by the British government has not led to the disintegration of the United Kingdom.

The Scottish National Party (SNP) wants full independence. But it does not have majority support among the voters in Scotland. Even some of the most ardent micro-nationalists remain loyal to the larger nation of which they are an integral part and resolutely oppose secession. Yet when denied autonomy, they can become some of the most rabid secessionists. Respect their identity, you have patriots on your side who can also serve as a catalyst in the pursuit of a larger union on a supra-national scale. Welsh writer, Bobi Jones, made some pertinent remarks on the subject of devolution when he talked about Celtic resurgence:

"The 'Celtic resurgence'...is part of a worldwide phenomenon. It belongs to the whole anti-colonial movement. Wherever there has been 'empire,' there has been...an attempt to win freedom....

The pattern, as I see it, is what we would call 'diversity within unity.' The unity in this equation is now becoming wider – for us, Europe is becoming more and more significant. As Europe becomes more important as a unit – both political and economic – the smaller units, too, are becoming more important.

So you have this 'diversity' increasing and becoming politically more essential. At the same time, people are forfeiting some of their personal power. It's already happening, but in a new way. Europe unconsciously encourages Welsh people to look over the head of London. For Wales that's a good thing, because it's always been a bad thing for us to be centrally directed from London.

Since the 16ᵗʰ century, the center of gravity – the center of economic, political, cultural and linguistic gravity – has been outside Wales. Wales has played toward the center, to a point outside of itself. That has been where the heart of things has been, anyway. Our blood leaks toward the center. Our population has gone in that direction. Our economy, too, has shifted; our unemployment is always worse than at the center. The energies of production, of some cultural riches, drift that way.

Wherever you have centralization, you tend to have

uniformity. Whenever you have movement toward revival or resurrection, there's a different kind of energy going on – toward more fruitfulness or variety."[44]

In the African context, Nigeria provides one good example where the leaders attempted to accommodate conflicting interests of different ethnic and regional groups by trying to restructure the federation.

One of the country's main leaders, Chief Obafemi Awolowo, came up with some ideas to decentralise power, maintain national unity and stability and protect the interests of minority groups in Africa's giant federation dominated by three ethnic groups: the Hausa-Fulani in the north, the Igbo in the east, and the Yoruba in the West. In 1947, Awolowo, a Yoruba from Western Nigeria, proposed in his book, *Path to Nigerian Freedom*,[45] that the country should be divided into 40 states, with cultural and linguistic affinity as the basis of division.

Nigeria was then a federation of three massive regions – North, East and West – formed in August 1946 by the British colonial government and remained so until 5 May 1967 when the country was divided into 12 states not long before the outbreak of the civil war (2 July 1967 – 15 January 1970) which was triggered by the declaration of independence for the Eastern Region as the Republic of Biafra on 30 May 1967. The federation also included the smaller Mid-West Region carved out of the Western Region in 1963. The Mid-West was mostly composed of the Edo who wanted their own region separate from the Western Region dominated by the Yoruba. After the Mid-West was carved out, the federation was restructured again a few years later in April 1967:

"A communique issued after the meeting of the (ruling) Supreme Military Council on April 22nd, stated that it had adopted a political and administrative 'programme of action' for preserving the Federation of Nigeria as one

489

country. The main items in the approved programme, according to the communique, included: 'creation of States as the basis of political stability in Nigeria.'"[46]

Long before then, the division of Nigeria was also suggested along similar lines (as Awolowo's) by the National Council of Nigeria and the Cameroons (NCNC) – renamed in 1960 the National Council of Nigerian Citizens (NCNC) – led by Nnamdi Azikiwe, an Igbo from Eastern Nigeria, who became Nigeria's first president when the country won independence on 1 October 1960; he first served as governor-general (1960 - 1963) before becoming president (1963 – 1966).

The party issued a Freedom Charter in 1948 advocating a federal form of government with the new states based on ethnic and linguistic affinity. Earlier, Azikiwe advocated in his book, *The Political Blueprint of Nigeria*[47] published in 1943, a federal form of government and the division of the federation into eight states.

Then in 1953, Awolowo proposed the division of Nigeria into nine states. In 1959, his party, the Action Group, called for the creation of more states. And everywhere across the country, minority groups demanded their own states as a safeguard against domination by the three major groups – the Hausa-Fulani, the Igbo and the Yoruba – who dominated the three massive regions of the federation.

It was therefore clear from the beginning when the Nigerian federation was formed that creation of more states to protect minority groups was critical to national unity and stability.

In 1967, the federation was divided into 12 states. The number went up to 19, 21, 30, and finally to 36. But more states may be created in the future.

That is what other African countries, especially those wracked by ethnic conflicts – including Rwanda and Burundi despite their identity primarily as biethnic states of Hutus and Tutsis, with a small minority of the Twa who constitute about 1% of the population – need to do to resolve these conflicts and maintain national unity and stability.

Create more states or provinces and grant maximum self-rule to disgruntled and oppressed groups. Otherwise expect perpetual conflict and even disintegration of these countries into non-viable entities dominated by warlords, looters, smugglers, kidnappers, rapists and cold-blooded murderers as happened in Somalia, Sierra Leone and Liberia where bandits treated these failed states as their personal fiefdoms.

The key to conflict resolution in Africa is consensus building by different ethnic groups and political parties as well as other interest groups including regional alliances in order to form governments which allow extensive devolution of power.

Besides granting extensive autonomy to ethnoregional groups – while maintaining a strong national government for the sake of national unity in spite of such diversity – much smaller and weaker groups such as the Twa in Rwanda and Burundi and the Mbuti in neighbouring Congo, collectively known as Pygmies, need extra protection from larger groups. Other groups which need such protection and access to the political process as well as inclusion in the government include the San and the Khoikhoi (so-called Bushmen) in the countries of southern Africa especially in Botswana and Namibia where they are on the periphery of the mainstream.

Almost none of the African countries across the continent provide this kind of protection, let alone extra-protection, for smaller and weaker minorities.

Multiethnic India is one of the countries which has this kind of guarantee of group rights for its weaker citizens embodied in the law, although, frankly speaking, her performance has been less than stellar with regard to the untouchables.

491

But a constitutional guarantee is necessary. It is a vital step towards equality for oppressed minorities. Without such a guarantee, they may never be able to win their rights in many areas if they try to go through conventional channels whose authority for such preferential treatment is derived from a constitutional text. Without such constitutional authority, the government can not legitimately claim to have the mandate to formulate and implement such a policy unless laws are passed to justify preferential treatment as happened in the United States where affirmative action is upheld by federal laws and regulations and by the courts.

In India, the constitution forbids the practice of "untouchability," and legislation has been used to reserve quotas for former untouchables – and also for tribal peoples – in the legislatures, education, and in public services. But the caste system remains a fact of life, as it has been for centuries, although somewhat eroded nowadays. In Africa, it has a rough but functional equivalence to tribalism – and to racism in the United States especially before the civil rights movement and the civil rights laws which were passed in the sixties to guarantee racial equality – especially in Rwanda and Burundi where the Tutsi aristocracy would be analogous to the Brahmans and other Indians of the upper castes.

But the Indian caste system is much more rigid. For example, marriage outside the caste is prohibited, while the Hutu and the Tutsi have intermarried for so long, through the centuries, that it is sometimes very difficult to tell the difference between a Hutu and a Tutsi from physical features alone: you could be right or wrong 6 times out of 10, may be even more than that. Yet, there are some parallels between the Indians of the upper castes and the Tutsi, as underscored by this statement from Tutsi leaders:

"The relations between we (Batutsi) and they (Bahutu)

492

have always until the present been based on servitude. There is, therefore, between we and they no foundation for brotherhood....Since it was our kings who conquered the Bahutu country and killed their petty little kings and thus subjugated the Bahutu, how can they now pretend to be our brothers?"[48]

As things turned out, the Hutu did not even try to pretend to be their brothers during the 1994 Rwandan genocide. Yet, they continue to live together because they have to. They have no choice. They must share the land. And they must live under the same government. But they don't have to be denied maximum self-rule, preferably in their own ethnic enclaves, if they continue to kill each other and oppress one another.

And Rwanda (or Burundi) does not have to be a unitary state in order to remain united as one country, especially when the unitary state is used by one group to dominate others. It should be decentralised.

Decentralisation in Rwanda and Burundi will probably work best if power is shifted from the centre to the periphery – at the grassroots level in the villages – to create autonomous entities linked together in some kind of confederation as a safeguard against oppression of one ethnic group by the other if one group is dominant at the centre. This will also enable the people – both the Hutu and the Tutsi as well as the Twa, a tiny minority – to manage their own affairs without undue interference from their leaders whether local or national.

There are many other cases in different parts of the world where devolution of power has not led to national disintegration but has, instead, helped to foster and maintain national unity and stability.

Also, in Africa, each country has its own unifying institutions – even if they are intangible, such as common cultural values, language, and history – which can be used to forge and strengthen national ties in spite of the fact that

493

Africans are divided along ethnic and regional lines. But a concerted effort can be made to institutionalise cultural values and other things shared by different ethnic groups across the nation and strengthen those institutions in order to use them as the basis for unity across ethnoregional lines.

One example is Kenya and Tanzania where language, Kiswahili, has served as a unifying factor. Extensive decentralisation along ethnoregional lines has not been used as the basis for unity and stability in those two countries, although it is valid in other contexts on the continent, probably even in Kenya, given the nation's history of ethnic rivalries.

In Tanzania during Nyerere's presidency, decentralisation was pursued along political lines, only coincidentally on ethnic basis for no other reason than that administrative boundaries in most districts and regions happen to coincide with ethnic identity, yet without assuming the attributes or character of ethnostates – political entities which may be necessary in some African countries to maintain national unity. For example, Ethiopia, a country of about 80 different ethnic groups, is a federation of provinces which are virtually ethnostates. Although autonomous only in theory since power is still concentrated at the centre, the provinces were created on ethnic basis as stipulated by the federal constitution – based on ethnic confederalism – which even allows them to secede.

This kind of federal structure was instituted in recognition of a people's right to self-determination, in fulfillment of a fundamental natural right of every people to rule themselves, and as a safeguard against domination and oppression by other groups. However, Ethiopia's national leaders have shown little tolerance for secessionist sentiments.

Nigeria is another country which also has, through the years since the civil war (1967 – 1970), gradually evolved

494

towards a federation of ethnostates as a durable basis for national unity.

Congo, former Zaire, may follow the same path as the only way of saving the country form breaking up. And probably that is the only way it can be saved, if it's not already too late to do so.

There may never be one Congo again other than being an area that is frozen indefinitely as a patchwork of *de facto* independent states which may only be brought together as an organic whole under a federal system or even a confederation to replace the highly centralised state whose power is not even felt in many remote parts of this vast country – the size of Western Europe – which has the unenviable distinction of being the bleeding heart of Africa.

One of the biggest advantages of decentralisation, or devolution, is the freedom and inspiration people have in finding solutions to their own problems without interference by the central government.

The people become more energetic under a decentralised system of government. They become more engaged, more creative and more dynamic because there is no one telling them what to do and what not to do. They are free to use their own skills and talents without waiting for instructions from some bureaucrats usually hundreds of miles away in the nation's capital.

It is these bureaucrats and national leaders who impede progress. They stifle individual initiative by directing virtually everything from the centre, thus ruining lives which could have been more productive in a variety of ways had the people been left alone to come up with their own solutions to their own problems instead of those solutions being provided by the central government without even knowing they will be suited to local circumstances which only the local people know best. They are the ones who are in the best position to know what they want and what kind of solutions will work for them.

Bureaucracy not only stifles individual initiative; it stunts growth at the local and national levels across the spectrum. And it thrives best under centralisation or centralised systems of government which are usually under bad leadership because leaders have nothing to fear in terms of accountability. There is no one to hold them accountable for their actions because power is concentrated in their hands.

Africa has been plagued by bad leadership for decades. But the problems of poor governance and lack of accountability, which have institutionalised corruption that has become synonymous with Africa, are not going to be tackled without strong institutions, the most prominent being democratic institutions and an independent judiciary. Democratic institutions demand transparency.

However, these institutions can not be built, and they can not function, under a political system which enables a few individuals to monopolise power, concentrated in their hands for their own benefit, thus blocking change which will reduce their power and even force them out of office. The system which enables them to abuse power and perpetuate themselves in office, and which insulates them from accountability including prosecution for the crimes they commit – especially corruption and trampling on human rights – is fostered by the centralised state.

Once power is decentralised and spread out all the way down to the grassroots level, it will be very difficult and in many cases even impossible for leaders to abuse their power. Most of the power will be in the hands of the people, not in the hands of their leaders. It will enable the people to rule themselves.

Under a decentralised system, leaders are going to have less power; the system will enable the people to manage their own affairs; it will also make power less attractive to aspiring dictators and other unscrupulous elements seeking office.

Leaders are also going to be held accountable for their actions because of transparency under a decentralised system, exposing wrongdoing, and punishing culprits, without fear of retribution from the leaders because they will no longer have the kind of power they had under a highly centralised state.

Africa can not even start to sort things out unless power is decentralised or devolved. That is because there is a need to get the people involved in sorting things out. But they can not get actively involved without having power in their hands. They can get it only under devolution or under a decentralised system of government.

That is one of the main issues, and one of the major challenges, Africa will have to address in the twentieth-first century in her quest for peace, stability and progress.

Even some of the strongest supporters of African unity who built their nations under highly centralised states which they justified on the grounds that African countries would break up along ethnic and regional lines if they did not have strong central governments support decentralisation or at least acknowledge its advantages. Although very few practise it, they see no contradiction between decentralisation and unity. As President Julius Nyerere of Tanzania stated in his work, *Decentralisation*:

"The purpose of both the *Arusha Declaration* and of *Mwongozo* was to give the people power over their own lives and their development....To the mass of the people, power is still something wielded by others....

The planning and control of development...must be exercised at the local level....Our nation is too large for the people at the centre in Dar es Salaam always to understand local problems or to sense their urgency. When all the power remains at the centre, therefore, local problems can remain, and fester, while local people who are aware of them are prevented from using their initiative in finding solutions. Similarly, it is sometimes difficult for local people to respond with enthusiasm to a call for development work which may be to their benefit, but which has been decided upon and planned by an authority hundreds of miles away....

We have to work out a system which gives more local freedom for both decision and action on matters which are primarily of local impact....The system must...reduce the amount of red tape and bureaucracy which is at present in danger of strangling our people's enthusiasm....(But) projects which are of national importance must remain under national control, even though they may be situated in one particular area – a decision which does not preclude greater delegation of authority to the responsible officers on the spot....

Regions and districts should plan and implement local development activities as well as administer local affairs with the very minimum of interference from Dar es Salaam. This will mean, for example, that a very large proportion of agricultural programmes will be made the direct responsibility of the Districts and Regions. Small industrial and commercial developments will be a local responsibility where these fall outside the programmes of...national parastatal organisations. Local roads, water supplies, health and primary education will also be dealt with at the local level....The Regions and Districts will be free to make their own decisions about priorities and methods of work....

We have to decentralise the control and decision-making now exercised from Dar es Salaam, and also centralise local control, decision-making and responsibility....

The present system of rural local government will be abolished, as will the present practice of each Ministry having its own officers working in Regions and Districts....The abolition of the present system of local government does not mean the abolition of local representation. On the contrary, the purpose of the new system is to increase the people's participation in decision-making, and it will therefore demand that the powers and responsibilities of local representatives are increased....

The new District Development Councils will be...responsible to the people for the use of the new powers at District level. It will be their job to lead the work of direct consultation with the people, so that this decentralisation really does result in the people themselves having a say in their own development and in their own affairs....One of the major purposes of this reorganisation is to ensure that future economic planning stems from the people and serves the people directly....

The transfer of power to the Regions and Districts must not also mean a transfer of a rigid and bureaucratic system from Dar es Salaam to the lower levels. Not is it the intention of these proposals to create new local tyrants in the persons of the Regional and District Development Directors....

Decentralisation...is based on the principle that more and more people must be trusted with responsibility – that is its whole purpose."[49]

No one would accuse President Nyerere of pursuing a policy – decentralisation – that would lead to the fragmentation of Tanzania or any other African country. His nationalist and Pan-African credentials were beyond dispute.

Decentralisation in Tanzania took place under a unitary state. Therefore, it is possible even for devolution – not just decentralisation – to take place under a strong central government which may still be good for the sake of national unity if African leaders make it more democratic instead of using it as an oppressive machinery as has been the case in most countries across the continent since independence.

Under devolution, regional governments and other component units of the state including local jurisdictions have the statutory power to make laws. Under decentralisation, such power remains at the centre – which is a unitary state – but is dispersed all the way to the grassroos level; for example, in Tanzania where there were ten-cell units each comprising ten households under its own leader.

Although the unitary system has many disadvantages, resulting mainly from abuse of power because power is concentrated in the hands of a few people at the centre, it also has its advantages which must be looked at in their proper historical context, especially in post-colonial Africa.

Therefore its benefits can not be ignored. Kwame Nkrumah used the unitary – centralised – state effectively in Ghana to contain separatist threats among the Ashanti in the central province, the Dagomba and others in the north (what was once known as the Northern Territories), and an irredentist movement among the Ewe in the Volta region in the east who wanted to unite with their kinsmen in neighbouring Togo. In Tanzania, Nyerere used it to build one of the most cohesive and most stable countries on the continent.

Unfortunately, most African leaders refuse to share power with their people and have tarnished the image of the centralised state even when it has proved to be useful in some cases. Hence the need for devolution.

Devolution of power can also be implemented in different ways depending on the circumstances of each country that is trying to pursue it. For example, African countries threatened by secession could grant non-sovereign independent status to restive regions and enable them to be freely associated with the national government as a way of satisfying disgruntled populations in those areas and neutralising separatist sentiments.

Equatorial Guinea could loosen its grip on the independence-prone island of Bioko, formerly known as Fernando Po, and even allow it to fly its own flag as a symbol of domestic sovereignty – short of international recognition – in addition to having its own government and its own president, premier or prime minister the way it has been done in Tanzania where Zanzibar has its own government, its own president and its own flag although subordinate to the union government of the United Republic of which Zanzibar remains an integral part.

The island nation of the Comoros can take the same approach towards resolving its conflict with the secessionist islands of Anjouan and Moheli; so can Senegal with regard to the separatist Casamance Province, and Namibia towards Caprivi Strip where separatists also want to establish their own independent state.

Cabinda Province which is separated from the rest of Angola by a strip of land which is a part of the Democratic Republic of Congo (DRC) is another major contender for full autonomy and domestic sovereignty for historical and geographical reasons as well, not just because of its unique identity as an ethnic and cultural entity.

Its demand for independence is one of the most stubborn cases on the continent because of strong separatist elements in the province.

But its quest for full sovereign status is also partly, if not largely, motivated by a desire to have full control of the region's resources instead of sharing them with the rest of Angola. Cabinda has some of the largest oil fields in the world. Most of Angola's oil revenues come from those oil fields. Cabinda is also rich in other resources. If the region did not have such abundant resources, the demand for independence would not have been as strong as it is now. It may not even have existed if Cabinda were a barren, desperately poor territory.

The secessionist movement in the province can be weakened or neutralised by granting extensive autonomy to the province, with a self-government that has all the attributes of sovereignty in all areas except defence, national security, foreign policy, immigration, monetary policy, and without international recognition as a sovereign state.

Besides its geography as a territory separate from the rest of Angola, which reinforces its unique identity, Cabinda's history also differs in some fundamental respects from the history of the rest of Angola in spite of the colonial ties which bind both as one colony once ruled by Portugal. But it is also a fact that Cabinda was once ruled separately by Portugal, as a protectorate, separate from the rest of Angola until it was later incorporated into the larger colony to create a single colonial entity.

Even the Berlin conference conceded the status of Cabinda as a separate territory, distinct from the rest of Angola which was known as Portuguese West Africa.

It was as if there were two distinct colonies in the region ruled by Portugal: Portuguese West Africa (Angola), and Portuguese Congo as Cabinda was known when it was a protectorate.

The Organisation of African Unity (OAU) itself once considered Cabinda to be a separate Portuguese colony, distinct from Angola. But it also refused to recognise the separatist movement in Cabinda, fearing that it would encourage secession in other countries on the continent.

So, Cabinda's history has reinforced the region's unique identity in a very significant way. And it has been one of the major factors fuelling the independence movement in the province. It can also be used by Cabindans to demand even more concessions - for greater autonomy - from the Angolan government, some of which should be granted, provided the people of the province also agree to remain an integral part of Angola – a concession, and a sacrifice, they should be prepared to make in order to win extensive autonomy from the central government in Luanda.

The fundamental aspiration among disgruntled groups, encompassing whole regions and tribes or ethnic groups – is the desire to rule themselves. They are disgruntled because they do not have the freedom to be what they are and to do what they want to do. They are also disgruntled because they are marginalised by the central government.

But even if they are not marginalised, they want to rule themselves because they have their own identities, aspirations and desires, and their own cultural values and traditions and traditional institutions which are not allowed to flourish or are deliberately suppressed by the highly centralised state which abhors unity in diversity and wants to mould the people into a monolithic whole under mass regimentation ostensibly for the sake of national unity. In many cases, the result is mass discontent and civil strife including civil wars.

The biggest fear among African governments is that if the demands of these groups are fulfilled, such a concession will have a domino effect and African countries are going to break up along ethnic and regional lines.

But both sides can have their wishes satisfied if they use dynamic compromise which entails acknowledging the legitimacy of both quests: separatist regions should be accorded "sovereign" status but without their own personality as full-fledged independent states in the international arena. They must remain within their present national boundaries as a part of the compromise with the countries from which they want to separate. Such an offer by national governments confronted with separatist threats will help to ward off secession and placate even some of the most uncompromising secessionists.

Separatist regions should also be allowed to fly their own flags, have their own anthems, and celebrate their own holidays – along with those of the larger nation of which they remain an integral part. They should have their own governments responsible for all aspects of administration within their regional boundaries – without any interference, none whatsoever, from the central government unless there is anarchy and violence which the region's security forces can not handle, or if they want to secede.

Each separatist region should also have its own constitution, its own regional parliament and local assemblies.

Those are usually the basic demands separatists expect to fulfill if they secede. They are also the basic demands of practically every government in the world; they are the attributes of national sovereignty. Once these demands are met in restive regions, the secessionist movement in those areas will be robbed of its momentum.

The only thing that disgruntled ethnoregions – such as Cabinda in Angola, Casamance in Senegal, Bioko Island in Equatorial Guinea, and Caprivi Strip in Namibia, all of which want to secede – will not have is an international personality of their own and recognition as independent nations. But most of their basic demands will have been fulfilled under this compromise formula. Not only will secessionist movements in those regions lose momentum; they will also lose their legitimacy and appeal among many – if not among the majority – of their supporters who may see the leaders of these movements as sheer opportunists and power-hungry individuals if they continue to demand secession after the national government has acceded to their basic demands as outlined above.

Once such a compromise formula is applied, African countries will no longer have to worry about splitting along ethnoregional lines, one of the main reasons most African leaders refuse to grant autonomy to the regions, besides their inordinate ambition for power.

But if African leaders really want to save their countries from degenerating into chaos and anarchy and from disintegrating into tribal independent states, they must be willing to share power and make major concessions to the regions agitating for independence, along the lines of the compromise formula outlined here. Denying them maximum self-rule will not solve the problem; it will only inflame passions among the people in the restive regions and fuel secessionist sentiments. And what African leaders have always feared – national disintegration – will become a self-fulfilling prophecy.

One of the most troubled countries which can benefit from such devolution of power through shared sovereignty – the nation sharing sovereignty with the regions – is Rwanda whose northwestern provinces of Gisenyi and Ruhengenri constitute traditionally Hutu strongholds which have never been totally subdued by the Tutsi rulers throughout the country's history.

Maximum self-rule for regions and ethnic enclaves in Rwanda will achieve several things:

It will ease ethnic tensions. It will ventilate grievances of individual citizens and ethnic groups who feel that they are dominated and oppressed by the central government which is controlled by the members of one ethnic group.

Maximum self-rule will guarantee justice and equality for all – Hutu, Tutsi, Twa, and others. It will help to promote peace and stability and maintain national unity.

It will encourage productivity by removing government control which stifles individual initiative and robs the people of the incentive to work.

It will also maximise performance in all areas and foster regional cooperation at the macronational level (East-central African), with the border districts and provinces of Rwanda bordering Congo, Uganda, Burundi and Tanzania functioning as vital links to these neighbouring countries once they are allowed to trade freely and even integrate their economies with them.

No restrictions should be imposed on currency flow across borders even if this creates havoc for weaker economies. It will be a blessing in disguise since a neighbouring country with a weaker currency and economy will be forced to be more competitive, hence more productive, and will be forced to devalue its inflated currency. The countries involved will also be encouraged by potential benefits of regional integration and will be compelled by need to institute a common currency.

What is proposed here for Rwanda should also be applied to Burundi, the two being twin states in terms of history and ethnic composition.

Extensive decentralisation will save many African countries from economic ruin, political chaos and anarchy and from disintegration – restive regions which have been denied autonomy opt for secession.

In the case of Rwanda and Burundi, already embroiled in conflict, the alternative to devolution of power is chronic instability – and civil war neither the Hutu nor the Tutsi can win, in absolute terms, although odds are in favour of the Hutu after a long war of attrition because of their superiority in numbers.

If the two countries can not end wars within their borders, then the international community should help to implement a radical solution to this perennial conflict between the Hutu and the Tutsi. The solution entails the partition of both Rwanda and Burundi into Hutuland and Tutsiland, but only if the people of both countries agree to do so in an internationally supervised referendum.

The partition will inevitably involve massive relocation of populations to create viable, independent ethnostates which will become safe havens for the members of their ethnic groups and which may even be compelled by economic needs and political circumstances to form a confederation in spite of the hostility between the two.

Otherwise the Hutu and the Tutsi will be locked in perpetual conflict. The rest of the world can't do anything about it if the people who are fighting don't want to stop fighting. Peace is possible only if the people involved in conflict want peace.

The goal should be peace at any price even if it means separation of the two groups – unless they accept war as a better alternative.

The conflict in Rwanda and Burundi, a microcosm of a

tragic continental phenomenon, is but one aspect of what Africa has failed to be, an entire generation after independence. The African continent has not done much to end its wars and solve other problems which have turned Africans into international beggars – not only begging for food but also for help to end their conflicts and even to maintain peace in conflict zones. And prospects are bleak the world's poorest yet richest continent will do better in the future after decades of rotten leadership, oppression, institutional decay and economic ruin unless the modern African state is restructured to reflect African realities and to make it responsive to the needs and aspirations of the people; a process that entails a complete overhaul of the system in most parts of the continent in order to replace it with a better one through creative destruction. Nothing short of revolution is going to change Africa and improve her condition.

Therefore, there may be some prospects, however dim, even in some of the most hopeless cases. And there are examples to vindicate this position.

Out of the ashes of Somalia, a wasteland, emerged a stable Somaliland which separated from the rest of the country and went on to become a viable state although no country has recognised it as a legal sovereign entity. But it has continued to function as a *de facto* state (so has its neighbour, Puntland, another stable enclave in northern Somalia) and is in better shape than the rest of Somali which has been ravaged by war. In fact, Somaliland is governed far better than many African countries are. They are failed states. Yet they enjoy international recognition. Why shouldn't Somaliland be accorded the same status? It deserves full recognition as a legal sovereign entity.

There are other examples. After being battered by war for years, Liberia and Sierra Leone returned to peace, staggering, and may even slide back into anarchy, especially in the case of Sierra Leone, a country that enjoyed only intermittent peace until the the former colonial power, Great Britain, intervened.

But they, at least, tried to end their conflicts with the help of the international community although it was not enough and it came too late in the case of Sierra Leone. It was not until 2000 that the United Nations intervened in Sierra Leone on a somewhat significant scale, almost 10 years after the war started in that country.

In the case of Liberia, the country showed that in spite of several failures during the course of its conflict, peace could be achieved. Out of the ruins of this old republic emerged a stable nation, although under a brutal despot, former warlord Charles Taylor who terrorised his fellow countrymen into voting for him to be president. They feared that if they did not elect him, he would go back to the bush and plunge the country into another civil war and shoot his way into office as he tried to do earlier until he was blocked by the Nigerian-led West African peacekeeping forces (ECOMOG) from seizing power. He wanted to rule without electoral mandate.

Durable and just peace in Africa is possible but not through intimidation. It can be achieved and sustained only when African countries adopt a system of power sharing to allay fears among different groups – especially ethnic groups, and not just political parties – which feel, and in most cases rightly so, that they have been deliberately excluded from meaningful participation in the political process and representation in the government. And that means the winner-take-all system, an alien institution brought to Africa by Europeans and based on Western political traditions, must be abolished.

Losers in elections should, together with the winners, form a coalition government to rule by consensus; an accommodation and reconciliation of conflicting views that has been the hallmark of African traditional institutions of governance.

It is a travesty of justice and a mockery of true representative government to claim that only the party that wins the election is entitled to rule because it has the mandate from the electorate to do so. Which electorate?

What about those who did not vote for it but instead voted for the candidates of the other party or parties? Are they not part of the electorate? If they are, why are they excluded from the government of their country?

If the winning party has the right to form a government whose legitimacy is derived from the consent of the governed, it has the right to govern only those who voted for it since it is they who have given it such consent. The other voters have given the other party or parties the mandate to govern them and implement their policies.

A party that wins only 48% - 50% or even 55% - 60% of the votes does not have the right to have 100% of the power to rule the country, excluding the 50% - 52% or 40% - 45% who did not vote for it and who do not support its policies. That is discriminatory and divisive especially in African countries where exclusion of some groups from power is a way of life.

Yet almost all African governments derive their legitimacy from such politics of exclusion while claiming to represent all the people.

Only rule by consensus, which mandates inclusion of all groups, can guarantee fair representation, justice and equality for all.

In addition to power sharing and rule by consensus typical of traditional Africa, there is also an imperative need to reduce the power of the central government. Le the people decide for themselves. They know what they want.

Extensive devolution of power will enable the people not only to release their creative potential; it will enable them to solve their own problems and incorporate into the modern political system an array of traditional institutions and values which served Africa well for centuries before the advent of colonial rule which led to the imposition of alien institutions on the continent, wreaking havoc.

In many cases, imperial rule distorted and destroyed

traditional institutions without which African societies could not have survived and functioned as viable entities in precolonial times. It is these same institutions, values and traditions which can help Africa to survive and thrive without rejecting all aspects of modern life in this global village.

Africa needs to reclaim her past. Africa must also recognise the enormous potential of her people, the vast majority of whom still live in traditional societies across the continent. But their potential can not be fully harnessed if they remain powerless. Power in African countries must be shared all the way down to the grassroots level instead of being concentrated in the hands of a few people at the top.

That is one of the challenges Africa faces in the twentieth-first century: to let the people determine their own destiny without interference by anybody, especially national leaders, most of whom oppress and exploit their own people and even collude with foreign interests to plunder the continent.

If the people start to have control over their lives and make decisions which affect them instead of being told what to do; if the leaders are held accountable for their actions including well-meaning incompetence; and if the people start to control their resources which are being ruthlessly exploited by unscrupulous elements in power together with external forces, then there is hope for Africa. Otherwise, all talk of an African renaissance is no more than empty rhetoric.

But enabling the people to have power – the power to make decisions for themselves and even to rule themselves – does not mean they are being encouraged to break up their countries and establish their own independent states.

The future of African lies *not* in secession but in regional integration and in the creation of federations or confederations, especially federations with strong federal institutions to achieve and maintain unity in diversity, and stability.

Formation of such large political units will inevitably lead to the abolition of national borders as we know them today. And the map of Africa will have to be redrawn to reflect the changes.

We may need our own Berlin conference not only to legitimise new borders resulting from unification but also from disintegration of some countries where entire populations of particular groups may be justified to have their own independent states. Again, Somaliland stands out as a classic example of such a group of people in this contetx.

Therefore, in some parts of the continent, the reconfiguration may result from secession. But the focus should be on the creation of larger political entities or macronations.

However, there are extreme – but very few – cases which may justify secession; the secession of South Sudan being a prime example. Another example is Eritrea when the people of that country voted for separation from Ethiopia although even before then, Eritrea, a former Italian colony, was a separate territorial entity forcibly incorporated into Ethiopia.

Western Sahara is another territorial entity which has a legitimate claim to independence denied by Morocco which has forcibly annexed the territory.

And where anarchy is endemic as in the case of Somalia, the breakaway region of Somaliland which has been able to function as a stable and prosperous *de facto* state – and whose boundaries are the same the territory had when it was a colonial entity known as British Somaliland – such a region may be a strong candidate for recognition although African countries and the rest of the international community have refused to recognise Somaliland as an independent state.

Another extreme case was the secession of the predominantly Igbo Eastern Region of Nigeria which declared independence as the Republic of Biafra. It was recognised by four African countries: Tanzania, Zambia, Ivory Coast and Gabon. It was also recognised by Haiti. Another country that came close to recognising Biafra was Uganda under the leadership of President Milton Obote. But Obote did not do so because he hosted peace talks in Uganda's capital Kampala between the Nigerian federal government and the secessionist leaders.

Ghanaian military head of state, Lieutenant-General Joseph Ankrah, was also sympathetic towards Biafra and reluctantly supported Federal Nigeria before and after his country hosted peace talks between the two sides.

President Habib Bourguiba of Tunisia also said he understood the position of the countries which recognised Biafra as "a protest against massacre."

Sierra Leone, Dahomey, Senegal, Rwanda and Burundi were also very sympathetic towards Biafra and acknowledged the merits of its cause although they did not formally recognise the secessionist region.

Fortunately, Africa has not had many cases which have justified secession. The few cited above are extreme, and justified, unlike the secession of Katanga Province in the former Belgian Congo which was externally engineered.

The rest of the secessionist movements or threats on the continent – there are hardly any credible ones in terms of legitimacy and military power – can be contained and neutralised by extensive devolution of power to let the people in restive or secessionist regions manage their own affairs as autonomous entities.

Highly centralised states which are in most cases intolerant of dissent, suffocate the opposition, and even discourage cross-fertilisation of ideas – however potentially fruitful – have been a major source of instability in many countries across the continent. And they have contributed to retarded growth across the spectrum precisely because they don't allow robust, vigorous debate and local input and discourage the people from finding solutions to their own problems, solutions suited to local circumstances.

Extensive devolution or decentralisation will not only contribute to growth and development but to peace and stability, all of which have been elusive in many countries across the continent since independence. Without peace and stability, any kind of progress, including regional integration, is impossible.

Already, there are regions with great potential for integration. In East Africa, the countries of Kenya, Uganda and Tanzania have been close for many years, culturally and historically including their shared colonial experience of being ruled by Britain. Rwanda and Burundi have historical and cultural ties to Tanzania and Uganda and even constituted one colony together with Tanganyika (now mainland Tanzania) known as Deutsch-Ostafrika – German East Africa – ruled by Germany.

Neighbouring Congo, once ruled by Belgium, has political, cultural and historical ties to East Africa, especially Tanzania, more than it does to its other neighbours such as the Central African Republic.

Swahili, Tanzania's national language also spoken in Kenya, Uganda, Rwanda and Burundi, is the *lingua franca* of the entire eastern Congo. It is also widely spoken in the southern part of Congo, in Katanga Province, and even as far west as the capital Kinshasa and elsewhere in the country. And Congolese music is as popular in Tanzania as it is in Congo itself, and to a smaller degree in Kenya, Uganda, Rwanda and Burundi.

With all those ties, Congo has the attributes to become an integral part of a large federation composed of Kenya, Uganda, Tanzania, Rwanda and Burundi.

Cong's ties to East Africa are also enhanced by the fact that during colonial rule, the country was ruled by the same colonial masters who ruled Rwanda and Burundi, what was then a single territory known as Ruanda-Urundi. And its capital Leopoldville (now Kinshasa) was also the colonial capital of Ruanda-Urundi.

The Belgian colonial rulers ruled Ruanda-Urundi from Leopoldville, far away, because they considered the territory to be a minor colonial possession unlike Congo.

Before then, Rwanda-Urundi was ruled by Germany. Before the Germans lost the territory in World War I, they also considered Ruanda-Urundi to be a minor possession and made it an integral part of Tanganyika.

Another region which has great potential for unification is what was once known as the Central African Federation or the Federation of Rhodesia and Nyasaland which broke up into what are now the countries of Zambia (formerly Northern Rhodesia), Zimbabwe (the former Southern Rhodesia), and Malawi (formely Nyasaland). The three countries have many political, cultural and historical ties and could form a strong federation.

The dissolution of the federation in 1963 was even opposed by President Milton Obote of Uganda who argued that had the federation survived and emerged from colonial rule as a single political entity under one leadership, it would have had the potential to become a strong nation and would have been a step towards African unity and continental unification.

In East Africa during British colonial rule, African leaders in Kenya, Uganda and Tanganyika were resolutely opposed to formation of an East African federation by the colonialists.

They argued that if such a federation were formed, it would, together with the federation of Rhodesia and Nyasaland, and apartheid South Africa, have constituted a vast belt of white-ruled territory – from Kenya, Uganda and Tanganyika all the way down to the Cape – which would have helped to consolidate and perpetuate white rule and domination on the continent.

In his book *Towards A Pax Africana: A Study of Ideology and Ambition*,[50] Professor Ali Mazrui states that Obote was the only African leader who was opposed to the dissolution of the Federation of Rhodesia and Nyasaland because he felt that dissolving the federation was a step backwards in the quest for continental unity.

But there is still great potential for its revival, only in a different form as a vehicle for regional integration and continental unification instead of being an instrument of racial domination as it once was during British colonial rule.

Farther south, colonial ties could also facilitate formation of a federation comprising Botswana (once known as Bechuanaland during British colonial rule), Swaziland, Lesotho (known Basutoland when it was under the British) and South Africa.

Namibia, formerly known as South West Africa and once ruled by apartheid South Africa, could join the federation, as would Mozambique.

The people of all those countries also have had extensive historical, cultural and political ties for a long time as is the case with the people of the former Federation of Rhodesia and Nyasaland and of East Africa.

In the western part of the continent, there is also great potential for formation of a West African federation or smaller federations; for example, a federation of the countries of the Mano River Basin: Guinea, Sierra Leone and Liberia.

Ivory Coast can also join the federation whose nucleus is the Mano River Union, an association for economic cooperation formed by Liberia and Sierra Leone in 1973. Guinea joined the union in 1980.

The people of the four countries have extensive historical, ethno-cultural and linguistic ties predating colonialism.

The confederation of Senegal and The Gambia, known as Senegambia, can be revived. It was formed in 1982 and collapsed in 1989. The people of the two countries are the same in terms of historical, cultural, ethnic and linguistic ties.

Those are only a few examples of possible federations on the continent. Anything short of that will be a tragedy for Africa.

Africans can not even begin to think seriously in terms of sustained development, peace and security, without regional integration which can eventually lead to formation of federations, or confederations, across the continent. That is one of the challenges Africa is going to face in the twentieth-first century.

Prospects are dim that national boundaries will be completely erased. That is because of "the sanctity of borders," a cardinal principal that has been upheld by most African leaders since independence.

Unfortunately, many Africans invoke the sanctity of borders – to maintain their territorial integrity and national identities – to their detriment because they have not transcended their differences for the sake of African unity. Therefore it is unlikely that borders will be changed.

But something may still happen that will facilitate continental or subcontinental unity. Instead of national boundaries being abolished, what will probably happen is the loosening of borders through regional integration which may eventually lead to formation of federations or confederations in different parts of Africa.

Therefore, there may come a time when national boundaries will be rendered meaningless by the imperative need for regional integration when Africans realise that their countries can not develop, and can not survive and thrive as viable political and economic entities, without full cooperation with their neighbours and others on the continent.

Such cooperation will require the establishment of institutions and infrastructures which transcend national boundaries and sovereignties, leading to the creation of larger political and economic units in which national identities will be virtually submerged eventually leading to unification of the countries involved.

But this will require Africans to realise that they are Africans first, before anything else, and that all their other identities – ethnic, national, regional or subregional and so on – are secondary to that. Then and only then will they give concrete expression to the professed belief that "We are all Africans."

Appendix I:

Julius Nyerere: Reflections

YOU WANTED me to reflect. I told you I had very little time to reflect. I am not an engineer (reference to the vice-chancellor of the University of Dar es Salaam who identified himself as an engineer in his introductory remarks) and therefore what I am going to say might sound messy, unstructured and possibly irrelevant to what you intend to do; but I thought that if by reflecting, you wanted me to go back and relive the political life that I have lived for the last 30, 40 years, that I cannot do.

And in any case, in spite of the fact that it's useful to go back in history, what you are talking about is what might be of use to Africa in the 21st century. History's important, obviously, but I think we should concentrate and see what might be of use to our continent in the coming century.

What I want to do is share with you some thoughts on two issues concerning Africa. One, an obvious one; when I speak, you will realise how obvious it is. Another one, less obvious, and I'll spend a little more time on the less obvious one, because I think this will put Africa in what is going to be Africa's context in the 21st century.

And the new leadership of Africa will have to concern itself with the situation in which it finds itself in the world tomorrow – in the world of the 21st century. And the Africa I'm going to be talking about, is Africa south of the Sahara, sub-Saharan Africa. I'll explain later the reason why I chose to concentrate on Africa south of the Sahara. It is because of the point I want to emphasise.

It appears today that in the world tomorrow, there are going to be three centres of power: some, political power; some, economic power, but three centres of real power in the world. One centre is the United States of America and Canada; what you call North America. That is going to be a huge economic power, and probably for a long time the only military power, but a huge economic power.

The other one is going to be Western Europe, another huge economic power. I think Europe is choosing deliberately not to be a military power. I think they deliberately want to leave that to the United States.

The other one is Japan. Japan is in a different category but it is better to say Japan, because the power of Japan is quite clear, the economic power of Japan is obvious.

The three powers are going to affect the countries near them.

I was speaking in South Africa recently and I referred to Mexico. A former president of Mexico, I think it must have been after the revolution in 1935, no, after the revolution; a former president of Mexico is reported to have complained about his country or lamented about his country. "Poor Mexico," said the president, "so far from God yet so near the United States."

He was complaining about the disadvantages of being a neighbour of a giant.

Today, Mexico has decided not simply to suffer the disadvantages of being so close to the United States. And the United States itself has realised the importance of trying to accommodate Mexico.

In the past there were huge attempts by the United States to prevent people from moving from Mexico *into* the United States; people seeking work, seeking jobs. So you had police, a border very well policed in order to prevent Mexicans who *seek*, who *look* for jobs, to *move* into the United States. The United States discovered that it was not working. It *can't* work.

There is a kind of economic osmosis where whatever you do, if you are rich, you are attractive to the poor. They will come, they'll even *risk* their own lives in order to come. So the United States tried very hard to prevent Mexicans going into the United States; they've given up, and the result was NAFTA. It is in the interest of the United States to try and create jobs in Mexico because, if you don't, the Mexicans will simply come, to the United States; so they're doing that.

Europe, Western Europe, is very wealthy. It has two Mexicos. One is Eastern Europe. If you want to prevent those Eastern Europeans to come to Western Europe, you jolly will have to create jobs in *Eastern* Europe, and Western Europe is actually *doing* that. They are *doing* that. They'll help Eastern Europe to develop. The whole of Western Europe will be doing it, the Germans are doing it.

The Germans basically started first of all with the East Germans but they are spending lots of money also helping the other countries of Eastern Europe to develop, including unfortunately, or *fortunately* for them, including Russia. Because they realise, Europeans realise including the Germans, if you don't help *Russia* to develop, one of these days you are going to be in trouble. So it is in the interest of Western Europe, to help Eastern Europe including Russia.

They are pouring a lot of money in that part of the world, in that part of Europe, to try and help it to develop.

I said Western Europe has two Mexicos. I have mentioned one. I'll jump the other. I jump Europe's second

Mexico. I'll go to Asia. I'll go to Japan. Japan – a wealthy island, *very* wealthy indeed, but an *island*. I don't think they're very keen on the unemployed of Asia to go to Japan. They'd rather help them where they are, and Japan is spending a lot of money in Asia, to help create jobs *in* Asia, prevent those Asians dreaming about going to Japan to look for jobs. In any case, Japan is too small, they can't find wealth there.

But apart from what Japan is doing, of course Asia *is* Asia; Asia has *China!* Asia has *India*, and the small countries of Asia are not very small. The population of Indonesia is twice the population of Nigeria, your biggest. So Asia is virtually in a category, of the Third World countries, of the Southern countries; Asia is almost in a category of its own. It is developing as a power, and Europe knows it, and the United States knows it. And in spite of the *huge* Atlantic, now they are talking about the Atlantic *Rim*. That is in recognition of the importance of Asia.

I go back to Europe. Europe has a second Mexico. And Europe's second Mexico is North Africa. North Africa is to Europe what Mexico is to the United States. North Africans who have no jobs will not go to Nigeria; they'll be thinking of Europe or the Middle East, because of the imperatives of geography and history and religion and language. North Africa is part of Europe and the Middle East.

Nasser was a great leader and a great *African* leader. I got on extremely well with him. Once he sent me a minister, and I had a long discussion with his minister at the State House here, and in the course of the discussion, the minister says to me, "Mr. President, this is my first visit to Africa."

North Africa, because of the pull of the Mediterranean, and I say, history and culture, and religion, North Africa is pulled towards the North. When North Africans look for jobs, they go to Western Europe and southern Western

Europe, or they go to the Middle East. And Europe has a specific policy for North Africa, specific policy for North Africa. It's not only about development; it's also about security. Because of you don't do something about North Africa, they'll come.

Africa, south of the Sahara, is different; *totally* different. If you have no jobs here in Tanzania, where do you go? The Japanese have no fear that you people will flock to Japan. The North Americans have no fear that you people will flock to North America. Not even from West Africa. The Atlantic, the Atlantic as an ocean, like the Mediterranean, it has its own logic. But links North America and Western Europe, not North America and West Africa.

Africa south of the Sahara is isolated. That is the first point I want to make. South of the Sahara is totally isolated in terms of that configuration of developing power in the world in the 21st century – on its own. There is no centre of power in whose self-interest it's important to develop Africa, *no* centre. Not North America, not Japan, not Western Europe. There's no self-interest to bother about Africa south of the Sahara. Africa south of the Sahara is on its own. *Na sijambo baya.* Those of you who don't know Kiswahili, I just whispered, "Not necessarily bad."

That's the first thing I wanted to say about Africa south of the Sahara. African leadership, the coming African leadership, will have to bear that in mind.

You are on your own, Mr. Vice President. You mentioned, you know, in the past, there was some Cold War competition in Africa and some Africans may have exploited it. I never did. I never succeeded in exploiting the Cold War in Africa.

We suffered, we suffered through the Cold War. Look at Africa south of the Sahara. I'll be talking about it later. Southern Africa, I mean, look at southern Africa; devastated because of the combination of the Cold War

523

and apartheid. Devastated part of Africa. It could have been *very* different. But the Cold War is gone, thank God. But thank God the Cold War is gone, the chances of the Mobutus also is gone.

So that's the first thing I wanted to say about Africa south of the Sahara. Africa south of the Sahara in those terms is isolated. That is the point I said was not obvious and I had to explain it in terms in which I have tried to explain it. The other one, the second point I want to raise is completely obvious. Africa has 53 nation-states, most of them in Africa south of the Sahara. If numbers were power, Africa would be the most powerful continent on earth. It is the weakest; so it's obvious numbers are not power.

So the second point about Africa, and again I am talking about Africa south of the Sahara; it is fragmented, fragmented. From the very beginning of independence 40 years ago, we were against that idea, that the continent is so fragmented. We called it the Balkanisation of Africa. Today, I think the Balkans are talking about the Africanisation of Europe. Africa's states are too many, too small, some make no logic, whether political logic or ethnic logic or anything. They are non-viable. It is not a confession.

The OAU was founded in 1963. In 1964 we went to Cairo to hold, in a sense, our first summit after the inaugural summit. I was responsible for moving that resolution that Africa must accept the borders, which we inherited from colonialism; accept them as they are.

That resolution was passed by the organisation (OAU) with two reservations: one from Morocco, another from Somalia.

Let me say why I moved that resolution.

In 1960, just before this country became independent, I think I was then chief minister; I received a delegation of Masai elders from Kenya, led by an American missionary. And they came to persuade me to let the Masai invoke something called the Anglo-Masai Agreement so that that section of the Masai in Kenya should become part of Tanganyika; so that when Tanganyika becomes independent, it includes part of Masai, from Kenya.

I suspected the American missionary was responsible for that idea. I don't remember that I was particularly polite to him. Kenyatta was then in detention, and here somebody comes to me, that we should break up Kenya and make part of Kenya part of Tanganyika. But why shouldn't Kenyatta demand that the Masai part of Tanganyika should become Masai of Kenya? It's the same logic. That was in 1960.

In 1961 we became independent. In 1962, early 1962, I resigned as prime minister and then a few weeks later I received Dr. Banda. *Mungu amuweke mahali pema* (May God rest his soul in peace). I received Dr. Banda. We had just, FRELIMO had just been established here and we were now in the process of starting the armed struggle.

So Banda comes to me with a big old book, with lots and lots of maps in it, and tells me, "Mwalimu, what is this, what is Mozambique? There is no such thing as Mozambique." I said, "What do you mean there is no such thing as Mozambique?" So he showed me this map, and he said: "That part is part of Nyasaland (before it was renamed Malawi in 1966). That part is part of Southern Rhodesia, that part is Swaziland, and this part, which is the northern part, Makonde part, that is *your* part."

So Banda disposed of Mozambique just like that. I ridiculed the idea, and Banda never liked anybody to ridicule his ideas. So he left and went to Lisbon to talk to Salazar about this wonderful idea. I don't know what Salazar told him. That was '62.

In '63 we go to Addis Ababa for the inauguration of the OAU, and Ethiopia and Somalia are at war over the Ogaden. We had to send a special delegation to bring the president of Somalia to attend that inaugural summit, because the two countries were at *war*. Why? Because

Somalia wanted the Ogaden, a *whole* province of Ethiopia, saying, "That is part of Somalia." And Ethiopia was quietly, the Emperor quietly saying to us that "the whole of Somalia is part of Ethiopia."

So those three, the delegation of the Masai, led by the American missionary; Banda's old book of maps; and the Ogaden, caused me to move that resolution, in Cairo 1964. And I say, the resolution was accepted, two countries with reservations, and one was Somalia because Somalia wanted the Ogaden; Somalia wanted northern Kenya; Somalia wanted Djibouti.

Throw away all our ideas about socialism. Throw them away, give them to the Americans, give them to the Japanese, give them, so that they can, I don't know, they can do whatever they like with them. *Embrace* capitalism, fine! But you *have* to be self-reliant.

You here in Tanzania don't dream that if you privatise every blessed thing, including the prison, then foreign investors will come rushing. No! No! Your are dreaming! *Hawaji*! They won't come! (*hawaji*!). You just try it.

There is more to privatise in Eastern Europe than here. Norman Manley, the Prime Minister of Jamaica, in those days the vogue was nationalisation, not privatisation. In those days the vogue was *nationalisation*. So Norman Manley was asked as Jamaica was moving towards independence: "Mr. Prime Minister, are you going to nationalise the economy?" His answer was: "You can't nationalise *nothing*."

You people here are busy privatising not *nothing*, we did *build* something, we built *something* to privatise. But quite frankly, for the appetite of Europe, and the appetite of North America, this is privatising nothing. The people with a really good appetite will go to Eastern Europe, they'll go to Russia, they'll not come rushing to Tanzania! Your blessed National Bank of Commerce, it's a branch of some major bank somewhere, and in Tanzania you say, "It's so big we must divide it into pieces," which is *nonsense.*

Africa south of the Sahara is isolated. Therefore, to develop, it will have to depend upon its own resources basically. Internal resources, nationally; and Africa will have to depend upon Africa. The leadership of the future will have to devise, try to carry out policies of *maximum* national self-reliance and *maximum* collective self-reliance. They have no other choice. *Hamna!* (You don't have it!)

And this, this need to organise collective self-reliance is what moves me to the second part.

The small countries in Africa must move towards either unity or co-operation, unity of Africa. The leadership of the future, of the 21st century, should have less respect, less respect for this thing called "national sovereignty." I'm not saying take up arms and destroy the state, no! This idea that we must *preserve* the Tanganyika, then *preserve* the Kenya as they *are*, is nonsensical! The nation-states we in Africa, have inherited from Europe. They are the builders of the nation-states par excellence. For centuries they fought wars!

The history of Europe, the history of the *building* of Europe is a history of war. And sometimes their wars when they get hotter although they're European wars, they call them *world wars*. And we all get involved. We fight even in Tanganyika here, we *fought* here, one world war.

These Europeans, powerful, where little Belgium is more powerful than the whole of Africa south of the Sahara put together; these *powerful* European states are moving towards unity, and you people are talking about the atavism of the tribe, this is nonsense! I am telling *you* people. How can anybody think of the tribe as the unity of the future? *Hakuna!* (There's nothing!).

Europe now, you can take it almost as God-given, Europe is not going to fight with Europe anymore. The Europeans are not going to take up arms against Europeans.

They are moving towards unity – even the little, the little countries of the Balkans which are breaking up, Yugoslavia breaking up, but they are breaking up at the same time the building up is taking place. They break up and say we want to come into the *bigger* unity. So there's a *building* movement, there's a *building* of Europe. These countries which have old, old sovereignties, countries of hundreds of years old; they are forgetting this, they are *moving* towards unity. And you people, you think Tanzania is sacred? What is Tanzania!

You *have* to move towards unity. If these powerful countries see that they have no future in the nation-states – *ninyi mnafikiri mna future katika nini*? (what future do you think you have?).

So, if we can't *move*, if our leadership, our future leadership cannot move us to bigger nation-states, which I *hope* they are going to try; we tried and failed. I tried and failed. One of my biggest failures was actually that. I tried in East Africa and failed. But don't give up because we, the first leadership, failed, no! *Unajaribu tena*! (You try again!). We failed, but the idea is a good idea. That these countries should come together.

Don't leave Rwanda and Burundi on their own. *Hawawezi kusurvive* (They cannot survive). They can't. They're locked up into a form of prejudice. If we can't move towards bigger nation-states, at least let's move towards greater co-operation. This is beginning to happen. And the new leadership in Africa should encourage it.

I want to say only one or two things about what is happening in southern Africa. Please accept the logic of coming together. South Africa, small; South Africa is very small. Their per capita income now is, I think $2,000 a year or something around that. Compared with Tanzanians, of course, it is very big, but it's poor.

If South Africa begins to tackle the problems of the legacy of apartheid, they have no money! But compared with the rest of us, they are rich. And so, in southern

Africa, there, there is also a kind of osmosis, also an economic osmosis. South Africa's neighbours send their job seekers *into* South Africa. And South Africa will simply have to accept the logic of that, that they are big, they are attractive. They attract the unemployed from Mozambique, and from Lesotho and from the rest. They have to accept that fact of life. It's a problem, but they have to accept it.

South Africa, and I am talking about post-apartheid South Africa. Post-apartheid South Africa has the most developed and the most dynamic private sector on the continent. It is white, so what? So forget it is white. It is South African, dynamic, highly developed. If the investors of South Africa begin a new form of trekking, you *have* to accept it.

It will be ridiculous, absolutely ridiculous, for Africans to go out seeking investment from North America, from Japan, from Europe, from Russia, and then, when these investors come from South Africa to invest in your own country, you say, "a! a! These fellows now want to take over our economy" - this is nonsense. You can't have it both ways. You want foreign investors or you don't want foreign investors. Now, the most available foreign investors for you are those from South Africa.

And let me tell you, when Europe think in terms of investing, they *might* go to South Africa. When North America think in terms of investing, they *might* go to South Africa. Even Asia, if they want to invest, the first country they may think of in Africa *may* be South Africa. So, if *your* South Africa is going to be *your* engine of development, accept the reality, accept the reality.

Don't accept this sovereignty, South Africa will reduce your sovereignty. What sovereignty do you have? Many of these debt-ridden countries in Africa now have no sovereignty, they've lost it. *Imekwenda* (It's gone). *Iko mikononi mwa IMF na World Bank* (It's in the hands of the IMF and the World Bank). *Unafikiri kuna sovereignty*

529

gani? (What kind of sovereignty do you think there is?).

So, southern Africa has an opportunity, southern Africa, the SADC group, *because* of South Africa.

Because South Africa now is no longer a destabiliser of the region, but a partner in development, southern Africa has a tremendous opportunity. But you need leadership, because if you get proper leadership there, within the next 10, 15 years, that region is going to be the ASEAN (Association of South-East Asian Nations) of Africa. And it is possible. But forget the protection of your sovereignties. I believe the South Africans will be sensitive enough to know that if they are not careful, there is going to be this resentment of big brother, but that big brother, frankly, is not very big.

West Africa. Another bloc is developing there, but that depends very much upon Nigeria my brother (looking at the Nigerian High Commissioner – Ambassador), very much so.

Without Nigeria, the future of West Africa is a problem. West Africa is more balkanised than Eastern Africa. More balkanised, tiny little states. The leadership will have to come from Nigeria. It came from Nigeria in Liberia; it has come from Nigeria in the case of Sierra Leone; it will have to come from Nigeria in galvanising ECOWAS. But the military in Nigeria must allow the Nigerians to exercise that vitality in freedom. And it is my hope that they will do it.

I told you I was going to ramble and it was going to be messy, but thank you very much.

Source:
Mwalimu Nyerere Memorial Site: Written Speeches, South Centre, Geneva, Switzerland, 2001.
This is an abridged version of Nyerere's speech at an international conference at the University of Dar es Salaam, Tanzania, December 15, 1997. The transcription of the non-written speech came from Mrs. Magombe of

the Nyerere Foundation, Dar es Salaam.

Translation of Kiswahili words, phrases and sentences in Nyerere's speech into English in the preceding text, done by the author, Godfrey Mwakikagile.

Appendix II:

Land Grab or Development Opportunity?

With land central to the livelihoods of millions of people in Africa, Lorenzo Cotula of the International Institute for Environment and Development examines the impact of large-scale land acquisitions on the continent's farmers.

"Land grabs" are now one of the biggest issues in Africa.

Over the past few years, companies and foreign governments have been leasing large areas of land in some of Africa's poorest countries.

Many commentators have raised concerns that poor villagers will be forced off their land and agribusiness will marginalise family farming.

Others say that foreign investment can help African countries create jobs, increase export earnings and use more advanced technologies.

Three years since media reports started raising public awareness on this issue, evidence has been growing on the scale, geography, players, features and impacts of the land rush. The emerging picture provides ground for concern.

Last year the World Bank documented media reports of land deals over the period between 2008 and 2009.

The deals were for nearly 60 million hectares worldwide, roughly the size of a country like Ukraine – and two-thirds of the land acquired was in Africa.

While new figures continue to emerge, all evidence points to a phenomenon of unprecedented scale.

Also, some individual deals are for very large areas. For example, Liberia recently signed a concession for 220,000 hectares.

Money to be made

Media attention has focused on investments by Middle Eastern and Asian government-backed operators but Western companies have also been heavily involved.

Companies acquire land because they expect world food and commodity prices to increase – so there is money to be made in agriculture.

Some governments have also promoted land acquisitions abroad as a way to secure affordable food for their people.

In many African countries, agriculture has suffered from years of neglect – and investment is needed to improve productivity and market access.

But not all investment is good – and growing evidence strongly indicates that large land deals are not the way to go.

Short-lived jobs

A synthesis of over 30 reports worldwide found that many investments have failed due to insufficient soil fertility, financing difficulties or over-ambitious business plans. For example, in Mozambique and Tanzania, some large biofuels projects have now been abandoned.

Even where investments are profitable, it is often difficult to see how they contribute to poverty reduction. The jobs created are few, short-lived and low-paid – and public revenues are limited by tax exemptions.

A report published last year raised serious questions about the terms of the contracts that governments are signing up to. Some of the world's poorest people are losing the land, water and natural resources that have supported their livelihoods for generations. In Uganda, for example, 20,000 people claim to have been evicted from their land and a legal case is pending before courts.

Not every deal is a "land grab" – much depends on local context, the investor's track-record, the terms of the lease, and whether these reflect the free, prior and informed consent of local landholders.

But for local people, the context in which the deals are being concluded tends to make negative outcomes more likely.

Best intentions

There are huge power imbalances among international companies, government and local landholders. Many land deals are being negotiated without transparency and local consultation.

In many parts of Africa, local farmers, herders and gatherers only have insecure legal rights to the land they see as theirs. Most have no written documents for their land. Much land is owned by the state, which can allocate it to outside investors even against local opposition.

And while international law provides relatively effective protection for foreign investment, international human rights law remains inaccessible and ineffective for people losing land.

So even when investors come with the best intentions, this means local groups are exposed to the risk of dispossession – and investors to legal disputes.

Family farmers have long provided the backbone of African agriculture – and, when given a chance, they have been able to compete on global markets.

Family farming

In Ghana, for example, a co-operative of 60,000 cocoa farmers has run a successful business for nearly 20 years and owns 45% of a UK company that manufactures and distributes chocolate.

The global demand for food and agricultural commodities creates new opportunities for African farmers.

Public policies and infrastructure to support family farming are needed today more than ever.

Evidence also shows that private investments to improve productivity or market access can be structured in ways that support local farmers.

Many companies successfully source agricultural produce from family farmers, and have invested in other activities along the production line – in ways that secure their supplies and improve local livelihoods.

In Mali and Zambia, some farmer associations own shares in the company they collaborate with, which gives them monetary benefits and a greater say.

Co-operatives or intermediaries can reduce the costs linked to working with large numbers of farmers. Public policy plays a key role in promoting fairer investment models.

The perception that large plantations are needed to "modernise" agriculture in poorer countries is dominant in many government circles.

But evidence shows that this perception is misplaced.

Promoting agricultural development in Africa and

addressing the world's food security challenges requires investing in farmers – not in farmland.

Source:
BBC Africa, London, 21 February 2012.

Appendix III:

Hedge funds 'grabbing land' in Africa

Hedge funds are behind "land grabs" in Africa to boost their profits in the food and biofuel sectors, a US think-tank says.

In a report, the Oakland Institute said hedge funds and other foreign firms had acquired large swathes of African land, often without proper contracts.

It said the acquisitions had displaced millions of small farmers.

Foreign firms farm the land to consolidate their hold over global food markets, the report said.

They also use land to "make room" for export commodities such as biofuels and cut flowers.

"This is creating insecurity in the global food system that could be a much bigger threat than terrorism," the report said.

The Oakland Institute said it released its findings after studying land deals in Ethiopia, Tanzania, South Sudan, Sierra Leone, Mali and Mozambique.

'Risky manoeuvre'

It said hedge funds and other speculators had, in 2009 alone, bought or leased nearly 60m hectares of land in Africa – an area the size of France.

"The same financial firms that drove us into a global recession by inflating the real estate bubble through risky financial manoeuvres are now doing the same with the world's food supply," the report said.

It added that some firms obtained land after deals with gullible traditional leaders or corrupt government officials.

"The research exposed investors who said it is easy to make a deal – that they could usually get what they wanted in exchange for giving a poor tribal chief a bottle of Johnnie Walker [whisky]," said Anuradha Mittal, executive director of the Oakland Institute.

"When these investors promise progress and jobs to local chiefs it sounds great, but they don't deliver."

The report said the contracts also gave investors a range of incentives, from unlimited water rights to tax waivers.

"No-one should believe that these investors are there to feed starving Africans. These deals only lead to dollars in the pockets of corrupt leaders and foreign investors," said Obang Metho of Solidarity Movement for New Ethiopia, a US-based campaign group.

However, not all companies named in the report accept that their motives are as suggested and they dismiss claims that their presence in Africa is harmful.

One company, EmVest Asset Management, strongly denied that it was involved in exploitative or illegal practices.

"There are no shady deals. We acquire all land in terms of legal tender," EmVest's Africa director Anthony Poorter told the BBC.

He said that in Mozambique the company's employees

earned salaries 40% higher than the minimum wage.

The company was also involved in development projects such as the supply of clean water to rural communities.

"They are extremely happy with us," Mr Poorter said.

Source:
BBC Africa, London, 8 June 2011.

Appendix IV:

Ethiopia forces thousands off land

Ethiopia's government has been accused of forcing tens of thousands of people off their land so it can be leased to foreign investors.

US-based Human Rights Watch says people are being forcibly relocated to new villages that lack adequate food, farmland and facilities.

Ethiopia has already leased out more than 3.6 million hectares (8.8m acres) of land – an area the size of The Netherlands – HRW says.

Addis Ababa rejects HRW's allegations.

"I can tell you that it is baseless – on both grounds – on both the land grab issue and resettlement of the people," Ethiopian Information Minister Bereket Simon told the BBC World Service.

"No-one is forced [to leave their homes]. This is an absolute lie. The people around Gambella are inhabiting the place in a very scattered manner."

"It is true that we are providing access to land on a lease basis for 25 years for local and foreign developers. We have about three million hectares of land which is not inhabited by anybody."

'Weaker and weaker'

HRW says it has evidence that some 70,000 indigenous people in the western Gambella region were relocated against their will to new villages that "lack adequate food, farmland, healthcare and educational facilities."

The group said it spoke to more than 100 people in May and June last year for the report.

"My father was beaten for refusing to go along [to the new village] with some other elders," a former villager told HRW.

"He said: 'I was born here – my children were born here – I am too old to move so I will stay.' He was beaten by the army with sticks and the butt of a gun. He had to be taken to hospital. He died because of the beating – he just became weaker and weaker."

HRW says that the residents of Gambella have never had formal title to the land they lived on and used – and the government often claimed the areas are "uninhabited" or "under-utilised,"

That claim, HRW says, enables the government to bypass constitutional provisions and laws that would protect these populations from being relocated.

The government in Addis Ababa has said in the past that all the moves are voluntary, the new villages will have adequate infrastructure and everyone who moves will be given assistance to help their transition to a new livelihood.

But HRW says many of the new villages have no access to government services at all, and people are arriving at the worst time of year – the beginning of the harvest – to find the land has not been cleared and prepared for growing.

"The government failure to provide food assistance for relocated people has caused endemic hunger and cases of starvation," HRW says.

Magn Nyang, who lives in Minneapolis in the US, says his mother was forcibly re-settled from a village close to Gambella town to a camp.

"When the investors came in they took over the land and they [the villagers] were kicked out," he told the BBC World Service.

"They were relocated under the pretext that they were going to get clean water, health clinics built for them, schools for their children – but none of that happened."

Food crisis

The Oakland Institute, a US think tank that released a report last year about foreign firms acquiring land in Africa, described the situation as a "land rush."

"Hundreds of investors from all over the world rushing to Africa – lured by cheap land prices, availability of land – all for the sake of taking over these productive lands to be able to grow foods for exports," Anuradha Mittal, Oakland Institute's executive director, told the BBC.

"Our research – and reports by other human rights organisations – shows that this is happening at the expense of the most vulnerable people," she said.

BBC business reporter Duncan Bartlett reported in June 2011 that Saudi Arabia and China planned to acquire large tracts of land, particularly in Gambella, to grow more than one million tonnes of rice to take back to their own countries.

Ethiopia's Deputy Prime Minister and Minister of Foreign Affairs Hailemariam Desalegn told him the arrangement was an advantage to the country.

He said the area being leased is lowland, where farmers are not willing to go and plough the land. It is often infested with malaria and the climate made it unsuitable for small holder farmers.

And he denied it would lead to food shortages and higher prices in a part of the world already suffering from a food crisis.

"Small holder farmers feed themselves first and sell when there is a marketable surplus," he said, adding that government subsidies helped those in urban areas.

Source:
BBC Africa, London, 17 January 2012.

Appendix V:

Land-grab phenomenon threatens Africa

Critics question the wisdom of producing food for foreign consumption in regions where many go hungry — especially when the land deals displace local subsistence farmers.

There is a gold rush happening in Ethiopia, but it is not a hunt for the yellow metal. It is a quest for the green gold of fertile farmland. A nation more associated with periodic famine and acute childhood malnutrition than with agricultural bounty is leasing millions of hectares — an area the size of Belgium — to foreign companies, who want to grow and export food to places like Saudi Arabia, China, India and Europe.

One-third of the fertile Gambella area in western Ethiopia, for example, is being leased for the next 50 years by the Bengaluru-based food company Karuturi Global. Forests are being clear-cut, swamps drained, rivers diverted and whole villages moved to make way for flower farms and palm-oil and rice plantations.

"It is very good land. It is quite cheap ... We have no land like this in India," effused Karuturi's project manager Karmjeet Shekhon to the *Guardian* soon after the lease was settled in 2011.

The government in Addis Ababa says it needs foreign companies like Karuturi Global to help create jobs, raise Ethiopia's income from food exports and develop the agricultural technology and infrastructure that can bring the impoverished country into the mainstream of the global market economy. It has enticed investors with tax breaks alongside rock-bottom lease rates (as little as $1, or Dh3.67, per hectare per year).

But at what cost — to land rights, to human health, to the environment, to national stability?

It is a question being asked not only in Ethiopia but across Africa. As I report in the current issue of the journal *Ethics and International Affairs*, many other countries are also welcoming big agricultural projects bankrolled by foreign investors whose goal is to send food abroad.

Liberia has reportedly signed concessions for nearly one-third of its national territory in recent years. (Liberia, like many other African nations, claims government ownership of all the country's arable land).

Half of the Democratic Republic of the Congo's agricultural lands are being leased to grow crops, including palm oil for the production of biofuels.

Perhaps the largest single venture to date is the ProSavana Project in northern Mozambique, where an area roughly the size of Switzerland and Austria combined has been leased by Brazilian and Japanese companies to produce soybeans and maize for export.

Critics question the wisdom of producing food for foreign consumption in regions where many go hungry — especially when the land deals displace local subsistence farmers.

In Mozambique, where more than 80 per cent of the overall population depends on family farming, authorities claim that the land seized for ProSavana is unoccupied. But surveys by the country's National Research Institute show that it is an area of shifting seasonal cultivation and grazing and the nonprofit group GRAIN estimates that millions of peasant farmers are losing their land as a result of forced resettlement schemes.

In Ethiopia, meanwhile, 1.5 million farmers and pastoralists have been moved off of their land to make way for new industrial farms.

According to Olivier de Schutter, the United Nations special rapporteur on the right to food, the reverse transfer of agricultural wealth is a new form of colonialism. Outside powers, with the help of local governments, claim that they are helping countries develop, de Schutter says, when their real motive is to exploit resources to ensure their own food security. "Small-scale family agriculture, on which most of the world's rural poor still depend," he argues, "is threatened by large-scale plantations, export-led agriculture and the production not of food but commodities."

To make matters worse, the land-grab phenomenon also threatens to foster instability and conflict over scarce resources, population shifts and the best way to feed expanding countries.

Lack of access to food and farmland will likely lead to social unrest in future years, warn scholars at the independent academic research organisation, the New England Complex Systems Institute. "Conditions of widespread threat to security are particularly present when food is inaccessible to the population at large," they write. "In [such cases] even the threat of death does not deter actions that are taken in opposition to the political order."

Wealthy countries have always looked to faraway, resource-rich lands for food exports.

Europeans established plantations throughout the world in the 19th century and multinational food companies have done the same in the post-colonial era.

However, recent land grabs are different and not just in scope: Whereas in the past, most export agriculture focused on products that could not be grown at home (bananas, citrus, coffee, cocoa), today's projects often grow staple food crops like soy, wheat, rice, as well as oils for biofuels.

The African land grabs began in earnest after the global food crisis peaked in 2008.

The start of the Arab Spring, which was in no small part a response to the price of wheat more than doubling in under a year, was a wake-up call heard around the world — especially in countries like the Gulf states and the Asian 'tiger economies' with limited capacity to grow their own food. Corporations in these countries started acquiring terrain in Africa, the continent with the highest percentage of available arable land, as an insurance policy against extreme price volatility on the global market. And African governments, desperate for infusions of cash and technology, were willing partners.

The UN has proposed some ground rules to regulate these land deals, but they are non-binding and frequently flouted, leading to a chaotic situation. "It appears to be like the Wild West," said Jos Graziano da Silva, the head of UN's Food and Agriculture Organisation, "and we need a sheriff and law in place."

This lack of effective regulation threatens the livelihoods and basic rights of millions of Africans.

In a scathing 2012 report on Ethiopia's Gambella region, Human Rights Watch documented arbitrary arrests, rapes, beatings and killings of those who have resisted leaving their villages to make way for foreign projects, as well as starvation among the newly landless.

This hunger is caused in part by the diversion of agricultural land away from local food production, which has boosted food prices.

Graham Peebles, the director of Create Trust, a Britain-based charity that runs education projects in Ethiopia, writes that the leasing of fields formerly used for the cultivation of the staple teff "is largely responsible for costs of teff (used to make *injera* — the daily bread) quadrupling in the last four years."

On the security front, controversial land deals have already sparked violence. In Ethiopia, members of the Suri tribe have taken up arms against the military to try to stop the diversion of the Koka River to irrigate a Malaysian plantation project, which threatens to drive them from their villages in a fertile floodplain.

And when the South Korean industrial giant Daewoo struck a deal to lease half of all the arable land in Madagascar for the production of corn and biofuels, a bloody uprising led to the ouster of the country's president, Marc Ravalomanana. (His successor's first act in office was to revoke the unpopular deal).

There may be trouble ahead for Liberia as well. An op-ed by two land rights activists in the *New York Times* last year argued that massive land transfers threaten Liberia's fragile stability. "These concessions come at a delicate time," Silas Kpanan'ayoung Siakor and Rachel Knight wrote, "as violent local-level land disputes both between and within villages are still widespread throughout Liberia." Emmanuel Jangebah, a tribal chief in Totoquelle, a village slated to be "developed" for oil palms by a Malaysian corporation, put the matter bluntly: "If we see bulldozers in the bush, we will take our machetes and run to meet them," he told *OnEarth* magazine.

There is also potential for violence in the newly formed nation of South Sudan, where the government has lost no time in leasing nearly 10 per cent of its territory to foreign investors — an alarming development, according to David Deng, research director of the South Sudan Law Society. "It is fairly clear to us all that poorly planned investments can contribute to conflict, particularly in fragile, post-conflict states," Deng told the *Guardian* in 2012. "But conflict can also attract investment, as opportunistic

551

companies come to take advantage of power vacuums and in the case of South Sudan, of a massive transfer of wealth to a bureaucratically weak government."

These are just a few of the places where instability looms, if land acquisitions are not better regulated and managed.

Troublingly, however, some African governments are expressing discontent over land grabs for reasons other than the threat of conflict and human rights violations. In Ethiopia, the Karuturi project is lagging behind schedule due to flooding, poor infrastructure and other issues. Addis Ababa, in response, says it will pull support and licences for utilising land from projects that do not develop as quickly as it wants. "If the failure is their failure then we will be obliged to take the measure," Agriculture Minister Tefera Deribew said in an interview with Bloomberg in late November (Research has estimated that some multinationals are also waiting for the right market conditions before they exploit land they have obtained, letting it lie fallow in the meantime).

Nobody denies that Africa's agriculture needs to be improved, and soon, if the continent is to feed its rapidly growing population. (The population of Ethiopia, for instance, is expected to triple from 90 million to more than 278 million by 2050.) But to ensure future food security, a fair balance needs to be struck between increasing agricultural exports and serving local needs.

Stephen O'Brien, parliamentary under-secretary of state for international development in Britain, says it is vital that "the interests of the poorest and most marginalised groups are taken into account, both in the decision-making process when looking at whether to sell agricultural land, and in getting their fair share of the subsequent benefits, whether financial or food produced."

One way that local farmers can be served is by sharing with them the latest knowledge about small-scale, "agroecological" or low-input sustainable farming, which does not require costly agrochemicals, genetically modified seeds, and mechanised farm equipment in order to succeed. Agronomists have developed inexpensive ways to boost the productivity of small family plots, which can produce equal and, in some cases, higher yields than large plantations do.

The Oakland Institute, a California-based think tank that focuses on agriculture and land-rights issues, cites the System of Rice Intensification (SRI) along the Niger River in Mali as a model operation. The SRI, a low-input cooperative irrigation system, involves tiny plots of only one-third of a hectare. Yet it grows an average of nine tonnes per hectare, more than twice the production of Moulin Moderne du Mali, a major multinational investor, and its farmers are able to earn $1,879 a year, more than double Mali's average per-capita income.

Such small-scale projects can potentially keep huge numbers of family farmers profitably employed and produce food for local markets while preserving land for future generations.

And critically, undertaking these projects does not mean abandoning the large-scale production of food for foreign markets. (Export dollars, after all, do matter economically.) Multinational corporations can help accomplish both goals: In exchange for being granted licences to grow food for export, corporations should be contractually required to invest in local agriculture and offer technical assistance and infrastructure improvements for small landholders.

For this to happen, however, the playing field between local and foreign interests must be levelled. Binding rules need to be established by international bodies — and agreed to by African governments and multinational corporations — which will protect the rights of indigenous farmers, as well as ensure the integrity of Africa's environment, soil and water. Otherwise, the hastily negotiated land deals will continue to shortchange the long-term interests of millions of Africans, leading to more hunger, displacement, even turmoil.

Source:
Richard Schiffman, "Land-grab phenomenon threatens Africa," *Gulf News*, December 26, 2013. The same article was published under the title, "Green Rush: How big agriculture is carving up Africa for industrial farmland," in *Foreign Policy*, December 17, 2013.

Chapter notes:

Chapter One

1. Ahmadu Bello, quoted by Odumegwu Ojukwu in his speech to the Organization of African Unity (OAU), seeking recognition of the secessionist region of Eastern Nigeria as the independent Republic of Biafra, in Addis Ababa, Ethiopia, August 5, 1968, in Colin Legum and John Drysdale, *Africa Contemporary Record: Annual Survey and Documents 1968 - 1969* (London: Africa Research Ltd., 1969), p. 670.

2. Northern Nigerian delegation to the Ad Hoc Conference on the Nigerian Constitution, Lagos, Nigeria, September 1966, in *Africa Contemporary Record*, ibid.

3. Odumegwu Ojukwu, ibid., p. 652.

4. Obafemi Awolowo, *Path to Nigerian Freedom* (London: Faber & Faber, 1947), chap.5. See also George Padmore, *Pan-Africanism or Communism?: The Coming Struggle for Africa* (London: Dennis Dobson, 1956), p. 276.

5. Kenneth Kaunda, quoted in *Africa Contemporary*

Record, op. cit., p. 245. See also Kenneth Kaunda, in *Times of Zambia*, Lusaka, Zambia, February 1968.

6. Obafemi Awolowo, *Path to Nigerian Freedom*, op. cit.

7. Julius Nyerere, quoted by James C. McKinley Jr., "Many Failures, and One Big Success," in the *International Herald Tribune*, September 2, 1996, p. 2.

8. Ibid.

9. Julius Nyerere, quoted in *Sunday Independent*, Johannesburg, South Africa, October 17, 1999; and by R.W. Johnson, "Nyerere: A Flawed Hero," in *The National Interest*, Washington, D.C., No. 60, Summer 2000, p. 73.

On Tanzania's achievements under his leadership despite many failures, see Nyerere in R.W. Johnson, "Nyerere: A Flawed Hero," ibid. As Johnson stated: "Until the end Nyerere was proud about how well he had served Tanzanians. As he told the World Bank: 'We took over a country with 85 percent of its adults illiterate. The British ruled us for 43 years. When they left, there were two trained engineers and 12 doctors. When I stepped down there was 91 percent literacy and nearly every child was in school. We trained thousands of engineers, doctors and teachers.'"

10. Nyerere, in his radio broadcast to the nation on the seventh anniversary of Tanzania's independence, Radio Tanzania, Dar es Salaam (RTD), December 9, 1968, quoted in *Africa Contemporary Record*, op. cit., pp. 216 - 217. See also full text of the speech released in Kiswahili, and translated into English, by the Tanzania Ministry of Information and Broadcasting, Dar es Salaam, Tanzania, December 10, 1968.

11. Nicephore D. Soglo, "Benin's Election Was A Victory for Democracy and the People," in *The Washington Post*, reprinted in the *International Herald Tribune*, August 24 - 25, 1996, p. 6.

12. Godfrey Mwakikagile, *Military Coups in West Africa since the Sixties* (Huntington, New York: Nova

Science Publishers, Inc., 2001), pp. 7 - 13. See also, pp. 211 - 232.

13. Crawford Young, "The Impossible Necessity of Nigeria: A Struggle for Nationhood," in *Foreign Affairs*, November/December 1996, p. 142. See also, Wole Soyinka, *The Open Sore of A Continent: A Personal Narrative of the Nigerian Crisis* (New York: Oxford University Press, 1996).

14. Wole Soyinka, *The Open Sore of A Continent*, op. cit., p. 8; George B.N. Ayittey, *Africa in Chaos* (New York: St. Martin's Press, 1998), p. 171.

15. Soyinka, ibid. See also, "Soyinka at SOAS (Schoo of Oriental and African Studies, University of London), in *Africa Analysis: Fortnightly Bulletin of Financial and Political Trends*, London, No. 259, 1 November, 1996, p. 5.

16. Ibid.

17. Crawford Young, "The Impossible Necessity of Nigeria: A Struggle for Nationhood," in *Foreign Affairs*, op. cit., p. 143.

18. Sekou Toure, quoted in *West Africa*, July 22, 1961, p. 799. See also Julius Nyerere, "One-Party Rule," in *Spreahead*, Dar es Salaam, Tanganyika, November 1961; Nyerere, "The Role of African Trade Unions," in *Labour*, Accra, Ghana, June 1961; Gwendolen M. Carter, editor, *African One-Party States* (Ithaca, New York: Cornell University Press, 1962); Thomas Hodgkin, *African Political Parties* (Baltimore, Maryland: Penguin Books, 1961); Immanuel Wallerstein, *Africa: The Politics of Independence* (New York: Random House, 1961); Herbert J. Spiro, *Politics in Africa: Prospects South of the Sahara* (Englewood Cliffs, New Jersey: Prentice-Hall, 1962).

See also, in his analysis of the creation of a new nation, David Apter, *The Gold Coast in Transition* (Princeton, New Jersey: Princeton University Press, 1955). And for a distinction between "mobilization" and "consociational" regimes, see David Apter, *The Political*

Kingdom of Uganda (Princeton, New Jersey: Princeton University Press, 1961). See also Thomas Hodgkin, "A Note on the Language of African Nationalism," in *African Affairs*, Carbondale, Illinois, No. 1, 1961, pp. 22 - 40.

For a general comparison between Africa and other developing regions of the world, see Gabriel Almond and James S. Coleman, *The Politics of the Developing Areas* (Princeton, New Jersey: Princeton University Press, 1960); Rupert Emerson, >*From Empire to Nation* (Cambridge, Massachusetts: Harvard University Press, 1960); Vera Micheles Dean, *Builders of Emerging Nations* (New York: Holt, Rinehart and Winston, 1961); Max F. Millikan and Donald L.M. Blackmer, editors, *The Emerging Nations* (Boston: Little, Brown & Co., 1961); John H. Kautsky, editor, *Political Change in Underdeveloped Countries* (New York: John Wiley & Sons, 1962); Barbara Ward, *The Rich Nations and the Poor Nations* (New York: W.W. Norton & Co., 1962).

19. Sekou Toure, in *La Lutte du Parti Democratique de Guinee pour l'Emancipation Africaine* (Conakry, Guinea: Imprimerie National, 1959), pp. 58, and 149; translated in Sekou Toure, "African Emancipation," in Paul E. Sigmund, Jr., editor, *The Ideologies of the Developing Nations* (New York: Frederick A. Praeger, 1963), pp. 154 - 169.

For an opposing view on the one-party system, see Nnamdi Azikiwe, "Parliament and Parties," and "Parliamentary Democracy," in Nnamdi Azikiwe, *Zik: A Selection from Speeches of Nnamdi Azikiwe* (New York: Cambridge University Press, 1961); Obafemi Awolowo, "A Critique of One-Party Systems," in *Awo: The Autobiography of Chief Obafemi Awolowo* (New York: Cambridge University Press, 1961); James S. Wunsch and Dele Olowu, editors, *The Failure of the Centralized State: Institutions and Self-Governance in Africa* (Boulder, Colorado: West View Press, 1996).

20. Robert S. Greenberger, "Africa Ascendant: New

Leaders Replace Yesteryear's 'Big Men,' and Tanzania Benefits," in *The Wall Street Journal*, December 10, 1996, pp. A1, and A5.

21. Thomas Sowell, *Race and Culture: A World View* (New York: Basic Books, 1994).

22. Godfrey Mwakikagile, *Africa and the West* (Huntington, New York: Nova Science Publishers, Inc., 2000).

23. Harold Cruse, *The Crisis of the Negro Intellectual* (New York: William Morrow, 1967).

24. Harold Cruse, *Rebellion or Revolution?* (New York: William Morrow, 1968), pp. 240 - 241. See also, Cornel West, *Race Matters* (Boston, Massachusetts: Beacon Press, 1993); Andrew Hacker, *Two Nations: Black and White, Hostile, Unequal* (New York: Ballantine, 1992).

25. Bailey Wyat, a former slave, quoted by Hugh Pearson, "The Birth of the New South," in *The Wall Street Journal*, June 24, 1996.

26. Ali A. Mazrui, *Towards A Pax Africana* (London: Weidenfeld & Nicolson, 1967), p. 97.

27. Kwame Nkrumah, *Ghana: The Autobiography of Kwame Nkrumah* (New York: Thomas Nelson and Sons, 1957). See also Julius Nyerere, "The Rational Choice," in Andrew Caulson, editor, *African Socialism in Practice* (Nottingham: Russel Press, 1979), pp. 19 - 26; "False Starts: Capitalist and Socialist," in Richard Sandbrook, *The Politics of Africa's Economic Recovery* (Cambridge: Cambridge University Press, 1993), chap. 2; Nigel Dower, "Is the Idea of Development Eurocentric?," in Richard Auty and John Toye, editors, *Challenging the Orthodoxies* (New York: St. Martin's Press, 1996), pp. 85 - 102.

The asymmetrical relationship between African countries and the former colonial powers and other industrialized nations, which is inherently exploitative, is analogous to the situation in the United States where African-Americans (black Americans), constituting a virtual colony within, are at the mercy of white Americans because of racism, an in-built component of the American political socio-economic system; an argument rejected by black American conservatives such as Thomas Sowell, and others, without any empirical evidence.

See, for example, Thomas Sowell, *Race and Economics* (New York: Longman, 1975), and *Markets and Minorities* (New York: Basic Books, 1981), in which he dismisses the significance of racism in the American context, contending that it is overcome by market forces in a capitalist economy because of the nature of the system which is driven by competition in the quest for profit.

This is a very myopic view, and deeply flawed analysis, which ignores the racist practices of many white business owners and employers who simply refuse to patronize or hire blacks even if it means losing them as customers or as prospective and highly productive employees. They don't need blacks because most of their customers and employees are white in a predominantly white nation. Otherwise there would have been no need for civil rights laws to open up opportunities for blacks and try to level the playing field, if market forces by themselves were enough to eliminate or effectively contain racism. They had not done that in 300 years, a simple historical fact black conservatives, for some inexplicable reason, fail to grasp.

Whites also view with apprehension the fact that they are going to be a minority within a few decades; which partly explains their siege mentality, hence their belief that they are being overwhelmed - swamped - by hordes of non-whites who must be kept at bay. Therefore they must help only their own kind in terms of employment, housing and whatever else; nothing but feeble attempts to justify racism.

28. Tom Mboya, in *Transition*, Kampala, Uganda, Vol. 3, No. 8, March 1963, p. 17. See also Tom Mboya, *Challenge of Nationhood* (London: Heinemann, 1970);

Julius Nyerere, *Freedom and Socialism: A Selection from Writings and Speeches 1965 - 1967* (Dar es Salaam, Tanzania: Oxford University Press, 1968).

29. Nnamdi Azikiwe, *Zik: A Selection from the Speeches of Nnamdi Azikiwe* (Cambridge: Cambridge University Press, 1961), p. 102.

30. Charity Ngilu, speaking in Bokoli village, Bungoma, Kenya, January 8, 2000. Quoted by Kenyan Professor Kivutha Kibwana, "Ethnic Politics: Curse or Blessing," Nairobi, Kenya, July 2001. As Kibwana states in his paper:

"I cannot resist joining debate with both Kwendo Opanga (The tribal card in the succession game plan) and Murungi Kiraitu (Gema and the politics of tribal solidarity). The question both writers were addressing is: Is it the tribe or the political party which matters in Kenya's politics and society?....

Kwendo Opanga bluntly concluded his piece by stating that he rather a political party told him what to do and not his tribe through a proxy political party. Kiraitu on the other hand concluded that tribal alliances have a key role in Kenya's politics.

If we organize politics through tribes, are we not conceding either poverty of ideas and issues or opting for a deliberate strategy of concealing our political vision or ideology? Or are we saying political parties will always be eclipsed by tribe? Should we then search for a new vehicle for our African democracy? Is President Yoweri Museveni's no-party system one of the viable alternatives? Or should we go back to the one-party model?

I think two dangerous trends are emerging in Kenya currently. We are entrenching the ethnic principle to such an extent that we shall have to live with it for many decades to come. Do we want to? All sectors of the elite including the media elite are popularizing ethnic politics. Secondly, those who attempt to shift Kenya's politics to the plane of issue politics are not encouraged and are often vilified. It would therefore seem to me that a conspiracy to banish issue politics is afoot.

Interestingly, however, GEMA is not one tribe. If one can bring several tribes together through GEMA, why not do so through broad issues and a party?....

Tribal alliances are another form of trying to recreate new political parties. Frankly, Kenya needs about three or even two political parties i.e. a conservative party, a liberal party and a radical party. We have to work on reducing the 40 or so registered political parties into two or three.

If we organize on the basis of tribal alliances, we could easily encounter a stalemate if one alliance does not put together most tribes together (sic). We would be fanning secession fires. What do tribes that lose do? How are the expectations of their people to be satisfied?

Where an ethnic group comes into power after mobilizing on ethnic basis, it must satisfy its ethnic following. Can it do so and equally satisfy all other ethnic groupings?....

My personal dream - and I agree with Kwendo Opanga - is that Kenyans should develop parties of issues. We must venture beyond tribe."

The question is, how is that going to be done, in the midst of such intense ethnoregional loyalties, not only in Kenya but in other African countries as well? People talk about issues, yet mobilize forces on ethnic basis.

See also one of my books in which I address the subject, suggesting, among other things, formation of coalition governments, and reduction of the number of political parties to two or three to broaden the base of support that cuts across ethnoregional lines. With only two or three parties allowed, members of different tribes - including enemies - will have to work together as members of the only political parties they can join in the country. After all, when we talk about a multi-party system for functional purposes, we are really talking about a two-party system, *not* a system of 5, 10, 20, or 40 parties.

That's nothing but chaos. And it is used to justify dictatorship or military intervention in government. Even third parties don't win elections; it's extremely rare. When was the last time the Liberal Party won a general election in Britain? Just remember that.

See Godfrey Mwakikagile, *Ethnic Politics in Kenya and Nigeria* (Huntington, New York: Nova Science Publishers, Inc., 2001).

See also, "Kenyan MPs Seeks End to Political Parties," in "BBC News: Africa," 7 December, 2000:

"A Kenyan opposition legislator has moved a motion in parliament seeking the abolishment of political parties and the creation of a partyless state.

Social Democratic Party (SDP) member for Juja, Stephen Ndicho, wants all political party activities in the country to be suspended for at least 10 years to curb tribalism.

Kenya, which has 47 (sic) tribes, ended its single party rule in 1991 and has since held two multi-party general elections.

Mr. Ndicho insisted that his motion did not advocate for a return to a single party political system but seeks to provide a stopgap measure in the country's politics to heal tribal and political divisons.

'Since the advent of multi-partism in this country in 1991, tribalism has really taken a tall order on this country,' Mr. Ndicho told the BBC. 'Every tribe in Kenya seems to be owning a political party,' he said, adding that 'if this trend continues, you can imagine Kenya will be a disintegrated country.'

The member said Kenya should borrow a leaf from Uganda where President Museveni banned political parties when he took power in 1986 in order to restore stability in a country that had been ravaged by war.

Mr. Ndicho said there was political enmity among Kenya's different party members, adding that during the 1992 and 1997 general elections, results showed that voting was done along tribal or regional lines."

Chapter Two

1. Julius K. Nyerere, in a speech delivered to the Second Pan-African Seminar, World Assembly of Youth, Dar es Salaam, Tanganyika, August 1961, in *WAY* (World Assemby of Youth) *Forum*, No. 40, September 1961; reprinted in Paul E. Sigmund, Jr., editor, *The Ideologies of the Developing Nations* (New York: Frederick A. Praeger, 1963), pp. 205, 208, and 209. See also *Tanganyika Standard*, Dar es Salaam, Tanganyika, August and September 1961.

2. Godfrey Mwakikagile, *Africa after Independence: Realities of Nationhood* (Atlanta, Georgia: Protea Publishing, 2002).

3. John Reader, *Africa: A Biography of the Continent* (New York: Alfred A. Knopf, 1998), pp. 659, 660, and 662.

4. Ibid., p. 662; Catherine Hoskyns, *The Congo since Independence: January 1960 - December 1961* (Oxford: Oxford University Press, 1965), p. 308; M. Meredith, *The First Dance of Freedom* (London: Hamish Hamilton, 1984), p. 150. See also Patrice Lumumba, *Congo: My Country* (London, 1962).

5. Quoted in Madeleine G. Kalb, *The Congo Cables: The Cold War in Africa: From Eisenhower to Kennedy* (New York: Macmillan, 1982), p. 27; J. Reader, *Africa: A Biography of the Continent*, op. cit., p. 659.

6. Adam Hochschild, *King Leopold's Ghost: A Story of Greed, Terror, and Heroism in Colonial Africa* (New York: Houghton Mifflin Co., 1998), pp. 301 - 302; Sean Kelly, *America's Tyrant: The CIA and Mobutu of Zaire* (Washington, D.C.: American University Press, 1993), pp. 57 - 60, 71, and 178.

7. Ibid. See also John Ranelagh, *The Agency: The Rise and Decline of the CIA* (New York: Simon & Schuster,

1986), p. 342; John Stockwell, *In Search of Enemies* (New York: W.W. Norton, 1978), p. 105; Report from the US Senate investigation, headed by Democratic Senator Frank Church of Idaho, into CIA covert activities against foreign leaders and governments, *Alleged Assassination Plots Involving Foreign Leaders: An Interim Report of the Select Committee to Study (US) Governmental Operations with Respect to Intelligence Activities*, Washington, D.C., November 20, 1975.

8. Ludo de Witte, *The Assassination of Lumumba* (New York: Verso, 1999).

9. Allen Dulles, quoted by Kevin Whitelaw, "A Killing in Congo: Lumumba's Death...," in *U.S. News & World Report*, July 24, 2000, p. 63.

10. "A Killing in Congo," in *U.S. News & World Report*, ibid.; Ludo de Witte, *The Assassination of Lumumba*, op. cit. See also (US) National Security Archive: "It is possible to kill a man with bare hands, but very few are skillful enough to do it well," reads a declassified 1954 CIA "Study of Assassination" on covert activities in Guatemala. And "persons who are morally squeamish" make bad assassins. This and other CIA documents can be seen at www.gwu.edu/-nsarchiv. Choose Electronic Briefing Books, and click on "CIA and Assassinations."

11. Zaire, in *1997 Almanac: Information Please* (Boston: Houghton Mifflin Co., 1996), p. 295.

12. Government of Tanganyika, in a message to UN Secretary-General U Thant, on the assassination of President Sylvanus Olympio of Togo, in *Tanganyika Standard*, Dar es Salaam, Tanganyika, January 26, 1963; quoted by Ali A. Mazrui, *Towards A Pax Africana* (London: Weidenfeld & Nicolson, 1967), p. 123.

13. Ronald Ngala, in *Uganda Argus*, Kampala, Uganda, April 25, 1964; A.A. Mazrui, *Towards A Pax Africana*, op.cit., p. 270.

14. Julius Nyerere, "The Honour of Africa," address to

the Tanzania National Assembly, December 14, 1965, before Tanzania broke off diplomatic relations with Britain the following day, the first African country to do so (followed by Ghana under Nkrumah), in J.K. Nyerere, *Freedom and Socialism: A Selection from Writings and Speeches 1965 - 1967* (Dar es Salaam, Tanzania: Oxford University Press, 1968), pp. 123 - 124.

15. *Sunday Times*, Johannesburg, October 3, 1999; R.W. Johnson, "Nyerere: A Flawed Hero," in *The National Interest*, No. 60, Washington, D.C., Summer 2000, p. 76.

16. *The Mercury*, Durban, South Africa, October 5, 1999; R.W. Johnson, "Nyerere: A Flawed Hero," ibid., pp. 67 - 68.

17. Julius Nyerere, quoted in *Sunday Times*, London, October 3, 1999; R.W. Johnson, "Nyerere: A Flawed Hero," ibid., p. 73. See also, "Farewell to the Father of Tanzania," in the *Mail and Guardian*, Johannesburg, October 15, 1999; "Julius Nyerere of Tanzania Dies; Preached African Socialism to the World," in *The New York Times*, October 15, 1999, p. B10; "Former Tanzanian President Julius Nyerere Dies at 77; African leader Led Independence Movement and Worked to Unify Nation, Continent," in *The Washington Post*, October 15, 1999, p. B-06; "Julius Nyerere: Former President of Tanzania Led Country to Independence," in the *Los Angeles Times*, October 15, 1999, p. 30.

18. Hackman Owusu-Agyemang, "Tribute to Dr. Julius Nyerere: Death Has Robbed Africa of A Leading Light," in *The Independent*, Accra, Ghana, October 27, 1999. See also "Tanzania Mourns Its 'Teacher'; Nyerere Remembered as A Leader Who Unified the Nation, " in *The Washington Post*, October 22, 1999, p. A-25.

Chapter Three

1. "Sekou Toure," in Paul E. Sigmund, Jr., editor, *The Ideologies of the Developing Countries* (New York: Frederick A. Praeger, 1963), p. 154.

2. Fred Greene, *Dynamics of International Relations*: *Power, Security, and Order* (New York: Holt, Rinehart and Winston, 1964), p. 676.

3. Okon Udokang, "The Third World as A Political Force," in *The Black Scholar*, Sausalito, California, May 1975, p. 12. See also Okon Udokang, editor and contributor, *African Politics and Foreign Relations* (Toronto: University of Toronto Press, 1975); and Julius Nyerere, on the Cold War and Africa, cited by *The New York Times*, April 1, 1964, p. 2.

4. Julius Nyerere, quoted by *The New York Times*, December 19, 1961; and Ali A. Mazrui, *Towards A Pax Africana* (London: Weidenfeld & Nicolson, 1968), p. 77. See also Nyerere, in *Tanganyika Standard*, Dar es Salaam, Tanganyika, December 18, 1961.

5. Julius Nyerere, *Freedom and Socialism*: *A Selection from Writings and Speeches 1965 - 1967* (Dar es Salaam, Tanzania: Oxford University Press, 1968), pp. 189, and 190.

6. Ibid., pp. 190, and 202.

7. Ibid., pp. 190 - 191.

8. "Sekou Toure," in Paul E. Sigmund, *The Ideologies of the Developing Nations*, op. cit., p. 154.

9. Julius Nyerere, *Freedom and Socialism*, ibid., p. 202. Kwame Nkrumah also discusses attempts by the CIA to overthrow Nyerere in the mid-sixties and how the American intelligence agency succeeded in overthrowing his Ghanaian government on February 24, 1966. See

Kwame Nkrumah, *Dark Days in Ghana* (New York: Monthly Review Press, 1966).

10. John F. Kennedy, quoted by Richard Reeves, *President Kennedy: Profile of Power* (New York: Simon & Schuster, 1993), pp. 227 - 228.

11. Richard Reeves, *President Kennedy*, op. cit., p. 227.

12. Oran R. Young, *The Politics of Force: Bargaining During International Crises* (Princeton, New Jersey: Princeton University press, 1968), pp. 132 - 133, 159 - 160. For analyses of the proceedings of the Belgrade Conference, see Paul Hoffman in *The New York Times*, September 3, 1961, Sect. IV, p. 4; and Harry Schwartz in *The New York Times*, September 10, 1961, Sect. IV, p. 3. And for a general analysis of the Belgrade Conference, see Peter Lyon, *Neutralism* (Leicester, England: Leicester University Press, 1963), Chap. VI.

13. Kwame Nkrumah, in his speech to the United Nations General Assembly, March 7, 1961. See also the full text issued by the Ghana Ministry of Information, Accra, Ghana, p. 8; and *Ghanaian Times*, Accra, Ghana, March 8, 1961.

14. John F. Kennedy, quoted by Ernest R. May and Philip D. Zelikow, editors, *The Kennedy Tapes: Inside the White House During the Cuban Missile Crisis* (Cambridge, Massachusetts: Harvard University Press, 1997), pp. 144, 150, 175, 176, 179, 183, 256, 272, and 275.

15. Jorge G. Castaneda, *Companero: The Life and Death of Che Guevara* (New York: Alfred A. Knopf, 1997), pp. 228 - 229.

16. Henry Tanner, reporting from Abidjan, Ivory Coast, in *The New York Times*, March 25, 1962. For contrast, see Victor D. DuBois, "The Role of the Army in Guinea," in *Africa Report*, Vol. 8, No. 1, January 1963. See also George Weeks, "The Armies of Africa," in *Africa Report*, Vol. 9, No. 1, January 1963.

For comparative analysis of military strength in Africa vis-a-vis white-minority-regime military preparedness during the sixties, see "Military Strength in Southern Africa" in *Central Africa Research*, London, August 10, 1968; and Colin Legum and John Drysdale, *Africa Contemporary Record: Annual Survey and Documents 1968 - 1969* (London: Africa Research Ltd., 1969), pp. 716 - 717.

17. "Declaration of Federation by the Governments of East Africa," signed by the President of the Republic of Tanganyika, Dr. Julius Nyerere; the Prime Minister of Uganda, Mr. Milton A. Obote; and the Prime Minister of Kenya, Mr. Jomo Kenyatta, in Nairobi, Kenya, June 5, 1963.

See full text in Anthony J. Hughes, *East Africa: The Search for Unity: Kenya, Tanganyika, and Uganda* (Baltimore, Maryland, USA: Penguin Books, 1963), Appendix pp. 265 - 269. The full text of the declaration is also found in Godfrey Mwakikagile, *Ethnic Politics in Kenya and Nigeria* (Huntington, New York: Nova Science Publishers, Inc., 2001), pp. 218 - 220.

18. Nnamdi Azikiwe, "African Unity," in Paul Sigmund, *The Ideologies of the Developing Nations*, op. cit., pp. 216 - 217, and 218 - 219. See also Nnamdi Azikiwe, *Zik: A Selection from Speeches of Nnamdi Azikiwe* (New York: Cambridge University Press, 1961).

19. Jorge Castaneda, *Companero: The Life and Death of Che Guevara*, op. cit., p. 277.

20. Nelson Mandela, his speech to the Pan-African Freedom Movement for East and Central Africa (PAFMECA), Addis Ababa, Ethiopia, February 1962.

21. Nelson Mandela, *Long Walk to Freedom: The Autobiography of Nelson Mandela* (New York: Little, Brown and Co., 1994), pp. 250, 251, 252, and 253.

22. Mamadou Dia, *The African Nations and World Solidarity* (New York: Frederick A. Praeger, 1961); Mamadou Dia, "Independence and Neocolonialism," in

Paul E. Sigmund, *The Ideologies of the Developing Countries*, op. cit., pp. 232, 235 - 236.

23. Kaye Whiteman, "France's Year in Africa," in *Africa Contemporary Record*, op. cit., pp. 29 - 30.

24. Ali Mazrui, *Towards A Pax Africana*, op. cit., p. 253.

25. Julius Nyerere, cited by James C. McKinley, "Tanzania's Nyerere Looks Back: Many Failures, and One Big Success: Bringing a Nation to Life," in *The New York Times*, September 2, 1996; and the *International Herald Tribune*, September 2, 1996, p. 2.

26. "Declaration of Federation by the Governments of East Africa," in Anthony J. Hughes, *East Africa: The Search for Unity*, op. cit., pp. 265 - 266; and Godfrey Mwakikagile, *Ethnic Politics in Kenya and Nigeria*, op. cit., pp. 218 - 220.

27. George Bennett, "Settlers and Politics in Kenya," in Vincent Harlow, E.M. Chilver, and Alison Smith, editors, *History of East Africa, II* (Oxford: Oxford University Press, 1965), pp. 304 - 305; see also p. 578.

28. "Uganda," in *Africa Contemporary Record*, op. cit., p. 230. See also "Dr. Obote's Decade - Ten Years in Parliament" (Kampala, Uganda: Milton Obote Foundation, 1968).

29. James C. McKinley, "Tanzania's Nyerere Looks Back," ibid.

30. Ronald Ngala, quoted in *Uganda Argus*, Kampala, Uganda, April 25, 1964.

31. "Declaration of Federation by the Governments of East Africa," Anthony J. Hughes, *East Africa: The Search for Unity*, op. cit., p. 266; and Godfrey Mwakikagile, *Ethnic Politics in Kenya and Nigeria*, op.cit., p. 219.

32. Ahmed Ben Bella, "The Future of Algeria," an interview with Maria Macciochi, *L'Unita*, an Italian newspaper, in Algiers, August 13, 1962; reprinted in Paul Sigmund, *The Ideologies of the Developing Nations*, op. cit., pp. 147 - 148.

33. Julius Nyerere, "The Stress is Now on Dignity," in *Sunday News*, Dar es Salaam, Tanganyika, September 8, 1963, p. 9.

34. Kwame Nkrumah, in *Ghana Today*, Vol. 8, No. 21, Accra, Ghana, December 16, 1964; and Ali Mazrui, *Towards A Pax Africana*, op. cit., p. 73.

35. Paul Lee, "Documents Expose US Role in Nkrumah Overthrow," ghanaweb.com, March 7, 2001.

36. Adebayo Adedeji, interviewed by Margaret A. Novicki, in *Africa Report*, September - October 1983, p. 14.

37. Ali Mazrui, *Towards A Pax Africana*, op. cit., pp. 65 - 66. See also *West African Pilot*, May 18, 1961, and *West Africa*, May 6, 1961.

38. Ali A. Mazrui, *Towards A Pax Africana*, ibid., p. 251. See also Ali A. Mazrui, "African Attitudes to the EEC," in *International Affairs*, Vol. 38, No. 1, London, January 1963. For a report on the Pan-African militancy of the Nigerian youth, see *The New York Times*, March 3, 1962.

39. *Ghanaian Times*, Accra, Ghana, April 27, 1965.

40. "Guinea," in *Africa Contemporary Record*, op. cit., pp. 505 - 506.

41. Julius Nyerere, "Nationalism and Pan-Africanism," speech to the Second Pan-African Seminar, World Assembly of Youth (WAY), Dar es Salaam, Tanganyika, August 1961. Published in *WAY Forum*, No. 40, September 1961; and Paul Sigmund, *The Ideologies of the Developing Nations*, op. cit., pp. 208 - 209. See also Nyerere, text of the same speech, in the *Standard*, Dar es Salaam, Tanganyika, August 1961.

Chapter Four

1. Richard J. Herrnstein, Charles Murray (contributor), *The Bell Curve: Intelligence*

and Class Structure in American Life (New York: Free Press, 1994).

2. George B.N. Ayittey, *Africa in Chaos* (New York: St. Martin's Press, 1998).

3. Keith B. Richburg, *Out of America: A Black Man Confronts Africa* (New York: Basic Books, 1997).

4. "Africa's Democratic Despots," in *The Economist*, January 3, 1998; Reginald Dale, "Finally, Some Good News From Africa," in the *International Herald Tribune*, December 13, 1996, p. 15; Yoweri Museveni, in a speech to the UN General Assembly, February 1997, cited by Tom Stacey, "African Realities," in *National Review*, May 19, 1997, p. 30; Godfrey Mwakikagile, *Economic Development in Africa* (Commack, New York: Nova Science Publishers, Inc., 1999), pp. 3, and 99.

5. Ernest Aning, "Let's Tackle the Turncoat Politicians First," in the *New African*, No. 352, May 1997, pp. 6 - 7.

6. Maxwell Oteng, "What About the Mobutus?," in the *New African*, ibid., pp. 4, and 6.

7. Simbowe Benson, "Mobutu Deserves No Sympathy," in the *New African*, ibid., p. 6.

8. Yoweri Museveni, in a speech to the UN General Assembly, February 1997, cited by Tom Stacey, "African Realities," in *National Review*, May 19, 1997, p. 30.

9. Thierry Naudin, "Europe Can Help Africa, But Only If Africa Helps Itself," in *The European*, November 21, 1996, p. 22.

10. West African diplomat in Abidjan, Ivory Coast, quoted by Howard W. French, "Shells Rain on Center of Brazzaville: France and U.S. Strive to Evacuate Citizens," in the *International Herald Tribune*, June 10, 1997, p. 4.

11. Julius Nyerere, "Reflections," South Centre, Geneva, Switzerland; full text of his speech reproduced in Godfrey Mwakikagile, *Nyerere and Africa: End of an Era* (Atlanta, Georgia: Protea Publishing Co., 2002), Appendix II, pp. 386 - 395. For this citation, see p. 394, ibid.

12. Ibid.

13. Ken Saro-Wiwa, *A Month and A Day: A Detention Diary* (New York: Penguin Books, 1993).

14. Ken Saro-Wiwa, quoted by David Rieff, "The Threat of Death: The Ruin of Nigeria, the Ruin of Africa," in *The New Republic: Africa Is Dying*, in June 16, 1997, p. 38.

15. Ken Saro-Wiwa, quoted by the *Guardian*, Lagos, Nigeria, October 1985.

16. Gordon Frisch, "Africa - Staring Into the Abyss: Send in The Mercenaries and Re-Colonize," in "Recolonize Africa?," http://www.rense.com/general13/re.htm, on CNN.com.

17. Ibid.

18. Max Hastings, "The Return of the Dark Continent," in *The Daily Mail*, Johannesburg, South Africa, August 13, 2002.

19. Henri Konan Bedie, quoted in "Sure, Africa's Troubled. But There is Good News," in *The New York Times*, June 15, 1997, p. E-16; see also Henri Konan Bedie, in *Le Figaro*, Paris, June 1997.

20. Charles Onyango-Obbo, "Only A Madman Would Recolonise Africa," in *The East African*, Nairobi, Kenya, June 5, 2000.

Chapter Five

1. Jawaharlal Nehru, "Portuguese Colonialism: An Aanachronism," in *African Quarterly*, Vol. 1, No. 3, October-December, 1961, p. 9. See also Nehru, "Emergent Africa," in *African Quarterly*, Vol. 1, No. 1, April-June, 1961, pp. 7 - 9.

2. Godfrey Mwakikagile, *The Modern African State: Quest for Transformation* (Huntington, New York: Nova Science Publishers, Inc., 2001), pp. 238 - 239.

3. Loonster, South Africa Discussion Forum - South African Politics: Book Review, *Mano Vision*, Issue 23,

London: Godfrey Mwakikagile, *The Modern African State: Quest for Transformation* (Huntington, New York: Nova Science Publishers, Inc., 201), March 22, 2002.

4. Ibid.

5. Wole Soyinka, *The Man Died: Prison Notes of Wole Soyinka* (London: Rex Collings, 1974).

6. Ngugi wa Thiong'o, *Detained: A Writer's Prison Diary* (London: Heinemann, 1978).

7. Michael Radu, "African Nightmare," in FrontPage magazine.com, January 15, 2003.

8. Godfrey Mwakikagile, *Africa and the West* (Huntington, New York: Nova Science Publishers, Inc., 2000).

9. George B.N. Ayittey, *Africa in Chaos* (New York: St. Martin's Press, 1998).

10. Godfrey Mwakikagile, *The Modern African State: Quest for Transformation*, op. cit.

11. Adebayo Adedeji, in an interview with *Africa Report*, New York, September-October, 1983, p. 14.

12. Adebayo Adedeji, quoted in "A Survey of sub-Saharan Africa," in *The Economist*, September 1996, p. 4 of the survey.

13. Wole Soyinka, in a speech at Wellesley College, Massachusetts, quoted by Zia Jaffrey, "The Writer in Exile as 'Opposition Diplomat,'" in the *International Herald Tribune*, May 2, 1997, p. 24; and in *The New York Times*, April 30, 1997.

14. Peter Anyang' Nyong'o, in *Popular Struggles for Democracy in Africa* (London: Zed Books, 1987), pp. 14 - 25.

15. George B.N. Ayittey, *Africa Betrayed* (New York: St. Martin's Press, 1992), pp. 235, 236, and 240. See also Tanzania in *New African*, London, April 1990, p. 16.

16. Gnassingbe Eyadema, cited by George B. N. Ayittey, *Africa Betrayed*, ibid., p. 238; *New African*, October 1991, p. 12.

17. Ibid.

18. Chinua Achebe, *The Trouble with Nigeria* (Enugu, Nigeria: Fourth Dimension, 1985), p. 3.

19. Keith B. Richburg, *Out of America: A Black Man Confronts Africa* (New York: Basic Books, 1997), pp. 247 - 248, xiv.

20. K. B. Richburg, ibid., pp. 169 - 173, 174 - 175, and 177.

Chapter Six

1. Francis N. Njubi, "African Intellectuals in the Belly of the Beast: Migration, Identity and the Politics of Exile," in *Mots Pluriels*, No. 20, University of Western Australia, February 2002.

2. Ali A. Mazrui, in Philippe Wamba, "An American African Scholar: An Interview with Professor Ali Mazrui," Africana.com, 2001.

3. Philip Ochieng', "How Africa Can Utilise its Intellectuals in 'Exile'," in *The East African*, Nairobi, Kenya, March 13, 2000.

4. Guchure wa Kanyugo, quoted by Philip Ngunjiri, "Africa Continues to Suffer from A Brain Drain," Africana.com, August 1, 2001.

5. Wene Owino, quoted ibid.

6. David Johnson, "Africa's Brain Drain Slows Development," Africana.com, March 2, 2000; Panafrican News Agency; United Nations Economic Commission for Africa (ECA); African Studies Center, Boston University.

7. Peter Da Costa, quoted by david Johnson, ibid.

8. 1993 United Nations Development Programme (UNDP) report cited by Lalla Ben Barka, deputy secretary of the UN Economic Commission for Africa (ECA), in David Johnson, "Africa's Brain Drain Slows Development," ibid.

9. Patrick Seyon, quoted by David Johnson, "Africa's Brain Drain Slows Development," ibid.

10. Patrick Seyon, ibid.

11. "South Africa's Brain Drain," in *Monday Paper*, Vol. 17, No.7, Department of Communication, University of Cape Town, South Africa, March 30 - April 6, 1998. See also "Commonwealth Business Tackle Africa's Brain Drain," in Commonwealth News and Information Service, London, November 25, 2002.

12. James S. Shikwati, "Brain Drain versus Africa's Economic Woes," in IREN (Inter-Region Economic Network) Kenya: Articles, May 20, 2000.

13. Gus Selassie, "The Brain Drain - Africa's Achilles Heel," World Markets Research Centre: In Focus 2002. See also Augustine Oyowe, "Brain Drain: Colossal Loss of Investment for Developing Countries," in *The Courier ACP-EU*, No. 159, September - October, 1996, pp. 59 - 60; "Brain Drain Costs Africa Billions," BBC News: Africa, October 17, 2001; Wachira Kigotho, "Brain Drain Stunts Africa," in *The East African Standard*, Nairobi, Kenya, October 5, 2002.

14. Katrin Cowan-Louw, quoted by Gus Selassie, "The Brain Drain - Africa's Achilles Heel," ibid.

Chapter Seven

1. Herman J. Cohen, interview, "Forging A Bipartisan Policy," in *Africa Report*, September-October 1989, p. 19.

2. Robert K.A. Gardiner, "Economic Commission for Africa," his address at the 15th Session of the UN Economic and Social Council, Geneva, July 12, 1968; reprinted in Colin Legum and John Drysdale, *Africa Contemporary Record: Annual Survey and Documents 1968 - 1969* (London: Africa Research Ltd., 1969), p. 746.

3. Stephen Buckley, "Some Places the Boon of Globalization Forgot: Africa - Investors Skip the sub-Sahara and Its Many Flaws," in the *International Herald Tribune*, January 2, 1997, pp. 1 and 4.

4. Lucia Quachey, head of the Ghanaian Association of Women Entrepreneurs, quoted by Stephen Buckley, in the *International Herald Tribune*, ibid., p. 4.

5. "ECA and Africa's Development, 1983 - 2008," cited in "Africa: A Statistical Profile," in *Africa Report*, September-October 1983, p. 58.

6. "ECA and Africa's Development, 1983 - 2008," ibid.; "Survey of Economic and Social Conditions in Africa" (E/ECA/CM. 9/5), UN Publications (New York: United Nations, 1983); "World Development Report, 1983" (Washington, D.C.: World Bank, 1982; New York: Oxford University Press, 1982). See also *Demographic Yearbook for 1983* (New York: United Nations, 1982).

7. Cited by Robert Gardiner, in *Africa Contemporary Record*, op. cit., p. 745. See also Arthur Lewis, "Development Planning," in *The Legon Observer*, Legon, Accra, Ghana, May 24, 1968.

8. Ugandan professor, Makerere University, Kampala, quoted by Lara Santoro, "West Cheers Uganda's One-Man Show: This Month, Clinton Will Visit A New Type of African Strongman, Yoweri Museveni," in *The Christian Science Monitor*, March 2, 1998, p. 6.

9. Robert Gardiner, "Economic Commission for Africa," in *Africa Contemporary Record*, op. cit., p. 746.

10. Stephen Buckley, "Africa: Investor Interest and the Boon of Globalization Skip sub-Saharan Countries With Their Flaws in Politics and Infrastructure," in the *International Herald Tribune*, January 2, 1997, p. 4.

11. Robert Gardner, "Economic Commission for Africa," in *Africa Contemporary Record*, op. cit., p. 746.

12. Walter Elkan, "East African Community," in *Africa Contemporary Record*, op. cit., pp. 13 - 14. See also Arthur Hazelwood, editor, *African Integration and Disintegration* (Oxford; Oxford University Press, 1967), esp. chap. 3; A. Hazelwood, "The Treaty of East African Cooperation," in the *Standard Bank Review*, London, September 1967; Philip Ndegwa, *The Common Market*

and Development in East Africa, East African Studies No. 22 (Nairobi, Kenya: East African Publishing House, 1965); and Peter Robson, *Economic Integration in Africa* (London: Allen & Unwin, 1968), esp. chap. 4.

13. Adebayo Adedeji, interview, *Africa Report*, September-October 1983, pp. 13 - 14.

14. Ibid.

15. Stephen Buckley, "Africa Investor Interest and the Boon of Globalization Skip sub-Saharan Countries With Their Flaws in Politics and Infrastructure," in the *International Herald Tribune*, January 2, 1997, p. 4.

16. Ibid.

17. Ibid.

18. John Koo, quoted ibid.

19. Henri Konan Bedie, ibid.

20. George B.N. Ayittey, ibid.

21. George B.N. Ayittey, "The UN's Shameful Record in Africa," in *The Wall Street Journal*, July 26, 1996, p. A10.

22. Alauwa Lobela, quoted by Nicholas D. Kristof, "Tiger Tales: Why Africa Can Thrive Like Asia," in *The New York Times*, May 25, 1997, p. E4. See also N.D. Kristof, "From Asia's 'Tigers,' A Lesson for Impoverished Africa: How to Turn Poor Into Rich: It's More Than Economics," in the *International Herald Tribune*, May 27, 1997, p. 1.

23. World Bank Reports, East Asia: Savings Rates and Foreign Investment Data, 1981 - 1990, cited by N.D. Kristof, "Tiger Tales: Why Africa Can Thrive Like Asia," in *The New York Times*, ibid.

24. Samuel Ndomba, quoted by N.D. Kristof, ibid.

25. N.D. Kristof, ibid.

26. Michael Moravcsik and J.M. Ziman, "Paradisia and Dominatia: Science and the Developing World," in *Foreign Affairs*, July 1975, pp. 704 - 705, and 702. For a more direct attack on the attempt to represent knowledge as a quantifiable economic category, see J.M. Ziman, Book

Review, *Minerva*, July 1974, p. 384.

27. N.D. Kristof, op. cit.

28. Michael Chege, "Africa Is Not One Country: Time to Put Away the Heroic Stereotypes," in *The Times Literary Supplement*, London, January 3, 1997, p. 14. See also Merilee S. Grindle, *Challenging the State: Crisis and Innovation in Latin America and Africa* (Cambridge: Cambridge University Press, 1997); Benno Ndulu and Nicolas van de Walle, editors, *Agenda for Africa's Economic Renewal* (Brunswick, New Jersey: Transaction Publishers, 1997); and Mamadou Dia, editor, *Africa's Management in the 1990s and Beyond* (Washington, D.C.: World Bank, 1997).

29. Benjamin Mkapa, quoted by Robert S. Greenberger, "Africa Ascendant: New Leaders Replace Yesteryear's 'Big Men,' and Tanzania Benefits," in *The Wall Street Journal*, December 10, 1996, p. A1.

Chapter Eight

1. Kwame Nkrumah, *Neo-Colonialism: The Last Stage of Imperialism* (New York: International Publishers, 1965).

2. *Detroit News*, 1975.

3. *Africa Report*, African-American Institute, New York.

4. Julius Nyerere, "Nationalism and Pan-Africanism," excerpts from a speech delivered to the Second Pan-African Seminar, World Assembly of Youth (WAY), reprinted from WAY *Forum*, No. 40, September 1960, in Paul E. Sigmund, Jr., editor, *The Ideologies of the Developing Nations* (New York: Frederick A. Praeger, 1963), pp. 205, 209, and 208.

5. Julius Nyerere, cited by Herschelle S. Challenor, chairman of the board of directors, National Summit on Africa, in a memorial tribute to Mwalimu Julius Nyerere, Washington, D.C., February 18, 2000. See The National

Summit on Africa.

6. James Baldwin, "Fifth Avenue, Uptown."

7. Immanuel Kant, *Eternal Peace and Other Essays* (Boston: Houghton Mifflin, 1914), p. 68; Kant in Will Durant, *The Story of Philosophy* (New York: Pocket Books, 1974), p. 284. See also Godfrey Mwakikagile, *Africa and the West* (Huntington, New York: Nova Science Publishers, Inc., 2000), p. 218; Walter Rodney, *How Europe Underdeveloped Africa* (Dar es Salaam, Tanzania: Tanzania Publishing House, 1972).

8. Kant, *Observations on the Feeling of the Beautiful and Sublime*, translated by John Goldthwait (Berkeley: University f California Press, 1960), pp. 111 - 113; Dinesh D'Souza, *The End of Racism: Principles for A Milticultural Society* (New York: Free press, 1995), p. 28. See also D'Souza, ibid., pp. 442, and 468.

9. Baron de Montesquieu, *The Spirit of the Laws, Vol. 1*, translated by Thomas Nugent (Cincinnati, Ohio: Robert Clarke & Co., 1973), pp. 274 - 275.

10. David Hume, "Of National Character," in D. Hume, *Essays: Moral, Political and Literary, Vol. 1*, edited by T.H. Green and T. Grose (London: Longman's Green and Co., 1975), p. 252.

11. Hegel, *The Philosophy of History* (New York: Dover Publications, 1956), pp. 95 - 99.

12. Arnold Toynbee, quoted by Felix Okoye, *The American Image of Africa: Myth and Reality* (Buffalo, New York: Black Academy Press, 1971), p. 7.

13. Albert Schweitzer, *The Primeval Forest* (New York: Pyramid Books, 1974), p. 99.

Conclusion

1. "Kamuzu Banda Dies: 'Big Man' Among Anticolonialists, " *The New York Times*, 27 November 1997.

2. Godfrey Mwakikagile, *Military Coups in West Africa Since the Sixties* (Huntington, New York: Nova Science Publishers, Inc., 2002).

3."Nigeria: Islamist Push," in *The Economist*, 6 November 1999, pp. 48 and 49. See also Minabere Ibelema, "Nigeria: The Politics of Marginalization," in *Current History: A Journal of Contemporary World Affairs*, May 2000, p. 211:

"These ethnoreligious tensions are reminiscent of the events in 1966 and 1967 that precipitated Nigeria's civil war in which more than 1 million Nigerians died when the Igbos created the secessionist state of Biafra.

Emeka Odumegwu Ojukwu, who led the 30-month secession, has been blamed by some northern leaders for fomenting this year's Kaduna crisis. Ojukwu has responded by calling the accusation a hallucination, and by suggesting psychiatric examination for the accusers. But he has also said of the Igbos that 'we have to get prepared, be on our toes and wait.'

Leaders used similar language directly preceding the declaration of secession in 1967."

4. Northern Nigerian politician, quoted in "Nigeria: Islamist Push," *The Economist*, ibid.

5. *The Economist*, 6 November 1999, p. ibid., p. 49.

6. "A Survey of Nigeria – Here's Hoping: Fissiparous Folk," in *The Economist*, 15 January 2000, p. 14 of the survey. See also David L. Bevan, Paul Collier and Jan Willem Gunning, *Nigeria and Indonesia: The Political Economy of Poverty, Equity and Growth* (Oxford: Oxford University Press, 1999).

7. *The Economist*, 29 January 2000, p. 4.

8. "Nigeria: Religious Blood," in *The Economist*, 26 February 2000, p. 55.

9. Ibid.

10. Minabere Ibelema, op. cit.

11. "Nigeria: Religious Blood," *The Economist*, ibid.

12. *The Christian Science Monitor*, 2 March 2000, p. 24. See also Nigeria in *The Economist*, 4 March 2000, p. 6: "Some 400 people...were killed in ethnic and religious violence after fighting between Christians and Muslims in the north. Troops eventually brought order. The government said that northern Muslim states had suspended plans to introduce full *sharia* law."

13. *The Christian Science Monitor*, 25 May 2000, p. 24.

14. "Africa News: Africa Nightline," voice of America (VOA), Washington, D.C., 25 March 2000.

15. *The Christian Science Monitor*, 25 May 2000, p. 24; *The Wall Street Journal*, 23 May 2000, p. A-1.

16. Steve U. Nwabuzor, in *Niger World*, 24 March 2000.

17. Minabere Ibelema, "Nigeria: The Politics of Marginalization," *Current History: A Journal of Contemporary World Affairs*, op. cit., p. 211.

18. Wole Soyinka, *The Open Sore of a Continent: A Personal Narrative of the Nigerian Crisis* (New York: Oxford University Press, 1996), pp. 31 – 32.

19. Minabere Ibelema, "Nigeria: The Politics of Marginalization," *Current History: A Journal of Contemporary World Affairs*, op. cit., pp. 211 – 212.

20. Godfrey Mwakikagile, *Economic Development in Africa*, op. cit.

21. *The Christian Science Monitor,* 26 May 2000, p. 20.

22. Joe Igbokwe, in *Tempo,* Lagos, Nigeria, 9 March 2000; *World Press Review,* May 2000, p. 28.

23. *Tempo,* and *World Press Review,* ibid.

24. *Guardian,* Lagos, Nigeria, 28 February 2000; *World Press Review,* ibid.

25. Odumegwu Ojukwu, quoted by M. Ibelema, *Current History: A Journal of Contemporary World Affairs*, op. cit., p. 213.

26. Tajudeen Suleiman, "The Man Behind the Sharia," in *Tempo*, Lagos, Nigeria, 11 November 1999; *World Press Review*, January 2000, pp. 31 – 32.

27. Cameron Duodu, Gemini News Service, London, 29 October 1999 in *World Press Review*, ibid., p. 31.

28. Michael Chege, "Africa's Murderous Professors," *The National Interest*, No. 46, Washington, D.C., Winter 1996/97, pp. 33 – 34; also quoted by Godfrey Mwakikagile, *The Modern African State: Quest for Transformation* (Huntington, New York: Nova Science Publishers, Inc., 2001), p. 190.

29. Quoted in "Kenyan Strongman Blames Political Foes for Surge in Violence," in the *International Herald Tribune,* 18 August 1997, p. 1. Also quoted by Godfrey Mwakikagile, *Ethnic Politics in Kenya and Nigeria*, Huntington, New York: Nova Science Publishers, Inc., 2001, p. 120.

30. Mallam Mukhtar Bello, quoted by Colin Legum and John Drysdale, eds., *Africa Contemporary Record:*

Annual Survey and Documents 1968 - 1969 (London: Africa Research Ltd., 1969), p. 664.

31. Ahmadu Bello, quoted in *Africa Contemporary Record,* ibid.

32. Mallam Muhammadu Mustapha Maude Gyari, ibid.

33. Mallam Bashari Umaru, ibid.

34. A. A. Abogede, ibid.

35. Iya Abubakar, ibid.

36. Mallam Ibrahim Muse, ibid.

37. Mallam Bashari Umaru, ibid.

38. Alhaji Usman Liman, ibid.

39. Alhaji Ibrahim Musa Gashash, ibid.

40. Gibson Kuria, quoted in "Explosion of Violence in Kenya Stirs Fears of Electoral Mayhem," in the *International Herald Tribune,* 21 August 1997, p. 6. Also quoted by Godfrey Mwakikagile, *Ethnic Politics in Kenya and Nigeria,* ibid., p. 121.

41. *International Herald Tribune,* ibid. G. Mwakikagile, ibid.

42. Ibid.

43. Richard Leakey, quoted by the *International Herald Tribune,* 21 August 1997, p. 6, and by Godfrey Mwakikagile, *Ethnic Politics in Kenya and Nigeria,* op. cit, p. 122.

44. "A Celtic Resurgence: A Conversation with Welsh writer Bobi Jones," in *The Bloomsbury Review,* Denver, Colorado, May/June 2000, pp. 3, and 25.

45. Obafemi Awolowo, *Path to Nigerian Freedom,* Faber & Faber, London, 1947.

46. "Nigerian Civil War: Aburi Conference and Subsequent Developments, January - July 1967," in *Africa Research Bulletin, Vol. 4, Nos. 1 - 7, 1967; Africa Contemporary Record: Annual Survey and Documents 1968 - 1969,* Africa Research Limited, 1969, p. 648.

47. Nnamdi Azikiwe, *The Political Blueprint of Nigeria,* African Book Co., 1943.

48. Quoted in Jack David Eller, *From Culture to*

Ethnicity to Conflict: An Anthropological Perspective on International Ethnic Conflict, University of Michigan Press, Ann Arbor, 1999, p. 221. See also Neil Jeffrey Kressel, *Mass Hate: The Global Rise of Genocide and Terror,* Plenum Press, New York, 1996, pp. 87 – 118.

49. Julius K. Nyerere, *Decentralisation*, National Printing Co., Ltd., 1972, Dar es Salaam, Tanzania, pp. 1, 2, 3, 5, and 10.

50. Ali A. Mazrui, *Towards A Pax Africana: A Study of Ideology and Ambition*, (London: Weidenfeld & Nicolson, 1967).

See also Juan Enriquez, "Too Many Flags," *Foreign Policy*, Washington, D.C., Fall 1999, pp. 30 - 48; George F. Will, "The Poor Are Unwanted in the 'Secessionist Age'," *The Washington Post*, June 24, 1998, and in the *Internatuinal Herald Tribune*, June 25, 1998, p. 5; Pascal Boniface, "The Proliferation of States," *The Washington Quarterly*, 1998; Francis Deng and Terrence Lyons, eds., *African Reckoning: A Quest for Good Governance* (Washington, D.C.: Brookings Institution Press, 1998); Carol Lancaster, *Aid to Africa: So Much to Do, So Little Done* (Chicago: university of Chicago Press, 1999).

Gidon Gottlieb, *Nation Against State: A New Approach to Ethnic Conflicts and the Decline of Sovereignty* (New York: Council on Foreign Relations, 1993); Robert Jackson, *Quasi-States: Sovereignty, International Relations and the Third World* (Cambridge: Cambridge University Press, 1990); Kenichi Ohmae, *The End of the Nation-State: The Rise of Economic Regional Powers* (New York: Free Press, 1995); David Elkin, *Beyond Sovereignty: Territory and Political Economy in the Twentieth-First Century* (Toronto: University of Toronto Press, 1995).

Saskia Sassen, *Losing Control? Sovereignty in an Age of Globalization* (New York: Columbia University Press, 1996); James Minahan, *Nations Without States: A Historical Dictionary of Contemporary National*

Movements (Westport, Connecticut: Greenwood Press, 1996); Joseph Nye Jr., "In Government We Don't Trust," in *Foreign Policy*, Washington, D.C., Fall 1997; "The World Economy: The Future of the State," in *The Economist*, 20 September 1997; Ted Robert Gurr, "Ethnic Warfare on the Wane," in *Foreign Affairs*, May/June 2000, pp. 52 – 64.

See also Obiora C. Okafor, "After Martydom: International Law, Substitute Groups, and the Construction of Legitimate Statehood in Africa," in *Harvard International Law Journal: International Law and the Developing World - A Millennial Analysis*, Harvard Law School, Cambridge, Massachusetts, Spring 2000; Stephen Ellis, *The Mask of Anarchy: The Destruction of Liberia and the Religious Dimension of an African Civil War* (New York: New York University Press, 2000).

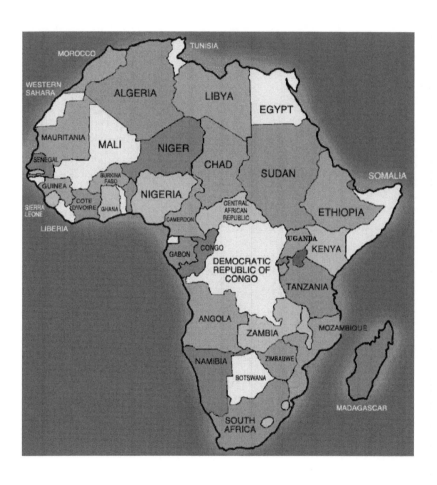

587

34919347R00324

Printed in Great Britain
by Amazon